OBJECT ORIENTATION

Concepts, Languages,
Databases, User Interfaces

Setrag Khoshafian

Razmik Abnous

John Wiley & Sons, Inc.

New York · Chichester · Brisbane · Toronto · Singapore

Library of Congress Cataloging-in-Publication Data:

Khoshafian, Setrag.
    Object orientation : concepts, languages, databases, user
  interfaces / Setrag Khoshafian, Razmik Abnous.
        p.   cm.
    Includes bibliographical references.
    1. Object-oriented programming.   I. Abnous, Razmik.   II. Title.
  QA76.64.K48   1990
  005.1–dc20   90–33364
  ISBN 0–471–51802–6   CIP
  ISBN 0–471–51801–8 (pbk.)

Printed in the United States of America

10 9 8 7 6 5 4 3 2

To our wives
Silva Khoshafian and
Suzanne M. Abnous

and children
Nishan, Jonathan, and Shahan Khoshafian,
Sevan and Haig Abnous

CONTENTS

3

INHERITANCE 79

4

OBJECT IDENTITY   143

5

C++   181

6
ADA
233

7

OBJECT-ORIENTED DATABASES

257

8

USER INTERFACES

323

PREFACE

The application environments of the 1990s are becoming increasingly fast-paced and complex. There is great diversity in the way information is accessed, manipulated, and presented. Information is no longer centralized; it is distributed on networks of heterogeneous environments. Different generic products and tools attempt to simplify a user's interactions with information systems. Unfortunately, the diversity and the lack of integration among these products often force users to learn multiple-user interface paradigms, obtuse operating system scripts, and different key-stroke commands.

There is an enormous need for integration, simplicity, and ease of use across all products. But simplicity and ease of use come at a price. The simpler and more intuitive the environment, the more complex the underlying software system must be to support and implement it. To meet the computational needs of the 90s, software must be modular, extensible, maintainable, and robust. It must be manageable. This means the model of the real world and its implementation in the system should not be too far off.

Object orientation is an enabling software technology that attempts to fulfill the computational needs of the 1990s. The potential of this relatively new methodology stems from:

1. The proficiency of its higher-level object-oriented model, which also reduces software cost and provides the designer with real-world programmable components

2. Its capability to share and reuse code with object-oriented engineering techniques, reducing the time required to develop an application

3. Its capability to localize and minimize the effects of modifications through object-oriented programming abstractions, allowing the software to encompass more diverse algorithms and technologies

Object orientation is relatively young. There is still considerable confusion and controversy over such basic concepts as *objects, object-oriented languages*, and *object-oriented databases*. Nevertheless, object orientation offers some well-established programming disciplines. These disciplines are laying the foundation of most of the software engineering activities of the 1990s.

This book clarifies the *basic concepts* associated with object orientation. It provides a clear yet comprehensive exposure to the fundamental ideas in object orientation. This is important since object orientation is often confused with certain languages, such as Smalltalk, or particular user-interface paradigms, such as windows and icons. Furthermore, a clear understanding of object-oriented concepts will allow the reader to use object-oriented constructs in *any* programming language (including conventional programming languages).

The book will give the reader a basic understanding of the main concepts of popular object-oriented systems: languages, databases, and user interfaces. Object orientation is above all a programming *style* that allows better organization and modularization of large application programs. The book emphasizes the concepts and the ideas for improving programming style, regardless of whether the programmer uses an object-oriented programming language. Special emphasis is given to C++ and Ada as object-oriented languages and to the newly emerging fields of object-oriented databases and user interfaces.

Many programming languages are labeled or claim to be "object-oriented." We felt it was important to show how object-oriented concepts are reflected in these languages. Simula and Smalltalk have played a historic role in the evolution of object-oriented systems and concepts. Nevertheless, we believe the most popular system development languages of the 1990s will be C++ and Ada. Hence we devote an entire chapter to each.

The book also demonstrates the object-oriented concepts that manifest themselves in database applications. We felt the need to present a clear exposure of the emerging field of object-oriented databases. These databases constitute the next evolutionary step after relational databases; post–relational database management systems will all have object-oriented features. This book demonstrates both the object-oriented characteristics and database characteristics of several systems that claim to be *object-oriented databases*.

User interaction with the systems of the 1990s will be more intuitive. Given the explosion in multimedia information management systems and graphical information displays, we decided to analyze the object-oriented capabilities of the next generation of user interfaces (UI). These UI environments provide direct object manipulation features. They allow users to represent and interact with visual objects using familiar physical metaphors. This book uncovers the object-oriented characteristics of the most popular UI systems.

This book is intended for a wide variety of audiences. At small and large corporations, MIS managers and professionals can use the book to understand the impact of object orientation on their end-users. This book will serve the needs of software engineers and computer scientists who are interested in object-oriented systems and want a global perspective on the subject. At universities, it could be a supplementary text for programming languages and software engineering courses, or a graduate course dedicated to object-oriented systems. The books is also suitable for short courses, continuing education, and professional self-study. Prerequisites in data structures, compilers, operating systems, performance evaluation, and databases will be useful.

Chapter 1 gives a brief introduction to object-oriented concepts. This chapter examines the evolution of object orientation in languages, databases, and user interfaces. It also presents examples used commonly throughout the book.

The key object-oriented concepts covered in this book are:

> abstract data typing
> inheritance
> object identity

Chapters 2 through 4 provide detailed and self-contained exposure to all the aspects of these foundational concepts.

Chapter 2 discusses the concept of abstract data typing. It describes in detail mechanisms of hiding the implementation of an object's interface routines. Abstract data typing enhances code extensibility and reusability. The chapter also clarifies and differentiates commonly used object-oriented terms, such as *classes, instances, methods*, and *messages*.

Chapter 3 discusses the concept of inheritance. Through inheritance, one can build new classes or software modules on top of an existing, less specialized hierarchy of classes, instead of redesigning everything from scratch. The new classes can inherit both the behavior and the representation of existing classes. Inheritance enhances software extensibility, reusability, and code sharing.

Chapter 4 surveys the concept of object identity. Object identity allows the objects in an application to be organized in arbitrary graph-structured object spaces. This chapter shows the superiority and generality of the strong notion of object identity when compared to the conventional techniques of referencing objects in programming languages and databases.

Three disciplines have been most influential in the evolution of object-oriented technologies: object-oriented languages, object-oriented databases, and object-oriented user interfaces.

Throughout Chapters 2, 3, and 4 are numerous illustrative examples in some of the most common object-oriented languages, such as Smalltalk. However, we dedicate an entire chapter to each of the most popular object-oriented languages today, namely C++ and Ada. Chapter 5 concentrates on C++. It describes the main features of C++ Version 2.0 through illustrative examples. C++ already is *the* system development language of the 1990s. The chapter, which is self-contained, will provide the reader with a firm grasp of the language. Chapter 6 explores the object-oriented features of Ada, another popular programming language. Ada is a standardized language that is used by the Department of Defense. It supports a number of object-oriented concepts, which are explained in the chapter through examples.

Chapter 7 covers the emerging field of object-oriented databases. Object-oriented databases combine the object-oriented concepts of abstract data typing, inheritance, and object identity with database capabilities. These database capabilities include the support of persistent object spaces, transactions, recovery, querying, and versioning of objects. The chapter discusses the object-oriented features of several object-oriented database management systems from both research and industry.

Chapter 8 illustrates the enormous impact of object orientation on the design and presentation of the modern user interfaces. This chapter covers such concepts as the direct manipulation of objects and the application of predefined class hierarchy libraries for user-interface components. It also discusses some of the modern graphical user interfaces in use today and describes the object-oriented interface layers presented to both end-users and application developers.

We would like to extend our appreciation to people who helped us with this book. Above all we want to thank our wives—Silva Khoshafian and Suzanne M. Abnous— for their support and patience. We would also like to express our gratitude to our editors: Dianne Cerra, Wendy Hoben, and Roger Blumer. We are grateful for the assistance of our copyeditor, Leon V. Jeter, and our production coordinator, Kristina Williamson, both from Publication Services. Finally, we would like to thank the people who reviewed or supplied information for the book, including Joe Ammirato, Brad Baker, Arvola Chan, Jack Hahn, Rene P. Siles, Jerry Silverman, Les N. Tabata, Gazel Tan, Tom Tullis, and Harry Wong from Ashton-Tate; Don Courtney and Craig Hensen-Sturm from Digital Equipment Corporation; Dan Fishman, Lee Garverick, Rich Tella, and Mike Webb from Hewlett-Packard; Charles H. Irby from Metaphor Data Systems; Mohammad A. Ketabchi from Santa Clara University; Allen Otis and Jacob Stein from Servio Logic Corporation; and Mark Achler from The Whitewater Group.

Walnut Creek, California
July, 1990

SETRAG KHOSHAFIAN
RAZMIK ABNOUS

1

INTRODUCTION

■ 1.1 INTRODUCTION TO OBJECT ORIENTATION

The 1990s will undoubtedly be called the decade of object-oriented programming. The need for this novel programming paradigm is rather simple: Users are demanding more functionality from their computing systems. They are asking for simpler, easier-to-use computing environments. Increased functionality and easier-to-use computing environments come at a price, however. They demand more complex underlying systems (there are no free lunches!). This means more lines of code to be organized, managed, and maintained. Figure 1.1 illustrates the exponential time needed to develop a system (in terms of labor-months) as a function of size (lines of code) or functionality. Time and again the validity of this exponential cost has been proven to be true. It is interesting to note that most software development companies were late in shipping their next generation, functionality-rich products in the late 1980s. Using the same software methodologies of the 1970s and 1980s will result in even more late product shipments, "buggy" products, and similar problems in the 1990s.

This book is about the *object-oriented techniques, languages, databases,* and *user interfaces* that attempt to solve and satisfy the computational needs of the 1990s. Object orientation provides better paradigms and tools for:

- Modeling the real world as close to a user's perspective as possible
- Interacting easily with a computational environment, using familiar metaphors
- Constructing reusable software components and easily extensible libraries of software modules
- Easily modifying and extending implementations of components without having to recode everything from scratch

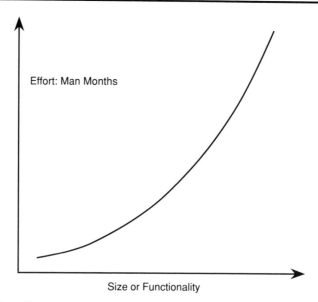

Figure 1.1 The effort to develop a system increases exponentially as a function of size or functionality.

Object orientation attempts to satisfy the needs of end-users as well as those of developers of software products. This is accomplished via real-world modeling capabilities, illustrated in Figures 1.2, 1.3, and 1.4. In object-oriented programming the central entities are data (vs. procedures or subroutines). The data objects communicate or invoke one another through sending *messages* to each other. This is illustrated in Figure 1.2a. Collections of objects that respond to the same messages are implemented through *classes*. A class describes and implements all the methods that capture the behavior of its *instances*. This is illustrated in Figure 1.2b. The implementation is totally hidden or encapsulated within the class. In other words, the implementations can be extended and modified without affecting the users of the class in any way. Thus, classes contribute both to the modeling of the real world and to software extensibility and reusability. Classes implement a very fundamental concept in object orientation, namely, *abstract data types*. Chapter 2 is dedicated to a detailed discussion of classes and abstract data types in general.

A class is like a module. With object orientation, these modules can be used not only in different applications, but also to *extend* or *specialize* a class. This is achieved through *inheritance*. Figure 1.3 provides three examples of inheritance: an inheritance hierarchy rooted at Person, an inheritance hierarchy rooted at Vehicle, and an inheritance hierarchy of user-interface objects rooted at Window. As the examples illustrate, class inheritance provides a very natural approach for organizing information. In addition, it allows software modules to share code and representation. Chapter 3 discusses all the aspects of class and object *inheritance*.

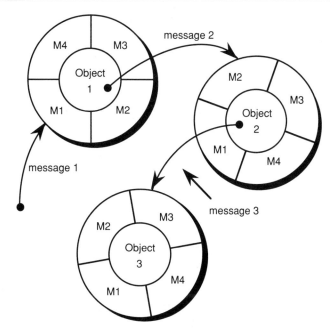

(a) Objects send messages to each other

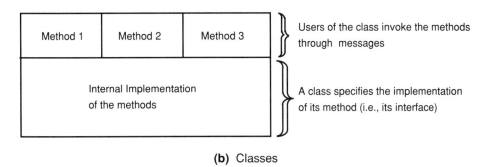

(b) Classes

Figure 1.2 Objects (instances) and classes.

Each class has a template that describes the *state* or *structure* of its instances. An object's state can contain other objects. For example, a car has an engine and a body; the engine of a car consists of a steering system, a propulsion system, and a braking system. The same object could be referenced or accessed through different objects. The same address object is often the address of more than one person; the same department contains many employees; the same dialog can be activated through different buttons, and so on. Figure 1.4 presents two employees, Tim and Terry, who are partners in a joint project. Tim and Terry work in the same toy department.

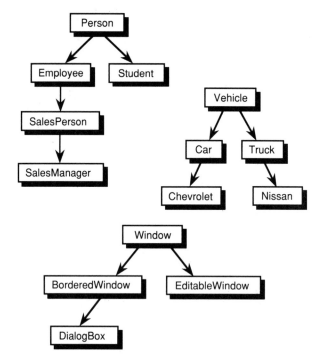

Figure 1.3 Examples of class hierarchies.

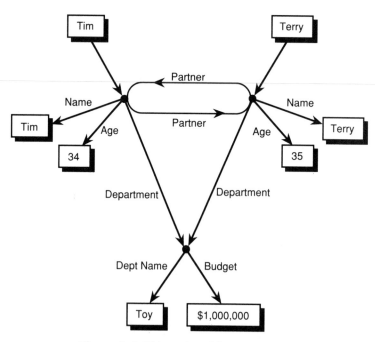

Figure 1.4 Objects describing two partners.

The Tim and Terry objects actually contain the same Toy department object, rather than containing two different copies of the same object, as in conventional systems. The object-oriented concept that supports such natural organizations of the object spaces is *object identity*. Chapter 4 is dedicated to object identity.

Using these object-oriented concepts in languages, databases, and user interfaces, we will eventually be able to achieve a linear expansion in effort as a function of size or functionality. This is illustrated in Figure 1.5, which shows that there is an initial rise in cost while learning the object-oriented technology and developing initial reusable components or class hierarchies, but later a more linear growth of effort is achieved.

1.1.1 Object Orientation for All Users

Since the introduction of digital computers, users have been searching for increasingly higher-level and natural programming languages. The aim is to communicate with, interact with, and employ these powerful machines in increasingly effective, simple, and natural ways.

Despite the overwhelming dominance of computers in industrial and office environments in the 1980s, home computing still remains an elusive goal. One of the often cited reasons is the difficulty of using and manipulating these personal machines. Although steady progress has been made, many have observed that current personal computers are still relatively hard to use for a novice. Computer builders are far from creating truly intelligent machines. As things stand now, user friendliness, higher-level languages, and most advanced features of automatic computation are typically

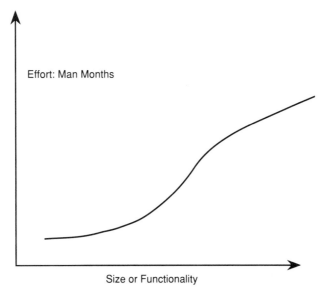

Figure 1.5 With object-oriented methodology we eventually achieve linear growth with increased functionality.

determined by the perceptions and the imaginations of computer developers. These language and user-interface designers determine what is best for the naive end-user, through analyzing what is best for *themselves*.

The roots of object-oriented programming can be traced back to the gradual attempts of programming language designers to develop language constructs, disciplines, and programming philosophies that would help write software more quickly. The object-oriented programming discipline promises (and has delivered) significant benefits to each of the following three major groups of computer users:

1. *End-users:* the public at large, including MIS managers, secretaries, house-wives, househusbands (these are the 1990s, after all!), users of teller machines, airline reservation systems, and so on. For this largest group of users, object orientation promises increasingly friendlier user interfaces. Object orientation will help integrate multimedia data types in computing environments. Thus voice, image, and animation sequences as well as text data will be part of the computer's repertoire of stored and manipulated objects.

2. *Application developers:* including database designers and administrators, vertical application developers, custom software developers, and so on. Object orientation promises to help the application developer by providing tools that are easier to use. Object-oriented hypermedia tools will help organize and link the multimedia nodes of an application. Object-oriented database design tools will help create the most natural abstractions of the end-user's object space.

3. *System programmers:* including developers of spreadsheets, word processors, operating systems, and databases. These are the power users of computing systems. For these expert programmers, object orientation enhances the engineering and configuration management tools. Through specialization of existing software components, these programmers will be able to build complex systems more quickly.

Several different features of object orientation will satisfy the varying computational needs of these three user groups. The modeling and programming of user requirements have driven programming languages, databases, and user interfaces toward object orientation. In the following sections we briefly describe the evolution of these disciplines.

1.1.2   What *Is* Object Orientation?

Object orientation can be loosely described as the *software modeling and development (engineering) disciplines that make it easy to construct complex systems from individual components.*

The intuitive appeal of object orientation is that it provides better concepts and tools with which to model and represent the real world as closely as possible. The advantages in programming and data modeling are many. As pointed out by Ledbetter and Cox (1985),

. . . object (oriented) programming allows a more direct representation of the real-world model in the code. The result is that the normal radical transformation from system requirements (defined in user's terms) to system specification (defined in computer terms) is greatly reduced.

Figure 1.6 illustrates this. Using conventional techniques, the code generated for a real-world problem consists of first encoding the problem and then transforming the problem into terms of a Von Neumann computer language. Object-oriented disciplines and techniques handle the transformation automatically, so the bulk of the code just encodes the problem and the transformation is minimized. In fact, when compared to

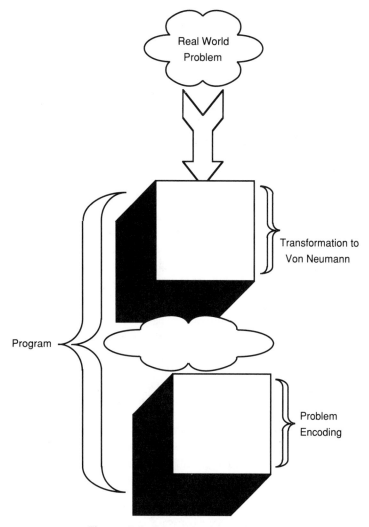

Figure 1.6 Conventional programming.

more conventional (procedural) styles of programming, code reductions ranging from 40 percent to an order of magnitude have been reported for a number of problems after adopting an object-oriented style of programming.

Therefore the object-oriented concepts and tools are enabling technologies that allow real-world problems to be expressed easily and naturally. Object-oriented techniques provide better methodologies to construct complex software systems out of modularized reusable software units.

The three most fundamental aspects of the object-oriented paradigm are *abstract data typing* (Chapter 2), *inheritance* (Chapter 3), and *object identity* (Chapter 4). Each of these concepts contributes to the software engineering *and* modeling properties of object-oriented systems. There are many object-oriented notions associated with these three. Furthermore, a specific object-oriented language, system, or database will emphasize one or two of these concepts without supporting the others directly. Ada, for instance, does not fully support inheritance; the support of object identity in C++ and Eiffel is rather limited; and there is a problem in the way Smalltalk supports inheritance and encapsulation. The rest of this section illustrates these three fundamental concepts through a simple example. (Chapters 2 through 6 are dedicated to a much more detailed discussion of the object-oriented concepts and their manifestation in popular object-oriented languages.)

1.1.2.1 Abstract Data Types

Data types describe a set of objects with the same representation. There are a number of operations associated with each data type. Abstract data types extend the notion of a data type through "hiding" the implementation of the user-defined operations (messages) associated with the data type. Languages that support abstract data types provide constructs to directly define data structures *and* the operations used to manipulate occurrences (instances) of the data structures. In addition, *all* manipulations of instances of the data type are done exclusively through operations associated with the data type.

Here is a simple example from automotive design to illustrate the object-oriented concepts. A car model typically has several related models that have common features and parts. Note that the operation of the car does not necessarily involve any knowledge of internal engineering design or structure. Every car model has a dashboard full of control mechanisms that combine with the pedals to constitute an interface with the car. Each car model has a particular set of mechanical interfaces depending on model, year, luxury items (such as air conditioning), and so on. To drive the car, the driver needs to interact only with the controls of the dashboard and the pedals. This basically captures the notion of abstract data typing or encapsulation. A language supporting abstract data typing will allow the instances of the data type to be manipulated only through a prescribed collection of operations associated with the type.

1.1.2.2 Inheritance

The second powerful object-oriented concept is *inheritance*. Through inheritance designers can build new software modules (such as classes) on top of an existing hierarchy of modules. Inheriting behavior enables *code sharing* (and hence reusability) among software modules. Inheriting representation enables *structure sharing* among data objects. As we shall see, the combination of these two types of inheritance provides a powerful modeling and software development strategy.

Consider a hierarchy of Ford Mustang models, as illustrated in Figure 1.7. The LX for example, inherits most of the features and subparts of the base model, but specializes the interior and the engine. Similarly, the GT inherits features from the LX but has a sportier exterior and engine. This is the essence of inheritance hierarchies, where object types inherit most of their attributes from generic or less specialized types.

1.1.2.3 Object Identity

The third powerful object-oriented concept is *object identity*. Identity is that property of an object that distinguishes each object from all others. With object identity, objects can contain or refer to other objects. Identity organizes the *objects* of the object space manipulated by an object-oriented program. Abstract data types and inheritance are used to model and organize the *types* or classes of objects.

We illustrate the benefits of object identity through a car model example (consider Figure 1.8). Each car consists of subparts: an engine and a body. The engine itself can be thought of as a composite of a steering system, a propulsion system, and

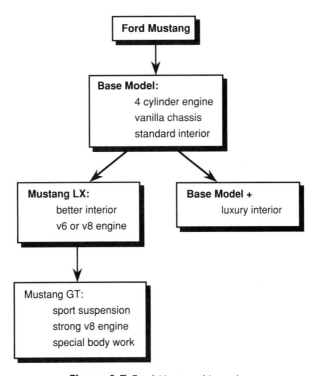

Figure 1.7 Ford Mustang hierarchy.

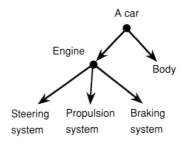
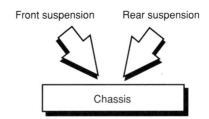

Figure 1.8 Components and subparts of a car.

a braking system. The subparts are attached to each other through wires and other hardware. For example, the chassis is shared and accessed by the front and rear suspension systems. Thus, the conceptualization of the car is a graph where subparts are accessed or referenced by other subparts. In object-oriented languages, this graph-structured representation is made possible through the notion of *object identity*.

1.1.3 Programming Languages, Databases, and Interfaces

The three main computer science areas that have been irreversibly influenced and affected by object orientation are:

1. *Programming languages.* The procedures of an application are encoded in a particular programming language. Each programming language has its own syntax and semantics. Examples of programming languages include FORTRAN, C, and Ada. All programming languages are translated (compiled) to machine languages. Each computer has its own machine language, the only one understood by that computer. The machine language of an IBM PC is very different from the machine language of an Apple Macintosh. However, the PC *clones* understand the machine language of IBM PCs.

2. *Database management systems.* Stored databases that are queried by many users concurrently are managed by complex systems called database management systems (DBMSs). Each DBMS supports a particular conceptual model. For example, the relational model depicts the stored data space as a collection of "flat" tables. Examples of database management systems include dBASE from Ashton-Tate for PCs and DB2 from IBM for mainframe computers.

3. *Visual and iconic user interfaces.* The user interface of an application handles the input and output of the user. Thus its main function is communication with the end-user. The input to the system can be controlled through command lines. This is the approach used in DOS and the UNIX operating system. Alternatively, the user can interact with the system with visual programming constructs such as icons and menus, as is the approach used in the Macintosh.

■ 1.2 HISTORY AND EVOLUTION

This section traces the evolution of programming languages, database management systems, and graphical user-interfaces. The authors demonstrate how the object-oriented paradigm is being incorporated in each of these disciplines.

1.2.1 The Evolution of Object Orientation in Programming Languages

Assemblers were the earliest computer languages that introduced symbolic representation of the underlying machine instructions. Some of the earliest assemblers include Soap for the IBM 650 (mid-1950s) and Sap for the IBM 704 (late 1950s). But the first milestone of high-level programming was undoubtedly the development of FORTRAN.

FORTRAN (mid-1950s) introduced several important programming language concepts including variables, arrays, control structures (iteration and conditional branching) and so on (Backus, 1978). FORTRAN is still one of the most popular programming languages. The language has an active ANSI (American National Standards Institute) standardization committee that periodically releases substantive enhancements of and extensions to the language.

Yet, in the late 1950s, one problem found when developing large FORTRAN programs was that variable names would conflict in different parts of a program. High-level programming languages that succeeded FORTRAN include PL/1, COBOL, and Algol. The designers of the language Algol decided to provide barriers to separate variable names within program segments. This gave birth to the Begin . . . End blocks in Algol 60 (Randell and Russell, 1964). Since the variable names appearing within a block are known only to that block, their use will not conflict with the use of the same variable name in other blocks of the program. This was a first attempt at providing protection or *encapsulation* within a programming language. Block structures are now widely used in a variety of languages.

In the early 1960s, the designers of the language Simula-67 (Dahl and Nygaard, 1966; Dahl, Myhrhaug, and Nygaard, 1970) took the block concept of Algol one step further and introduced the concept of an *object*. Although Simula's roots were in Algol, it was mainly intended as a simulation language. Thus, Simula objects had "an existence of their own" and could (in some sense) communicate with each other during a simulation. Conceptually, an object contained both data and the operations that manipulate its data. The operations were called *methods*. Simula also incorporated the notion of *classes*, which are used to describe the structure and behavior of a set of objects. Class inheritance was also supported by Simula. Inheritance organizes the classes into hierarchies, allowing the sharing of implementation and structure. Simula also distinguished between two types of equality, identical and shallow, reflecting the distinction between *reference-* (identity) based versus *value-* (content) based interpretations of objects. Therefore, Simula laid the foundation of object-oriented languages and some of the object-oriented terminology. In addition to using object-oriented concepts, Simula was a "strongly typed" language. This means that the type of each variable is known at the time of compiling so that errors involving type are found then, and not when the program is run. In retrospect, if Simula implementations had better marketing, Simula could have become a much more widespread language.

Another important milestone in the development of programming languages was the LISP (McCarthy et al., 1965) functional programming language. LISP was introduced in the late 1950s and early 1960s. LISP was, and still remains, one of the most elegant languages, using a few simple programming constructs (lists and function application) to perform complex computations. LISP remains the language of choice for many artificial intelligence applications. There are a number of companies that actively support LISP versions, and there are some companies, such as Symbolics, that build LISP machines.

In the early 1970s, the concept of *data abstraction* was pursued by a number of language designers for the purpose of managing large programs (Parnas, 1972). There are two fundamental aspects of abstract data typing. One is to cluster the structure of the type with the operations defined on the type. For instance, with Algol or Pascal, the language does not encourage the grouping of all the operations on a record type in the same module with the definition of the record type. Simula achieved clustering, or grouping of structure and operations, through classes.

The other aspect of abstract data typing is *information hiding*, where the details of implementation and representation of the objects are hidden and cannot be directly accessed through the users of the object. Languages such as Alphard (Wulf, London, and Shaw, 1976) and CLU (Liskov et al., 1977) introduced data abstraction. In CLU, for instance, abstract data types were implemented through *clusters*, an appropriate name. As these languages were developed, a good deal of the foundational and mathematical theory for abstract data types began to evolve. This helped establish the concept of abstract data types by providing a rigorous mathematical basis for using object orientation (Goguen, Thatcher, Wegner, and Wright, 1975; Guttag, 1977; Burstall and Goguen, 1977). The theory was then developed further for application to specification (Ehrig, Kreowski, and Padawiz, 1978), and for higher-order abstract data types (Parsaye, 1982).

One of the most important programming languages to support abstract data typing was Ada (Booch, 1986). The U.S. Department of Defense (DoD) commissioned the design of Ada to reduce and control cost of software development. The DoD intended Ada to be the language of choice for the development of new embedded systems. The language contains the usual control flow constructs (*if . . . then . . . else, while,* and so on), and the ability to define types, functions, and subroutines. Object-oriented constructs in Ada include packets and packages, which are discussed in more detail in Chapter 6. The DoD defined the requirement in a document called STEELMAN. Based on the requirement stated in STEELMAN, several language proposals were submitted, all based on the Pascal language. A large collection of people contributed to the design of the Ada language. Most of the language designers were from European nations; Jean Ichbiah from France was the primary language designer, and several other authors were from France, the United Kingdom, West Germany, and the United States.

It has been (and still continues to be) debated for a long time whether Ada is an object-oriented language. Ada supports several object-oriented concepts such as abstract data types, overloading of functions and operators, parametric polymorphism, and even specialization of user-defined types. Yet, Ada does not fully support inheritance. Chapter 6 explores Ada more.

During the 70s and 80s, the object-oriented concepts from Simula and other earlier prototypes were embodied in one of the most influential object-oriented languages: Smalltalk. Smalltalk (Goldberg and Robson, 1983) was initially a research project at Xerox Palo Alto Research Park (PARC). During the 70s, a group of researchers at Xerox PARC were revolutionizing the future of the computer industry. Xerox PARC researchers invented or solidified many technologies now recognized as object-oriented, both in the realms of languages and user-interfaces. For languages, Smalltalk was developed at PARC during this time. In the realm of user-interface, both the Star workstation (also developed at PARC) and its predecessor the Alto, influenced the design and look and feel of the Apple Macintosh, Aldus PageMaker desktop publishing software, Microsoft Windows, and Metaphor DIS software environment.

In fact, Smalltalk was (and is) not just a language. It incorporates a whole programming environment and a menu-based interactive user interface. The Smalltalk environment includes an extensive initial class hierarchy. Programming in Smalltalk entails opening a working window, browsing and extending the class hierarchy through another window, and so on. The programmer interacts with the system through dialogs and pop-up or pull-down windows, depending on the particular implementation of the environment. Learning how to use the initial Smalltalk class hierarchy is a substantial but important investment in time.

There were several versions and dialects of Smalltalk: Smalltalk-72, -74, -76, -78, -80, and more recently Smalltalk/V from Digitalk. The most important and stable version remains Smalltalk-80. The computer scientists who were most influential in the development of the Smalltalk language include Alan Kay, Adele Goldberg, and Daniel Ingalls. The Goldberg and Robson book on Smalltalk-80 (1983) remains one of the most important and frequently referenced pieces of literature in object orientation.

The Smalltalk language incorporates many of the object-oriented features of Simula, including classes, inheritance, and support of object identity. However, in Smalltalk information hiding is enforced more rigorously than Simula. Furthermore, Smalltalk is not a typed language. The types of the variables in Smalltalk *are not specified* at variable-declaration time. The same variable can assume different types at different times in the same program. The type of a variable is the class of the object referenced by the variable. Classes are like factories which create *instances* from templates. Methods can be defined for class instances or can apply to the class itself. A substantial amount of this book is dedicated to the clarification of these concepts.

Smalltalk is extremely rich in object-oriented concepts. In Smalltalk everything is an object, including classes and base types (integers, floating point numbers, and the like). This means that throughout the entire Smalltalk environment, programming consists of sending messages to objects. A message can add a number to another number, or it can create a new instance of a class, or it can introduce a new method in a given class. Smalltalk will remain a powerful influence in object-oriented programming. There is continuous design and development of different variations and dialects of Smalltalk, implemented on a host of different hardware platforms.

Besides Smalltalk, there were other influences and concepts that illuminated the amazing world of object orientation. Object orientation attempts to model the real world as closely as possible. Another aspect of the real world is *concurrency*. For example, in an office environment, secretaries, managers, and other employees function simultaneously and independently. They communicate with each other through conversations, memos, electronic mail messages, and so on. Although some object-oriented languages (most notably Smalltalk) introduced terms such as *messages* to describe the *activation* or *invocation* of a method by an object (thereby giving the illusion that objects are acting independently and concurrently), the underlying semantics and execution model of the language is purely sequential; the semantics of messages are nearly identical to the semantics of procedure calls. In order to support concurrency, Smalltalk employs another construct, namely a *process*. Therefore, there are two concepts to concentrate on: objects and processes (Yokote and Tokoro, 1987).

To alleviate this problem, there have been some attempts to incorporate parallelism and design concurrent object-oriented languages. The most notable and influential of these was Hewitt's actor model (Hewitt, 1977; Agha and Hewitt, 1987). Other concurrent object-oriented languages include Lieberman's Act 1 (Lieberman, 1981) and ABCL/1 (Shibayama and Yonezawa, 1987). Objects in ABCL/1 execute concurrently. An object is either dormant, waiting, or active. Objects are activated only upon receiving messages. After an object has processed all its messages, it becomes dormant. The model represented by ABCL/1 and other concurrent object-oriented languages reflects the intuitive notion of objects sending and responding to messages more directly.

Throughout the 1980s, object-oriented concepts (abstract data types, inheritance, object identity, and concurrency), Smalltalk, Simula, and other languages began to merge and give birth to a number of new object-oriented languages, with extensions and dialects. Next we categorize the strategic direction of object-oriented programming language development.

1. *Extensions, dialects, and versions of Smalltalk.* There have been several proposals (and prototypes) to extend Smalltalk with typing (as mentioned earlier, variables in Smalltalk are not typed), multiple inheritance (original dialects of Smalltalk allowed a class to inherit from only one parent or superclass), or *concurrent programming* constructs (Yokote and Tokara, 1987). These are primarily research projects or prototypes.

   In terms of actual products, Xerox and Tektronix offer Smalltalk-80 on some of their machines. Another notable vendor of Smalltalk is ParcPlace systems, which supports Smalltalk-80 versions on a number of platforms. Digitalk offers Smalltalk/V for IBM-compatible personal computers and Macintoshes. Many of the examples in this book use Smalltalk/V. Since PCs are widespread and Smalltalk/V is relatively inexpensive, the examples will allow readers to experiment with some object-oriented programs.

2. *Object-oriented extensions of conventional languages.* One of the most popular object-oriented languages is C++. This language was designed by Bjarne Stroustrup at AT&T in the early 1980s (Stroustrup, 1986). The first implementation of the C++ language was released as a preprocessor to C compilers. C++ provides two constructs for class definitions. The first method is an extension of the *struct* construct and the other, through the new *class* construct. C++ allows hierarchies of classes, and allows subclasses to access methods and instance variables from other classes in their hierarchy. The language permits ad hoc polymorphism by allowing overloading of function names and operators. But, unlike Smalltalk, C++ does not come with a large collection of predefined classes. This task has been left to vendors supplying C++ libraries.

   Another popular dialect of C is Objective-C (Cox, 1987). This language is a superset of C incorporating object-oriented features from Smalltalk. It uses a modified version of Smalltalk syntax to add these features. Just like Smalltalk, it comes with a large collection of predefined classes to simplify the software development process. Objective-C supports abstract data types, inheritance and operator overloading. Unlike C++, however, Objective-C does not extend the definition of any existing C language construct. It relies totally on the introduction of new constructs and operators to perform tasks such as class definition or message passing. The recently announced NeXT computer chose Objective-C as its primary development language.

   For Pascal, popular object-oriented extensions include Object Pascal for the Macintosh from Apple Computer and Turbo Pascal from Borland for IBM personal computers. Object Pascal (Schmucker, 1986) was designed by Niklaus Wirth and a group of Apple Computer engineers. It extends the Pascal language to support the notions of abstract data type, methods and inheritance. It extends the Pascal *type* and variable declaration statement to support the notion of object and class definition. MacApp, presented in Chapter 8, is a large collection of class definitions developed mostly in this language.

3. *Strongly typed object-oriented languages.* This chapter has already mentioned the father of object-oriented languages, Simula. It was standardized in 1986, and a number of companies (mostly in Sweden—Lund Software and Simprog AB) offer Simula implementations on a host of platforms.

There have been some novel strongly typed object-oriented languages. A very interesting and commercially available language is Eiffel (Meyer, 1988), from Interactive Software Engineering, Inc. In addition to encapsulation and inheritance, Eiffel integrates a number of powerful object-oriented capabilities such as *parametric types*, and *pre-* and *post-conditions* for methods. Both concepts are described in more detail in Chapter 2. Other strongly typed object-oriented languages include Trellis/Owl (Schaffert et al., 1986) from Digital Equipment Corporation, and Ada, which is discussed in more detail in Chapter 6.

4. *Object-oriented extensions of LISP.* There have been several extensions of LISP. The most notable object-oriented extensions include Flavors (Moon, 1986) which is supported by Symbolics; CommonLoops from Xerox, Common Objects (Snyder, 1985), and the Common List Object System (CLOS).

Common Objects is interesting because it attempts to resolve an apparent conflict between encapsulation and inheritance, as discussed in Chapter 3. CLOS is significant since there is an ANSI X3J13 committee that is standardizing the language (Bobrow et al., 1988). Both Xerox and Symbolics are involved in its development. CLOS introduces novel and interesting approaches to some of the object-oriented concepts, such as method combination for resolving method conflicts in multiple inheritance. This is discussed in more detail in Chapter 3.

Object-Oriented Languages in the 1990s

In 1982 it was predicted that "object-oriented programming will be in the 1980s what structured programming was in the 1970s" (Rentsch, 1982). The 80s will probably be known as the decade that launched the object-oriented era of computation.

The year 1986 saw the first major conference, OOPSLA (Object-Oriented Programming Systems and LAnguages), entirely dedicated to object orientation. And 1988 brought the first journal entirely dedicated to object orientation: *The Journal of Object-Oriented Programming.*

Attendance at OOPSLA conferences steadily increased. Simultaneously, object-oriented languages such as C++ (Stroustroup, 1986), Objective-C (Cox, 1986), Smalltalk-80 (Goldberg and Robson, 1983), Eiffel (Meyer, 1988), and object-oriented extensions of LISP became commercially available. Several major computer companies such as AT&T, Sun, and Microsoft started pursuing object-oriented styles of programming in developing their own software.

In the 1990s, object-oriented languages, techniques, databases, and user interfaces will be even more popular. Most software development will be affected by object orientation one way or another. The 1990s will be the decade of the proliferation of object-oriented languages and technologies.

1.2.2 The Evolution of Object Orientation in Databases

The forerunners of database management systems were generalized file routines. These file management systems were able to discretely perform common operators on files, independent of their data. Some examples of these routines include sorting, file maintenance, and report generation.

In the 1950s and 1960s, *data definition* products were developed by large companies such as IBM, General Electric, and Honeywell. These products permitted the description of the structure of databases which were accessed by many users. The earlier data definition products evolved into COBOL, which was developed by CODASYL (Conference On DAta SYstems and Languages) in 1960. The COBOL language had a data division construct, which separated the description of the data or database from the routines that accessed and updated the data.

The CODASYL Language Committee eventually proposed an extension of COBOL for databases. The actual group commissioned for this task was the Data Base Task Group (DBTG). In 1969, DBTG defined the Data Description Language (DDL) and the Data Manipulation Language (DML) for databases. These laid the foundation for *network* database management systems. The DBTG specifications were actually preceded and influenced by a product from General Electric called IDS (Integrated Data Store), which was sold in the early 1960s. Other early network database products were IDMS from Cullinet (1970), DMS 1100 from Sperry (1971), and IDS-2 from Honeywell Information Systems (1975).

The underlying data model of all these products presented the user with a network view of the databases. A network view consists of record types and one-to-many relationships among the record types. For example, an organization can have an employee record type, where each employee has a name, address, social security number, and salary. It can also have a department record type that has the department name and department budget. The network representation includes a one-to-many relationship between department and employee record types, indicating that each department will contain many employees who will be working in that department. Database data models are discussed in more detail in Chapter 7.

The network model allows a record type to be involved in more than one relationship. A less general model is a tree-structured hierarchical relationship among record types, which is the basis of the hierarchical data model. The hierarchical data model allows a record type to be involved in *only one* relationship as a "parent" and also *only one* relationship as a "child." The earliest hierarchical database management systems were the IMS (Information Management System) family of products developed by IBM. The IMS was the result of a project that began in the 1960s in response to the massive information-handling needs generated by NASA's Apollo moon program. Another popular hierarchical database management system product was the Time-

Shared Database Management System developed by the System Development Corporation.

Both the hierarchical and network data models were primarily "navigational": a user would start from a parent or owner record and navigate through the members of a relationship through *get next*, *get first*, or *get last* constructs. Furthermore the owner/member relationship (for the network model) or parent/child relationship (for the hierarchical model) were explicitly stored in the database records. More specifically, the network and hierarchical database implementations did not have physical data independence. This meant the user's view of the navigational and hierarchical databases reflected the way the data was organized, stored, and accessed from the underlying physical storage media. In some cases, the user or the database management system administrator (DBA) was required to specify details of record placement, storage areas, record ordering, record locations, and so on. Besides the specification hassle, this approach severely limited the extensibility, maintainability, reusability, and portability of the database management system applications developed from these models.

In order to provide more flexibility in organizing large databases and alleviate some of the problems of the earlier models, Ted Codd introduced the *relational data model* in the early 1970s. Relational database management systems became increasingly popular in the 1980s, and their use and popularity will steadily increase in the 1990s. Relational databases are prevailing because of several inherent advantages. The first is that relational query languages such as SQL (Structure Query Language) are much more *declarative* than the navigational languages of the earlier models. This means the user specifies what is wanted from the database in a high-level declarative style of programming, specifying *what* is to be accessed from the database rather than *how* to access it. The relational model is simple and elegant. The underlying theory is based on the mathematically well-founded and well-understood concepts of relational algebra and first-order predicate calculus. Relational algebra consists of only a few operations: set operations (union, intersection, difference, cartesian product) and the relational operations (selection, projection, join).

Commercial relational systems and the propagation of relational databases stem from the System/R (Astrahan et al., 1976) and INGRES (Stonebraker et al., 1976) relational database implementation efforts. System/R was an ambitious research project at the IBM San Jose Research Center. It paved the way for the DB2 commercial relational database management system from IBM. The INGRES (INteractive Graphics and REtrieval System) project at the University of California, Berkeley, was also very influential in encouraging the growth of this technology. INGRES eventually became a commercial relational database product and INGRES corporation one of the major players in the relational database industry.

IBM eventually came up with commercial relational database products called SQL /DS in the early 80s. In 1983, IBM marketed the DB2 relational database products for the MVS platforms. DB2 is significant because many relational database vendors have been attempting to be compatible with DB2's dialect of SQL. The American National

Standards Institute SQL proposal was ratified in 1986, and is based on DB2's dialect. Besides IBM, several other companies marketed relational database management systems. One of the earliest vendors was Relational Software Inc. (now called Oracle Corporation) with its ORACLE relational database management systems products. Other major vendors include Digital Equipment Corporation (VAX RDB/VMS), Relational Technologies Inc. (INGRES), Unisys Corp. (UDS RDMS 1100), Data General Corp. (DG/SQL), Sybase Inc., Ashton-Tate, and so on.

In the late 1980s, almost all commercial database management systems were based on either the hierarchical, network, or relational model. Relational databases continue to become more widely used, at the expense of the earlier network and hierarchical products. Still, there have been several alternative database modeling proposals. Most of these post-relational data models were prototyped in research labs and were never commercialized.

One of the earliest alternative database data modeling proposals was the *semantic* data model. The motivation of semantic data models (and most data models for that matter) is very similar to the goal of object orientation: model the real world as closely as possible.

Examples of early introductions to semantic models include Abrial's data semantics model (1974), a 1976 paper (Hall et al.), and the famous entity-relationship (ER) model, introduced by Chen (1976). The ER model is quite simple. The earlier ER models do not incorporate the notion of inheritance. In particular, nodes in an ER diagram are either entity nodes, printable attribute nodes, or relationship (aggregate) nodes. The entity-relationship approach is a widely accepted technique for data modeling. In the ER model, an entity is an object or a thing that exists and can be distinguished from other entities. An entity might be a person, an institution, a flight, and so on. Entities are described through attributes or properties. In terms of the regular database constructs, entities generally conform to records while their attributes are represented as the fields of those records.

Other semantic database data models closely related to the entity relationship model include the Semantic Data Model of Hammer and McLeod (1981), and TAXIS (Mylopoulos, Bernstein, and Wong, 1980; Wong, 1983). TAXIS integrates database management, programming language, and AI techniques. Semantic networks are used to organize database objects such as relations and transactions.

As mentioned earlier, semantic data models (especially the ER data model) are used primarily as database design tools. Often a *schema* (structure) of a database is designed using an ER model. The semantic schema is then mapped onto a relational schema using a relational database language's data definition language (such as the DDL of an SQL). The user then retrieves and updates the data stored via the schema using a relational data manipulation language (such as the DML of an SQL). This is somewhat inconvenient and unnatural. There were some attempts to incorporate data manipulation capabilities in a semantic data model, using *functional* relationships. This resulted in a number of functional data models (Kerschberg and Pacheco, 1976).

Perhaps the most often referenced functional model is DAPLEX (Shipman, 1981). In this model, attributes are treated as functions. Values are retrieved through applying functions to entities.

The semantic data modeling approach was not the only one that tried to add more semantics to traditional data models. There were a number of data models that attempted to incrementally extend the relational data model in order to allow more flexibility, while maintaining a solid theoretical foundation.

The object space in the relational model consists of a collection of flat tables. Each table is a set of rows (tuples). The column values in each row (attributes of tuples) can only be instances of base atomic types such as integers, floats, or character strings. The flat-table representation is known as the *first normal form*. *Complex object* models attempted to relax the first normal form restrictions. Complex object models are alternatively called non-first normal form data models, nested relational models, set and tuple models, or logic-based data models with complex terms.

With a nested relational model, the user will be able to have a relation-valued (that is, based on a set of tuples) attribute and thus represent, store, and retrieve a set of tuples directly. There have been a number of nested relational models, including VERSO (Bancilhon et al., 1983) and the nested relational model of Schek and Scholl (1986).

More general complex object models (involving the nesting of *arbitrary objects*) can be constructed by building object spaces on top of a collection of base atomic types, using two object constructors: sets and tuples. (Bancilhon and Khoshafian, 1986; 1989), (Khoshafian, 1989), and (Abiteboul et al., 1990) present more general complex objects using set and tuple object constructors.

The post-relational complex object models mentioned so far only allow tree-structured object spaces. Although rich in conceptual foundation, these models did not allow the same object to be a sub-object of multiple parents. They do not support graph-structured object spaces. To have this ability, object models need to support the object-oriented concept of object identity (Chapter 4). One of the earlier object-oriented models that fully supported object identity was FAD (Bancilhon et al., 1987), which was implemented at the MCC research consortium in Austin, Texas. Objects in FAD are constructs from sets, tuples, and atomic objects. Each object has an identity, independent of its type (set, tuple, or atomic) or value. Other object models that allow the construction of general graph-structured object spaces include GEM (Zaniolo, 1983), LDM (Kuper and Vardi, 1984), and (Leclusc et al., 1988).

As explained earlier, the semantic data models and the complex object models were mostly research proposals, projects, or prototypes. The complex object models and the semantic data models laid a firm foundation for the development of a number of object-oriented databases, both in research and the marketplace. Concepts such as complex objects, object identity, inheritance, and set and tuple valued attributes propagated these powerful object-oriented database systems. Each object-oriented database was influenced by one or more of the complex and semantic data modeling alternatives.

Perhaps through eagerness to explore novel and emerging technologies, computer scientists took quick notice of the opportunities and potential of the integration of object-oriented concepts with database capabilities (concurrency, persistence, access methods, querying, and the like).

With the introduction of object-oriented database systems such as GemStone from Servio Logic, Gbase from Graphael, and Vbase from Ontologic, object-oriented databases became commercially available around 1986. The first object-oriented database workshop in Asilomar during the summer of 1986, also demonstrated that great enthusiasm (similar to that in the object-oriented programming communities) was permeating the database community. The following years witnessed the development of several commercial object-oriented databases including Statice from Symbolics (Symbolics, 1988), SIM from UNISYS, Ontos also from Ontologic, and many others.

Currently there are at least six approaches for the incorporation of object-oriented capabilities in databases:

1. Novel database data model/data language approach
2. Extending an existing database language with object-oriented capabilities
3. Extending an existing object-oriented programming language with database capabilities
4. Providing extendable object-oriented database management system libraries
5. Embedding object-oriented database language constructs within a host language
6. Application-specific products with underlying object-oriented databases

Each of these alternatives is discussed in more detail in Chapter 7.

Object-Oriented Databases in the 1990s

Noted earlier was the prospect that the 1990s will be known as the decade that launched the object-oriented era of computation. This applies to object-oriented languages, systems, databases and interfaces. For languages and user interfaces, we are already witnessing the emergence of a number of standards: C++, Smalltalk-80, CLOS, and Ada for object-oriented languages; Microsoft's PM, Hewlett-Packard's NewWave, and IBM's OfficeVision for user interfaces and environments.

In the area of databases, things are not so clear. Standards are *not* emerging. The market share of object-oriented databases in the foreseeable future is negligible, when compared to the relational, network, and hierarchical market shares. In fact, relational databases are just taking off and they will continue to dominate in the 1990s. Yet, relational database management systems *are* starting to incorporate object-oriented features. This option falls under the second approach just listed. Because many companies are incorporating object-oriented features in their products, the dominant standard will be object-oriented extensions of SQL.

When discussing databases, however, readers should look at a broader perspective and remember that the future of databases is in fact *intelligent* databases (Parsaye, et al., 1989). These are databases which tightly integrate artificial intelligence, information-retrieval, object-oriented, and multimedia technologies into traditional databases. Therefore the extension of databases with additional capabilities is not limited to object orientation. Support of inferencing (artificial intelligence), full-text retrieval (information retrieval) and multimedia data types (voice, text, graphics) is equally important. These capabilities will be standardized as extensions of SQL. The authors discuss intelligent databases in detail in Chapter 7.

1.2.3 The Evolution of Object Orientation in User Interfaces

The primary means of communication with computers until recently has been through command-based interfaces. In command interfaces, users have to learn a large set of commands to get their job done. In early computer systems, paper tapes, cards, and batch jobs were the primary means of communicating these commands to the computers. Later, timesharing systems allowed the use of CRT terminals to interact/communicate with the computer. These early systems were heavily burdened by users trying to share precious computer resources such as CPU and peripherals.

The batch systems and time sharing led to command-driven user interfaces. Users had to memorize commands and options or consult a large set of user manuals. The early mainframe and minicomputer systems required a large set of instruction manuals on how to use the system. In some systems, meaningful terms were used for command names to help the end-user. But in other systems the end-user had to memorize arcane sequences of keystrokes to accomplish certain tasks.

Early users of computers were engineers, and what we now call expert users; users that had a lot of interest in knowing more about the computer systems and the technology. Command line interfaces were acceptable or tolerated by the majority of these users. In the 1970s, computers were introduced to a new class of users: secretaries, managers, and "non-techies." These new users were less interested in learning computer technology and more interested in getting their job done through the machine. The command based interfaces caused many of these new users to develop computer phobia. Imagine the thought of memorizing commands made up of "Control-Shift-D" to delete a word or "Control-Escape-D" to restore a word.

To make life easier for the end-user, a large collection of devices have been invented to control, monitor, and display information. The early (and still widely used) peripherals are the keyboard and the video terminal. But, it was not until the late 70s that the commercial introduction of the mouse changed user-interfaces dramatically.

The mouse was around before the 70s, but only in research groups. In the 60s, projects at SRI International, MIT, and other universities led to the invention of pointing devices and windowing systems (Perry and Voelcker, 1989). The mouse and joystick were among some of the few pointing devices that were invented in this period. Also, these research pioneers invented the notion of splitting the screen to allow multiple windows and direct manipulation of objects.

In the 70s, researchers at Xerox PARC were busy designing powerful new workstations armed with graphical user-interfaces. Their experiments concentrated on applying the associative memory of the end-user combined with direct manipulation capabilities (Johnson et al., 1989). The basic assumption of these new workstations was that one user could have a powerful desktop computer totally dedicated to that user's task. Thus, the computer is not only used to perform the task, but can also provide a much more intuitive and easy-to-use environment.

To apply the associative memory of the user, menus and dialog boxes are used to interact with the user. Instead of memorizing commands for each stage, the user selects a command from a menu bar displaying a list of available commands. For example, Figure 1.9 displays the menu bar from the Microsoft Write utility. This menu bar displays a list of commands available such as File, Edit, and Search. When the mouse is clicked on any one of these menu commands the appropriate action is taken. Pull-down and pop-up menus display options (commands) available for each selection. Figure 1.10 shows the pull-down menu displayed when the Character menu item is selected. The user can then select from different character styles.

Figure 1.9 Microsoft Write menu bar.

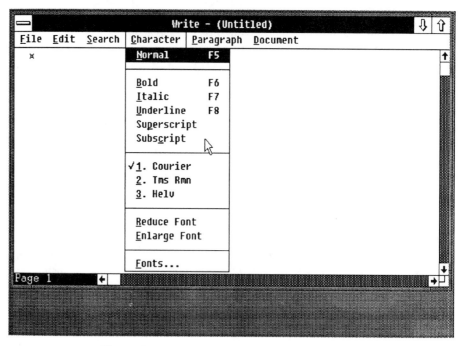

Figure 1.10 Typical Microsoft Write pulldown menu.

Dialog boxes allow more complex interaction between the user and the computer. Dialog boxes employ a large collection of control objects such as dials, buttons, scroll bars, and editable boxes. For example, in Figure 1.11, a dialog box is used to open a file. This dialog box is composed of two buttons called Open and Close, an edit box that allows a file name to be entered, and a scroll region that allows navigation through the list of files and directories available on the disk. Clicking on the Open button causes the file to be viewed.

In graphical user-interfaces, textual data is not the only form of interaction. Icons represent concepts such as file folders, waste baskets, and printers. Icons symbolize words and concepts commonly applied in different situations. Figure 1.12 shows the Microsoft Paint utility with its palette composed of icons. Each one of these icons represents a certain type of painting behavior. Once the pencil icon is clicked, for example, the cursor can behave as a pencil to draw lines. Application of icons to the user-interface design are still being explored in new computer systems and software such as the NeXT computer user interface (see Figures 1.13*a* and 1.13*b*).

The idea of metaphors has brought the computer closer to the natural environment of the end-user. The concept of physical metaphor paradigm developed by Alan Kay, initiated most of the research for object-oriented user interfaces. "The physical meta phor is a way of saying that the visual displays of a computer system should present the images of real physical objects, with some degree of abstraction" (Veith, 1988).

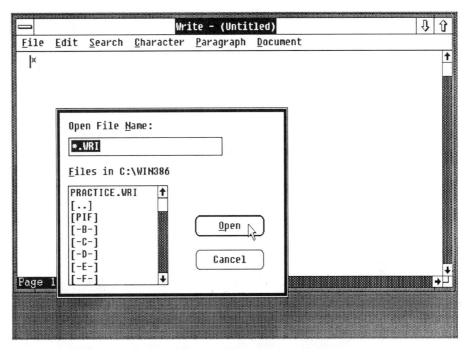

Figure 1.11 Typical Microsoft dialog box.

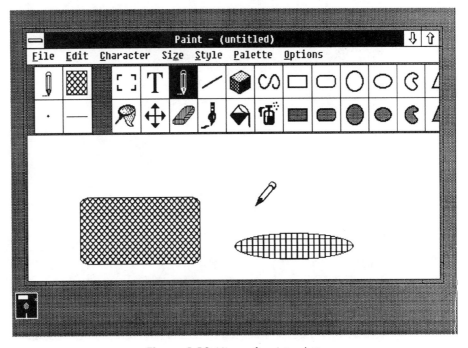

Figure 1.12 Microsoft paint palette.

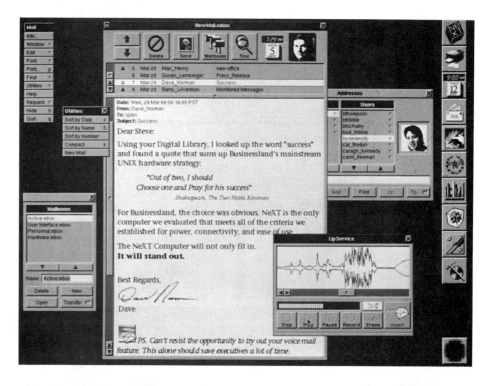

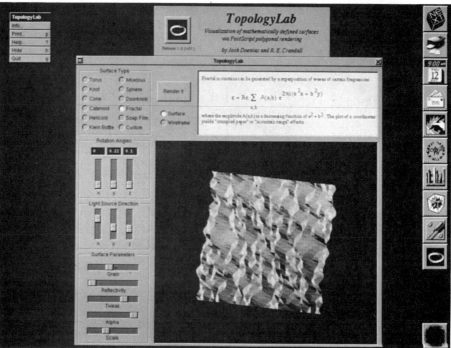

Figure 1.13 Typical NeXT user interfaces.

For example, the wastepaper basket icon can be used to discard objects from the system by simply dragging the unwanted objects into the wastepaper basket, as in real life. The desktop metaphor probably has been the most famous paradigm. Because of the large set of potential office users, this metaphor can have the most dramatic effect. In this paradigm, the computer presents information and objects as they would appear and behave in an office, using icons for folders, in-baskets, out-baskets, and calendars. OfficeVision from IBM relies heavily on the desktop metaphor in its graphic user-interfaces. It provides an environment for secretaries and executives to represent and manipulate office objects such as files, folders, and even the telephone.

In systems employing the desktop metaphor and direct manipulation, end-user data and the application are not separate entities. The object representing the end-user information encapsulates the data as well as the procedure required to modify it. In Hewlett-Packard's NewWave for example, an icon representing a report not only contains data but it contains information about the word processor used. Upon clicking the mouse on this icon, the appropriate word processor is started and loaded with the user data (see Figure 1.14a).

Object orientation (via physical metaphor) allows novice users to create new applications and compound documents. In Metaphor's DIS, an end-user can create ad hoc applications graphically by connecting icons representing tools such as database management systems, spreadsheets, and graphics (see Figure 1.14b). Further, the user

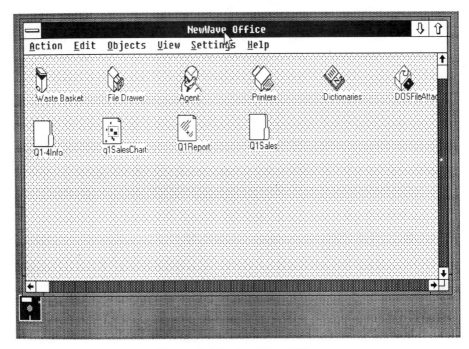

Figure 1.14a NewWave Office.

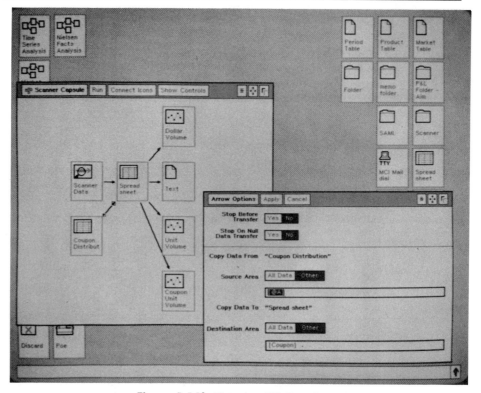

Figure 1.14b Metaphor DIS Capsules.

can graphically direct individual icons to produce certain results. For example, the database management utility can be visually programmed to produce the result of an SQL query from a corporate database (see Figure 1.14c). Users can create documents composed of different objects such as text, graphics, and images.

Object orientation also comes to the rescue of the software engineer, by lightening the burden of user-interface development. New user-interface concepts require the development of complex software to display screen objects and handle their events. Simple tasks such as displaying a featureless window require several pages of code in a high level language such as C. User-interface development environments such as MacApp and Actor provide libraries composed of object hierarchies. Each class within the hierarchy defines the attributes necessary for its objects in addition to inheriting features from its superclasses. Each object within the hierarchy communicates with other objects in the system through transmission of messages. The user-interface designer can further extend the class hierarchy by adding their own screen object designs. These new screen objects can inherit properties from existing classes. In addition, they can refine old properties or define new properties as needed.

The most recent advances in user-interface design come from the newly formed NeXT Corporation. Using the NextStep Interface Builder, a designer can quickly develop

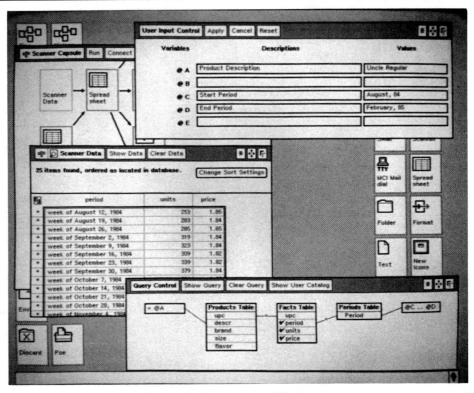

Figure 1.14c Metaphor DIS Query.

a user interface graphically by selecting, placing, and resizing user-interface objects (Webster, 1989). Figure 1.14*d* depicts the NextStep *Interface Builder*.

Object-Oriented User Interfaces in the 1990s

In the 90s, computer systems will include much more powerful processor(s), higher resolution displays, and even more memory. A larger portion of the computing power of the future machines will be used to make computers more aesthetic. The user interfaces in the 1990s will be more intuitive, handle diverse types of objects, and provide visual programming environments.

Graphical user interfaces will play a dominant role in the industry. Direct manipulation of objects will be widespread and will make computers accessible to a broader audience. In the future, direct manipulation will allow developers to design user interfaces by selecting and resizing screen objects directly on the screen. Tools such as NextStep will be commonly used to develop sophisticated user interfaces. Also, the end-user will be able to build an application graphically by connecting preconstructed parameterized components.

Emerging technologies such as Digital Video Interactive (DVI), optical disk drives, and digital signal processors will permit the end-user to interact with multimedia

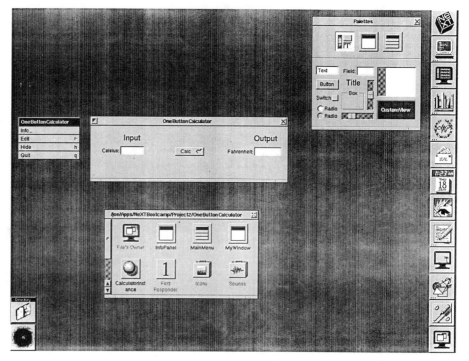

Figure 1.14d NeXT Interface Builder.

applications. Object-orientation will be exploited to integrate diverse sets of objects ranging from text and voice to images and video. Apple's HyperCard and other hypermedia tools will be used more often to interconnect these disparate objects.

Visual programming will help both nonprogrammers and programmers develop applications. Iconic and visual languages will allow programmers to create object types and quickly design the flow of control for the application. Visual SQL (Trimble and Chappell, 1989) and QBE (Zloof, 1977) will allow an executive to generate a report or navigate through corporate databases on mini and mainframe computers without being computer-literate.

■ 1.3 EXAMPLES

Today's programming and database languages provide little help for direct representation of user-defined types or for operations on those types. Most of the languages provide a set of operators that deal with system-defined types such as integer, float, and character strings. In most cases, the application developer resorts to complex and bulky code to represent user-defined entities. As stated previously, one of the major goals of object orientation is to allow the programming language or database language to be extendable and thus be able to deal with user-defined entities directly.

Throughout this book, we use a wide range of application areas to demonstrate object-oriented concepts. This section introduces examples often used in this book to demonstrate the application of object orientation in office automation, scientific application, and computer-aided design (CAD). These three application areas, along with many others, are apt to benefit most from object orientation. Each one of these areas requires representation of complex objects and can benefit from object orientation concepts such as abstract data types, inheritance, and object indentity.

1.3.1 Office Automation

The office automation example encompasses objects commonly found in a sales office—employees, salespersons, accounts, and secretaries. This application area will be used to demonstrate abstract data types, inheritance, and object identity. Figure 1.15 depicts the hierarchy of object types used in this example. For each one of these types, a set of attributes is defined. Each one of these attributes represents

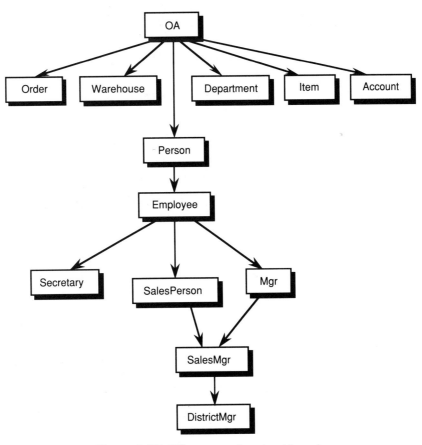

Figure 1.15 Office automation class hierarchy.

structural or behavioral components of the type. Structural attributes are used to represent factual information, such as quota or set of accounts for *SalesPerson* objects. Behavioral attributes are used to represent information that is derived from fact. For example, with *Employee*, *Evaluate Bonus* may be computed based on *rank* and *salary* of employees. In addition, each object type definition inherits attributes from its supertype(s). *SalesPerson* inherits its *Salary, Department,* and *Rank* attributes from *Employee.* And *SalesMgr* inherits attributes from both *SalesPerson* and *Mgr* object types. The major object types included in this example are:

1. *Account:* each account represents a corporation that buys items from the sales office. For each account, some of the attributes kept are *Name, Number* and *SetOfItemsOrdered.*

2. *Order:* at any given time, a set of orders are active. For each active order, the following information is kept: *Account, SetOfItems,* and *Discount.*

3. *Item:* each office sells one or more items: printers, mouse, personal computers, and so on. For each item, *Cost* and *Name* of the item are kept.

4. *Employee:* all employees of the sales office belong to one of the subtypes defined within the *Employee* hierarchy. The attributes for *Employee* objects (and sub-objects) include *Salary, Department, Rank, EvaluateBonus,* and *AccumulatedVacationLeave. Employee* subtypes include:

   a. *SalesPerson*—for each *SalesPerson* object (besides inheriting the *Employee* attributes), attributes include *Quota, Orders, Accounts, Commission, TotalActiveOrders,* and *AddNewAccount.*

   b. *SalesMgr*—attributes are inherited from both *SalesPerson* and *Mgr* object types, including *Skill, Quota,* and *Commission.* In addition, *SalesForceSize* is kept for each *SalesMgr* object.

   c. *DistrictMgr*—for each object of *DistrictMgr* type, *DistrictBudget* is defined, in addition to all attributes inherited from its *SalesMgr* supertype.

1.3.2   Scientific Application

Complex numbers are used to demonstrate application of object orientation in scientific areas. Complex numbers are used in scientific applications like thermodynamics or the study of electrical and electronic circuits. The set of complex numbers is a mathematical numbering system. A given complex number contains a set of two numbers: a real and an imaginary number. Similar to integers and real numbers, complex numbers can be used in arithmetic (addition, subtraction, . . .) and relational (equality, greater than, . . .) operations. This application area will be used to demonstrate abstract data types, operator overloading, and object identity.

The following notation is commonly used to demonstrate complex numbers:

$a + bi$

where a is the real part and b is the coefficient of i, which stands for the (imaginary) square root of -1.

Given two complex numbers $x = a + bi$ and $y = c + di$, the sum of x and y is $x + y = (a + c) + (b + d)i$. The multiplication of x and y is $x * y = (a + bi)(c + di) = (a*c - b*d) + (b*c + a*d)i$. For example, given $x = 1 + 3i$ and $y = 4 + 5i$, $x + y = 5 + 8i$ and $x * y = -11 + 17i$.

Given two complex numbers $x = a + bi$ and $y = c + di$, the equality of x and y is determined by $x == y$ if $a == c$ and $b == d$. For example, given $x = 1 + 2i$ and $y = 1 + 2i$ the result of $x == y$ is *true*. If $x = 1 + 3i$ and $y = 2 + 3i$ the result is *false*, as 1 is not equal to 2.

1.3.3 Computer-Aided Design

Computer-aided technologies ranging from mechanical, electrical, and electronic CAD to computer-aided software engineering (CASE) will likely benefit tremendously from object orientation. These technologies require representation of complex objects, and that is what object-oriented systems do best! The example in this section demonstrates the use of object orientation to represent complex CAD objects. This application area will be used to demonstrate abstract data types and inheritance.

The example chosen here is electronic CAD (ECAD), where a hardware designer has components that perform boolean operations such as **AND** gates and arithmetic operations such as **adder** gates. For demonstration purposes, we limit ourselves to 8-bit data only. Thus, all the components operate on 8-bit data. The basic building blocks for an electronic CAD design are the following:

> *Gates*—components that perform some operation. Some of these components are:
> And2 (AND gate with two inputs)
> And3 (AND gate with three inputs)
> Or2 (OR gate with two inputs)
> Add2 (Adder with two inputs)

> *Pad*—components used to stimulate or obtain results from a logic circuit. There are two types of pads in use:
> InPad (used to drive input to a circuit)
> OutPad (used to get results from a circuit)

> *Ports*—the inputs and outputs of gates and pads are represented by ports. Each port, in turn, can be connected to one or more other ports. For example, the output of an And2 gate can be connected to inputs of an And2 gate and an outPad simultaneously.

Figure 1.16 demonstrates a circuit composed of some of these components. Given the values I1 = 3 and I2 = 10, O1 will be 11 and O2 will be 2.

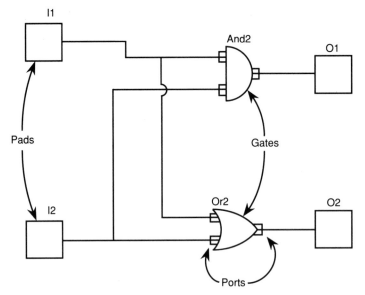

Figure 1.16 An ECAD example.

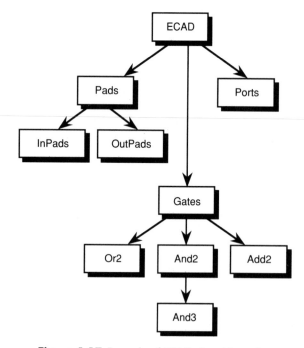

Figure 1.17 Example of ECAD class hierarchy.

Large computer software systems are used to develop and simulate an electronic design. A class hierarchy, as depicted in Figure 1.17, models different types of ECAD objects. Some of the functionalities provided by these object types are:

1. *Testability:* once a logic circuit is designed, verify the correct result. To perform this verification, the input pads are stimulated with data and the values of the output pads are observed and compared against a known result.

2. *Determine circularity:* some circuits are required to be acyclic. Given any component, determine if output ports are directly or indirectly connected to the input ports.

3. *Draw:* each component has its own standard shape that can be drawn at a specified position.

4. *Move:* move the current position of a component.

■ 1.4 SUMMARY

This chapter provided a brief introduction to object orientation. Object orientation models the real world as close to a user's perspective as possible. Object orientation provides better paradigms and techniques for constructing reusable software components and easily extensible libraries of software modules. This enhances the extensibility of programs developed through object-oriented methodologies. End-users, systems programmers, and application developers are all benefiting from object-oriented modeling and programming technologies.

The fundamental object-oriented concepts are abstract data types, inheritance, and object identity. An abstract data type describes a collection of objects with the same structure and behavior. Abstract data types extend the notion of data types through hiding the implementation of the user-defined operations (messages) associated with the data type. Abstract data types are implemented through classes. Classes can inherit from each other. Through inheritance we can build new software modules (such as classes) on top of an existing hierarchy of modules. Inheriting behavior enables code sharing (and hence reusability) among software modules. Inheriting representation enables structure sharing among data objects. Identity is that property of an object that distinguishes each object from all others. With object identity objects can contain or refer to other objects. Object identity organizes the objects of the object space manipulated by an object-oriented program.

The chapter examined the impact of the object-oriented technology on three different areas of computer science: programming languages, database management systems, and user interfaces. For each of these areas, the evolution of object orientation through the past decades was traced. Also outlined was the future direction of each field in the current decade.

At the end of the chapter, we presented three examples that will be used throughout the book. These examples were chosen from diverse application areas: office automation, scientific applications, and computer-aided design. For each one of these examples, this chapter defined the problem and gave the definitions and terms that will be used throughout the following chapters.

2

ABSTRACT
DATA TYPES

■ 2.1 INTRODUCTION

Chapter 1 gave an overview of the object-oriented concepts and the evolution of object orientation in programming languages, databases, and user interfaces. This chapter examines the first fundamental object-oriented concept: abstract data typing. Section 2.1 provides the basis for understanding the role of abstract data types within object-oriented systems. This section also elucidates the object/message paradigm. Section 2.2 discusses classes, the language constructs used to define abstract data types in most object-oriented languages. This section also covers the related concepts of instance variables, methods, and messages.

Sections 2.3 and 2.4 turn to the topics of *overloading* and *dynamic binding*. In conventional languages an operation such as " + " could be used for objects of different data types. In object-oriented systems this sort of polymorphism, called overloading, is available to every user-defined abstract data type. From dynamic binding, Section 2.5 moves on to the powerful concept of *parametric polymorphism*. Also known as generic types, parametric polymorphism allows sharing of code among data types that have a common structure.

Finally, some object-oriented systems introduce mechanisms to create *integrity constraints* associated with objects or their operations. These constraints help ensure correct implementations of systems using abstract data types. Constraints are discussed in Section 2.6.

Throughout this chapter, we also compare the abstract data type approach to more traditional procedural models.

2.1.1 Data Types

All programming languages provide some support of data types. For example, the conventional programming language Pascal supports base types such as integers, reals, and characters as well as type constructors such as arrays and records. Abstract data types extend the notion of a data type; they hide the implementation of the user-defined operations associated with the data type. This information hiding capability allows the development of reusable and extensible software components. Such merits of abstract data typing will be illustrated throughout this chapter.

A data type in general describes the representation of a set of objects. For example, an item consists of:

Name: The name of the item
Number: The identifying number of the item
Description: The item's characteristic features
Cost: The cost of the item

Name, *Number*, *Cost*, and so on are the attributes (also called fields, slots, or instance variables) of the *Items* data type. Every item will have specific values for each of these attributes. Here are some specific *items:*

Name: Wrench
Number: 1
Cost: $20.00

Name: Hammer
Number: 2
Cost: $10.00

Notice that the name of an item is a string of characters, the number of an item is an integer, and the cost of an item is expressed in dollars. "Characters," "integers," and "dollars" are themselves data types. Every programming language comes equipped with a collection of base data types, usually including integers, reals, characters, and so on. Programming languages also support a number of built-in type constructors to generate more complex types. For example, Pascal supports records and arrays.

So far the term *data type* has been used to describe a set of objects with the same representation. There are also a number of operations associated with each data type. It is possible to perform arithmetic on integer and float data types, concatenate character strings, or retrieve or modify the cost of an item.

An informal definition of a data type is:

Representation + Operations

In conventional languages such as C or Pascal the operations on a data type are compositions of type constructor and base type operations.

Operations = Constructor Operations + Base Operations

For example, to increase the cost of an item by 10 percent, the Cost attribute of the item must be accessed and updated. Assume *ITM* is the item record; the Pascal implementation of the operation will be:

ITM.Cost := ITM.Cost * 1.1;

The type constructor operators typically are generic extraction operations. For example, the selection operation for retrieving a field from a record needs two arguments:

1. The name of the object (*ITM* in the previous example).
2. The name of the record's field (*Cost* in the previous example).

Field selection is generic in the sense that the same mechanism is used for all record types. Some common type constructors include records, arrays, lists, sets, and sequences.

2.1.2 From Data Types to Abstract Data Types

Abstract data types (ADTs) provide an additional mechanism whereby a clear separation is made between the interface and implementation of the data type. The implementation of an abstract data type consists of:

1. The representation: choosing the data structures.
2. The operations: choosing the algorithms.

The interface with the abstract data type is brought about through its associated operations.

Consider the definition of the abstract data type for *SalesPerson* in the office automation example:

Representation:
Name
Address
TelephoneNumber
OfficeLocation
Salary
Commission
Accounts
Quota
Orders

Operations:
    AddNewAccount
    RemoveOrder
    GiveRaise
    ChangeQuota
    ChangeCommission
    ChangeAddress
      and so on

The actual data structures chosen to store the representation of an abstract data type are invisible to its users or clients. The algorithms used to implement each of an ADT's operations are also encapsulated within the ADT. The information-hiding feature of abstract data typing means that objects have "public" interfaces. However the representations and implementations of these interfaces are "private." This is illustrated in Figure 2.1.

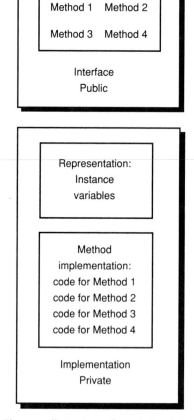

Figure 2.1 The overall structure of an abstract data type (Class).

The basic idea behind this type of abstraction is rather simple. Consider a base type such as an integer in a conventional programming language like C or Pascal. The language provides a finite number of operations such as $+$, $*$, and $-$ that represent the addition, multiplication, and subtraction operators of integers. Some additional operations are *remainder* and *quotient*, which evaluate the remainder and quotient of integer division. (For example, 15 remainder 4 is 3, 15 quotient 7 is 2.) These operators have well-defined associative, commutative, and distributive properties which fully define the behavior of integer objects.

Most reasonable users simply invoke these operators to manipulate integers (although some lower-level languages like C allow the bitwise manipulation of base types). Indeed, in some languages *only* these operations are permitted on objects of the type integer. In Pascal, for instance, the internal bit/string representation of an integer (such as, using 32-bit two's complement) is completely hidden. Pascal programs manipulating integers can easily be ported and compiled on systems using entirely different internal representations for integers. This is illustrated in Figure 2.2.

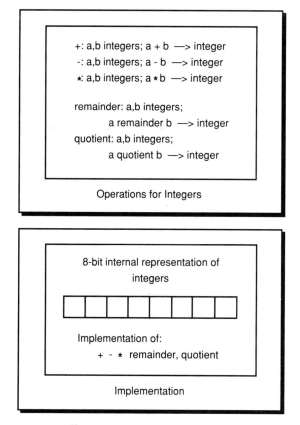

Figure 2.2 The integer data type.

A language incorporating abstract data types extends these benefits to every object or datum in a program. The abstraction mechanism that enforces the access and update of objects with user-defined types is encapsulated. Hence it can only be performed through the interface operations defined for the particular type. Contrast this with conventional programming languages like C or Pascal where the set of integers defined in the following can be manipulated by any function or procedure within the scope of the record's type.

```
type SetOfIntegers = ^ListElem;
    ListElem = record
                IntegerElement: Integer;
                Next: ListElem
            end;
```

In other words, we can traverse an object that is a *SetOfIntegers* as a list. We can directly retrieve or update any particular *Integer*, that is, any one of the object's elements. This is illustrated in Figure 2.3 where the *Find* function traverses the linked list to see if a given element is in the linked list. Now suppose that the representation

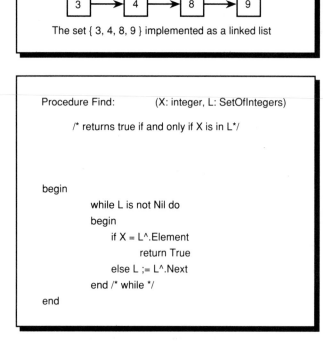

Figure 2.3 The function *Find*.

of a set of integers is changed, perhaps implemented through an array of integers. The *Find* function and all other functions that depend on the data structures used to manipulate the object type must be modified.

If instead, abstract data typing is used, a number of set operations can be defined for sets. Manipulations of sets will be done only through these external operations. These operations should completely govern the behavior of sets of integers. Internally, a set of integers can be stored and implemented as a linked list of records, as an array of integers, or by any other representation. It will make absolutely no difference as far as the users of these sets of integers are concerned. However, when the representation is modified the function *Find* and all other functions and operations of the abstract data type have to be modified.

In the Office Automation example, sets are used to store accounts, active orders, salespeople managed by a district manager, districts, and so forth. To perform set operations such as insert element, delete element, union, and intersection the abstract data type interface operations must be used: *AddNewAccount*, *HireSalesPerson*, *FireSalesPerson*, *ChangeCommission*, and *AddNewOrder*.

The internal representation and implementation of these operations could be modified at any time without affecting the interface with the abstract data type *SalesPerson*. For instance, the sets storing accounts for salespeople could use an array or list representation without affecting the public interface of salespeople. Or an entirely different representation could be possible for sets storing the salespeople reporting to a sales manager. Changes in attribute implementation do not result in changes for the ADT interface.

2.1.3 The Object/Message Paradigm

Object orientation is often described using the object/message paradigm. Objects make up the computational universe for this paradigm. Each object responds to a prescribed collection of messages that comprise that object's interface.

In procedural models of computation, routines or functions call each other to return data values or update input data parameters. In the object/message model, every datum is an object that is capable of processing requests known as messages. These messages may do either of two things. They may ask the object to perform a computation and return a value. Or they may modify the object's content, changing its state or value. Figure 1.2*a* in Chapter 1 illustrated three objects sending messages to each other: object 1 received a message 1 and decided to send a message 2 to object 2. In its turn object 2 sent a message 3 to object 3. In terms of computational power, the two models are equivalent. In terms of modeling, software development, software extensibility, and reusability the object/message model is far superior.

Graphical interfaces represent the most natural method of using the object/message approach in human/computer computational interactions. The Macintosh, the OS/2 Presentation Manager, NeXT, and Metaphor all use object-based graphical user-interface environments. These products and others present the user with screens populated by icons and windows. An icon can represent a terminal window, a trash can (in which we can dispose of other objects), a word processor, spreadsheet, chart, or any other application.

Imagine sending the message, "Open thyself! I want to interact with thee!" to an icon (by clicking on the icon with a mouse). In response, the icon opens as a window and offers a menu of choices. These choices represent the messages that can be handled by the object. If the user opens a word processing file, it would be possible to save the file, change the fonts, print the file, or other operations.

The object's icon provides a physical metaphor for another, underlying object. For example, in the Macintosh environment a trash can is the icon used to depict the object disposal function. This physical representation helps the user easily understand and recognize the functionality provided by the object behind the icon.

One of the earlier pioneers of the physical metaphor concept was Alan Kay, who had considerable influence in the development of the Smalltalk, the Star, and the Macintosh programming environments (White, 1983). Object-oriented, graphical user interfaces and environments are discussed in more detail in Chapter 8.

Compared to conventional models, the object/message paradigm is a different computational model. The premise is that the data universe consists of a collection of objects where each object has as its interface a set of messages to which it responds. All objects can thus communicate with each other by sending messages to one another.

Objects in this model have internal states. As indicated earlier, external messages can cause objects' internal states to change. Messages can also retrieve values calculated from an object's internal state. These concepts will be clearly illustrated throughout this chapter.

The *data* is the active computational entity in the object/message model of computation. A program entails a number of objects sending messages to one another. By contrast, the *procedure* is the main computational entity in conventional models. A conventional program consists of a number of procedures which call one another, sometimes passing data as arguments.

Underlying the object/message paradigm is the powerful abstract data typing discipline. As mentioned earlier, abstract data types define encapsulated sets of similar objects with an associated collection of operations. Therefore abstract data types specify the structure, as well as the behavior of objects. The structural specifications describe what objects look like. The behavioral specifications describe what messages are applicable to each object.

In summing up, abstract data typing hides the internal representation of objects from the outside world and protects from external meddling the internal algorithms used to implement the objects' behavior. An object sends a message to another object. It is up to the recipient to figure out how to respond to the message. In effect, the objects say to one another, "Tell me what you want me to accomplish. I'll do it in my own way." Abstract data typing and the object/message computational model provide a more delegatory mode of computation.

2.1.4 Modularization through Procedures versus Objects

Modularization is a well-established engineering principle. It is well-known that an intricate problem often yields to a "divide and conquer" strategy. This principle is by no means exclusive to engineering problems in science or computer science. For instance, in the 18th and 19th centuries, European colonialists used divide and conquer tactics to subdue ethnic groups in the areas they controlled. As the complexity of software approaches the complexity of the real world, modularization becomes imperative. Equally important, we must define our modules intelligently. Modularization alone is not the answer; long after decolonization, some third-world countries have yet to recover from wrecklessly exploitative uses of the ancient divide and conquer strategy.

In classical programming languages modularization is centered around procedures (functions, subroutines). In object-oriented languages, modularization or problem partitioning are often accomplished through abstract data typing. The object-oriented approach is a better abstraction mechanism for the following reasons:

1. Modeling of the real world.
2. Autonomy.
3. Generation of correct applications.
4. Reusability.

Each of these reasons is discussed in the subsections to follow.

2.1.4.1 Modeling of the Real World

The decomposition of the object space in an object-oriented application is data based. This means the data objects are the central entities in an object-oriented program. By contrast, conventional programming is procedure-based. Objects such as items, accounts, sales people, and managers have well-defined behavior and encapsulated algorithms implement these behaviors as object interfaces. This property of the object-oriented methodology cannot be over-emphasized. Most of the other advantages stem from this fundamental modeling potential. By contrast, procedure-based decomposition is unnatural in most applications.

Abstract data typing provides a more direct representation of the real world. The clarity, robustness, debugging, and maintenance of programs is greatly improved. This property of object orientation is illustrated throughout the book.

2.1.4.2 Autonomy

Abstract data typing allows objects to behave as autonomous agents, responding to coherent collections of messages. Consider the work flow in an automated office

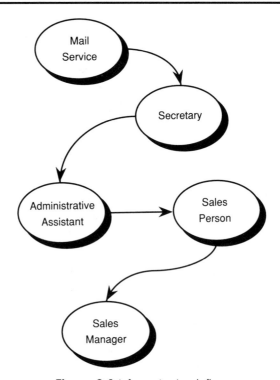

Figure 2.4 Information/work flow.

environment. As illustrated in Figure 2.4 information flows from one node to the other. The nodes are:

mail service
secretary
administrative assistant
salesperson
sales manager

Each of these nodes has specific authority and responsibilities for handling certain of the many types of information that come into the office. For example, ultimate control of the budget can only be authorized by the sales manager. And most managers learn rather quickly (sometimes painfully) that the control of their appointment calendar is best delegated to the administrative assistant.

Imagine a procedural abstraction of this work-flow model. Each node has to "learn" three things for each piece of information being processed:

1. The form of the information: invoice, accounts receivable form, or requisition form, and so on.

2. The authorization (or lack of it) on the particular information form.

3. The procedure of the particular task to be performed.

If a company goes through a reorganization, the forms, procedures, authorizations, and even the work-flow model may be modified. Then each node in the network has to re-learn **1**, **2**, and **3**. This parallels what happens in conventional programming. The modification of even a record data type has a rippling effect through all procedures that use the data type.

Now imagine the same work-flow model using abstract data typing. Not only the nodes, but the forms themselves will be autonomous objects with encapsulated behavior. For example, each information object (such as an invoice) responds to a prescribed collection of messages. The forms "know" the authorization level of each work-flow node and can place themselves on the appropriate person's desk for signature.

Similarly, the people performing the work-flow node functions respond only to the set of messages relevant to their position. They are concerned only with their own particular procedures and tasks. In fact, these algorithms are completely local to each node: "I don't care which word processor you use, but please have my letter typed and ready by 9:00 A.M. Thank You!"

Similarly the processing of the data is performed through messages to the data: "Invoice #3, please staple yourself with Expense form of Mr. Jones. Thank You!" Or an administrative assistant might request: "Expense form in folder 2, please give me total expense. Thank You!" (Please note that unlike conventional programming, object-orientation is very polite and civilized.)

2.1.4.3 *Generation of Correct Applications*

The modularization in object-oriented programming allows the development of more robust code bases:

1. Encapsulated abstract data types can easily be "stubbed." Stubbing means the actual code that implements an operation (method) is commented out and replaced by a diagnostic message (such as "You have invoked operation 01"). Through stubbing, modules that use or invoke the operation are not affected by bugs in the code implementing the operation.

2. We can easily incorporate exception-checking and error-handling mechanisms with either the data or the operations of the abstract data type.

3. Object-oriented modularization helps isolate errors within the abstract data type.

Besides hiding the implementation details, abstract data typing also protects objects from inadvertent modifications of their state. A user or client of the object must explicitly invoke an operation that modifies the state of the object. This ensures that the procedure updating the object's state has some understanding of the object's semantics.

2.1.4.4 *Reusability*

The conventional mechanism for generating reusable code is through libraries of routines. There are several drawbacks to this approach (Meyer, 1988). For example, the routines may be written in a language that does not incorporate parametric polymorphism and overloading. Then the reusable library will consist of either a large number of very similar routines or very long and non-extensible routines involving huge case statements. Sections 2.3 and 2.5 discuss the reusability of software components constructed in an object-oriented framework using overloading and polymorphism, respectively.

2.1.5 Summarizing the Benefits of Abstract Data Typing

Data typing already provides numerous benefits to the programmer. Through encapsulation, abstract data typing extends these advantages considerably. The advantages of abstract data typing can be summarized as follows:

1. Allows better conceptualization and modeling of the real world. Enhances representation and understandability. Categorizes objects based on common structure and behavior.

2. Enhances the robustness of the system. If the underlying language allows the specification of the types for each variable, abstract data typing allows type checking to avoid run-time type errors. Furthermore, integrity checks on data and operations greatly enhance the correctness of programs.

3. Enhances performance. For typed systems, knowing the types of objects allows compile time optimization. It also permits better clustering strategies for the persistent objects as discussed in Chapter 7.

4. Better captures the semantics of the type. Abstract data typing clusters or localizes the operations and the representation of attributes.

5. Separates the implementation from the specification. Allows the modification and enhancement of the implementation without affecting the public interface of the abstract data type.

6. Allows extensibility of the system. Reusable software components are easier to create and maintain.

2.1.6 Chapter Organization

The rest of the chapter discusses the basic concepts associated with abstract data typing. Section 2.2 shows how classes implement abstract data types. This section defines instances, methods, messages, and many other important notions, with illustrative examples. Section 2.3 shows how overloading can be used to enhance extensibility. Section 2.4 discusses a related concept, namely dynamic binding. Section 2.5 exposes the power of parametric polymorphism. Section 2.6 shows how constraints can be used to construct more complete abstract data types.

■ 2.2 CLASSES

Class is the language construct most commonly used to define abstract data types in object-oriented programming languages.

One of the earlier uses of classes was in Simula (Dahl and Nygaard, 1966; Dahl, Myhrhaug and Nygaard, 1970), to declare sets of similar objects. In Simula, classes were used primarily as templates to create objects of the same structure. The attributes of an object can be base types such as integers, reals, and booleans. Or they may be arrays, procedures, or instances of other classes. Thus the behavior *and* structure of objects are attributes in Simula.

In Simula, the attributes of an object can be accessed directly through a dot (period) notation. If *JOHN* is an instance of *Person* we can access his name directly through *JOHN.name*. (Note the similarity to the mechanism used to access fields in Pascal records.) This applies both to attributes which are values as well as to attributes which are procedures. For example, if *JOHN* is actually an employee, we could have given him a 10 percent raise with the statement:

> JOHN.GiveRaise(10)

In the above statement, *GiveRaise* is a procedure which modifies the *Salary* attribute of *JOHN*.

Simula localized or clustered the procedures associated with a type through class constructs. However, in allowing direct access to attributes, it failed to provide information hiding.

Smalltalk (Goldberg and Robson, 1983) and other object-oriented languages refined and extended the concepts of class and inheritance introduced by Simula in several ways. In Smalltalk, access to and updates of attribute values (also referred to as instance variables) could be done only through messages. Smalltalk also introduced message/object syntax. This syntax significantly differs from the procedure-oriented syntax of most conventional programming languages. The Smalltalk message/object paradigm is illustrated in this and subsequent sections.

A class incorporates the definition of the structure as well as the operations of the abstract data type. Thus, a class defines an abstract data type. Elements belonging to the collection of objects described by a class are called *instances* of the class.

Section 2.1.3 illustrated the representation and operations of *SalesPerson*. Figure 2.5 illustrates some of the methods of class *SalesPerson*. Figure 2.6 shows a number of instances of this Class: the salespersons "John Chan," "Mary Agrawal," "Suzan El-Fanzo," and "Jim Khatchian." (After all, this book was written in California!)

A class definition (minimally) includes the following:

1. The name of the class.
2. The external operations for manipulating the instances of the class. (These operators typically have a target object and a number of arguments.)

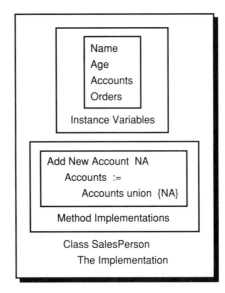

Figure 2.5 The class SalesPerson.

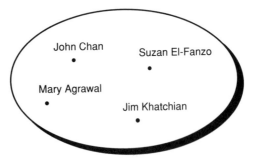

Figure 2.6 Instance of SalesPerson.

3. The internal representation.

4. The internal implementation of the interface.

For now, assume there is an implicit target object to which the operator applies. The target object is explained in more detail in Section 2.2.2. In an intuitive sense it is the recipient of the message or operator. In other words, each invocation of an operator applies to one and only one instance of the class. That instance is the target. For this example, the target will be one of the salespeople: John, Mary, Suzan, or Jim.

Here are descriptions of some of the interface operators (methods) of the class *SalesPerson*:

> Name: *AddNewAccount*
> Argument: The account to be allocated to the salesperson.
> Effect: Add and allocate a new account to the salesperson.
> Name: *RemoveOrder*
> Argument: The order that is no longer active.
> Effect: Remove the order from the set of pending orders allocated to the salesperson.
> Name: *TotalAccounts*
> Effect: Return the total number of accounts allocated to the salesperson

A class definition must also include the code needed to implement its interface operators. And it must include descriptions of the internal representation of objects, that is, object states.

We must remember that the values of the variables in the internal representation of the instances of the class pertain to individual objects. For instance, John's internal representation consists of his description (name, address, social security number, base salary) as well as the accounts and active orders handled by him. Some of the particular values that describe John might also describe other objects: For example, John shares his address with his spouse. However, the aggregation of the full set of these values captures the state of John as an instance of *SalesPerson*.

As discussed in the next section, values of the variables in the internal representation vary for each instance of a class. However, all the instances share the codes that implement the interface operators. Thus, there will be a single code base that implements the operators such as *AddNewAccount*, *RemoveOrder*, and *TotalAccounts*. These operators are always invoked with a target object as argument. The object-oriented system knows how to apply the appropriate operations to the target objects without violating their internal states. Interface operators have a purpose similar to procedure calls in conventional programming languages.

2.2.1 Instance Variables

The internal representation of a class is encompassed by the instance variables. In the previous example, instance variables are all the variables that hold the state of objects that are instances of the class *SalesPerson*. *Name*, *Address*, and *Salary* are all examples of instance variables. They take on different values for each instance, in this case each salesperson of the class *SalesPerson*. In other words, for each instance of a class, memory storage will be allocated to maintain the internal representation. Figure 2.7 illustrates the values and the resulting memory allocation for the salespeople instances John, Mary, Suzan, and Jim.

In some object-oriented languages, each instance variable declaration consists of:

<instance-variable-name> *<instance-variable-class-type>*

where the latter is the name of a class. It is an error to assign any type of object to these instance variables other than that specified in their declaration. Type constraints such as these are commonly used in many typed programming and database languages. In these languages, the types of the variables or record fields are explicitly declared and specified. The type may be a class, rather than a base type.

Through type constraints and algorithms that infer the types of expressions and variables, languages become strongly typed. Strongly typed languages' ability to trap type errors is one of their advantages. A type error occurs when an operator expects

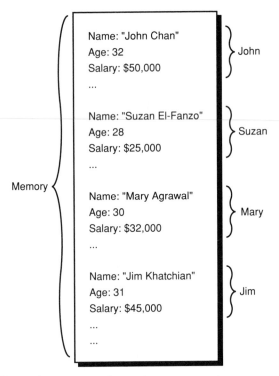

Figure 2.7 Memory allocated to instances of SalesPerson.

an argument to be an instance of a particular class C1, but is called with an argument that is an instance of a totally unrelated class C2. In a strongly typed language, type errors are detected at compile time. Successful compilation of a program in a strongly typed language guarantees that no type errors will be generated during actual program execution (Cardelli and Wegner, 1985). Examples of object-oriented languages that do extensive type checking during compilation include C++, Ada, Eiffel, and Trellis/Owl (Schaffert et al., 1986).

In the strongly typed object-oriented language Eiffel, the instance variables (known as *attributes* in Eiffel) of *Salesperson* would be declared as follows:

```
class SALESPERSON feature
     Name:                STRING;
     Address:             ADDRESS;
     TelephoneNumber:     INTEGER;
     OfficeLocation:      ADDRESS;
     Salary:              DOLLAR;
     Commission:          REAL;
     Accounts:            SET[ACCOUNT];
     Quota:               INTEGER;
     Orders:              SET[ORDER];
end –class SALESPERSON
```

STRING, *ADDRESS*, *INTEGER*, *DOLLAR*, are *REAL* are names of classes. *SET[ACCOUNT]* and *SET[ORDER]* are instances of the parameterized (generic) class *SET[T]*, with actual generic parameters *ACCOUNT* and *ORDER*, respectively. This parametric polymorphism is a powerful construct for typed languages and is discussed in more detail in Section 2.5.

The class name on the right side of the colon indicates that the instance variable named on the left will be an instance of that class. Thus for any instance of *SalesPerson* such as John Smith, *Name* will be a *STRING*, and *Address* will be an instance of the class *ADDRESS*. *TelephoneNumber* will be an integer. *OfficeLocation* will also be an instance of *ADDRESS*. Salary will be an instance of *DOLLAR*, while *Commission* will be a real number. *Accounts* will be an instance of *SET[ACCOUNT]*. *Quota* will be an *INTEGER*, and *Orders* will be an instance of *SET[ORDER]*.

The example of the class *SalesPerson* also illustrates the fact that the definition of instance variables can be either in terms of built-in classes or types such as *INTEGER* and *STRING*, or user-defined classes such as *ADDRESS*.

Not all object-oriented languages require the specification of a class name for the instance variables. There are "typeless" languages such as Smalltalk, APL, or LISP which do not specify types or classes for their variables. Indeed, in Smalltalk the programmer cannot specify the class of the object named by an instance variable. The same variable X, for instance, could be bound to the integer 5 and then subsequently to the string "XY" within the *same* session or program.

The declaration of the instance variables for *SalesPerson* in Smalltalk/V would be:

```
Object subclass: #SalesPerson
    instanceVariableNames: 'name address
        telephoneNumber officeLocation salary
        commission accounts quota
        orders'
```

Note that the classes (types) of the instance variables are not specified. Within the same program or method it is possible to bind the same instance variable to different types of objects. A single instance variable could be bound first to a set and subsequently to an integer.

2.2.2   Methods and Messages

Classes declare the structure (that is, the instance variables) of a set of objects (that is, the class instances). A class definition also specifies the methods that define the behavior of its instances. Classes define the methods which update instance variables. Such a method might be an operation to raise a salesperson's salary.

Methods can also return instance variable values, or values calculated from instance variables. For example, the class *SalesPerson* should include a method to return the *Name* of a salesperson. It should also include a method to return the total number of accounts allocated to a salesperson.

As discussed in the beginning of the Chapter, methods are invoked by sending messages to objects. Specifically, invoking a method involves:

1. A target object.
2. The *selector*, or name, of the method.
3. The arguments of the operator.

Here is an example:

```
C initializeReal: 3 Imaginary: 2
```

C is the target object. *initializeReal:Imaginary:* is the selector with arguments *3* and *2*, respectively.

The Smalltalk syntax for messages is somewhat unusual. Messages with more than one argument are called *keyword* messages. The selector of *initializeReal:Imaginary* consists of two keywords: *initializeReal* and *Imaginary*. When invoking a multiple keyword message, the keywords are separated by the arguments of the message. Each keyword must precede the corresponding argument. Thus in the example above, *initializeReal* precedes *3* and *Imaginary* precedes *2* to create the complex number $3 + 2i$.

Other object-oriented languages extend more conventional procedure-calling syntax to send messages to objects. In Eiffel, for instance, sending a message to a target object is just a form of calling a routine. The target object identifier or expression is merely preappended to the routine call as follows:

C.initializeRealImaginary(3, 2)

A similar syntax is used in C++. In Trellis/Owl (Schaffert et al., 1986) the syntax for operations is very similar to Pascal procedures. The target object is identified as the first argument of the operation when it is invoked:

initializeRealImaginary(C, 3, 2)

The selector of a message chooses the appropriate method from all the methods associated with the target object. Each object has a *protocol*. The protocol of an object is the set of messages to which the object can respond. This, in turn, is determined by the class to which the object belongs. The protocol of an object describes its interface. It is the collection of methods defined for the instances of its class.

Figure 2.8 illustrates the message, with selector "+" and argument *C2*, sent to the target object *C*. This message will cause the real and imaginary parts of *C2* to be added to the real and imaginary parts of *C*, respectively. Since it is in the protocol of *C*, the message will be accepted and executed. If we send a message which is not

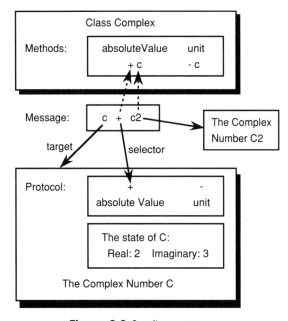

Figure 2.8 Sending a message.

part of the protocol of an object, the object will be unable to respond. In short, an error occurs. The object is saying, "Sorry, I do not understand your request!"

2.2.2.1 The Method Body

An object's class definition contains the code that implements the methods needed to respond to messages. When a message is sent to an object, the method corresponding to the message's selector is executed. Methods typically have formal parameters. The values of the message's argument *bind* the formal parameters of the method, before executing the method's code. Of course, this is exactly what happens when calling a procedure in a conventional programming language!

However, the choice of the actual code to execute for a message depends on the target object's class, a determination typically made at run time. This difference distinguishes the object-oriented approach from most conventional programming. We shall return to this important property of dynamic binding in Section 2.4.

Now, suppose we send the message *initializeReal: 3 Imaginary: 2* to the object *C*. The objects *3* and *2* are assigned to the arguments *r* and *i* in:

```
initializeReal: r Imaginary: i
    real := r.
    imaginary := i.
```

The variables *real* and *imaginary* are the instance variables of the object *C*. The binding of the argument *r* to *3* and the argument *i* to *2* is obvious. The binding of the variables *real* and *imaginary* to the actual instance variable values of the particular object *C* is more subtle.

Note that the assignments *real := r* and *imaginary := i* are actually modifying the state of the object *C*. Yet the object *C* itself is not indicated in the code. In other words, the target object is implicit when the method is invoked. The instance variables will denote the instance variables of the target object. The method can update or retrieve the values of the instance variables directly.

In Smalltalk, only methods defined in an object's class, or in its subclasses (see Chapter 3), can directly access and update its instance variables. Likewise, a method can directly access only the instance variables of the class, or superclasses of the class, in which it is defined.

For example, the following method evaluates the absolute value of a complex number:

```
absoluteValue
| sumSquares |
sumSquares := (real * real)  + (imaginary * imaginary).
^sumSquares sqrt.
```

The absolute value is the square root of the sum of the squares of the real and imaginary parts of a complex number. The method returns the square root of the (temporary) variable *sumSquares*, which contains the sums of the squares of the instance variables *real* and *imaginary*.

2.2.2.2 *Implicit Parameters and the Pseudovariable "Self"*

The examples in the previous sections raise an important object binding issue. Namely, how is the target object of the message identified?

A unique method, determined by the message's selector, contains the code implementing the message for a particular object class. This same code applies to *all* instances of the class. However the method header only specifies the method's name and formal arguments. How is the target object identified in the method body? It is possible to access and update the instance variables directly within a method. But occasionally it is preferable to refer to the target object itself within the method body.

Suppose, for instance, that for a given complex number C we want to evaluate the complex number which is parallel to it and whose absolute value is 1. In other words, we want to normalize the complex number. We evaluate the corresponding complex number on the unit circle by dividing the real and imaginary parts of the complex number with its absolute value.

```
unit
| unitComplex unitReal unitImaginary |
unitReal := real / (self absoluteValue).
unitImaginary := imaginary / (self absoluteValue).
unitComplex :=
    newComplexReal: unitReal Imaginary: unitImaginary.
^unitComplex.
```

Here the pseudovariable **self** is an implicit formal parameter which gets bound to the target object. For example, in:

C unit

self will become *C* in (*self absoluteValue*). Other object-oriented languages also have a similar pseudovariable mechanism to indicate the target object. In C++, for example, the counterpart of Smalltalk's **self** is **this** (see Chapter 5). Therefore, in Smalltalk's methods the implicit target object parameter is represented through:

1. The pseudovariable **self**.
2. The instance variables of the target object.

In object-oriented languages such as Smalltalk or C++ these pseudovariables are useful for at least three purposes:

1. As a return value of a method (such as adding another complex number to the target object and returning the target object)

2. To invoke other methods on the target object (such as *self absoluteValue* in the preceding example)

3. to distinguish between the object as an instance of the class versus the object as an instance of a super-class (see Chapter 3).

2.2.2.3 Accessor and Update Methods

The state of an object (that is, the values of its instance variables) can be retrieved and updated through methods. In fact, the methods of the instances of a class can be categorized as:

1. Those methods whose primary purpose is to retrieve or update instance variables.

2. More general methods performing complex computations, possibly involving many objects and methods.

In category **1**. *accessors* are methods which retrieve or access values of instance variables. *Update* methods change the state or value of instance variables.

Accessor and update methods are very useful since they allow a user or client to access and update the state of an object *through a method*. The need for accessing and modifying the value of an instance variable is rather obvious: objects have states which must be examined and modified. In conventional programming languages (and even in some object-oriented languages such as Simula) fields of records are accessed and updated directly.

Imposing the discipline of always accessing or modifying the values of instance variables through accessor and update methods provides considerable flexibility in class implementations.

For instance, in the class *SalesPerson*, the method *TotalAccounts* returns the total number of accounts assigned to a salesperson. A client of the class does not know (or care) how the value of *TotalAccounts* is evaluated. One implementation of the method could evaluate the total number of accounts as the cardinality of the *Accounts* instance variable. Alternatively, the total number of accounts could be stored in an instance variable *TotAcc*. In this case *TotalAccounts* is an accessor that returns the value of *TotAcc*. Depending on the users' access patterns, implementations of the class can switch between the alternative strategies (evaluation versus a *TotAcc* instance variable), *without changing the interface of the class*. For example, if the value of *Accounts* is fairly stable and the total number of accounts is retrieved very frequently, then it makes sense to introduce and maintain the *TotAcc* instance variable. This will enhance the performance of *TotalAccounts*; it will just access and return the value of *TotAcc*.

Accessor and update methods are so common that some object-oriented languages generate them automatically. For example, if the class of complex numbers is defined in Trellis/Owl, with instance variables *real* and *imaginary* as before, automatically the accessors are:

get_real
get_imaginary

and the update methods:

put_real
put_imaginary

to retrieve and/or update the real and imaginary parts of complex numbers, respectively.

2.2.3 Creating and Destroying Objects

In conventional programming languages such as C or Pascal, there are two ways to create instances of a record type:

1. Declare a variable or a field to be of the specified record type.
2. Allocate space from a memory heap and create a pointer to a structure of the specified record type.

For example, in Pascal a complex number can be defined as:

```
TYPE
    ComplexPtr = ^Complex
    Complex =
RECORD
    Real: real;
    Imaginary: real;
END;
```

A variable can then be declared to be of the type Complex, and initialize its real and imaginary parts as in procedure *Recproc:*

```
Procedure Recproc( );
    VAR
        C1, C2: Complex;

    BEGIN
        C1.Real := 1.0;
        C1.Imaginary := 2.0;
        C2.Real := C1.Real;
        C2.Imaginary := 3.0;
    END;
```

where $C1$ and $C2$ represent the complex numbers $1 + 2i$ and $1 + 3i$, respectively. Since $C1$ and $C2$ are declared locally within the procedure, they get "garbaged" once the execution returns from *Recproc*.

The alternative is to have variables of type *ComplexPtr*. Then records are created of the given type in a heap space as follows:

```
Procedure PtrProc( );
    VAR
        pC1, pC2: ComplexPtr;

    BEGIN
        new(pC1);
        pC1^.Real := 1.0;
        pC1^.Imaginary := 2.0;
        new(pC2);
        pC2^.Real := pC1^.Real;
        pC2^.Imaginary := 3.0;
    END;
```

Here, the built-in function **new** creates a record of the type of its argument. It then sets its pointer argument as a handle to the object, as illustrated in Figure 2.9. Even though $pC1$ and $pC2$ are declared locally within the procedure, upon returning from the procedure the memory space allocated for the records pointed to by $pC1$ and $pC2$ will *not* be automatically reclaimed. Thus if we call *Recproc* five times, the total memory space used for $C1$ and $C2$ will be eight bytes (assuming each real number is four bytes). By contrast, if we invoke *PtrProc* five times, the total memory space allocated for $pC1$ and $pC2$ will be 40 (5×8) bytes.

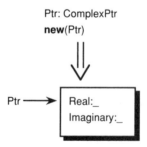

Figure 2.9 The function **new** creating a record.

2.2.3.1 *Creating Objects in Object-Oriented Languages*

In Smalltalk, objects are created by asking a "factory," the class, to "stamp out" an instance. The class stamps out the new object using the instance variable declaration as a template. For example, the complex-number class will be created through:

> *Object subclass: #Complex*
> *instanceVariableNames: 'real*
> *imaginary'*

In addition to some "instance" methods, Smalltalk also supports class variables and class methods. These classes and methods are associated with the class rather than the instances of the class. In the uniform "everything is an object" universe of Smalltalk, classes are also objects.

When a class is treated as an object, class variables and methods correspond to the class's structure and behavior, respectively. An important category of class methods are those methods invoked to create and initialize instances of the class. Note that these methods are invoked when messages are sent to a class as an object.

Objects in Smalltalk are created through sending the message **new** to the object's class. This is somewhat similar to the creation of pointer spaces in Pascal and other conventional programming languages. For example, the following creates a complex number object *C* with uninitialized instance variables:

> *C := Complex new*

When executing the method **new** the Smalltalk interpreter will assign a new identifier for the object *C* (see Chapter 4) and allocate memory space for *C*'s instance variables. To create the complex number 3 + 2*i* we can invoke:

> *C initializeReal: 3*
> *C initializeImaginary: 2*

This allocates space for the integers *3* and *2*, stored in the instance variables *Real* and *Imaginary*, respectively. In fact, the initialization of the real and imaginary parts of a complex number can be combined as in:

> *C initializeReal: 3 Imaginary: 2*

It is also possible to combine the creation and initialization of an object. We can define the method as follows (comments in the code are delimited by quotation marks):

> *newComplexReal: r Imaginary: i*
> *| uComplexNumber iComplexNumber |*
> *"temporary variables in*
> *the method"*

> uComplexNumber := self new
>> "create an uninitialized
>> complex number; 'self' stands
>> for the class Complex"

> iComplexNumber := uComplexNumber initializeReal: r
>> Imaginary: i
>> "initialize the complex number
>> real and imaginary parts"

> ∧iComplexNumber
>> "return the initialized
>> complex number"

The up-arrow "∧" indicates the return value of the method. In this example, the method will return the newly created and initialized complex number.

Therefore there are two strategies for creating objects and assigning values to instance variables:

1. Have a special object-creation class method that assigns initial values to some or all of the instance variables. This is shown above with the *newComplexReal: Imaginary:* example. Other instance variables can be subsequently initialized or updated using methods.

2. Use a generic **new** method to create an instance of the class with uninitialized instance variables. For example, first execute *C := Complex new*. Subsequently initialize the instance variables through methods: *C initializeReal:3* and *C initializeImaginary: 2*.

2.2.3.2 Destroying Objects in Object-Oriented Languages

To get rid of the space allocated to records through **new**, Pascal provides a *dispose* function. To free the space allocated for *pC1* and *pC2* of the previous example, the user would call:

> dispose(pC1);
> dispose(pC2);

Some object-oriented languages such as Smalltalk use an approach similar to the "heap pointer" approach. It differs in that they employ a slightly different strategy to dispose of objects or reclaim their storage space.

Smalltalk does not provide an explicit *dispose* method to get rid of an object or to reclaim the storage space allocated to it. Instead, similar to LISP, Smalltalk uses an implicit object disposal or storage reclamation strategy often referred to as *garbage collection:* If there are no more objects or variables referencing an object, the object is garbage and the Smalltalk execution environment will automatically reclaim the space allocated to that object.

For example, assume the creation of a set:

S := *Set new*

and insert the complex number *C* into *S*

S *add: C*

Now there are two references to the object indicated by *C*

- the set *S* (the object is an element in this set)
- the variable *C*

We might subsequently delete the complex number from the set:

S *remove: C*

and assign a different object to *C*

C := *Complex new*

Now there will be no more direct or indirect ways (references) to access the complex number $3 + 2i$. The space allocated to it can be reclaimed.

To summarize, there are two strategies for getting rid of objects and reclaiming their memory space:

1. Through an explicit dispose or delete operation.
2. Though implicit disposal or reclamation of the object when it is no longer reachable from any variable or parent object in the programming environment.

The first strategy (used in Pascal and C) has the advantage that it is done on demand by the user. Hence it incurs very little overhead in the execution environment. Explicit deletions are the most common means of object disposal in database languages. For example, the most popular relational database language, SQL, provides an explicit delete operator to get rid of table rows.

There is one serious disadvantage to the explicit delete strategy. Since it is up to the user to explicitly delete the objects, the user can inadvertently keep references to a deleted object. This is known as the problem of "dangling" references. Reliance on explicit deletes leads to the possibility that a program may reference objects which have already been deleted. Databases have struggled with this problem and provided various constructs to help eliminate the dangling object reference problem. Some dialects of SQL enable the user to explicitly specify which attributes serve as references to other table rows. Chapter 7 discusses this further.

The second strategy, implicit object disposal, solves the problem of dangling references. However, object-oriented languages that pursue this strategy must pay a run-time overhead to figure out when objects become disposable. In other words they must keep track of all object references. Are there any more references to an object? Is any variable referencing the object? Is the object an attribute value of any other object? Or is the object contained in any other collection object? The execution environment must know the answers to all these questions in order to know which objects are garbage.

There are different strategies for automatic storage reclamation or "garbage collection." A comprehensive survey and analysis of this important implementation issue is beyond the scope of this book. However, for completeness, the next paragraphs list the most commonly used strategies.

1. *Reference Counting* (Collins, 1960; Knuth, 1973; Stamos, 1982; Deutsch and Bobrow, 1976; Ungar and Patterson, 1983): The simplest strategy is to keep a count of the number of references to the object. Objects are referenced through the instance variables of other objects, through global or environment variables, or through membership in a collection object (such as a set or an array). When the reference count of an object becomes zero, the object is "dead" (since no one can access it—it is unreachable). The storage allocated to the object can be reclaimed.

   Note that with object identity (discussed in Chapter 4), the object space in an object-oriented environment is a graph. The same object can be a value of an instance variable in multiple objects. In fact, an object can even reference itself. For example, (besides the pseudo-instance variable *self*) the value of an instance variable I can be the object itself. Self-referencing objects cannot be reclaimed through standard reference counting algorithms.

   Another drawback of the reference counting algorithm is its CPU or execution time overhead. Earlier implementations of Smalltalk have used this algorithm (Goldberg and Robson, 1983; Kaehler and Krasner, 1983; Stamos, 1982). It has been demonstrated that storage reclamation through reference counting can consume up to 20 percent of the CPU cycles (Ungar and Patterson, 1983; Ungar, 1987).

2. *Mark and Sweep* (McCarthy, 1960; Knuth, 1973; Stadish, 1980): Another simple but expensive algorithm is the mark and sweep storage reclamation strategy. The mark and sweep algorithm has two phases. The first phase (the "marking" phase) marks all the objects that are reachable from the active execution environment root objects. The second phase (the "sweeping" phase) deletes all the dead objects (that is, the objects that are not reachable). Unlike

reference counting, mark and sweep algorithms can reclaim the storage of self-referencing dead objects.

3. *Scavenging Algorithms* (Baker, 1978; Ballard and Shiron, 1983; Lieberman and Hewitt, 1983): The scavenging algorithms and their recent "generation" scavenging descendants are becoming increasingly popular. The scavenging algorithms get rid of the second sweeping phase of the mark and sweep strategy, through moving the "live" objects to a new memory area. In the original Baker algorithm (Baker, 1978) the dynamic memory space is partitioned into two semispaces. Before the scavenge the objects are located in one semispace. A scavenge can occur either on demand (for instance, the system runs out of dynamic memory space) or incrementally. The scavenge traverses all the reachable ("live") objects and copies them contiguously to the other semispace of memory. Of course, all references to objects are resolved. Once all the objects are moved, the first memory semispace becomes completely empty. Thus, in addition to storage reclamation, scavenging algorithms achieve memory compaction and avoid the fragmentation of the dynamically allocatable memory space.

Storage reclamation based on scavenging algorithms has shown much better performance than reference counting or mark and sweep algorithms. Scavenging algorithms have many variants, including generation garbage collection (Lieberman and Hewitt, 1983), generation scavenging (Ungar, 1987), and opportunistic garbage collection (Wilson, 1988). The generation scavenging algorithm distinguishes between *old* objects and *new* objects. It has been observed that objects that are newly created usually die young. Older objects tend to survive. Therefore, rather than moving and swapping *all* the objects of the dynamic memory space indiscriminately, the generation scavenging algorithms concentrates on reclaiming the storage of the more recently created objects. Using generation scavenging, Ungar (1987) has demonstrated an eight-fold performance improvement over reference counting.

2.2.4 Class Extensions

Conceptually, a type or an abstract data type represents the set of all possible objects with the prescribed structure and behavior. Thus INTEGER represents the infinite set of integers. FLOAT represents the infinite set of floating-point real numbers. STRING OF CHARACTER represents the infinite set of strings of characters, and so on.

By contrast, the *extension* or *extent* of a class corresponds to the actual instances of a class which have been created but not destroyed. It is comprised of the existing instances of a class. Thus the extent of class *SalesPerson* corresponds to all the existing instances of *SalesPerson*: John, Mary, Suzan, and Jim.

We learned in Section 2.2.3 how some object-oriented systems create class instances by sending the message **new** to the class. This message tells the class to create an instance of itself. Since the class is an object itself, it has the potential to keep track of all the objects (instances) it has created. The class could also be informed of the removal or disposal of its instances. Therefore, a class could be constructed such that it monitors its own extension.

In conventional programming languages, a type represents the set of *all* possible objects of the given structure. For example in Pascal we define type *Complex* as follows:

```
TYPE
    Complex =
        RECORD
            Real: real;
            Imaginary: real;
        END;
```

This defines the set of all complex numbers, which is infinite. In fact, in Pascal *Complex* denotes the set:

{ (Real, Imaginary) | Real is real; Imaginary is real}

In object-oriented programming languages such Smalltalk or C++, the user defines a class expressly as a template to generate objects. Although these object-oriented languages provide the primitives to create and (implicitly or explicitly) destroy objects, they do not support class extensions.

Why do we ever need to know or access the extension of a class? Actually, for some types such as INTEGER or FLOAT, the notion of an extent does not make sense. Indeed in Smalltalk/V the class method **new** generates an error for the classes Integer and Float.

The most important use of class extensions is for the kind of bulk information processing traditionally performed by database management systems. One of the main functions of a database management system is to process large numbers of objects of the same type. This leads to an interesting contrast between database management systems and programming languages with respect to use of types and classes.

Consider the user of a database management system who creates a table in a database language such as SQL. This user is primarily interested in accessing the extension of the table. The following SQL Data Definition command defines the structure of an instance (or table element) of *SalesPerson*:

```
CREATE TABLE SalesPerson
    (Name            CHAR(20),
    Address          CHAR(40),
    TelephoneNumber  INTEGER,
    Salary           FLOAT
    ...)
```

At the same time, it also makes *SalesPerson* the "handle" to the set of all existing salespeople in the database. For example, we retrieve the *Name* and *Address* of salespeople whose salary is more than $50,000 with the SQL query:

```
SELECT Name, Address
FROM SalesPerson
WHERE Salary > 50000
```

We can also insert values into the SQL table:

```
INSERT INTO SalesPerson VALUES ("John Smith",
                                "1212 Dayton",
                                45000, ...)
```

And we can delete rows from the table. To delete John's record, assuming he is the only person called John Smith, we use:

```
DELETE FROM SalesPerson WHERE Name = "John Smith"
```

Thus we can explicitly delete records from and insert them into the extension *Sales-Person* (which contains the set of all salespeople).

This means that all type declarations in the database schema actually identify the extensions of all the tables defined in that schema. As discussed in Chapter 7, there are many object-oriented databases that support class extensions.

2.2.4.1   Collections

None of the most popular object-oriented languages (Smalltalk, C++, Ada) support the notion of a type or class extension explicitly. However, through *collection* objects we can achieve the same goal. As with class extension, we can create a collection (set, bag, array) that includes all instances of objects of the same class.

Most object-oriented languages support several built-in types or classes that are containers of other objects. The instances of these classes are actually collections of objects. In most cases, a collection object can be used instead of an extension to achieve the same functionality.

Thus the user can create instances of a set:

```
SalesPeople := Set new
```

Then instances of *SalesPerson* such as John could be inserted in the set explicitly as:

```
SalesPeople add: John
```

Since Smalltalk is "typeless," sets can contain objects of different types (instances of different classes). Strongly typed object-oriented languages, on the other hand, can require that all the elements of a collection object are of the same type.

In Eiffel a parametric type *SET[T]* can be defined:

SalesPeople: SET[SalesPerson]

Collection objects may be sets, arrays, or bags (sets that can have duplicate values). Users can employ them in place of class extensions as handles for collections of objects that are all instances of the same class.

Hence there are two strategies to access and traverse the existing instances of a class:

1. Through the class extensions (*if* the language supports extensions).
2. Through a collection object that contains the existing instances of the class (almost all object-oriented languages support collection objects).

Different applications will prefer to use one or the other of these choices. If the application incorporates only one interesting collection of objects, say salespeople, the extension approach is preferable. If, instead, object collections are naturally partitioned and accessed in disjoint subsets, the collection-object approach is better. For example, each warehouse in an order-entry database will contain a set of items. The application traverses and manipulates the set of items in a particular warehouse but rarely or never the set of all items in all warehouses. In this case, class extension for items is useless. However, set objects may well be used to collect the items within one warehouse.

In Section 2.2.1, the instance variables (attributes) of salespersons were described. Two of these attributes were *set valued*:

Accounts: *SET[ACCOUNT]*;
Orders: *SET[ORDER]*;

A class extension would not help here; traversing the set of all existing accounts or orders is not very useful! However, having a set of accounts and orders for *each* salesperson is imperative in this application.

■ 2.3 OVERLOADING

One of the most powerful and useful concepts of object orientation is operation or method *overloading*. Overloading allows operations with the *same name* but different semantics and implementations, to be invoked for objects of different types.

Overloading is neither new nor particular to object orientation. In conventional languages such as C or Pascal, programmers frequently encounter and use overloaded operations. Some common examples are arithmetic operators, I/O operations, object creation functions, and value assignment operators.

In almost all languages, the arithmetic operators "+", "−", and "*" are used to add, subtract, or multiply integers or floating-point numbers. These operators work even though the underlying machine implementations of integer and floating-point arithmetic are quite different. The compiler generates object code to invoke the appropriate implementation based on the kind (integer or floating point) of the operands.

Likewise, the same I/O operation is often used to read either integers, characters, or floating-point numbers. In Pascal Read(x) may be used, having x be an integer, a char, or a real. Of course, the actual machine code executed to read a character string is quite different from the machine code for reading, say, integers. However, Read(x), an overloaded operation, works for multiple types. Even basic operations such as assigning values to variables (": =" in Pascal or "=" in C) are overloaded. The same assignment operators are used for variables of many different types.

Conventional programming languages support overloading for some of the operations on built-in types such as integer, real, and character. *Object-oriented systems take overloading one step further and make it available for any operation of any object type*.

For instance, binary operations can be overloaded for complex numbers, arrays, sets, or lists. We already saw how "+" was used to add the corresponding real and imaginary parts of two complex numbers. If *A1* and *A2* are two arrays of integers we can define

$A := A1 + A2$ through $A[i] := A1[i] + A2[i]$ for all i.

Similarly, if *S1* and *S2* are sets of objects we can define

$S := S1 + S2$

to be the set union of the sets *S1* and *S2*.

How is a particular operation or message name bound to a particular implementation or method? Typically, this is determined by the target object of the message or operation dynamically (that is, at run time or after the message is sent to the target object). Dynamic binding to methods is discussed in the next section.

■ 2.4 DYNAMIC BINDING

Dynamic binding (also called *late binding*) is one of the most frequently cited advantages of the object-oriented style of programming. Dynamic binding means the system binds message selectors to the methods that implement them at run time (instead of compile time). The particular methods used in binding depend on the recipient object's class. As will be shown, the concept of dynamic binding is closely associated with that of overloading.

The run-time binding capability is needed for two reasons:

1. The object-oriented language supports operator overloading as described in the previous section. Consider the message $C + C2$. To determine the method that

needs to be executed for the message $+C2$, the system sends the message to the target object C. The target object checks whether the selector is in its protocol and if so executes the appropriate method. Therefore, the determination of the particular method to be executed for a message is done dynamically at run time.

2. A variable's object class or type may not be known until run time. This is true of languages that do not type the variables, like Smalltalk. In these languages it is very difficult and in some cases impossible to determine at compile time the type of the object referenced by a variable.

To illustrate the advantages of dynamic binding, imagine a "print" message applied to every element of a heterogeneous collection of objects. Assume there is a stack that can contain any kind of object and that every entry in the stack is to be printed. Further assume different print methods are associated with each class. All these print methods rely on different implementations and are totally unrelated.

In the statements shown below, the stack is **St**, and is implemented as an array 1 to Top of objects. The Smalltalk/V code for printing every element of the stack is:

for i := 1 to Top St[i] Print

Thus, each object *St[i]* would execute its appropriate print method, depending on the class to which it belongs. This is illustrated in Figure 2.10.

The key point is that the object decides what piece of code to execute for the print message. Unlike procedure names in more conventional programming languages, the

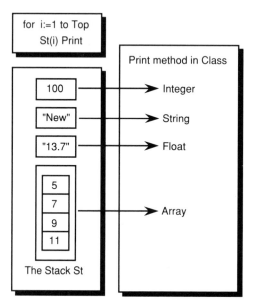

Figure 2.10 Dynamically binding Print.

selector *Print* does not by itself identify a unique piece of code. Instead, the actual code used is determined by the class of the target object to which the print message is sent. The object responds to the *Print* selector by using the printing method appropriate for its class.

If the language did not support overloading and dynamic binding, a large *case* statement would be needed. The appropriate print routine would then be invoked based on the selected object's type. Using a case construct, each entry in the stack would be a pair:

<object-type-class> <object>

Depending on the number of types, we would have a corresponding collection of print operators like *PrintInteger*, *PrintString*, *PrintFloat*, and so on. Printing each element of the stack would involve checking the type of the stack and calling the appropriate routine. The pseudocode using a Pascal-like syntax would be:

```
for i := 1 to Top do
    case St[i].type
        Integer:    PrintInteger(St[i].Object)
        Float:      PrintChar(St[i].Object)
        String:     PrintString(St[i].Object)
        Boolean:    PrintBoolean(St[i].Object)
```

Note that if a new type X were added, the case statement would have to be extended with PrintX. This addition would force recompilation of the whole routine that prints the elements of a stack.

In contrast, any number of new classes may be added to a system that uses overloading and dynamic binding. These extensions will never affect the method that prints all the elements of a stack. Nor will they force modification of any other previously defined method that uses generic selectors like *Print*.

Of course, manipulating collections of objects of different types (heterogeneous collections) implies that the language is not strongly typed. The previous example illustrated the power of overloading and dynamic binding. It also showed that this power is best utilized by typeless languages. Advocates of Smalltalk often reiterate the increased flexibility and extensibility of the language because of its lack of typing.

In summary, the advantages of dynamically binding overloaded operations are:

1. *Extensibility:* The same operator applies to instances of many classes without modifying its code.
2. *Development of more compact code:* As illustrated by the *Print* example, overloaded operators can be combined with dynamic binding. This allows us to avoid conditional branch constructs such as IF...THEN...ELSE or CASE statements that check the object type and invoke the corresponding operator.

3. *Clarity:* Not only more compact, the generated code is more readable and comprehensible. This enhances the robustness and efficiency of the development effort.

Performance costs are the main disadvantage of dynamically binding, overloaded operations. A penalty is paid for the run-time binding and/or type checking that must be done to guarantee correctness. Dynamic binding performed through a search for each invocation of each method can be expensive. Accelerators such as hash tables or indexes could be used to lessen the performance penalty of dynamic binding. However, the cost may still be high when compared with compiled strategies of languages like Pascal whose corresponding cost is just an address jump.

■ 2.5 PARAMETRIC POLYMORPHISM

According to Webster's, *polymorphism* generally represents the quality or state of being able to assume different forms. When applied to programming languages it indicates that the same language construct can assume different types or manipulate objects of different types. We have already encountered one form of polymorphism, namely overloading. With overloading, the same operator ("+") or the same message (*Print*) can apply to different types of objects. Indeed, the object types can be totally unrelated, such as, *Print* abstract of Shakespeare's *Henry V*, or *Print* employee salaries (or whatever turns you on).

This "anything goes" characteristic of overloading makes it a form of polymorphism (Cardelli and Wegner, 1985). This section discusses the more constrained, *parametric* polymorphism (or *genericity*) which is supported by many object-oriented languages including Eiffel and Ada.

Parametric polymorphism uses types as parameters in generic type declarations or classes. Some conventional programming languages provide one level of support for parameterized types. Pascal, for example, allows creation of specific instances of generic array or record types in type declarations. A user can declare a specific array type of 10 elements, each of which is an *Account* record through:

    ActiveAccounts: array[1..10] of Account

Object-oriented languages, which support parametric polymorphism, take it one step further. They allow use of parameterized types (or classes) in both built-in and user-defined programming constructs.

CLU was one of the earliest and most significant programming languages to incorporate parameterized polymorphic types (Liskov et al., 1977; Liskov and Guttag, 1986). CLU allows parameterization of both procedures and abstract data types. If a type supports the binary operator "+" (integers, reals, and so on) a list-sum operator can be declared as:

list-sum = **proc**[t: type] (a: list[t])
    returns(t)
    requires the type t has a binary operator
       + : **proctype**(t, t) **returns**(t)
          that "adds" two objects of type
          t.
    effects it returns the sum of the elements
       in the list using the binary ' + '

If *IL* is the integer list $1 \to 3 \to 7 \to$ NILL then the sum of the elements of *IL* can be evaluated through:

list-sum[int](IL)

Here the user has passed the actual parameter *int* for the formal type parameter *t*.

Similarly if *RL* is the list of real numbers $1.5 \to 3.7 \to 2.8 \to$ NILL, then the sum of the elements of *RL* can be evaluated through:

list-sum[real](RL)

As this simple example illustrates, the most important advantage of parametric polymorphism is code sharing. In strongly typed languages such as CLU and Eiffel the user has to declare the types of variables and objects. This means that a *list* type cannot be created that contains objects of arbitrary types.

In a strongly typed language that does not support parametric polymorphism, the user would have to replicate code and would be forced to construct *ListOfInt* and *ListOfReal* types. These would have extremely similar implementations of the overloaded routine *sum-list*. The only difference would be in the formal parameter type of the routine. In effect, procedures would be used to implement the same functionality for different types. Thus little would be gained over conventional programming languages.

Clearly, parametric polymorphism combines the flexibility and advantages of code sharing for generic types with the power of strong typing.

2.5.1 Parametric Abstract Data Types

Summing the elements of a list with a parametric type is an example of a method (routine, operation, procedure) with a parametric type. Actually, in CLU the **List** data type can itself be declared as a parameterized abstract data type. As described in Liskov and Guttag (1986; p. 82), the declaration will be of the form:

list = **data type** [t: **type**] **is**
    create, cons, first, rest, empty, equal, ...

The procedures *create*, *cons*, *first*, and so on constitute the interface of the abstract data type. *Create* constructs a new instance of a list, *first* returns the first element of a list, and so on. Like *list-sum* each of these procedures is itself a parametric procedure. Variables whose type is parametric must be declared by supplying specific type values for the parameter. For example the integer list *IL* and the list of real numbers *RL* must be declared as:

```
IL  =  list[int]
RL  =  list[real]
```

In the *sum-list* example, the procedure required the parameterized type to have a binary ("+") operation. Sometimes, however, requirements of particular operations are associated with the parameterized abstract data type as a whole. Requirements for operations that call for specific types of input and output parameters can be associated with either:

1. Procedures with parametric types or
2. The parametric abstract data type.

Equality predicates offer a good example of when a requirement should be associated with the abstract data type itself. To define a procedure that checks for the equality of two lists of type *t*, first the user must have an (overloaded) "equal" predicate for the type *t*. Now suppose this is a common requirement in many of the procedures of the abstract data type. It makes more sense to associate the requirement with the abstract data type itself than with each procedure:

> **requires** the type t has a binary operator
> equal: **proctype**(t, t) **returns**(bool)

2.5.2   Just Syntactic Sugar?

In the preceding examples, specific values for the parameters were supplied before invoking the parameterized procedure or using the parameterized abstract data type in type declarations.

Most languages supporting parameterized types enforce the *static* specification of the type parameters. This means that all the types will be known at compile time. Therefore some may view parametric polymorphism as an unnecessary syntactic sweetener. People have argued, for example, that parameterized macros provide the same functionality. The parametric types can be expanded by a macro before invoking a compiler. Indeed there are numerous pre-processing strategies (including macro expansions) which give us *some* of the functionality of parameterized types.

However, the full power of type parameterization is enjoyed only when the construct is incorporated in the semantics of the language. This section concludes with a summary of the arguments in favor of parameterization. First, the parameterized generic types provide clustering of representation (structure) and behavior (operations). This makes generic type declarations very similar to other (non-generic) abstract data type declarations. It provides a coherent object-oriented language with a natural construct: generic types. The user need not struggle with a pre-processor/macro language embedded in the host/native language. Making parametric types part of the language greatly enhances clarity and hence maintainability of the code.

Second, pre-processing of all procedures involving parametric types (such as macro expansion) will result in considerable duplication. The code spaces allocated for similar procedures will contain almost identical codes. (Think back to the example of summing up the integer elements of a list of integers and summing up the real numbers in a list of reals.) The overhead will be both in terms of space and compilation time.

Third, there are cases where it is difficult, or impossible to support the functionality of generic types through a pre-processing strategy. Recursive types are one example. Run-time binding of type parameters is another.

■ 2.6 CONSTRAINTS

Ideally, full support of abstract data typing requires the operations associated with an abstract data type to be *complete* and *correct*. A real abstract data type represents a type of object, be it an ECAD object, an Employee, or a data structure such as a stack. The full semantics of this abstract data type exist only in the mind of its creator. Therefore, realistically, the completeness or correctness of the ADT is only as good as the completeness or correctness of the code which captures its behavior.

To help the programmers better express the behavior of abstract data types, object-oriented programming languages need to provide constructs to indicate the constraints that test the correctness or completeness of the abstract data type.

There are two approaches to providing such language constructs:

1. Constraints placed on objects and instance variables.
2. Pre- and postconditions of methods.

Both approaches enable the programmer to express constraints that reflect the semantics of the abstract data type. These constraints, in turn, guarantee the completeness and correctness of the database application.

2.6.1   Constraints on Objects and Instance Variables

The first approach places constraints on objects. Access and update constraint routines are executed when manipulating instances of the abstract data type. These constraint routines are incorporated into the definition of the class. They may be associated either with the object instance as a whole or with particular instance variables of the object.

This is similar to the use of integrity constraints on tables in relational databases. Integrity constraints for object-oriented databases are discussed in detail in Chapter 7. An integrity constraint can specify, for example, that a column value (which corresponds to an instance variable value) cannot be nil. Another integrity constraint can specify that a column value must be within a certain value range (for instance the age of a person cannot be a negative integer). A more general constraint would be the specification that an employee's salary should not exceed that of the manager. Every time the salary of an employee is updated, the system checks the constraint. When it is violated, it is an error. The system will reject the update.

Attached predicates are a related concept used in some AI systems such as the Intelligence/Compiler (Parsaye and Chignell, 1988). They can be used to restrict access, evaluate missing information, or enforce constraints on an instance variable.

An attached predicate can be an:

> *if-accessed,* or
> *if-updated*

predicate. The if-accessed predicate gets fired whenever an instance variable is accessed. The if-updated predicate gets fired whenever an instance variable is updated. Through these predicates arbitrary conditions on the instance variable values can be checked to see if they are violated. For example, a user can check that the number of accounts assigned to a salesperson is at least 10, whenever the Accounts instance variable is assessed. Similarly, a user can verify that the balance of a checking account is nonnegative, whenever we update the balance.

2.6.2 Pre- and Postconditions of Methods

The second approach relies on pre- and postconditions of methods. This alternative associates preconditions and postconditions with the operations (methods) of the abstract data type, rather than with the objects. Preconditions allow one to introduce certain constraints on the instance variables that must be satisfied before a particular method is executed. Postconditions allow articulation of other constraints that must be satisfied upon terminating the execution of the method.

This is the approach taken in Eiffel (Meyer, 1988). For example, in Eiffel a user can attach pre- and postconditions to the Push and Pop operations to guarantee the semantics of a stack. A precondition for Push is the requirement that the stack instance must not be full. A precondition for Pop is the requirement that the stack instance must not be empty. Similarly, a post condition for Push is the requirement that the stack instance is no longer empty and its total number of elements is increased by one.

The choice between object constraints and conditions on methods is mainly a matter of convenience and judgment. The two approaches attempt to achieve the same effect; both help the programmer express the semantics of the abstract data type as directly as possible. However, there is no magic in constraints and conditions on either objects or operators. The completeness or correctness of the abstract data type is still only as good as that of the code used to prescribe its behavior. It remains the programmer's responsibility to use these constructs to express the semantics of the abstract data type explicitly.

▪ 2.7 SUMMARY

This chapter discussed the first fundamental concept of object orientation, abstract data typing. Abstract data types describe a set of objects with the same representation and behavior. With abstract data types there is a clear separation between the external interface of a data type and its internal implementation. The implementation of an abstract data type is hidden. Hence, alternative implementations can be used for the same abstract data type without changing its interface.

In most object-oriented programming languages, abstract data types are implemented through classes. A class is like a factory that produces instances, each with the same structure and behavior. A class has a name, a collection of operations for manipulating its instances, and a representation. The operations that manipulate the instances of a class are called methods. The state or representation of an instance is stored in instance variables. The methods are invoked through sending messages to the instances. Sending messages to objects (instances) is similar to calling procedures in conventional programming languages. However, message sending is more dynamic.

The same method name can be overloaded with different semantics and implementations; the method *Print* can apply to integers, arrays, and character strings. Operation overloading allows programs to be extended gracefully. Because of overloading, the binding of a message to the code implementing the message, is done at run time. This is called dynamic binding. The particular methods invoked when a program binds message names to methods depend on the recipient object's class.

In some systems, classes can be created with parametric types. Parametric polymorphism allows the construction of abstract classes, with type parameters; for instance, *Set[T]* represents a parametric class that can be instantiated to *Set[integer]* or *Set[Person]*. Both sets share the code which is implemented in *Set[T]*. Code sharing is the most important advantage of parametric polymorphism.

Finally, some systems allow programmers to define constraints on either methods or objects. These constraints help the programmers design correct and complete systems, reflecting the true semantics of the abstract data types.

3

INHERITANCE

■ **3.1 INTRODUCTION**

Object orientation attempts to model real-world applications as closely as possible. Object orientation also attempts to achieve software reusability and software extensibility. The powerful object-oriented concept that provides *all* these capabilities is inheritance.

Through inheritance designers can build new software modules (such as classes) on top of an existing hierarchy of modules. This avoids redesigning and recoding everything from scratch. New classes can inherit both the behavior (operations, methods, and so on) and the representation (instance variables, attributes, and so on) from existing classes.

Inheriting behavior enables code sharing (and hence reusability) among software modules. Inheriting representation enables structure sharing among data objects. As will be shown, the combination of these two types of inheritance provides a very powerful software modeling and development strategy.

Inheritance also provides a very natural mechanism for organizing information. It "taxonomizes" objects into well-defined inheritance hierarchies. Figure 3.1 illustrates some common real-world relationships: students and employees are persons; pads, gates, and parts are ECAD objects; and both raster and vector images are special image types.

3.1.1 Inheritance in Knowledge Representation

Inheritance has its roots in "common sense" knowledge representation paradigms used in Artificial Intelligence. One example is Ross Quillian's (1968) psychological model

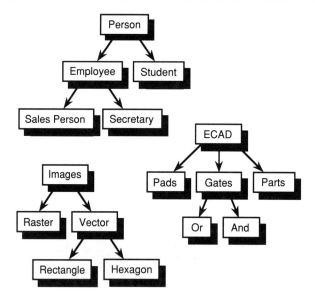

Figure 3.1 Examples of inheritance hierarchies.

of associative memory. The "node-and-link" model introduced by Quillian is one of the earliest *semantic network* knowledge representation models.

Semantic networks consist of nodes which represent concepts (objects) and links which represent relationships. In semantic network representations, both nodes and links have labels. The most powerful label representing inheritance relationships is the IS-A link. Figure 3.2 illustrates a semantic network for salespeople, where a SalesPerson

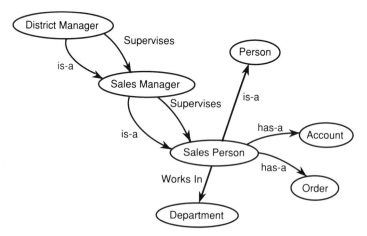

Figure 3.2 A semantic network for SalesPerson.

IS-A person. Similarly, a SalesManager IS-A salesperson, and a DistrictManager IS-A sales manager. A salesperson has Account and Order attributes. A salesperson works in a Department.

Inheritance is just *one* kind of relationship among concepts. Other relationship links can represent attributes (instance variables) of concepts (objects). In fact, Minsky (1975) introduced record-like structures called *frames* that allow the definition of new concepts in terms of previously defined frames. Frames contain *slots* which are similar to record fields or attributes. Frames can inherit slots from other frames. Figure 3.3 illustrates the frame Employee inheriting the slots Name, Age, and Address from the frame Person.

An Employee frame inheriting (*specializing*) from a Person frame illustrates *structural* inheritance: Employees are specialized Persons who, in addition to Name, Age, and Address slots, also have Salary, Rank, and Department slots. Frames support attached predicates, which were discussed in Chapter 2. Attached predicates are activated when a slot is accessed or updated, and so can serve as operations or methods attached to the frame. Some frame-based expert system shells also allow *instantiating* specializations (Parsaye and Chignell, 1988; Parsaye, et al., 1989). This is very similar to instances of the class templates discussed in Chapter 2. Thus the Employee John, who is 32 years old, inherits from the frame Employee. As will be shown, object-oriented languages distinguish between specialization through creating instances, and specialization through creating subclasses. Briefly, instances are created by sending the message *new* to a class, while subclasses are created by explicitly declaring superclasses for a class.

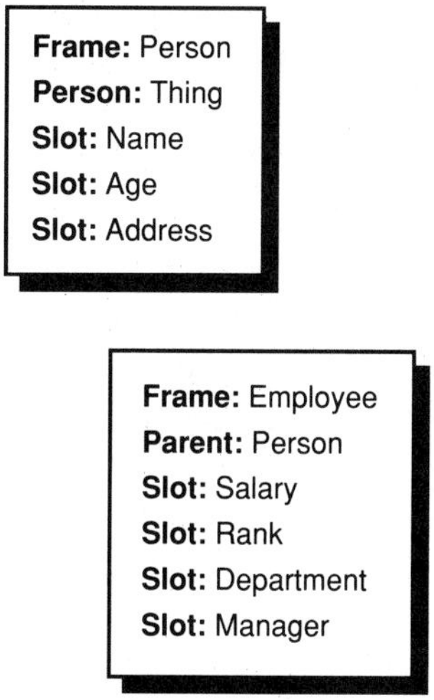

```
Frame: Person
Person: Thing
Slot: Name
Slot: Age
Slot: Address
```

```
Frame: Employee
Parent: Person
Slot: Salary
Slot: Rank
Slot: Department
Slot: Manager
```

Figure 3.3 Frame Employee inherits from Person.

3.1.2 Inheritance in Object-Oriented Languages

Besides being used in the common sense knowledge representation of AI, inheritance is incorporated into object-oriented languages through *class inheritance*. As shown in Chapter 2, classes can implement encapsulated sets of objects that exhibit the same behavior (abstract data types). The earliest object-oriented programming language, Simula, allowed classes to inherit from one another. For example, in Simula the program can indicate that the class *Employee* inherits from class *Person*:

```
Person class Employee(Salary, Department);
    real Salary; integer Department;
    begin
    ... procedures of Employee ...
    end
```

With the Simula jargon, the class *Person* is called the *outer* class (superclass) and the class *Employee* is called the *inner* class (the subclass). Besides its own attributes (*Salary*, *Department*, and the procedures of *Employee*) the inner class *Employee* contains all the attributes of *Person* (Name, Age, and so on). As mentioned in Chapter 2, the class parameters (that is, instance variables) in Simula are accessed and updated directly. In other words, Simula classes do not support information hiding.

In the most common object-oriented languages such as Simula, Smalltalk, Eiffel, and C++, classes can inherit both methods (behavior) and instance variables (structure) from superclasses. Besides providing a brilliant mechanism for organizing information, the most important contribution of inheritance is code sharing or code reusability.

To illustrate code reusability and the appropriateness of class inheritance in object-oriented systems, we can further specialize the classes rooted at *Person*. The additional classes and inheritance hierarchy is illustrated in Figure 3.4. Evident are secretaries and salespeople who are employees; graduate students and undergraduates are persons; salesmanagers further specialize salespeople, and district managers specialize salesmanagers. The classes *Secretary* and *SalesPerson* are called *subclasses* of *Employee*. The class *Employee* is a *superclass* of *Secretary* and *SalesPerson*. The subclass and superclass relations are transitive. Thus, if X is a subclass of Y and Y is a subclass of Z, then X is also a subclass of Z. For example, since *DistrictManager* is a subclass of *SalesManager*, it is also, by transitivity, a subclass of *SalesPerson*, *Employee*, and *Person*. Incidentally, employees are very appreciative of inheritance since their superiors are just instances of one of their subclasses!

Now if the class *Employee* implements the methods:

```
EvaluateBonus
GiveRaise
ChangeDepartment
```

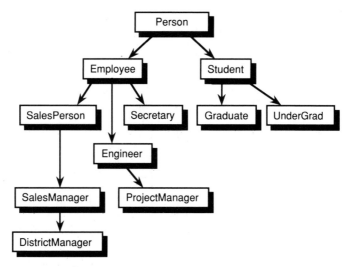

Figure 3.4 More comprehensive Person hierarchy.

then subclasses of *Employee* such as *SalesPerson*, *SalesManager*, and *DistrictManager* can inherit these methods without their having been re-implemented. In fact, the class *SalesPerson* can have its own additional methods such as:

>*TotalOrders* (returns the total number of orders)
>*TotalAccounts* (returns the total number of accounts)

which in turn would be inherited by its subclasses, *SalesManager* and *DistrictManager*.

The class inheritance hierarchy of object-oriented languages such as Smalltalk and C++ provides an excellent means of organizing complex code bases. Some object-oriented languages such as Smalltalk come with a comprehensive initial class hierarchy. Figure 3.5 gives the class hierarchy of collection classes which is included in the Smalltalk/V environment. The users of the language then specialize some of the classes in the initial class hierarchies to create classes that are more appropriate for their applications. Smalltalk programmers spend a substantial amount of time familiarizing themselves with the workings of the initial class hierarchies of the Smalltalk programming environment.

Therefore, there are two main aspects of class inheritance:

>*Structural*. Instances of a class such as *SalesPerson*, which is a subclass of *Employee*, will have values for instance variables inherited from *Employee* such as *Name*, *Address*, *Salary* and so on. Note that the instance variables *Name* and *Address* are actually inherited (transitively) from class *Person*, a superclass of *Employee*.

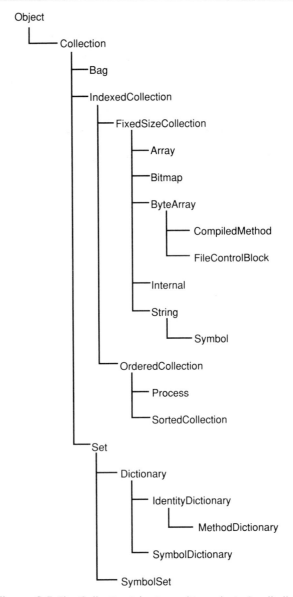

Figure 3.5 The Collection inheritance hierarchy in Smalltalk/V.

Behavioral. The class has methods such as *AccumulatedVacationLeave*, *GiveRaise*, *ChangeAddress* and so on, which are inherited by its subclasses such as *SalesPerson* and *Secretary*. This means we can send a message with selector *GiveRaise* to an instance *Margaret* of *Secretary* and execute the method *GiveRaise* in *Employee* with *Margaret* as the target object.

3.1.3 The Different Facets of Inheritance

Inheritance is a powerful technique that organizes complex code bases. It allows the construction of new classes on top of existing class hierarchies. Through inheritance richer semantic relationships among entities in an object space can be expressed directly and naturally. Thus, in addition to code sharing, inheritance also organizes the object spaces in an application domain.

Inheritance introduces some complexities, however, especially when integrated with other object-oriented concepts such as encapsulation, typing, visibility, and object states. Here are seven areas of inheritance that characterize most of the different approaches used by existing object-oriented languages:

1. **Inheritance and Subtyping:** In most object-oriented languages the two concepts are used interchangeably. Yet, it is useful to distinguish them. A few languages even provide different constructs to support each concept. Section 3.2 illustrates the differences between inheritance and subtyping.

2. **Visibility of Inherited Variables and Methods:** Some object-oriented languages such as Simula allow the direct manipulation of instance variables. Other languages such as C++ distinguish between public and private manipulation. With inheritance there is yet a third alternative, those deemed to be subclass visible. The different visibility alternatives are discussed in Section 3.3.

3. **Inheritance and Encapsulation:** The visibility of instance variables violates information hiding (class encapsulation). In fact, there is a conflict between inheritance and encapsulation if the instance variables of superclasses are accessed directly. Furthermore, encapsulation and overloading can be used to support some of the functionality of inheritance. However, inheritance is a much more direct and natural mechanism to share code and structure.

4. **How to Specialize:** Inheritance is achieved by specializing existing classes. Classes can be specialized by extending their representation (instance variables) or behavior (operations). Alternatively, classes can also be specialized through *restricting* the representation or operations of existing classes. The different specialization alternatives are also discussed in Section 3.3.

5. **Object Inheritance:** Most object-oriented languages support class inheritance (the ability of one class to inherit representation and methods from another class). An alternative approach is to allow objects to inherit from one another. Object inheritance allows an object to inherit the state of another object. There are models of computation that also incorporate operations with objects and use *only* object inheritance for organizing object spaces. These are called *prototype* systems. In these models objects *delegate* messages to one another, thereby inheriting methods or values stored in other objects. Object inheritance and delegation are discussed 3.5.

6. **Multiple Inheritance:** In many situations it is desirable to inherit from more than one class. This is called *multiple inheritance*. When a class inherits from more than one parent there is the possibility of conflict: methods or instance

variables with the same name but different or unrelated semantics that are inherited from different superclasses. Conflict resolution strategies are discussed in Section 3.6.

3.1.4 Chapter Organization

The rest of the chapter is organized as follows. Section 3.2 contrasts inheritance and subtyping. Subtyping is a behavioral relationship among object types. Inheritance hierarchies are implementational hierarchies. Section 3.3 discusses class inheritance. Classes inherit instance variables and methods from their superclasses. Section 3.4 elucidates the metaclasses. Classes, when treated as objects, are instances of metaclasses. Section 3.5 demonstrates how in some systems objects inherit from one another. The section explains delegation and compares prototype systems with class-based systems. Section 3.6 shows how a class can inherit from multiple parents or superclasses, through multiple inheritance.

■ 3.2 INHERITANCE AND SUBTYPING

Section 2.1.2 defined types as sets of objects with sets of operations on them. The common elements of different types can be abstracted to form *subtype* hierarchies. The concepts of subtyping and inheritance are often confused. As Moss and Wolf (1988) pointed out:

> . . . the two concepts (*inheritance and subtyping*) are merged into one mechanism in many programming languages. . . . As language designers have switched from the term class . . . to the term type . . ., it is natural for some that they also switch from the term *subclass* to refer to inheritors. The term *subtype*, therefore, can have different meanings in different languages. In sum, there has yet to arise any widely accepted set of definitions and terminology for inheritance and subtyping.

With inheritance, programmers can construct more specialized systems from existing class hierarchies. It is a mechanism that allows software modules to refer to and reuse existing modules. In general, inheritance deals with implementation, while subtyping is a semantic relationship among the types of objects.

3.2.1 Subtyping

A type T_1 is a subtype of type T_2 if every instance of T_1 is also an instance of T_2 (Cardelli and Wegner, 1985). For example, every prime number is also an integer, so the set of prime numbers is a subset of the set of integers. The definition of subtype implies that an instance of T_1 can be used whenever an operation or a construct expects an instance of type T_2. For example, prime numbers can be used in integer addition, multiplication, or division. The ability to use an instance of a subtype in a context where an instance of its supertype is expected is called the *principle of substitutability*.

Subtyping is a reflexive (every type is a subtype of itself) and a transitive relation (if T_1 is a subtype of T_2 and T_2 is a subtype of T_3, then T_1 is a subtype of T_3). Subtyping is also anti-symmetric: if T_1 is a subtype of T_2 and T_2 is a subtype of T_1, then (for all practical purposes) T_1 and T_2 are the same. Thus the subtyping relation imposes a partial order on the types of a system. In object-oriented languages this partial order expresses itself in the inheritance hierarchy. The hierarchy is a *tree* if the language supports single inheritance (as in Smalltalk). If the object-oriented language supports multiple inheritance (see Section 3.4), the inheritance hierarchy is actually a directed acyclic graph (DAG).

The subtyping relationship can be established through:

> subsets
>
> subtyping of Structured Types (such as tuples)
>
> subtyping of functions

In the following sections, the authors concentrate on subsets and subtyping of structured types. Subtyping of functions will be discussed in Section 3.3.2.3 (on Constrained Overriding). Function or method subtyping is crucial when a subclass (subtype) overrides or redefines an inherited method in a superclass (supertype). These redefinitions cannot be arbitrary. Hence, function subtyping is also discussed in the section on constrained overriding.

3.2.1.1 Subsets as Subtypes

Since types are *sets of objects*, the most obvious candidates for subtypes of a type are its subsets. For example, consider the type Integer. Each of the following are subsets of the set of integers:

1. R = the integers in the range 1..100
2. P = the prime numbers
3. E = the set of even integers

Each set satisfies the principle of substitutability: An element of R, P, or E can be used in any context that an Integer is used. But there is a fundamental difference between set E and the sets R and P (besides the contents of the sets). Sets R and P do not have the property of closure, which will now be explained.

Remember that a type is a set of objects *and a set of operations on these objects*. Thus, for the set of integers, there are the usual arithmetic operations: addition, multiplication, subtraction, or integer division. These operations have algebraic properties with respect to one another (associativity, distributivity, and so on). With a formal algebraic specification, the data type will be described through:

1. the *signatures* of its operators (that is, the types of the input and output parameters to the operators) and

2. the *axioms* that define the semantics of the operations (and hence the semantics of the type). These axioms are also called *reduction rules*, *rewrite rules*, or *equations*.

For example, the associativity of addition, multiplication, and the distributivity of multiplication with respect to addition can be expressed by the equations:

$$X + (Y + Z) = (X + Y) + Z$$
$$X * (Y * Z) = (X * Y) * Z$$
$$X * (Y + Z) = X * Y + X * Z$$

Besides these algebraic properties, the operations "+" and "*" have the important *closure* property: their signature maps pairs of integers onto integers. In other words, the sum or product of two integers is also an integer.

For the sets R and P this important property is violated. For R, there are cases where the sum or product of two integers in R is greater than 100 (and hence *not* in R). For P it is worse, since the sum or product of two primes (other than 1) is never a prime!

The set of even integers E, however, satisfies the closure property for addition, subtraction, and multiplication. Thus these three operations on E behave the same way as do their corresponding operations on Integers. For a type T_1 to be a *complete subtype* of T_2, the operators of T_2 should behave compatibly with arguments from T_1. The closure of inherited operations is the most important area where behavioral compatibility can be found.

Strict closure is not always necessary for the subtyping of relationships, though. The subtyping relationship of subsets may be maintained in two other ways:

1. by defining a set of constraints that will indicate on which pairs of values the operations are well behaved (satisfy the closure property). This is possible with the integers in R; but is awkward with P, since the result of "+" is never a prime and the result of "*" is a prime if and only if one of the arguments is 1 (hardly an interesting case)!

2. by inheriting the operators of the supertype but abandoning the closure requirement and refining/restricting the signature of the operators. This is a more reasonable approach. For example, for P we can define "+" to be an operator from a pair of primes to integers. The problem with this alternative would be that inherited operators on the subtype would not act quite the same way as the corresponding operators on the supertype.

3.2.1.2 Subtyping of Structured Types

When the semantics of a type is properly defined, the *inclusion* semantics of subtypes can be extended to more complex types such as tuples (records) or arrays.

Assume $t_1, \ldots, t_n$ are types and $a_1, \ldots, a_n$ are attribute names. Further, assume each type t_i has an interpretation that we indicate by $dom(t_i)$ (the domain of t_i).

Then we define:

$$[a_1 : t_1, a_2 : t_2, \ldots, a_n : t_n]$$

to be a tuple type whose interpretation is the set of all tuples that at least have attributes $a_1, \ldots, a_n$ whose values are in $dom(t_1), dom(t_2), \ldots, dom(t_n)$. Note that a tuple can have other attributes in addition to $a_1, \ldots, a_n$ and still be a member of this type.

For example, consider the type:

Type **Person**
  [Name: Character String
   Age: Integer
   Address: Character String]

The domain of *Character String* is the set of all strings of characters. The domain of *Integer* is the set of integers. The domain of *Person* is the set of all tuples that at least have the attributes (fields) *Name*, *Age*, and *Address* such that the value of *Name* is a string of characters, the value of *Age* is an integer, and the value of *Address* is a string of characters. Thus

  [Name: "Mary Beth"
   Age: 21
   Address: "202 Spring St., Madison, WI, 76503"]

is of type *Person*. But so is:

  [Name: "John Smith"
   Age: 20
   Address: "101 Spring St, San Pedro, CA, 94563"
   Social Security Number: 111-222-333
   Salary: $25,000
   Major: "Music"]

With this semantics any instance of a tuple type that includes the attributes "Name" of type *Character String*, "Age" of type *Integer*, and "Address" of type *Character String* is automatically an instance of the type *Person*. Actually, *Person* is just a shorthand for indicating the (conceptual) type.

In general, the subtyping relationship ($\leq$) for tuples is defined as follows:

If $t_i \leq u_i$ for $i = 1, \ldots, n$
then
$$[a_1 : t_1, a_2 : t_2, \ldots, a_n : t_n, \ldots, a_m : t_m]$$
$$\leq$$
$$[a_1 : u_1, a_2 : u_2, \ldots, a_n : u_n]$$
where $m \geq n$

For example:

> [Name: Character String
>   Age: 1..21
>   Address: Character String
>   Salary: Dollar]

$$\leq$$

> [Name: Character String
>   Age: Integer
>   Address: Character String]

This subtyping relationship is very close to the inheritance relationship in object-oriented programming languages. In Smalltalk, for example, the set of instance variables of a subclass is a superset of the set of instance variables of its superclass. Thus, the subclass is a subtype of the superclass.

Similar subtyping relationships hold for:

1. Collections, and/or
2. Parametric types

For example, if $S = \{t\}$ indicates a "set" type whose instances are sets with elements of type t then:

$$S_1 = \{t_1\} \leq S_2 = \{t_2\}$$
$$\text{if and only if } t_1 \leq t_2$$

For example $\{SalesPerson\} \leq \{Employee\}$; the set whose instances are salespeople is a subtype of the set whose instances are employees. The reason is that the SalesPerson type is a subtype of Employee.

The same subtyping relationship holds for other container types such as arrays, stacks, or tables.

3.2.2 Contrasting Inheritance with Subtyping

As indicated earlier, the concepts of subtyping and inheritance are often confused and used interchangeably. Therefore it is not uncommon to find languages which claim to support subtyping, yet provide just a form of class inheritance that is more constrained than subtyping.

The discussion on subtyping in the previous sections presented the concept as an ordering relationship among type structures and/or functions. In an object-oriented framework, subtyping needs to be analyzed in conjunction with abstract data typing. For an ADT1 to be a "subtype" of an ADT2:

1. The structure of ADT1 as captured in its instance variables must be a subtype of the structure of ADT2.
2. The behavior of ADT1 as captured in the signature and specification of its methods must conform to the behavior of ADT2.

Since an ADT is fully defined through its interface (that is, its methods), the more important requirement is the behavioral relationship. In fact, if we strictly follow the encapsulation paradigm, it should be possible to establish subtyping relationships among data types or abstract data types without worrying about the representation (structure) at all; each type could have an entirely different implementation of representation but maintain the behavioral subtype compatibility.

With **2.**, ADT1 is a subtype of ADT2 if, for each method M of ADT2, there is a corresponding method M of ADT1 that conforms. When does a method in a subtype conform to a method in a supertype? Unfortunately the conformance rules are not the same across all strongly typed object-oriented languages. In Section 3.3.2.3 we shall discuss two alternative conformance strategies.

It is conceivable for one abstract data type ADT1 to be a subtype of another abstract data type ADT2, and yet have an entirely different implementation for each of its methods (even for the methods that have the same signature as the corresponding methods in the supertype).

For example, Set is a subtype of Bag (bags are collections that can have duplicates; in sets, an object can occur only once). The operations (methods) on Set (union, intersection, difference, insert, delete, and so on) have signatures that are subtypes of the corresponding operations for Bag. Nevertheless, we can have entirely different internal representations for Set and Bag. Instances of Set could be implemented as arrays and instances of Bag could be implemented as linked lists. Figure 3.6 illustrates the same collection as an instance of an array (a set) and a linked list (a bag). With these different representations, the implementations of the same operators for Bag and Set are completely different. With respect to its behavior, however, Set is a constrained Bag, and thus a subtype of Bag.

This behavioral definition is independent of implementation, and subtyping can be viewed as a *behavioral hierarchy*. Inheritance, on the other hand, is an *implementational hierarchy*.

3.2.2.1   *Implicit Subtyping versus Explicit Inheritance*

The subtyping relationship can be established in one of three ways:

1. Explicitly, by naming a type to be a subtype of another type (actually indicating that the subtype is inheriting from the supertype).

Array

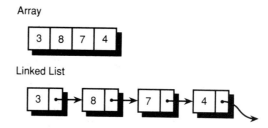

Linked List

Figure 3.6 Alternative representations of the same collection.

2. Implicitly, by inferring the subtype relationship from the properties of the types (using the definitions of the previous sections).

3. Through hybrid schemes, where the subtype relationship is sometimes inferred and other times stated explicitly.

Inheritance is always indicated explicitly. With method **2.**, the subtyping relationship uses *structural* equivalence. It is very rare to find a language where the subtyping relationship is not explicitly expressed in the type (class) definitions, but one language that uses implicit subtyping is Emerald (Black et al., 1987).

Some object-oriented languages use a hybrid scheme. The most frequently used scheme is the inheritance of parameterized or generic types. Thus,

Set[Employee] ≤ Set[Person]

because Employee is explicitly declared to be a subtype of Person, and the set construct preserves the subtype relationship. Subtyping of generic types is used in the type conformity rules in the Eiffel language.

Most conventional programming languages use explicit type *name* equivalence to establish type relationships. For example, two variables x and y in Pascal are of the same type if and only if their types have the same name:

x: T;
y: T;

Semantically, structural equivalence is really all that matters: Names of types are nothing but convenient *abbreviations* for the types. Yet even in strongly typed object-oriented languages, the type relationships are established explicitly through naming. In Trellis/Owl (O'Brien, 1985) for example, the specification that *SalesPerson* is a subtype of *Employee* is established explicitly through:

type_ module SalesPerson
subtype_ of (Employee)

.

.

.

end type_module;

Note that in addition to specifying the subtype relationship, this declaration is indicating that *SalesPerson* is inheriting *Employee*'s components (instance variables) and operations (methods).

Thus inheritance is typically indicated explicitly through a "superclass"/"supertype" clause. The superclass(es) is indicated by name. In Smalltalk/V we can indicate that *Employee* is a subclass of *Person*, and *SalesPerson* is a subclass of *Employee* through the declarations:

Object subclass: #Person
*   instanceVariableNames: 'name address age'*

Person subclass: #Employee
*   instanceVariableNames: 'salary rank*
*   department manager*
*   telephone officeLocation'*

Employee subclass: #SalesPerson
*   instanceVariableNames: 'accounts orders*
*   commission quota'*

3.2.2.2   Subtyping and Dynamic Binding

In Sections 2.3 and 2.4 the advantages of overloading and the need for dynamic binding in object-oriented languages were presented. Binding messages to methods at run time for those languages that do not specify object or argument types makes a lot of sense. In Smalltalk, for example, the same variable X in the same program block can reference (or represent) an instance of a Person and later an instance of a Fish. Therefore, messages sent to X are bound to particular methods dynamically (that is, at run time, not at compile time).

Can some sort of dynamic binding be supported with strongly typed languages such as Eiffel, Trellis/Owl, or C++? In these languages, the type of variables are declared statically. For example, if variable *John* is of type *Person*, I is an *integer*, *Mary* is an *Employee*, and *Jim* is a *SalesPerson* in the same program module, we must have the declarations:

John: Person;
I: integer;
Mary: Employee;
Jill: SalesPerson;

It would seem to be a clear violation of strong typing (and even typing in general) to be able to assign objects of a different type to any of these variables. Furthermore, in conventional languages such as Pascal, the assignments:

Jim := I;
Mary := Jill;
I := John;

would not even be executed since the compiler will detect a type error long before the program could be run.

Nevertheless, within the confines of subtyping it is indeed possible to assign an object reference Y of type T':

Y : T ';

to a variable X

X := Y;

which was statically defined to be of type T:

X : T;

as long as T' is a subtype of T. Note that the assignment **X := Y** is dynamically binding X to an object of a different type (that is, different from its static type). Therefore, if *Employee* is a subtype of *Person* and *SalesPerson* is a subtype of *Employee* the following assignments are all valid:

John := Mary;
John := Jill;
Mary := Jill;

Dynamic binding can also apply to methods. Assume the method *EvaluateBonus* is defined in class *Employee* and is redefined with an entirely different implementation in class *SalesPerson* (see Section 3.3.2.1 on overriding). Then if *EvaluateBonus* is invoked on *Mary* (using syntax similar to C++):

Mary.EvaluateBonus(...);
Mary := Jill;
Mary.EvaluateBonus(...);

before and after the assignment *Mary := Jill*, we will end up executing the code defined in *Employee* before the assignment, and the code defined in *SalesPerson* after the assignment!

As long as the overridden methods and instance variable redefinitions are confined to the subtyping constraints (as discussed in Sections 3.3.1.1 and 3.3.2.3) there will be *no* type errors generated at run time (strong typing). The implications of these dynamic bindings are tremendous. Now we can have our cake and eat it, too! The programmer can have the flexibility of dynamic binding added to the advantages of strong typing.

3.2.2.3 *What Do Classes Inherit?*

The relationship between inheritance and subtyping is similar to the relationship between abstract data types and classes. This is illustrated in Figure 3.7. Just as classes are used to implement abstract data types, in most object-oriented languages inheritance is used to support the subtyping relationships among classes. Using inheritance, programmers extend and refine existing software components. Thus inheritance provides software construction and reuse mechanisms.

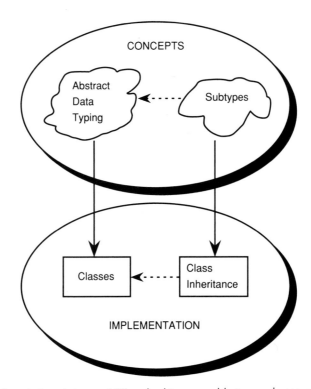

Figure 3.7 Correlations between ADT and subtypes, and between classes and class inheritance.

There are three components that could be inherited from a superclass:

1. The *Interface* of the superclass. All the methods of the superclass can be invoked with instances of the subclass as target objects.
2. The *Code* that implements the methods of the superclass. This is perhaps the most important contribution of inheritance for code sharing and reusability.
3. The *Representation* (instance variables) of the superclass. More specifically, if $C_2, \ldots, C_n$ are superclasses of C_1, then C_1 includes:

$$\text{Instance Vars of } C_2 + \cdots + \text{Instance Vars of } C_n$$

The next section covers all three aspects of inheritance and illustrates them through examples.

■ 3.3 CLASS INHERITANCE

Inheritance of classes is established through explicit declaration of the inheritance relationship. Thus the user declares explicitly:

Class SalesPerson is a subclass of class Employee

Each class is declared to be a subclass of one or more superclasses (more than one superclass is allowed only if the system supports multiple inheritance). Thus the object space of the user is organized in *class hierarchies* where each object is a member of all the classes reachable (through the *superclass* relationship) from the most specialized class of the object. Thus when an object O is created through:

O := C new

then O is a member of C and every superclass of C, as illustrated in Figure 3.8. As a specific example consider the inheritance hierarchy rooted at *Employee*. When an instance of DistrictManager is created through:

John := DistrictManager new

then *John* becomes a member of the class *DistrictManager*, as well as classes *Sales-Manager*, *SalesPerson*, *Employee*, and *Person*. This means the "state" of *John* will be stored in instance variables declared in *DistrictManager* (such as *DistrictBudget*), as well as additional instance variables declared in *Person* (Name, Address), *Employee* (Salary), *SalesPerson* (Quota), and *SalesManager*. Similarly the *behavior* of *John* is characterized by the union of all the methods of *John*'s superclasses.

Class inheritance can be completely ad hoc as in Smalltalk or other type-less languages. Alternatively, it is possible to introduce numerous type and visibility constraints on a class hierarchy. In the most general ad-hoc approach of class inheritance, the subclasses can override inherited instance variable or method definitions

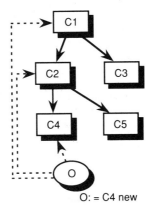

O: = C4 new

Figure 3.8 O is a member of C1, C2, and C4.

arbitrarily. The ability to override instance variables and methods adds considerable flexibility to handle exceptions and special cases. After all, one of the main features of inheritance is to model specialization.

In fact, some frame-based knowledge representation systems in AI allow some inherited slots (instance variables) to be *cancelled*, creating such interesting special objects as three-legged elephants (instance of the generic elephant inheriting from four-legged mammals), honest used-car salesmen (inheriting, alas, from the human race), or safe Middle East cruise trips. Some critics have argued that this arbitrary overriding or cancellation of inherited properties is counterproductive, to put it mildly. As Brachman (1985) points out:

> When *all* rules are made to be broken, then they aren't rules at all. The call to arms sounded . . . for the need to represent three-legged elephants and dead ducks (or those with their feet set in concrete), while crucially important if AI is ever to get a hold of "common sense," has led to naive mechanisms that both admit arbitrary, bizarre representations and force the ignorance of crucial, obvious facts (e.g., the rule that elephants with three legs are elephants is *not* made to be broken). AI representation systems have thrown out the compositional baby with the definitional bath water.

The flexibility of object-oriented systems to override declarations of instance variables and methods in class hierarchies can be categorized as follows:

For Instance Variables:

1. **No redefinition.** The simplest strategy is to inherit the instance variable but disallow any kind of redefinition by the inheriting client (that is, subclass).
2. **Arbitrary redefinition.** The second extreme is to allow a subclass to redefine the type of an instance variable without any constraints. This is the approach taken by Smalltalk and other type-less object-oriented languages.

3. **Constrained redefinition.** The instance variables can only be redefined to be *subtypes* of the type of the instance variables in the superclass. This ensures that the strong typing of the language is maintained when methods defined in the superclass manipulate the instance variables of the subclass.

4. **Hidden definitions.** To avoid conflicts between information hiding (encapsulation) and inheritance, instance variables can be hidden from the inheriting subclasses. This provides independent definitions of instance variables in the inheritance class hierarchy. One system that uses this strategy is CommonObjects (Snyder, 1986).

For Methods:

1. **Arbitrary redefinition.** The subclass can provide an entirely different and unrelated implementation of the method. When a message is sent to an object, the most specialized method is applied. This method overrides methods with the same name in the superclasses, without any restrictions on argument types or behavior.

2. **Constrained redefinition.** The type, or even the behavior of methods in the subclass, must have signatures that are subtypes of the signatures of the methods they override. For strongly typed languages it is important to maintain the subtyping relationship of method signatures for the overriding methods. For example, if method M in C_2 overrides method M in C_1, and C_2 is a subclass of C_1 then the signature of M in C_2 must *conform* (be a subtype of) to the signature of M in C_1. Also, if pre- and postconditions are specified for M in C_1, then the overriding pre- and postconditions of M in C_2 must conform to the C_1 definitions.

Arbitrary overriding of instance variables and methods provides flexibility. But if we allow arbitrary redefinitions, we cannot guarantee strong typing. This implies that object-oriented programs will be less safe and the system will incur a run-time type checking overhead. Constrained overriding is less flexible but guarantees strong typing. There are two main reasons that constraints are needed when overriding variables and methods in strongly typed object-oriented languages.

The first reason results from substitutability; if C' is a subclass of C, then an instance of C' can be used in any context that expects an instance of C. Therefore, in the same program we *must* be able to use instances of a class or any of its subclasses and *not* generate a run-time type error!

Another reason constraints are needed is to allow dynamic binding of variables to subclass instances. More specifically, a variable X can be declared to be an instance of a class C and subsequently have X be bound to an instance of a descendant C' of C. After the binding, methods invoked for X will be invoked for C'. For example, Sp can be declared to be a variable of type SalesPerson and subsequently be bound to an instance Sm of SalesManager, through Sp := Sm. In order to avoid run-time type errors, all the methods redefined in C' must conform with (such as, have a signature that is a subtype of) the corresponding methods in C, as discussed in Section 3.3.2.3. The constraints on instance variable and method argument types as discussed in the following sections will guarantee this conformance.

3.3.1 Inheriting Instance Variables

How subclass instances get their structure will be shown first. The class of an object describes its structure by specifying the object's instance variables. In all object-oriented languages, instances of a subclass must retain the same types of information as instances of their superclass.

One way to achieve this is to inherit the instance variables of the superclass directly and allow methods in the subclass to access and manipulate the instance variables of its superclass(es) without any constraints. This is the strategy in Smalltalk.

In this scheme, each subclass declares the *additional* instance variables that it introduces (as specialization or extension). Thus if class C_1 declares:

> *Class* C_1
> *Instance Variables:* X_1,
> X_2,
> X_3

and class C_2 is a subclass of C_1, then C_2 declares just the additional instance variables that it introduces:

> *Class* C_2 *subclass of* C_1
> *Instance Variables:* X_4,
> X_5,
> X_6

The state of each instance of C_1 will be stored in variables X_1, X_2, and X_3. The state of each instance of C_2 will be stored in variables X_1, X_2, X_3, X_4, X_5, and X_6. This is illustrated in Figure 3.9, which also depicts the state of Employee, a subclass of Person. In general, the instance variables of a class consist of the *union* of the instance variables of all its superclasses.

3.3.1.1 Redefining Instance Variables

In typed object-oriented languages such as C++, Trellis/Owl, or Eiffel the instance variable declarations also specify the types of the instance variables. Therefore the instance variable declarations take the form:

> *Class* C_1
> *Instance Variables:*
> X_1: CT_1,
> X_2: CT_2,
> X_3: CT_3

Class C_2 subclass of C_1
    Instance Variables:
        X_4: CT_4,
        X_5: CT_5,
        X_6: CT_6

where CT_1 is the name of the class (type) of X_1.

When the object-oriented language specifies the types (classes) of the instance variables (as does Eiffel), it is possible to redefine (and thus override) the type declaration of an instance variable in a subclass. This overriding can be

      (a) arbitrary, or
      (b) constrained.

For example, we can have class C_2 declared as:

Class C_2 subclass of C_1
    Instance Variables:
        X_2: CT_7,
        X_4: CT_4,
        X_5: CT_5,
        X_6: CT_6

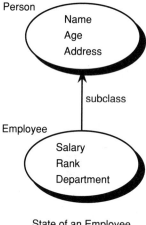

Figure 3.9 An Employee's state.

where the type of X_2 in C_2 (CT_7) is *totally unrelated* to the type of X_2 in C_2 (CT_2). For example, assume the instance variable *CAddress* in the class *Person* is of class *CAddress*, as show below.

```
Class CAddress:
    Instance Variables
        StreetNumber:   integer
        StreetName:     String[Char]
        Apartment #:    integer
        City:           String[Char]
        State:          String[Char]
        ZipCode:        integer
```

With arbitrary overriding, the subclass *Employee* of *Person* can redefine *Address*, and declare it to be of type *String[Char]*.

The tradeoff between arbitrary and constrained overriding is between flexibility and type-safe programming: arbitrary overriding provides more flexibility. However, inherited methods in the superclass that "assume" the type of the object as declared in the superclass can generate type errors, if the type of the object is changed in a subclass. For example, if we have a method *PrintAddress* defined in class *Person* that assumes the class *CAddress* representation, then this method must be overridden in class *Employee*. Otherwise, invoking *PrintAddress* on an instance of *Employee* will generate a type error.

In strongly typed languages such as Trellis/Owl or Eiffel the redefinition is more constrained: The type in the subclass must be a subtype of the corresponding type in the superclass. In other words, the class type CT_7 in the preceding example must be a subclass of the class type CT_2.

For example, say that a user would like to allow foreign employees in the class *Employees*. If we define a class *ForeignAddress* as subclass of *CAddress*:

```
Class ForeignAddress subclass of CAddress:
    Instance Variables
        Country:    String[Char]
        Continent:  String[Char]
```

the class of instance variable X_2 can be redefined with *ForeignAddress*. It would *not* be permissible to redefine X_2 to be of class *String[Char]* under these constrained rules, as *String* is not a subclass of *CAddress*.

3.3.1.2 Hiding Instance Variables

With encapsulated abstract data types, the instance variables are hidden from the users of the instances. So far, we have shown examples of how subclasses inherit and access the instance variables of their superclasses. There is no reason this has to be true. The superclass can hide its instance variables from the subclass, too.

In other words, a class has two sorts of "clients":

1. *Instantiating* clients—those who just create instances of the class and manipulate those instances through methods associated with the class.
2. *Inheriting* clients—those who are subclasses and inherit methods (behavior) and structure from the class.

Object-oriented languages have differed in the strategies for giving access and visibility to these two types of clients.

Smalltalk, for example, allows unrestricted access to instance variables by the inheriting clients, but completely restricts instantiating clients. Going back to previous examples, assume the *Accounts* instance variable of *SalesPerson* is implemented as an array of *Account*. *SalesManager* is a subclass of *SalesPerson*, and so is an inheriting client of *SalesPerson*. Each sales manager has a set of accounts, in addition to the accounts of the salespeople he or she manages. With the Smalltalk approach, any method defined in *SalesManager* or *DistrictManager* can directly access or update this *Accounts* instance variable *as an array*.

If an instantiating client has just created an instance Sp of *SalesPerson*, however, it can only access or update the instance variable *Accounts* indirectly. It must use messages with selectors *AddNewAccount* or *GetAccounts* in order to manipulate the *Accounts* instance variable.

Some have correctly argued that making the instance variables visible to the subclasses violates both uniformity and encapsulation (Snyder, 1986). If having done so, when the implementation of the superclass is modified through modifying the instance variables, all the subclasses utilizing these instance variables have to be modified! In her OOPSLA-1987 keynote address, Barbara Liskov gave a most elegant description of this conflict between abstract data typing (encapsulation) and inheritance:

> One problem with almost all inheritance mechanisms is that they compromise data abstraction to an extent. . . . When encapsulation is violated, we lose the benefits of locality. We must consider the combined code of the sub- and superclass in reasoning about the subclass, and if the superclass needs to be re-implemented, we may need to re-implement its subclasses.

For example, if the implementation of *Accounts* is modified to be a linked list instead of an array, then all the methods in subclasses of *SalesPerson* that directly access or update *Accounts* have to be modified. To illustrate this, consider the method *TotalAccounts* in *Salesperson*, which evaluates the total number of accounts allocated to a *SalesPerson*. Using a pseudo-Pascal syntax with an array implementation, the total number accounts will be accumulated through:

```
TotalAccounts := 0;
For i := 1 to MaxArraySize
    if Accounts[i] < > NIL
        TotalAccounts := TotalAccounts + 1;
end
```

where *MaxArraySize* is the statically defined maximum possible size of the array *Accounts*. If an entry in the array does not contain an account it is set to NIL.

If a linked-list implementation is used, the total number of accounts will be accumulated through:

```
TotalAccounts := 0;
NextAccount := Accounts;
While (NextAccount < > NIL) do
Begin
    TotalAccounts := TotalAccounts + 1;
    NextAccount := NextAccount^.Next;
End
```

where the *Next* field in the linked list of *Accounts* points to the record of the next account.

These two alternative implementations of *Accounts* illustrate the fact that a method in the subclass *SalesManager* of *SalesPerson* has to be modified since an implementation in the parent (superclass) of an instance variable was modified. Thus *all* inheriting clients that utilize the modified instance variable have to be modified.

CommonObjects (Snyder, 1986b), on the other hand, supports independent definitions of instance variables in the inheritance class hierarchy. The inheriting clients cannot directly access or manipulate the instance variables of their superclasses. In fact, instance variables in the inheritance hierarchy are independent of each other:

> . . . if the type child inherits from a type parent, then each object of type child automatically includes as part of its representation the local state (instance variables) of an object of type parent. These inherited instance variables are distinct from instance variables defined by the type child and any instance variable inherited by child from other types regardless of the names of the instance variables.

Therefore, as illustrated in Figure 3.10 an object of type (class) Chevrolet that is a subtype of type Car, in turn a subtype of Vehicle, will have instance variables pertaining to its state as a Vehicle, Car, and Chevrolet. The states are stored in the instance variables of the corresponding classes but are totally unrelated. It is important to note that with this approach, methods of a subclass (subtype) cannot access the instance variables of the superclass directly: like instantiating clients, the instance variables of the superclass must be accessed and/or updated through the methods of the superclass. As discussed in Chapter 2, some object-oriented languages automatically generate access and update methods to manipulate the hidden instance variables. The subclass can use these access functions to manipulate the instance variables defined in the superclasses.

The most general approach, which combines efficiency and flexibility, is to support the notions of public, private, and subclass visible and leave it to the implementation to specify the desired protection. A class can have two kinds of clients. These three options are defined as follows:

1. *Public*. If an instance variable or a method is declared to be public, then *any* client can directly access, manipulate, or invoke it.

2. *Private*. If an instance variable or a method is declared to be private, then *no* client can directly access, manipulate, or invoke it.

3. *Subclass Visible*. If an instance variable or a method is declared to be subclass visible, then it can be accessed, manipulated, or invoked directly only by inheriting clients (that is, they are private as far as instantiating clients are concerned).

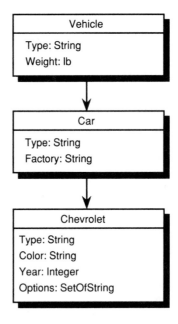

The state of MyCar

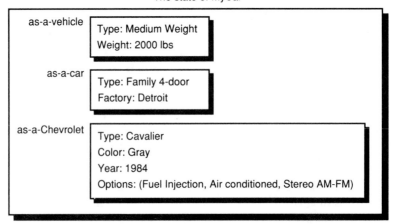

Figure 3.10 The type variable repeated in each class.

As will be described in Chapter 5, C++ supports the notions of public, private, and protected (subclass visible) *members* (methods or instance variables).

Trellis/Owl supports the notion of *subtype visible*. For example, to indicate that the instance variable (*component*, in Trellis/Owl terminology) *Address* of *Person* is to be subtype visible:

component me *address : address-type*
subtype visible

here **me** indicates the component is an instance variable (versus class or type component), and *address-type* is the type of the address instance variable. With this definition, only methods in a subtype of *Person* can obtain or update the value of the *address* instance variable.

If these three options are supported, then the designer can initially choose to be conservative and make most of the instance variables and some of the methods private. After establishing some stability in the code base of some classes, the instance variables and methods can be made public or subtype visible, providing more efficient and direct manipulation by the instantiating and inheriting clients.

3.3.2 Inheriting Methods

As indicated earlier, a class defines both the structure and behavior of a collection of objects. The behavior is specified in the methods associated with the instances of the class. Methods are operations that can either retrieve or update the state of an object. The state of an object is stored in its instance variables.

In an inheritance hierarchy, a method defined for a class is inherited by its subclasses. Thus, the inherited methods are part of the interface manipulating the instances of the subclass.

For example, we can have the class Window with BorderedWindow and Text-Window as subclasses as illustrated in Figure 3.11. MenuWindow is a subclass of BorderedWindow. The methods such as MoveWindow, ResizeWindow, and RotateWindow can also be invoked on instances of TextWindow and BorderedWindow. In the TextWindow subclass, more specialized methods for editing and modifying the font, character size, and so on of the text strings in the window are defined. These methods are not defined on instances of Window that are not also instances of TextWindow (such as, instances of BorderedWindow). BorderedWindow can have its own methods Edit, Font, and so on that are totally unrelated to the methods with the same selector names of, say, TextWindow. Thus, classes that are "siblings" (that is, have the same parent or ancestor class) can have operators (methods) with the same name that are totally unrelated.

3.3.2.1 Method Overriding

In addition, a subclass can override an inherited method. In other words, a method called M in class C can be overridden by a method also called M in a subclass C'

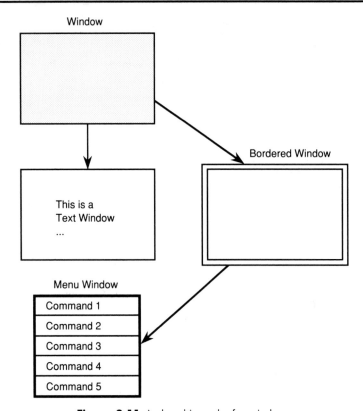

Figure 3.11 A class hierarchy for windows.

of C. Thus, when a message with selector M is sent to an object O, the underlying system will bind M to the method with the same name in the most specialized class of O.

For example, consider the hierarchy of *Persons*, with *Employee* a subclass of *Persons*, *SalesPerson* a subclass of *Employee*, and *SalesManager* a subclass of *SalesPerson*. Assume that the formula to evaluate the end-of-year bonus for salespeople is completely different than that of regular employees. In particular, the evaluation of the bonus of a regular employee is a function of the employee's manager's ranking (a number between 1 and 5) as well as the number of years the employee has worked for the firm:

EvaluateBonus code in class Employee:
    Bonus := Rank ∗ 1000 + NumberOfYears ∗ 100

The formula to evaluate the bonus of salespeople is a function of the total sales and the number of years the salesperson has worked for the firm:

EvaluateBonus code in class SalesPerson:
        *Bonus := TotalSalesAmount * 0.01 +*
                      *Rank * 1000 + NumberOfYears * 100*

Finally, the formula to evaluate the bonus of a sales manager is a function of:

1. The total sales of all the salespeople under the sales manager's supervision.
2. The total amount of direct sales done by the sales manager.
3. The number of years the sales manager has worked for the firm.

Therefore

EvaluateBonus code in class SalesManager:
        *Bonus := TotalSalesForceSales * 0.005 +*
                      *TotalDirectSalesAmount * 0.01 +*
                      *Rank * 1000 + NumberOfYears * 100*

Now, when the method *EvaluateBonus* is invoked, which piece of code is used? For example, assume:

   Mary Lou is an instance of SalesManager
   John Smith is an instance of SalesPerson

Note that besides being a sales manager, *Mary Lou* is a member of the abstract set *SalesPerson* and, by transitivity, she is also an *Employee*, and a *Person*. Similarly *John Smith* is a *SalesPerson*, an *Employee* and a *Person*.

However, *Mary Lou* is created as an instance of *SalesManager*. This means if we send to *Mary Lou* the message "What is your class?" the answer will be "*SalesManager*." Similarly *John Smith* is created as an instance of *SalesPerson*.

So, when we send a message such as:

   Mary-Lou EvaluateBonus

the search for a method called *EvaluateBonus* will start at the class *SalesManager*. Since such method is found in the declaration of this class, the search will stop there; the appropriate method has been found and can be executed.

The general algorithm for executing a message sent to an object involves a bottom-up (specialized to general) search for the appropriate method in the class hierarchy. More specifically assume the message *m* is sent to object *O*:

   O m

Let *C* be *O*'s class. For simplicity, assume we are dealing with a single inheritance hierarchy. Let *M* be the appropriate method that needs to be executed for *m*. Let S be the selector of *m*. Then *M* is determined as follows:

Method Invocation Algorithm

1. Initially set **cC** (the "current" class) to *C*.
2. If a method called S is declared in the definition of **cC**, then it is *M*. Stop searching and execute (invoke) it.
3. If **cC** is the root of the class hierarchy, generate an error and stop; the method is undefined.
4. Else set **cC** to its parent and go to step 2.

Here is another example: Assume the method *AddNewAccount* is defined only in class *SalesPerson*. Then if we send the message:

   Mary Lou AddNewAccount: NewAccount

the search will start at class *SalesManager*. Since such a method was not defined in *SalesManager*, step **4.** of the algorithm sets the current class to *SalesPerson*. The method is found in *SalesPerson,* so the search stops and *AddNewAccount* is invoked.

Now assume the method *SalesForceSize* is defined only in class *SalesManager*. The method evaluates the total number of salespeople that report to a sales manager. What happens when the message *SalesForceSize* is sent to John Smith? Such a method does not exist in John's class *SalesPerson*, so the search continues in *SalesPerson*'s parent, *Employee*. Again, the method is undefined, and the search goes to the class *Person*. The method is still undefined in *Person*. Since *Person* is the root of this class hierarchy, the system will generate an error (step **3.**).

3.3.2.2 *Invoking Superclass Methods*

Sometimes it is useful to call within a method of the subclass an overridden method of the superclass. For example, consider the formulae for *EvaluateBonus* in *SalesPerson* and *SalesManager*. If we let:

   StandardEmployeeBonus =
      *Rank * 1000 + NumberOfYears * 100*

then it is seen that the formula to evaluate the bonus in *SalesPerson* is:

   SalesPersonBonus =
      *StandardEmployeeBonus + TotalSalesAmount * 0.01*

Similarly,

   SalesManagerBonus =
      *SalesPersonBonus + TotalSalesForceSales * 0.005*

Therefore, the bonuses in classes *SalesManager* and *SalesPerson* use sub-expressions that are actually defined in their superclasses.

There are two basic strategies for invoking overridden superclass methods:

1. Use the pseudovariable **super**.
2. Qualify the method with the name of the class.

As shown in Chapter 2, the pseudovariable **self** is used to indicate the target object in a method; some object-oriented languages such as Smalltalk have an additional pseudovariable **super**, which is used to invoke overridden methods of the superclass. Like **self**, the pseudovariable **super** represents the target object of the message. But when a message is sent to **super**, the search for the method starts with the *superclass* of the target object's class. This means that in the Method Invocation Algorithm above, first the current class is set to the superclass of the object's class and *then* proceed with step **2**.

For example in Smalltalk/V, the method *EvaluateBonus* in the class *Employee* will be defined as:

```
EvaluateBonus
    ^((rank * 1000)  +  (numberOfYears * 100))
```

The *EvaluateBonus* method in the class *SalesPerson* will use the method in its superclass (that is, *Employee*):

```
EvaluateBonus
    ^((super EvaluateBonus)  +  ((self TotalSalesAmount) * 0.01)))
```

Here *TotalSalesAmount* is a method in *SalesPerson* that evaluates the total dollar amount of sales during the year. The "*super EvaluateBonus*" call will use the *EvaluateBonus* method in class *Employee* and return (rank * 1000) + (numberOfYears * 100) as evaluated there.

Similarly the *EvaluateBonus* method in the class *SalesManager* will use the method in *its* superclass (that is, *SalesPerson*):

```
EvaluateBonus
    ^((super EvaluateBonus) +
        ((self TotalSalesForceSales) * 0.005)))
```

where, in this application, *TotalSalesForceSales* is a method in *SalesManager* that evaluates the total dollar amount of sales from all the salespeople that report to the manager. Here the *super EvaluateBonus* call will use the *EvaluateBonus* method in the class *SalesPerson* (which in turn will call *EvaluateBonus* in *Employee*)).

A more obvious and general way to invoke a particular method is by qualifying its name with a class name. Thus, if the method is *EvaluateBonus* and it is desired to invoke its implementation in *Employee*, simply use the selector *Employee.EvaluateBonus*. Note that methods with the same name can appear in many places in a class hierarchy. A qualified method name will indicate the implementation that is either defined in the indicated class or is in the most immediate predecessor of the qualifying class name. Chapter 5 illustrates how this is done in C++.

3.3.2.3 Constrained Overriding

As described in Chapter 2, classes implement abstract data types. To define an abstract data type we need to describe the structure as well as behavior of the abstract data type. The structure is captured in the instance variables; the behavior of the class is expressed through its interface: the methods of the class.

In strongly typed object-oriented languages, the types of parameters and the type of the returned value are also specified for each method. For example, the input parameter of *TotalOrders* must be of type *SalesPerson*. Its output will be of type *Integer*. The specification of the types of the input and output (returned value) of a method (operation or function) is called the *signature* of the function. In languages that do not specify the types of the message arguments (such as Smalltalk) the signature of a method is the number of arguments, the method name, and the specification of the object returned by the method. The notation $T_1 * T_2 \rightarrow T_3$ indicates that a function accepts arguments of type T_1 and T_2 and produces a result of T_3.

Here are the signatures of some of the methods encountered thus far:

> *TotalOrders: SalesPerson → Integer*
> *TotalAccounts: SalesPerson → Integer*
> *AddNewAccount: SalesPerson ∗ Account → SalesPerson*
> *GiveRaise: Employee ∗ Float → Employee*

We can also have an alternative syntax for method signatures:

> *TotalOrders:* **argument** *SalesPerson* **returns** *Integer*
> *TotalAccounts:* **argument** *SalesPerson* **returns** *Integer*
> *AddNewAccount:* **arguments** *(SalesPerson, Account)*
>   **returns** *SalesPerson*
> *GiveRaise:* **arguments** *(Employee, Float)* **returns** *Employee*

Actually, since the first argument is always the class of the target object in a message, signatures of methods can also be specified as:

> *TotalOrders* **of** *SalesPerson:* **returns** *Integer*
> *TotalAccounts* **of** *SalesPerson:* **returns** *Integer*
> *AddNewAccount* **of** *SalesPerson:* **argument** *Account*
>   **returns** *SalesPerson*
> *GiveRaise* **of** *Employee* **arguments** *Float* **returns** *Employee*

The signatures of the methods of an abstract data type are really an *approximation* of the behavior of the abstract data type: They are basically a syntactic specification of the types of the input and output parameters. As was shown in Section 2.6, we need other mechanisms to specify the semantics of the methods (and hence the abstract data type). One mechanism is the use of pre- and postconditions for methods, which provides better realizations of the behavioral semantics of the abstract data type. As discussed in the next section, there are certain constraints on pre- and postconditions for methods that are redefined.

The notion of subtyping can also be extended to methods (operations, functions). The question is: When is a signature

$$T_1 \rightarrow T_2$$

a subtype of a signature

$$T_3 \rightarrow T_4 \ ?$$

The specification of subtyping for functions or methods comes into play when subclasses *redefine* or *override* an inherited method, as discussed in Section 3.3.2.1. In these cases the conformity constraints for function or method redefinition should be specified.

There are two alternative approaches for specifying when the signature of a function (method) conforms (such as, is a subtype of) the signature of another function (method). The most natural definition is to require that the arguments and the result of the method in the subclass be subtypes of the arguments and the result of the corresponding method in the superclass. In the case above this means:

T_1 should be a subtype of T_3
T_2 should be a subtype of T_4

This is called the *covariant* rule and is used in some object-oriented languages such as Eiffel.

Although the covariance rule seems intuitive, it violates static type checking. In fact, with covariance a program can be statically type checked at compile time and yet generate a type error at run time. Here is a simple example.

Assume there are two types of accounts:

regular accounts for a SalesPerson: Account
special accounts for a SalesManager: MgrAccount

MgrAccount is a subclass of Account. The subclass SalesManager *redefines* Add-NewAccount with signature:

$$AddNewAccount: SalesPerson * MgrAccount$$
$$\rightarrow SalesPerson$$

In the implementation of *AddNewAccount*, the class *SalesManager* uses the specialized features of *MgrAccount*. In particular, *MgrAccounts* has an instance variable called *Delegate*. When a new account is given to a manager, the manager delegates the account to one or more subordinates. This action does not make sense for accounts in general. It only makes sense for sales managers and *MgrAccount* instances.

Now consider the program (a mixed Pascal/Smalltalk-like syntax is used):

```
A : Account
Sp : SalesPerson
Sm : SalesManager
x : Employee
    . . .
/* initialize Sm and A */
    . . .
101:    Sp := Sm
102:    x := Sp AddNewAccount: A
```

Statically there are *no* type errors. However, at run time statement *101* will bind *Sp* to an instance of *SalesManager*. In other words, when *102* is executed, *Sp* will actually be a *SalesManager* instance. This means the method that will be executed for the message *AddNewAccount: A* will be the redefined method in class *SalesManager*. This method expects and uses the specialized features of a *MgrAccount* instance. Unfortunately it will be given an instance *A* of the more general *Account* class. Hence a type or incompatibility error will be generated at run time!

To guarantee strong type checking and avoid run-time type errors we should use the *contravariance* rule for the method or function subtype compatibility example. This rule states that the arguments of the more specialized function (method) should be *supertypes* of the arguments of the last specialized function (method). For our generic example, this means we should have:

T_1 should be a supertype of T_3

in order to have:

$$T_1 \rightarrow T_2 \leq T_3 \rightarrow T_4$$

In addition to the strong-typing argument there is a another intuitive reason for this relationship. The arguments of the function (method) represent the *domain*. The return value is an element in the *range* of the function. If S is a subtype of T, then the set of all instances of S is a subset of the set of all instances of T. Furthermore, if a function is defined on a set, it is certainly defined on any subset of the set. In general, a function from a domain D1 *is also* a function from domain D2 if D1 is a superset of D2. Similarly, a function whose range is R1 *is also* a function with range R2 if R2 is a superset of R1. Therefore, as illustrated in Figure 3.12, a function with domain D1 and range R1 *is also* a function with domain D2 and range R2, provided D1 is larger than D2 and R1 is smaller than R2.

3.3.2.3.1   Constraining Pre- and Postconditions

As discussed in Section 2.6, besides the specification of the number and types of arguments of each method of a class, there are additional constraints that can be used to delineate a method's (and hence a class's) behavior. These additional specifications are the pre-and postcondition predicates.

What constraints, if any, should be imposed on the pre- and postconditions of over-ridden methods? In other words, if a method *M* in class *C* is defined with:

> Method M:
>   Precondition P1
>   . . .
>   Postcondition P2

where P1 and P2 reference only the method's formal parameters and the target object, then what happens when M is redefined in a descendant C' of C? Are pre- and postconditions ignored, arbitrarily redefined, or redefined with constraints?

To guarantee strong typing, there must be constraints on how pre- and postconditions of methods can be redefined. The main reason for the constraints is to make dynamic binding possible. For example, assume *AddNewAccounts* which is defined in *SalesPerson*, is redefined in *SalesManager*.

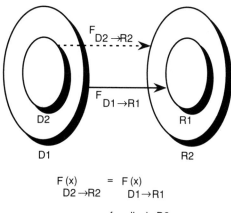

$$F(x)_{D2 \to R2} = F(x)_{D1 \to R1}$$

for all x in D2

Figure 3.12 F:D1→ R1 is also a function from D2→ R2.

The precondition of *AddNewAccount* in *SalesPerson* is:

> the current total number of accounts assigned to the salesperson must be less than the salesperson's quota

The postcondition of *AddNewAccount* in *SalesPerson* is:

> the total number of accounts is greater than or equal to one

If *SM* is a variable that was declared to be of type *SalesManager*:

> SM: SalesManager

and *SP* is a variable that was declared to be of type *SalesPerson*:

> SP: SalesPerson

then, with dynamic binding, the following is valid and must not generate a run-time type error:

> if < condition > then SP := SM
> SP AddNewAccount: Account1

To ensure this, the precondition of the redefined *AddNewAccount* in *SalesManager* must be *weaker* than the precondition of *AddNewAccount* in *SalesPerson*. The postcondition, on the other hand, must be *stronger*. There is no way to tell statically whether the *SP* in:

> SP AddNewAccount: Account1

references an instance of *SalesPerson* or an instance of *SalesManager*. Therefore, any call that was acceptable in the superclass *SalesPerson* must also be acceptable in the subclass: this means the precondition in the subclass must be weaker. An example of a weaker precondition is:

> the current total number of accounts assigned to the sales manager must be less than the sales manager's quota of accounts handled directly

> OR

> the total number of accounts currently assigned to salespeople managed by the sales manager fall below a threshold T.

For the similar reason, when the superclass guarantees a certain postcondition, the subclass redefining the method must also guarantee the postcondition. This means the postcondition in the redefined method must be stronger. An example of a stronger postcondition is:

the total number of accounts handled directly by the sales manager is greater than or equal to one

AND

the total number of accounts assigned to each of the salespeople managed by the sales manager remains unchanged

3.3.2.4 Inheriting the Interface

Inheritance is used to specialize: Employees are more specialized persons, salespeople are employees who are involved in selling items, or sales managers are salespeople who manage one or more salespeople. Nevertheless, characterizing inheritance as specialization has caused some confusion. A class C_1 inherits from class C_2 but the *interface* of C_1 (the subclass) is a *superset* of the interface of C_2!

This is illustrated in Figure 3.13. Viewing class types as sets of objects with the same structure and behavior, the set of *Employees* is a subset of the set of *Persons*. Similarly the set of *SalesPersons* is a subset of the set *Employees*. The set of secretaries is also a subset of the set of *Employees*. The set of sales managers is a subset of the set of salespersons and the set of district managers is a subset of the set of sales managers. However, when it comes to the interfaces and the representation, the inclusion hierarchies are reversed. For example, the set of attributes of salespersons includes all the attributes of *Employees* as well as additional attributes such as *Accounts* and *Orders*. Also the interface of *SalesPerson* is also a superset of the interface of *Employees*. It includes additional methods like *AddNewOrders*, *TotalAccounts*, and so on.

Thus, apart from specialization, inheritance can also be viewed as an *extension*: when a class C_1 inherits from a class C_2 it provides additional interface routines (methods) and/or attributes to the external environment. Viewing software as a contract between the designer of a class and its "clients" (such as, those who create instances of the class), inheritance extends the contract with additional "terms" and "clauses" of execution. These contractual addenda can be viewed as restrictions (specialization) or additional capabilities (extension).

3.3.2.5 Excluding Superclass Methods

As pointed out earlier, inheritance typically extends the interface of a superclass through defining new methods. Inherited methods can also be overridden through excluding some of the inherited methods in the subclass definition. For example, assume the following methods have been defined for the class Bag:

Insert
Delete
Intersect
Union
Difference
CartesianProduct
NumberOfOccurrences

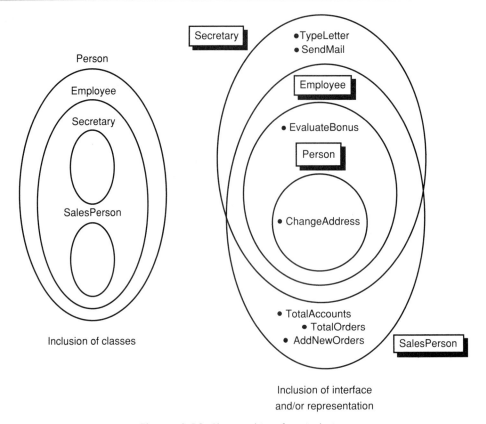

Figure 3.13 Class and interface inclusions.

A bag is a collection of objects that can have duplicates (that is, the *same* object can occur in a bag more than once). To evaluate the number of occurrences of an object in a bag we use the method *NumberOfOccurrences* which is a message sent to a bag object with an element object as argument. For example, the message:

B NumberOfOccurrences O

will return the number of occurrences of the object *O* in the bag *B*.

We want to create the subclass Set that will inherit from Bag. A set is also a collection, except that *an object can occur at most once* in the collection. Therefore the subclass Set specializes Bag through overriding the method *Insert*: before performing the actual insert we will check if the object is already in the Set. If yes, we will return a message saying "object already in the set." Thus *Insert* has an entirely different implementation in Set.

With *NumberOfOccurrences* there is a problem. Conceptually this method must not be part of the interface of Set. The value of *NumberOfOccurrences* for set objects is either 0 (the element is not in the set) or 1 (the element is in the set). Instead, we can have a predicate *IsElement* that returns true if an object is in a set. What is most important is that it is highly desirable to exclude *NumberOfOccurrences* from the *interface* of the class Set.

There are two basic ways for excluding inherited methods:

1. *Override the method* and send a diagnostic message when it is invoked on an instance of a subclass. This strategy is very general and can be used with almost any object-oriented language, since most languages support method overriding in the inheritance hierarchy. Another advantage is that if the language is strongly typed and the overriding is valid (that is, signatures and pre/postconditions are conforming) then there will be no problems with substitutability or dynamic binding. The disadvantage of the strategy is that it is at best a "hack": the method is still (a useless) part of the interface of the subclass.

2. *Specifying implicitly or explicitly* that the inherited method should not be inherited. This could be done either through an **exclude** construct as in Trellis/Owl or through specifying which are the methods that are inherited, and thus implicitly excluding the ones that are not inherited. The implicit or explicit specification is much cleaner. It enables better modeling since the interface of a class is cleanly captured. However, it could lead to run-time errors because of dynamic binding and substitutability. For example assume C' is a subclass of C that explicitly excluded the method M of C. If at run time a variable X which was declared statically to be of type (class) C was bound dynamically to an instance of the subclass C', then invoking M for X will cause a run-time error. Note that statically the call is valid, since X was declared to be of type C and M *is* defined for C.

Therefore, although the ability to exclude operations is desirable in some applications, explicit exclusion should be incorporated *only* if the application does not use dynamic binding.

■ 3.4 METACLASSES

Earlier discussions described objects as instances of classes. A class contains the description of the structure and behavior of its instances. In most object-oriented languages, classes are factories that create and initialize instances. In Smalltalk, for example, an instance of a class C is created through sending it the message *new*:

    iC := C new

Here a class is treated as an object that can instantiate (create instances) other objects. Therefore, in some object-oriented languages there are two types of objects:

1. *class objects*—objects that can act as templates and create instances of themselves.

2. *terminal objects*—objects that can only be instantiated but cannot instantiate other objects.

The state of a class *as an object* contains information about the *template* used by the class to create instances. For example, the template for complex numbers involves instance variables for the real and imaginary parts of a complex number instance—the *Real* and *Imaginary* instance variables. The template also incorporates the methods or operations for manipulating complex number instances. Similarly, the template for *Person* involves the name, age, social security number, and address of people who are instances of *Person*. The template for *Employee* includes additional instance variables such as salary, manager, and department.

If the class describes the instance variables and methods that are applicable to its instances, who or what class describes the state (instance variables) and behavior (methods) of the class *as an object?* More specifically, what is the class of a class?

Metaclasses are classes whose instances are also classes. Several (but not all) object-oriented languages support the concept of a metaclass. There are at least two advantages in treating classes as objects.

The first is that classes can be used for storing group information. If a class is treated as an object, then information global to all the instance variables of the class can be stored in class instance variables (or simply called *class variables* in Smalltalk). Methods associated with the class (called *class methods*) can be used to retrieve or update the values of class variables. For example, for the class *Employee*, *AverageSalary* is an important piece of global information that is used by instances or other clients of the class. Therefore, besides storing the template for creating and manipulating individual employees, the *Employee* class also includes information for the collection of employees as a group. Aggregate information for the existing instances of a class is very convenient if the extension of the class is maintained. Although some of the aggregate values (such as total number of instances, average salary of all existing employees, and so on) could be calculated, storing them in the instance variables of the class object (that is, the class variables) greatly improves the efficiency in calculating these values.

The second advantage (and most common usage) of class objects is their use in the creation/initialization of new instances of the class. The message *new* which is sent to class objects to create new instances can incorporate additional arguments to initialize the instance variables of the newly created instance. As discussed in Section 2.2.2.1, each class can have its own overloaded *new* method for creating and initializing instances. Recall that for complex numbers we had:

newComplexReal: r Imaginary: i

This method created a complex number and initialized its instance variables to r and i, respectively.

In supporting metaclasses, existing object-oriented languages pursue either:

1. Explicit support for creating and instantiating metaclasses.
2. Implicit support of metaclasses.

Some object-oriented languages do not support metaclasses at all, and their approach is discussed in Section 3.4.3.

3.4.1 Explicit Support

The first category is typified by ObjVlisp (Cointe, 1987). This object-oriented extension of LISP incorporates uniform support for classes and metaclasses; ObjVlisp treats objects, classes, and metaclasses uniformly as objects. Objects are instances of classes and each class has a metaclass. Both classes and metaclasses are objects. This means, for example, that metaclasses can be created as objects. It also means in order to create a class, we need to send a *new* message to its metaclass (a class is an instance of a metaclass). For example, to create the class Complex we send the *new* message to a special metaclass object called Class. In the message we include the:

1. Name of the class.
2. Instance variables of the class.
3. Methods (name *and* code) of the class.

For example, the messages to create the class *Complex* for complex numbers in ObjVlist are given by:

```
(send Class 'new
      :name       'MetaComplex
      :supers     '(Class)
      :i_v        '()
      :methods    '(())

(send MetaComplex 'new
      :name       'Complex
      :supers     '(Object)
      :i_v        '(real imaginary)
      :methods    '( ... )

      ... )
```

Here **:name**, **:supers**, **:i_v**, and **:methods** are all names of instance variables: **:name** indicates the name of the class being created, **:supers** indicates its superclasses, **:i_v** indicates its instance variables and **:methods** indicates its methods.

As illustrated in the example above, ObjVlisp incorporates two special built-in classes: *Object* and *Class*. These are the *only* built-in classes that are needed to create an object-oriented program in ObjVlisp. All other objects are created through either instantiating or creating a subclass of a class derived from *Object* or *Class*. Therefore in ObjVlisp:

> *Class:* is its own instance, and like any other object, it is a subclass of *Object*. A metaclass is both a subclass and an instance of *Class*. The special class *Object* is an instance of *Class*.

> *Object:* is the root of all classes. It is the most general class. Classes that are *not* metaclasses do not descend from *Class*. They are either subclasses of *Object* or subclasses of a class that is transitively a subclass of *Object*.

The relationship between *Class*, *Object*, the metaclass *MetaPerson* and classes *Person*, *Employee*, *SalesPerson* is depicted in Figure 3.14. Here all three classes *Person*, *Employee*, and *SalesPerson* are instances of *MetaPerson*.

One advantage to the explicit metaclass support strategy is its simplicity; it has uniform and homogeneous treatment of objects and classes. Metaclasses and classes are treated like any other objects. The only difference is that the instances of metaclasses are *classes*: objects that are templates for creating other instances. Other advantages are

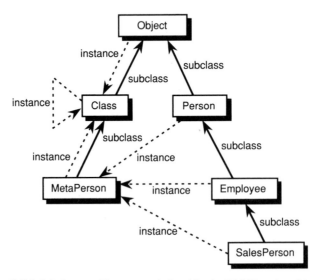

Figure 3.14 Subclass and instance relationships in ObjVlisp class hierarchies.

the flexibility and the capability of performance enhancement of the system (Graube, 1989): metaclasses contain the description of the class instances and information on class hierarchies and thus "metaclasses are perfectly suited to the task of optimization."

Although exposing metaclasses to the user enhances the understandability, flexibility, and extensibility of the object-oriented language, it also puts additional burdens on the user. One such burden is that the user has to perform class and metaclass instantiations in two separate steps; to manipulate and maintain three levels of objects.

Another disadvantage of explicit specification of metaclasses is that compatibilities must be maintained for inheritance. On one hand users are free to create and instantiate metaclasses. On the other hand classes are organized in inheritance hierarchies. An instance method defined in a class can invoke a class method.

To send a message to a class, object-oriented languages have a class message that returns the class of the object. For example, if E_1 is an employee then in:

$cE_1 := E_1$ *class*

cE_1 will be bound to the *Employee* class object. To send the message *GetAverageSalary* to the class of an employee:

cE_1 *GetAverageSalary*

or

$(E_1$ *class) GetAverageSalary*

Earlier it was illustrated how the *AverageSalary* class method can be called through an employee instance of the class *Employee*. Assume EMC is the metaclass of *Employee* and SPMC is the metaclass of *SalesPerson*. *SalesPerson* is a subclass of *Employee*. We define an instance method:

diffFromAverage
  ^self class averageSalary − salary

in class *Employee*. The message *GetAverageSalary* will be sent to the class of self. Its implementation (the method) will be specified *in the metaclass of the instance* (the class of the class). If *self* is bound to an *Employee* instance, the invoked method will be specified in EMC. Since *SalesPerson* is a subclass of *Employee* (assuming *SalesPerson* does not override *GetAverageSalary*), *self* could also be bound to an instance of *SalesPerson*. In that case the implementation of *GetAverageSalary* is specified in SPMC! If EMC and SPMC are different, then there *must be* a method with similar behavior in the *metaclass of the subclass*. This requirement is even more restrictive if the object-oriented language is strongly typed. As will be shown, Smalltalk solves this problem by having a metaclass hierarchy parallel to the class hierarchy.

It should be pointed out that the theory of metaclasses is still in its infancy. There have been some attempts to specify and formalize metaclass compatibility rules. For example, the problem just described is handled by the following compatibility rule by Graube (1989):

> *Metaclass Compatibilities*: A metaclass Mc_j is compatible with another metaclass Mc_i if, for all C_j instances of Mc_j which inherit from any C_i instances of Mc_i, every possible legal method which does not lead to an error for any iC_i instances of C_i inherited by C_j will not lead to an error for any iC_j instances of C_j.

Needless to say there are many more such rules and conditions to guarantee compatibility and safe executions of object-oriented programs involving metaclasses.

3.4.2 Implicit or Hidden Metaclasses

Smalltalk was the first object-oriented language to introduce metaclasses. However, the metaclasses in Smalltalk are hidden from the user. They are used in the uniform implementation of the kernel of the Smalltalk environment. In Smalltalk, metaclasses cannot be declared and created explicitly. Metaclasses are anonymous and *do not* have an existence independent of their class. In fact, each metaclass has exactly one instance, which is its class. Thus there is a one-to-one correspondence between classes and metaclasses and the definition of a metaclass is intertwined in the definition of the class.

When defining a class, the user distinguishes between class methods and class variables (as opposed to instance methods and instance variables). Although there are some subtle differences, class methods are basically the instance methods declared in a metaclass. Similarly a class variable is an instance variable of the class (as an object) also declared in the metaclass. Yet, unlike ObjVlisp, the specification of the class variables and class methods in Smalltalk are not made through an explicit metaclass creation mechanism. Classes are not created through sending a **new** message to a metaclass. Instead, the Smalltalk programming environment provides built-in menu driven options for creating classes.

For example, in Smalltalk/V classes are created through:

1. Opening a class browser.
2. Selecting a class.
3. Selecting the *add subclass* menu choice.

A dialog will ask for a class name. The class will be a subclass of the class that was initially selected. (Subclasses are discussed in great detail in this chapter.) Once the class name is provided, Smalltalk/V will come up with a template of a new class. The template will indicate:

- Instance variable name declarations
- Class variable name declarations

Smalltalk/V also provides menu choices to create *new* methods for classes and instances. The instance methods will apply to instances of the class. The class methods can be invoked on the class itself. As was said earlier, the most commonly used class method is *new* which creates and in some cases, initializes instance variables.

How is the class hierarchy reflected on the metaclasses? Each class is the unique instance of its metaclass and the metaclass hierarchy is parallel to the class inheritance hierarchy! Figure 3.15 illustrates this for the class hierarchy rooted at *Person*. Therefore, the problem of metaclass compatibility discussed in the previous section is avoided: A class method is supported either by the metaclass or through inheritance, by a predecessor of the metaclass.

The dynamics between objects, classes, and metaclasses is rather complex in Smalltalk. The architecture of the object/class/metaclass relationship is captured in built-in classes such as *Class*, *Metaclass*, *Object*. The relationship between these special classes is rather confusing.

Object: Every object is an instance of *Object* and every class is a subclass of *Object*. The metaclass of every object is the *Object* class. The *Object* class is a subclass of *Class*. The *Object* class, however, does not have a metaclass.

Class: Every metaclass is a subclass of *Class*. The metaclass *Class* (of Class) is a subclass of the *Object* class which, as we said earlier, is itself a subclass of *Class*! Thus the *Class* class, by transitivity, is a subclass of itself.

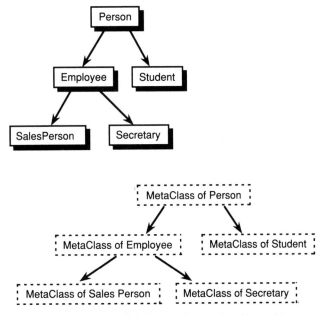

Figure 3.15 Parallel class and metaclass hierarchies.

Metaclass: All metaclasses are instances of the *Metaclass* class. The metaclass of Metaclass is *Metaclass class* which is a subclass of Class.

Due to the complexity of metaclasses in Smalltalk one study on the comprehension of Smalltalk-80 had the following conclusion (Borning and O'Shea, 1987):

> In our empirical studies, metaclasses were regarded as the most significant barrier to learnability by both students and teachers. We propose they be eliminated.

3.4.3 Object-Oriented Languages Without Metaclasses

Fortunately, not all object-oriented languages support metaclasses. In C++ classes are not objects. Although instances of classes are created through a *new* operator, the intention in C++ is the allocation of dynamic memory rather than the creation of an instance object. The *new* in C++ is similar to *malloc()* in C. The argument for *new* indicates the number of bytes from the heap space that needs to be allocated. The operation *new* returns a pointer to the newly allocated memory block. As discussed in Section 2.2, this memory block can subsequently be freed through a *delete* operation, which corresponds to *free()* in C.

Hence C++ classes are much more similar to types in conventional programming languages (especially C!) than to class objects that are dynamically created. In other words the only entities that are dynamically created (and hence require a *create* or *new* message) or destroyed in the C++ environment are the instances of classes. The instances correspond to the terminal instances; that is, the objects that are created dynamically cannot be templates of other objects (that is, classes).

There are other object-oriented languages that do not support the "class as object" paradigm. These include Simula and Eiffel. Simula also has a *new* operator, with nearly the same semantics as C++ (and C or Pascal, for that matter). Similarly, Eiffel has two operations, *Create* and *Forget* corresponding to allocation and de-allocation of dynamically allocatable memory.

In these languages, ordinarily a variable is declared to be of a certain type (or class):

> *P Person;*

This declaration is just a type specification. There is no actual memory allocated for P. To perform the memory allocation we need to perform (using C++ syntax):

> *P = new Person*

Now the run-time system allocates the appropriate memory and P points to that memory. If there are other "object-valued" instance variables of P, the memory for these must be dynamically allocated. For instance, memory for the Address of P must be allocated through:

> *P.Address = new Address*

Thus in C++ the *only* operation that accepts a class name as argument is *new*. In Eiffel, we do not even need to specify the class name. After declaring:

P: Person;

we can just create the actual object space and have P point to it through:

P.Create

Therefore in these strongly typed languages, classes are declared and initialized at compile time. Only objects can be created at run time.

In summary, although there seems to be some advantages in treating classes as objects, the theory, properties, and performance issues associated with the "classes as instances of metaclasses" paradigm is still in its infancy. Metaclass systems are difficult to understand (and, alas, explain!). Neither the Smalltalk (hidden metaclass approach) nor the explicit metaclass approach seems to be satisfactory. The C++ "classes as types" approach is a clear and mature technology that has been successfully implemented in numerous conventional as well as object-oriented languages.

■ 3.5 OBJECT INHERITANCE

The previous section discussed metaclasses. Object-oriented languages that support metaclasses have three categories of objects:

1. Metaclass objects whose instances are classes.
2. Non-metaclass class objects whose instances are terminal objects.
3. Terminal objects that are not classes.

Inheritance applies only to classes. Thus a class C_1 inherits representation and behavior from class C_2. Section 3.3 discussed the instance variable and method inheritance aspects of class inheritance in great detail.

In Smalltalk and other languages that support metaclasses, class variables are also inherited. This implies a limited form of inheritance for the state of objects. For instance, class *SalesPerson* inherits from class *Employee*. If *AverageSalary* is a class variable of *Employee*, then *SalesPerson* methods can access the class variable. For example, the method *IncAverageSalary* in *Employee* increments the *AverageSalary* by a given percentage:

IncAverageSalary: inc
    averageSalary := averageSalary * (1 + (inc/100))

We can invoke this method on *Employee*:

Employee incAverageSalary: 10

to increment *AverageSalary* by 10 percent. Subsequently we can invoke the instance method *spEvaluateDeviation* in *SalesPerson* given by:

SpEvaluateDeviation
      ^Salary − AverageSalary

on an instance *SP* of *SalesPerson*:

SP SpEvaluateDeviation

This shows how a variable holding a value that stores part of the state of an object is used (inherited) in a method of a subclass.

Unfortunately, Smalltalk has some basic problems and limitations in this ability to inherit the state of an object:

1. The semantics of class variable inheritance is not very clean. More specifically, subclasses can actually modify the class variables of their superclass! For example, a class *or* an instance method in *SalesPerson* can actually *update* the value of *AverageSalary*, part of the state of the *Employee* object!

2. The inheritance of objects is rather restricted: instances of arbitrary classes *cannot* inherit from one another.

Let us clarify problem **2**. In Figure 3.16*a* a class C′ inheriting from a class C; iC is an instance of C and iC′ is an instance of C′. The two relationships: inheritance and instantiation are illustrated in the figure. Of course, there will be many instances of C and C′. Only one instance of each has been illustrated. Now in Smalltalk and most object-oriented languages we *cannot* close the diagram and have an instance of a class inherit the state of an instance of another class. In other words, existing object-oriented languages do not support Figure 3.16*b*.

Inheriting states of objects is called *instance inheritance*. Instance inheritance is a powerful concept. In general terms, an object O inherits the state of an object O′ if the value of an instance variable i′ defined in O′ *determines* the value of the same instance variable in O. Here are a couple of simple examples. Again consider the class

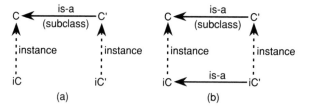

Figure 3.16 Inheritance and instance relationships between classes and instances.

hierarchy rooted at *Person*. An *Employee* is a *Person*, a *SalesPerson* is an *Employee*, and a *Student* is a *Person*. If we allow inheritance of object states then for each *Employee* instance E_1 there will be a *Person* instance P_1 such that E_1 inherits from P_1 the values of *Person* instance variables. Similarly for each *SalesPerson* SP_1 instance there will be an *Employee* instance EP_1 from which it inherits.

Consider the example of the person, student employee, and salesperson John Smith. In real life there is actually one John Smith. But, as illustrated in Figure 3.17, we have personJohn, empJohn, studentJohn, and salesJohn. The Person instance variable values of Name, Age, Address of empJohn, studentJohn and salesJohn are actually obtained from personJohn. In the same way, salesJohn obtains the values of instance variables such as Salary, Manager, Department from empJohn. Therefore, objects inherit actual *values* of instances variables.

Instance inheritance is a general and powerful mechanism that extends the class inheritance mechanism. Its usefulness has been demonstrated in office automation and engineering applications. Instance inheritance is a constrained application of object inheritance: an instance O' can inherit from an instance O only if the class of O' is a subclass of the class of O. The next section presents a more flexible form of inheritance called *delegation*, where arbitrary objects can inherit from one another.

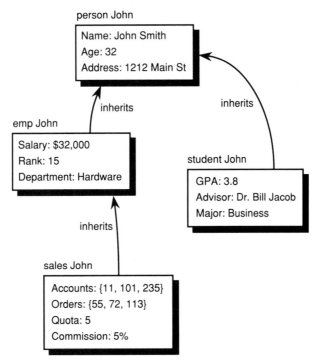

Figure 3.17 An example of instance inheritance.

3.5.1 Prototype Systems and Delegation

The object-oriented models of computation discussed so far were based on the notion of a class: Classes were used to implement abstract data types and the inheritance mechanism was based on the IS-A relationship of classes. A class represents a set or a group of objects with the same structure and behavior. Software development based on more traditional class-based languages such as Simula, Smalltalk, or C++ prescribes a top-down approach: The developer has to first conceive of the more general classes and then specialize or instantiate them.

If we overlook classes for a moment and concentrate just on objects, we can derive an entirely different bottom-up object-oriented computational model based on *prototypes*.

In prototype systems there is no distinction between instance objects and classes. Note that this is very different from saying that classes are themselves instances of metaclasses, as in the object-oriented languages Smalltalk, CLOS, or ObjVlisp. In those systems, a class describes a collection of objects of similar structure and behavior. The only type of instance that can fabricate objects is a class (an instance of a metaclass). But with prototype systems, the distinctions between instance objects and class objects are removed.

In a prototype system, one first thinks of a particular prototypic object and then draws similarities and/or distinctions for other objects. Any object can become a prototype. The idea is to start with individual cases and then subsequently specialize or generalize them. Lieberman (1986) elegantly describes the distinction between this approach and the object-oriented (set-oriented) approach.

> Prototype systems allow creating concepts first, then generalizing them by saying what aspects of the concept are allowed to vary. Set-oriented (object-oriented) systems require creating the abstraction description of the set (class) before individual instances can be installed as members.

In a sense, prototypes may be closer to the way humans learn—through association and specialization. This is illustrated in Figure 3.18. Pictured is a collection of objects that are shapes. These are shapes that exist in any environment: a computer screen, in a toy box, or the imagination. Shapes have common elements; circles and ovals look similar, although the curves of circles are more regular; rectangles and squares look similar, except that all the sides of a square are equal.

Therefore, having seen and observed a rectangular object (one particular rectangular object), a subsequent encounter with a square will prompt the shape analyst to draw an analogy: The square looks like the rectangle—it has four edges and four corners at 90 degree angles. Encountering another square, perhaps of a different size, the analyst will deduce that the analogy with the first square is even stronger, the only difference between the two squares is their sizes. Besides their individual shape and size properties there are a number of actions or operations that can be performed on each object: they can be moved, rotated, colored, and so on. Interestingly, the same operations are applicable to all three objects.

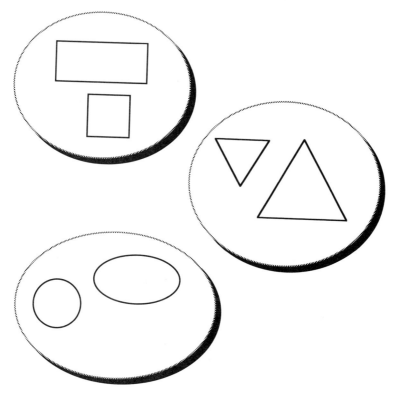

Figure 3.18 Different types of shapes.

The first rectangle is a prototype for the first square. Similarly the first square is a prototype for the second square. The mechanism used to implement prototypes is called delegation. As illustrated in Figure 3.19, the rectangle object *REC* has state information for the center, perimeter, and the ratio of the sides of the rectangle. The rectangle object also has a number of operations reflecting its behavior: Move, Rotate, Resize, and so on. Note that this rectangle object is not an instance of a Rectangle class. The particular state and operations pertain to this one particular object. The selectors and messages applicable to the rectangle object include the operations Move, Rotate, Resize, as well as accessor methods Center, Perimeter and Ratio. Thus, using a Smalltalk-like syntax:

REC Perimeter

returns the value of the Perimeter variable, and

REC Rotate 30

rotates the rectangle by 30 degrees.

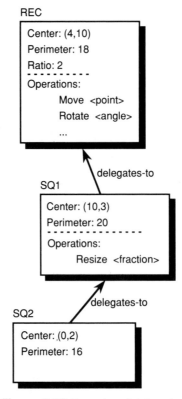

Figure 3.19 Examples of delegation.

The square object SQ_1 is similar to the rectangle object; the operations on the square are the same as those on the rectangle. The only difference is in the values of the perimeter and the ratio of the sides (which for squares is 1). The SQ_1 object has a delegates-to relationship with the *REC* object. This means state variables or operations that are not overridden in SQ_1 will be inherited from *REC*. Thus the method for execution of the message:

SQ₁ *Rotate 45*

is actually in *REC*. In other words, SQ_1 delegates to *REC* the execution of the message *Rotate 45*. When SQ_1 receives this message, it realizes it must be forwarded to the prototype object *REC*. When the message is forwarded to *REC*, the method *Rotate* is told that the rotation should be performed on SQ_1 (and not *REC*). Thus, like class-based and conventional languages, methods of delegation-based systems have formal parameters.

Similarly, SQ_2 forwards all its messages except *Perimeter* and *Center* to its prototype SQ_1. Note that the operations *Rotate* and *Move* will actually be handled by *REC*. For example the message

> SQ₂ Move < 3, 2 >

will first be forwarded to SQ_1. Since the message cannot be handled by SQ_1 it is in turn forwarded to *REC*. The message moves the center of the rectangle to the given argument coordinate. Needless to say when *Move* is executed it actually operates on SQ_2.

Note that what is happening here in terms of forwarding messages is very similar to the algorithm used in class inheritance; the main difference is that the actual *objects* are forwarding or delegating the messages. Note that the delegate-to relationship is more generic than the IS-A relationship of classes, it can be used between *any* two objects and not just classes. Also, both operations *and* state information can be inherited or delegated. Thus delegation systems can share the states of objects in addition to code. But the sharing is much more dynamic and flexible than class-based systems. The delegates-to relationship can be established dynamically, while the inheritance relationship of class-based languages such as Smalltalk is established and fixed when a class is created.

There are several object-oriented languages that support delegation. The most flexible of these are the actor-based systems. The original development of actor-based languages is attributed to Carl Hewitt (Hewitt et al., 1973). Some examples of concurrent actor-based languages include Actors (Agha and Hewitt, 1987), Act 1 (Lieberman, 1981 and 1986), and ABCL/1 (Yonezawa et al., 1987). Pure actor-based systems provide a uniform model of computation based on objects and messages. There is no explicit support of classes or types. The objects (called actors) are computational agents that can operate in parallel. Using the simplified Act 1 syntax (Lieberman, 1981) we can create a rectangle object (one object):

> Create an actor called REC by
>   Sending to OBJECT a message to EXTEND himself,
>   with new acquaintances named:
>   Center, with value <4,10>
>   Perimeter, with value 18
>   Ratio, with value 2

The actor *OBJECT* is the most general object, very similar to the most general class in class-based systems. The methods that handle the messages are defined for this object. For example, the *Move* method just updates the *Center*:

> If I'm REC and I get the message MOVE to New-Center
> I update my Center to the New-Center

Now *REC* could be extended to create SQ_1. The only changes in SQ_1 are the values of the *Perimeter*, the *Center*, and the *Ratio*:

Create an actor called SQ₁ by
    Sending to REC a CREATE message,
        with Center value <10, 3>
        with Perimeter value 20
        with Ratio value 1

Messages such as *MOVE* sent to SQ_1 will be delegated to *REC*. Similarly we can define:

Create an actor called SQ₂ by
    Sending to SQ₁ a CREATE message,
        with Center value < 0, 2>
        with Perimeter value 16

Here, for SQ_2 the message *MOVE* will be forwarded to SQ_1 who, in turn, will forward it to *REC*. However, the message to retrieve the *Ratio* for SQ_2 will be handled by SQ_1.

3.5.2 The Orlando Treaty

Lieberman has argued that delegation is more powerful than inheritance since it can easily be shown that inheritance can be modeled through delegation. The sharing of methods that is supported by the class-based systems can be achieved by having objects delegate their operations or methods to a common ancestor. Delegation appears to be more powerful than class inheritance because it is more general; in addition to sharing behavior, objects can also share state. Delegation also appears to be more general than object inheritance because arbitrary objects can delegate to one another.

Stein (1987), however, has shown that classes can be used to model delegation. As mentioned earlier, classes are instances of metaclasses in many object-oriented systems. But, unlike the instances, the classes have an inheritance hierarchy. Thus classes have class variables and class methods that are inherited from their superclasses. A class can inherit not only the structure but also the value of its super-class variables. This is exactly what happens in delegation. Hence, the effect of delegation can be achieved through the class hierarchy.

During OOPSLA 1987, which took place in Orlando, Florida, Lynn Stein, Henry Lieberman, and David Ungar discussed their differences and came up with a statement reflecting the need for two modes of sharing. The resolution of their differences is known as the Orlando Treaty (Stein, Lieberman, Ungar, 1989). The essence of the Orlando Treaty is that there are two modes of code sharing: anticipatory sharing and unanticipated sharing. Class-based systems are best for anticipatory sharing. Delegation-based systems are more suitable for unanticipated sharing.

The treaty characterized three dimensions for sharing:

1. *Static* versus *dynamic:* is sharing determined when an object is created or can it be determined dynamically?
2. *Implicit* versus *explicit:* are there explicit operations to indicate the sharing?
3. *Per object* versus *per group:* is sharing defined for whole groups objects (classes) or could sharing be supported for individual objects?

Traditional object-oriented languages such as Smalltalk, Simula, or C++ use static, implicit, and per-group strategies. By contrast, delegation-based systems use dynamic, explicit, and per-object sharing strategies. The Orlando Treaty acknowledges that:

> . . . no definite answer as to what set of these choices is best can be reached. Rather, that different programming situations call for different combinations of these features: for exploratory, experimental programming environments, it may be desirable to allow the flexibility of dynamic, explicit, per object sharing; while for large relatively routine software production, restricting to the complementary set of choices—strictly static, implicit, and group-oriented—may be more appropriate.

There is a tradeoff of space versus execution time between the two strategies, with prototype systems typically requiring less space but more time to bind methods or obtain attribute values. By contrast, systems using class inheritance have faster method lookup but may require more space. Also, if the class-based system is strongly typed, there is an additional tradeoff, that of safety versus flexibility. The bottom line is that dynamic systems can be used to build prototype systems, but production quality and high performance systems will have to use strongly typed class-based systems such as C++ or Eiffel.

■ 3.6 MULTIPLE INHERITANCE

So far most of the inheritance examples have used *single* inheritance: Each subclass had one and only one immediate superclass. The class inheritance hierarchy with single inheritance is a tree, with the most general class (typically the class Object) at the root of the tree. In many situations, though, it is very convenient to allow a subclass to inherit from more than one immediate superclass. In the Person class hierarchy, for example, there can be people who are both employees and students. With single inheritance it is impossible to express this multiple parent relationship directly. There are numerous such real-life examples of multiple inheritance: a Japanese car manufacturer has properties (instance variables and methods) that pertain to its characteristics both as a Japanese company and as a car manufacturer; a BorderedTextWindow that allows editing of text in a bordered window inherits both from TextWindow and BorderedWindow; a "Transformer" can act both as robot and a car. These examples are illustrated in Figure 3.20.

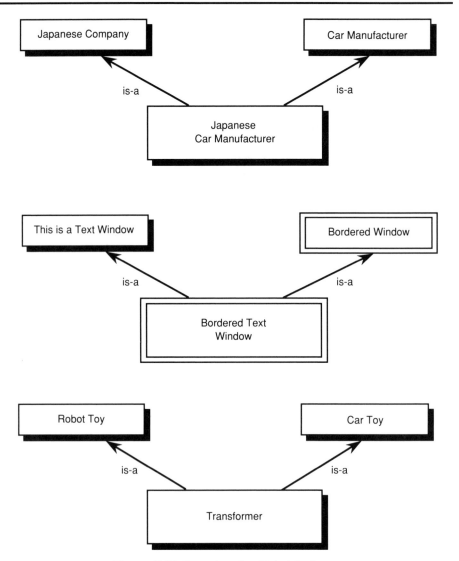

Figure 3.20 Examples of multiple inheritance.

The mechanism that allows a class to inherit from more than one immediate parent is called *multiple inheritance*. With multiple inheritance, we can combine several existing classes to produce combination classes that utilize each of their multiple superclasses in a variety of usages and functionalities. Then the class inheritance hierarchy becomes a DAG (directed acyclic graph), since a class can have more than one immediate predecessor.

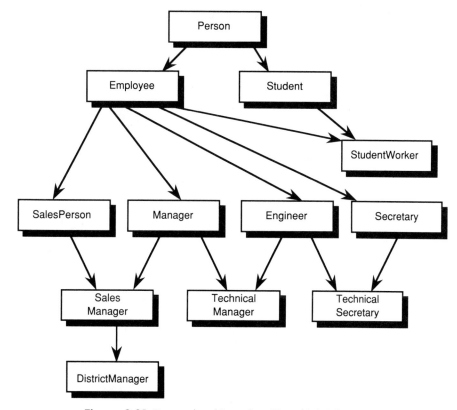

Figure 3.21 Person class hierarchy with multiple inheritance.

Figure 3.21 gives a more comprehensive example of the Person class hierarchy, using multiple inheritance. As illustrated, SalesManager inherits from both Manager and SalesPerson; similarly TechnicalManagers are Engineers and Managers; Student-Worker inherits from Employee and Student; finally TechnicalSecretaries are both Engineers and Secretaries.

We saw earlier that if a language allows subclasses to manipulate the instance variables of their superclasses directly (as in Smalltalk), then the set of instance variables for the subclass is the union of the instance variables of its immediate superclass and the additional instance variables defined in the subclass. Similarly, the set of methods for the subclass is also the union of the methods of its immediate superclass and the additional methods defined in the subclass. Of course, methods in the subclass can override methods in the superclass.

With multiple inheritance, these strategies are extended to the union of all immediate parents. More specifically,

Instance Variables of C = Local C Instance variables $\cup$ C_i Instance variables

where each C_i is an immediate predecessor of C.

Similarly, the methods of C are defined by:

Methods of C = Local C Methods $\cup$ C_i Methods

Suppose a Rectangle has two instance variables: LowerLeft and UpperRight representing the coordinates of the lower left corner and upper right corner. A ColoredRegion also has two instance variables: Color and Brightness. A ColoredRectangle, therefore, will have:

UpperRight, LowerLeft, Color, Brightness

Unfortunately, combining instance variables or methods of immediate predecessors is not that simple. The problem is that predecessors could have instance variables or methods with the *same name*, but with totally unrelated semantics. For example, a TechnicalConsultant and a Manager can have values for Skill which are totally unrelated: for the technical person Skill reflects the technical abilities and experience in a particular technical domain. For a manager, it reflects people management skills, knowledge of project management techniques, and so on. Therefore the units and domains of the values of Skill in these two classes are unrelated. Now, what happens when a class such as TechnicalManager inherits from both? What happens when there is a conflict? "Conflict" arises when different methods or instance variables with the same name are defined in a totally unrelated way by two or more superclasses.

The bulk of the problems of multiple inheritance deals with conflict resolution strategies. There are many such strategies, and each object-oriented language supporting multiple inheritance provides a slight variation of a strategy in its implementation. Some of the alternative conflict resolution strategies for multiple inheritance are presented. We expect other alternatives and variations on these alternatives to evolve over time.

There are two kinds of conflicts:

1. The conflicting instance variables or methods come from a common ancestor.
2. The conflicting instance variables or methods are totally unrelated.

The conflicting Skill instance variables for TechnicalManager illustrate the second kind of conflict. To see the first kind, consider the class StudentWorker inheriting from Employee and Student. An employee's instance variables are:

{Name, Age, Address, Salary, Rank, Department}

and a student's instance variables are:

{Name, Age, Address, GPA, Major, Courses, Advisor}

The conflicting instance variables are {Name, Age, Address}. But all three variables were actually inherited from the same class—Person. Person is a common ancestor of Employee and Student.

The overall strategy in many object-oriented languages supporting multiple inheritance is to provide a conflict resolution strategy for conflicts of totally unrelated variables, and resolve those with common ancestry *by using only one copy* of the instance variables from a common ancestor. Both Trellis/Owl and Eiffel use this strategy.

For example, since {Name, Age, Address} came from the same ancestor Person, the instance variables of StudentWorker will be:

> {Name, Age, Address, Salary, Rank, Department, GPA, Major,
> Courses, Advisor}

The following are the basic strategies for resolving the conflict of unrelated methods, and will be described in the next few sections:

- linearization
- forbidding conflicts
- renaming instance variables and methods
- qualifying instance variables and methods
- the Meet operation for subtypes

3.6.1 Linearization

The linearization strategies specify a linear, overall order of classes, and then specify that application of a class attribute (a method or instance variable) start from the most specific class. Note that this is exactly what happens during single inheritance. Therefore a linearization strategy for conflict resolution provides an algorithm for mapping the DAG of the predecessors of a class into a linear order. When a class indicates its superclasses, the superclass names are given in a particular order. The linearization strategy uses the ordering of class names and a "precede the more specific" algorithm to generate a linear total order. Consider the DAG that represents the predecessors of *StudentWorker*. If we declare:

StudentWorker superclasses Employee, Student

then the superclass linear order will have *Employee* precede *Student*, as shown in Figure 3.22. This is the approach taken in Flavors (Moon, 1986) and CommonLoops (Bobrow et al., 1986). As pointed out by Snyder (1986a), the main problem with this approach is the ordering of superclasses in a class declaration has significant semantic implications. For example, the declaration for the *StudentWorker* will effectively make the *Employee* a subclass of student, which was not the intent of the designer of the *Employee* class!

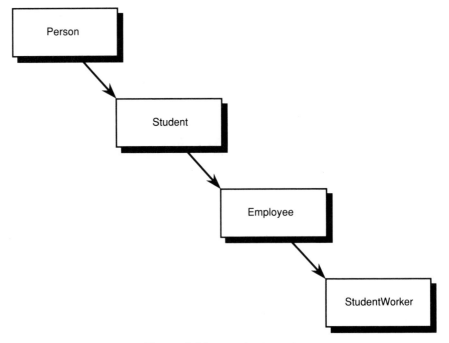

Figure 3.22 Linearization order.

3.6.2 Forbidding Conflicts – Renaming Strategies

The second approach is to issue an error if totally unrelated instance variables or methods are inherited through the multiple inheritance mechanism. Again consider the *Skill* instance variable of *TechnicalConsultants* and *Managers*. When we indicate:

TechnicalManager superclasses TechnicalConsultant, Manager

then the underlying system will complain, indicating that *Skill* is defined both in *TechnicalConsultant* and *Manager*. The strategy also applies to conflicting methods. Thus if both *TechnicalConsultant* and *Manager* have a method called *AugmentSkill*, the system will complain. This is similar to the approach taken in Eiffel and Trellis/Owl.

Generating an error for conflicting instance variables or methods is, of course, too restrictive. If anything, it should be a hint to the user that the conflicting instance variables must be *renamed*. For example, the management skill as well as the technical skills of a *TechnicalManager* are both important attributes. With a renaming scheme we can inherit *both* instance variables, giving them different names. Using Eiffel syntax the declaration will be:

```
class TechnicalManager ...    inherit
       Manager               rename Skill as ManagerSkill
       TechnicalConsultant   rename Skill as TechnicalSkill
```

Then both instance variables can be used by the subclass. Note that it is not necessary to rename both conflicting instance variables. If one of them is renamed the name conflict disappears. For instance, we can have:

```
class TechnicalManager...   inherit
     Manager                rename Skill as ManagerSkill
     TechnicalConsultant
```

without any conflict; both *Skill* instance variables will be inherited by *Technical-Manager*. *Skill* from *Manager* will be called *ManagerSkill* and *Skill* from *Technical-*Consultant will still be called *Skill*.

The same renaming strategy applies also to methods. Requiring renaming of conflicting instance variables or methods provides a lot of flexibility to the user. It lets the user determine whether indeed there is a conflict. It allows the user to rename the conflicting variables or methods with the most meaningful names for the application.

3.6.3   Qualified Instance Variables and Methods

Another straightforward solution to multiple inheritance conflicts is qualification of variable or method names with the name of the class. With this strategy, whenever there is an ambiguity in the access or usage of an instance variable or method, it must be resolved through qualifying the variable or method with the appropriate class name. C++ uses this strategy in supporting multiple inheritance.

For example, the C++ syntax for using the *Skill* of *Managers* and *TechnicalConsultants* would be:

```
Manager::Skill
TechnicalConsultant::Skill
```

This is similar to the renaming strategy, in the sense that with both strategies there will actually be two skills—one pertaining to *Manager* and the other to *TechnicalConsultant*. The only difference is that here an explicit renaming is not required. The "Implicit" name of a conflicting instance variable or method is the name of the attribute quantified by the superclass name. Thus when *TechnicalManager* inherits from *Manager* and *TechnicalConsultant* as in:

```
class TechnicalManager: public Manager,
                        public TechnicalConsultant
   { ... }
```

then methods and other clients of *TechnicalManager* can freely use *Skill* from any of the superclasses, as long as it is qualified by the superclass name.

3.6.4   The Meet Operation

The final strategy, combining superclasses, is actually a *meet* strategy for subtypes, as described by Cardelli (1984). This strategy applies only to typed attributes (instance variables) of records. The subtyping of records was discussed in Section 3.2. The idea of a meet stems from the subtype-ordering relationship of types.

Consider the tuple types:

$$T_1 = [a_1: t_1, a_2: t_2, a_3: t_3]$$

and

$$T_2 = [a_3: t_3', a_4: t_4]$$

The meet of T_1 and T_2 is the *greatest lower bound* of T_1 and T_2 using the subtyping relationship. In other words:

$$T_3 = T_1 \text{ meet } T_2$$
$$= [a_1: t_1, a_2: t_2, a_3: t_3 \text{ meet } t_3', a_4: t_4].$$

To understand the idea of a meet consider the simple example:

YoungAdultAge = 20 − 40

and

AdultAge = 30 − 70

then the meet:

YoungAdultAge meet AdultAge = 30 − 40

For tuple types consider:

Employee = [*Name: Character(30)*,
    Age: integer,
       Address: [StreetNumber: integer,
            StreetName: Character(20),
            State: Character(2),
            Zip: integer],
      Salary: integer,
      Rank: integer,
      Department: integer]

Foreigner = [*Name: Character(40)*,
      Age: integer,
      Address: [StreetNumber: integer,
          StreetName: Character(30),
          Zip: integer,
      Country: Character(20)]
      VisaStatus: Character(4)]

Therefore:

ForeignEmployee = Employee meet Foreigner =

> *[Name: Character(30),*
> *Age: integer,*
> *Address: [StreetNumber: integer,*
> *StreetName: Character(20),*
> *State: Character(2),*
> *Zip: integer,*
> *Country: Character(20)],*
> *Salary: integer,*
> *Rank: integer,*
> *Department: integer,*
> *VisaStatus: Character(4)]*

There are many similar attempts that have imposed a partial order on the type hierarchies (Ait-Kaci and Nasr, 1986).

3.6.5 Evaluating the Strategies

Linearization hides the conflict resolution problem from the user. But it introduces a superfluous ordering of class inheritance semantics. The user must employ indirect means to use methods that have been overridden by the linearization.

Renaming attributes or qualifying attributes puts the burden of conflict resolution on the user. In reality, however, these strategies provide more flexibility to the user; only the user knows the applicability of an inherited method or instance variable. Therefore the user can freely rename or qualify the inherited attributes.

Finally, the meet strategy provides a clean semantics for multiple inheritance. Yet its application is limited to record or tuple types for strongly typed languages.

Multiple inheritance is a powerful and useful tool. Yet care should be taken in defining consistent and intuitive semantics when conflicting methods and instance variables from different classes are inherited by the same class. There are many strategies for resolving these conflicts. In terms of flexibility, generality, and ease of understanding, renaming attributes and qualifying attributes seem to be the most promising strategies.

■ 3.7 SUMMARY

Inheritance is perhaps the most useful object-oriented concept. Inheritance achieves software reusability and extensibility. Through inheritance new software modules (such as classes) can be built on top of an existing hierarchy of modules. This avoids redesigning and recoding everything from scratch. New classes can inherit both the behavior (operations, methods, and so on) and the representation (instance variables, attributes, and so on) from existing classes.

Inheriting behavior enables code sharing (and hence reusability) among software modules. Inheriting representation enables structure sharing among data objects. The combination of these two kinds of inheritance provides a very powerful software modeling and development strategy.

Inheritance is achieved by specializing existing classes. Classes can be specialized by extending their representation (instance variables) or behavior (operations). Alternatively, classes can also be specialized through restricting the representation or operations of existing classes.

Most object-oriented languages support class inheritance (the ability of one class to inherit representation and methods from another class). An alternative approach is to allow objects to inherit from one another. Object inheritance allows an object to inherit the state of another object. There are models of computation that also incorporate operations with objects and use only object inheritance for organizing object spaces. These are called prototype systems. In these models objects delegate messages to one another, thereby inheriting methods or values stored in other objects. Prototype systems are more dynamic and flexible. Class-based systems have better performance. Therefore in building prototypes, object sharing or delegation is very useful. For building high performance products class-based systems are preferred.

In many situations it is desirable to inherit from more than one class. This is called multiple inheritance. When a class inherits from more than one parent there is the possibility for conflicts, which are methods or instance variables with the same name but different or unrelated semantics inherited from different superclasses. There are many conflict resolution schemata. The simplest and most obvious strategy is to forbid conflicts and require the programmer to rename the conflicting methods. Another alternative is to pre-append the method names with class names.

4

OBJECT IDENTITY

■ 4.1 INTRODUCTION

Chapter 2 discussed abstract data typing. With ADTs programmers can define sets of objects with similar behavior. The implementation of the methods associated with the ADT is encapsulated: Object states can be accessed and updated only through external interface operations. Chapter 3 covered inheritance. Inheritance can be used to organize the classes implementing the abstract data types. The inheritance hierarchies organize the object-oriented code and support extensibility and reusability. This chapter discusses the third fundamental object orientation concept *object identity* (Khoshafian and Copeland, 1986). With object identity, objects can contain or refer to other objects. Object identity organizes the objects of the object space manipulated by a program. Object identity clarifies, enhances, and extends the notions of pointers in conventional programming languages, foreign keys in databases, and file names in operating systems. Using object identity programmers can dynamically construct arbitrary graph-structured composite or complex objects, objects that are constructed from sub-objects. Objects can be both created and disposed of at run time. In some cases, objects can even become persistent and be re-accessed in subsequent programs.

4.1.1 So What's the Big Deal about Object Identity?

There are three primary techniques for identifying objects in conventional programming languages, databases, and operating systems:

1. Memory references/addresses
2. User-specified names
3. Identifier keys in collections

Each of these mechanisms compromises identity. Most programming and database languages use either one of the first two techniques to distinguish objects. This mixes addressability and identity. The address of an object is an external mechanism to name or reference the object. Its purpose is to provide a way to access an object within a particular environment and is therefore environment-dependent. Furthermore, it often reflects a lower-level computational model. Databases also use identifier keys (third technique) to distinguish objects in tables. Keys are "special" descriptive attributes or groups of attributes that identify individual objects. There are several problems in using descriptive data for identity. Typically, keys cannot be modified. Also costly and unnatural "joins" have to be performed to retrieve values of non-key attributes.

In a completely object-oriented system, each object will be given an identity that will be permanently associated with the object, immaterial of the object's structural or state transitions. Identity is internal to an object. Its purpose is to provide a way to represent the individuality of an object independently of how it is accessed, what it contains, or where it resides. An address-based or a descriptive data-based identity mechanism compromises identity, and corrupts the computational model of the language. Identity is a machine or implementation independent notion associated with objects.

Here is a simple example. Each of us as a person undergoes structural or state transitions. We grow older. We graduate from several schools and then join the routine of a professional career. We acquire new attributes such as a spouse, children, or excess weight. We might change our names, or even our social security number. Yet, no matter how many additional attributes we acquire, modify, or drop, there is presumably something unique about each one of us that is permanently associated with us.

Object identity brings these characteristics of the real world to languages and computation. Without object identity, it will be awkward (if not impossible) to assign self-contained objects to class attributes or instance variables. Also, without object identity it will be impossible to let the same object be part of multiple objects.

4.1.2   Chapter Organization

The rest of the chapter is organized as follows. In Section 4.2 we discuss how objects are referenced in programming languages. Section 4.3 explains why user-defined names compromise identity. Section 4.4 illustrates the problems of identifier keys for identity. Section 4.5 describes a powerful object model, where each object has a type, state, and identity. Section 4.6 explains the equality, copy, and merge operators associated with identity-based object models.

■ 4.2 REFERENCING OBJECTS IN PROGRAMMING LANGUAGES

An identity is a handle that distinguishes one entity from another. Any programming language must have some sort of identity. The earliest high-level programming language of the 1950s, namely FORTRAN, had very few object type constructs. The types in FORTRAN consisted of the alphanumeric types INTEGER, FLOAT, and so on and ARRAY. Arrays were collection objects whose elements could be accessed positionally. Memory in FORTRAN was allocated statically: At compile time the entire memory requirements for the objects accessed in the program was allocated statically. Thus the dimensions (and hence size) of arrays were also known statically. During the execution of the program it was impossible to expand or shrink the pre-allocated memory. The main mechanism to reference objects was through variable names. Object sharing among sub-routines was done through the COMMON and EQUIVALENCE constructs. Thus object types were very limited, as was the capability to construct, dynamically create or delete, and share objects.

High-level programming languages that succeeded FORTRAN include: PL/1, COBOL, and Algol. Algol language introduced much cleaner programming concepts such as context-free grammars, block-structured programming, and scoping. As far as flexibility with the object space, Algol 60 allowed arrays to have dynamic bounds. Thus the memory allocated for arrays was done at run time. Algol 60 also introduced the **own** decelerator, which allowed persistence of variable values across procedure calls.

The successor of Algol 60, namely Algol 68 (Tanenbaum, 1976), incorporated additional concepts. The most significant of these was the idea of a *record* or *structure*. The fields in structures are like the instance variables of classes: They are used to prescribe the state of objects. An equally important concept introduced by Algol 68 was the notion of *pointers* to objects through the **ref** (that is, object reference) construct. Pointers correspond to (virtual) memory addresses. Pointers enable the construction of generalized object spaces. Algol 68 and other languages such as Pascal and C, used a *heap* to dynamically allocate memory for data types referenced through pointers. A heap is a linear address space that is used to dynamically (at run time) allocate memory to objects.

Chapters 2 and 3 discussed some of the features of Pascal (Wirth, 1971). This simple yet elegant and powerful language incorporated such basic notions as call by reference, a much cleaner block-structured programming support, persistent files, records and pointers to records, and so on. As mentioned in Section 2.2.2, Pascal incorporated the *new* and *dispose* constructs to create and destroy objects.

The ever popular development language C (Kernighan and Ritchie, 1988) also has similar features: support of pointers, *malloc/free* functions, heap management, and so on. However, C is a "lower-level" functional programming language. For example, in C it is possible to manipulate the individual bits of values. Also C does not support call by reference (or "var" parameter passing). Instead, users have to pass pointers to structures allowing functions to modify the state of their parameters indirectly. The popularity of C is due to efficient implementations of the language, as well as the fact that there is an ANSI standard for C.

The object construction, destruction, and referencing properties of high-level languages such as C, Pascal, and even their successor Ada can be summarized as follows:

1. Support of structures or records as well as pointers to structures and records.
2. The storage space for pointers to records is dynamically allocated through a *new* operator. The pointers reference a storage area in a heap. Pointers correspond to memory addresses in a virtual address space.
3. The reclamation or cleanup of dynamically allocated storage is under the user's control, typically through a *dispose* operator. Therefore the user has to keep track of the number of references to a record in the heap. Premature de-allocation of storage space with multiple references cause some pointers to reference invalid data or "garbage."
4. The equality predicate in these languages can compare either base values such as integers or floating point numbers or addresses (pointer values). In most cases, equality of structures and different equality for composite objects is not supported (although dialects of some languages such as Pascal support equality of sets, arrays, and records).

The record management features of these languages clearly reflect the Von Neumann architecture of the underlying engines: Part of the execution model is centered on the notions of procedures allocating, updating, and de-allocating a memory space.

We said *part* of the execution model and not *all* because dynamic memory allocation implements a lower-level computational model *within* a higher-level language. We shall illustrate this through a simple example.

Consider Figure 4.1. Here is a simple record for the complex object example of Section 2.2.2. Both *C1* and *C2* are of type *ComplexPtr*:

```
TYPE
    ComplexPtr = ^Complex
    Complex =
        RECORD
            Real: real;
            Imaginary: real;
        END;
```

Figure 4.1*a* represents the heap space after executing:

```
new(C1);
C1^.Real := 3.5;
C1^.Imaginary := 2.7;
C2 := C1;
```

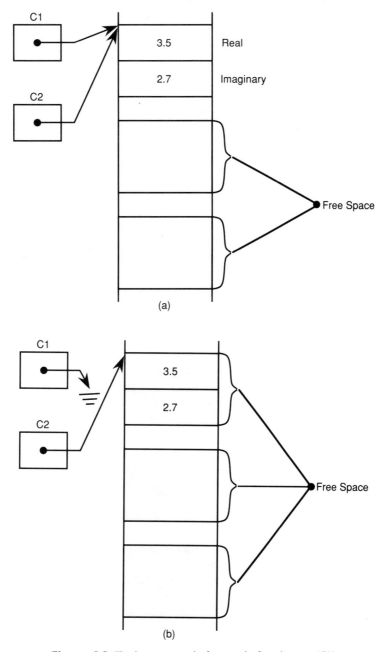

Figure 4.1 The heap space before and after dispose (C1).

Therefore *C1* and *C2* will reference the same heap memory location. After executing:

```
dispose(C1);
```

the heap area referenced by *C1* and *C2* will be freed, as illustrated in Figure 4.1*b*. This means a subsequent request for new storage from the run-time memory manager can allocate the space (or part of the space) referenced by *C1* and *C2*. The user should explicitly set *all* pointers referencing to the disposed memory space to NIL. Otherwise the user will be accessing either invalid or erroneous data.

Setting *C1* to NIL in the *dispose(C1)* call does not resolve this "dangling" reference problem (which was also alluded to in Section 2.2.2), since other references (such as *C2*) will not be automatically set to NIL. This is illustrated in Figure 4.1*b*.

Now assume we create and initialize another complex object (before disposing *C1*):

```
new(C3);
C3^.Real := 3.5;
C3^.Imaginary := 2.7;
```

The equality predicate (= in Pascal and == in C) is defined for basic scalar (integer, character, float, boolean) and pointer types. For some dialects of Pascal it is also defined for sets, arrays, and (in some cases) even record types.

For scalar types, the equality predicate returns TRUE if and only if the two values are the same. For pointer types, it returns TRUE if and only if the two addresses referenced by the pointers are the same. Therefore, in this example:

$$C1 \; = \; C2 \text{ is TRUE}$$

$$C1.Real \; = \; C3.Real \text{ and } C1.Imaginary \; = \; C3.Imaginary \text{ are both TRUE}$$

$$C1 \; = \; C3 \text{ is FALSE}$$

Equality of record types will compare the *contents* of two records (that is, the values of corresponding fields). As explained in Section 4.6.1, this corresponds to shallow equality in object-oriented languages. When equality of record type is supported:

$$C1^ \; = \; C3^ \text{ is TRUE}$$

where $Ci^$ represents the de-referenced object pointed to by the pointer Ci. Unfortunately, the most popular standardized conventional language C does not support equality of records (structures). In fact, neither do most dialects of Pascal.

When record equality is not supported the user needs to write his own program to compare the records field by field. Therefore to implement complex number object equality a user would need a function:

```
FUNCTION CompareComplex(C1, C2: Complex): boolean;
begin
    if C1.Real = C2.Real and
        C1.Imaginary = C2.Imaginary
    then
        CompareComplex := TRUE
    else
        CompareComplex := FALSE
end; { CompareComplex}
```

The dynamic memory allocation and the equality predicate issues are symptoms of many semantic problems in conventional languages:

> *Semantics of Dynamic Memory Allocation Primitives.* Many times the semantics or the effect of dynamic memory allocation operators is left to the implementation of the language. For example, in some implementations *dispose* is ignored. In other cases, the implementation of the language frees the memory allocated by *new* for the pointer type but does not set the pointer to NIL. In other cases, it frees the memory and sets the pointer to NIL.

> *Dynamic Memory and Scoping.* High-level structured languages such as C or Pascal have scoping rules that determine the data visibility, allocation, and access rules through a nesting of scopes. When it comes to dynamic memory allocation, however, scoping rules are no longer applicable; independent of the scope, if the user dynamically allocates memory, the user is also responsible to explicitly free it. Exiting the scope will *not* automatically reclaim the storage of dynamically allocated memory.

> *Dual Semantics.* This is the more serious problem of object referencing and dynamic memory allocation in conventional languages. There are actually two computation models integrated with two different semantic models.

The semantics problem is with the abstract machine of the high-level language (C, Pascal, Ada). The language has data types such as integer, real, or character string and type constructors such as arrays and records. The computational model of the high-level language also incorporates programming constructs such as *while* loops, *if-then-else* conditionals, *assignment statements*, *predicates*, and *routines* (procedures and functions).

These constructs are mapped onto the lower-level Von Neumann machine whose semantics are defined through the lower-level *assembly* language operations. These operations include basic arithmetic computations, register load and save operations, memory access operations, and so on. The key point is that when it comes to dynamic memory allocation primitives, the high-level language reflects the workings of the underlying low-level machine.

More specifically, *pointers* reference memory locations and not objects or instances of structures. The allocation (*new* in Pascal and *malloc()* in C) and deallocation (*dispose()* in Pascal and *free()* in C) of memory manage the heap space. The heap or the dynamic memory is not and should not be part of the semantics of the language.

These "high-level" languages have the capability to directly represent structures. They should also incorporate the capability to assign structure values to variables *or* fields of other structures. The notion of disposing or freeing memory should not even be part of the language. Instead, objects or instances of structures should be managed by the underlying implementation of the language. This is exactly what happens with most object-oriented languages. The construct that enables the arbitrary assignment of *object*-valued attributes or fields is object identity, which also supports a much richer semantics for object equality.

■ 4.3 OBJECT NAMING

The most commonly used technique for identifying objects in programming languages, databases, and operating systems is *user-defined names* for objects. There are practical limitations to the use of variable names without the support of object identity. One problem is that a single object may be accessed in different ways; it may be bound to different variables. These variables have no way to find out if they refer to the same object (Saltzer, 1978).

For example, a salesperson identified by the name P1 may be characterized as the employee of the sales manager John Smith who had the best sales in June of 1988. The *same* salesperson bound to a different name, P2, may be characterized as the salesperson who made three overseas trips during 1988. Assuming P1 and P2 can only be bound to objects (not to pointers), conventional languages do not provide predicates to directly correlate such identical objects. As will be shown, object-oriented languages such as Smalltalk provide a simple *identity* test with the expression X == Y, which is different from the *equality* test X = Y. The identity test checks whether two objects are the same. The equality test checks whether the contents of two objects are the same.

4.3.1 Path Names in Operating Systems

In operating systems, names are used to identify files and subdirectories within a directory. Both UNIX and DOS have hierarchical directory structures, where each directory contains a collection of files and possibly other directories. The name of a file must be unique within a directory. Each file is accessible through a directory *path*, which is basically a concatenation of directory names.

For example, assume a warehouse has organized its computer inventory in Software (Soft) and Hardware (Hard) directories. This is illustrated in Figure 4.2. All the files describing HP laser printers will be accessible through the path:

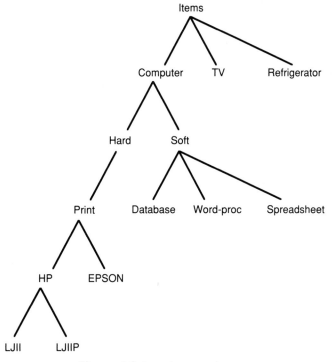

Figure 4.2 Items in a warehouse.

ITEMS/COMPUTER/HARD/PRINT/HP

Paths and "where things are stored" cause considerable headaches for both novice and advanced users of operating systems. Resolving ambiguous file references is one of the most frequently occurring problems for users of operating systems.

Another problem with concatenated names is that the object (file) space is a tree. To store or access the *same* file within multiple directories the user must make multiple copies of the file.

Besides replicating storage, copying requires user interaction to maintain consistency. For example, if the information pertaining to a particular printer is updated in the PRNT subdirectory, then *all* files referencing the printer must be explicitly updated by the user.

Some advanced operating systems such as UNIX do provide a linking mechanism through the LINK/UNLINK command (AT&T, 1986) to create and remove links to existing files. The general form of the link command:

link path1 path2

where path1 points to an existing file and path2 indicates the new directory entry which will be linked to the same file indicated by path1.

For example, to create a link between an HP LaserJet II printer file in PRINT subdirectory of HARD and PRINT in an integrated system subdirectory SYST1 the command is:

> link ITEMS/COMP/HARD/PRNT/HP/LJII
>   ITEMS/INTEG/SYST1/PRINT

The counterpart of LINK is UNLINK. The general form of UNLINK is:

> UNLINK path

This command removes the directory entry of the file indicated by the path. If *all* links to a file have been removed, the file is actually deleted and the space allocated to the file can be reclaimed.

Besides being cumbersome, there are more basic problems with object/file naming as supported by most operating systems today. The underlying problem, of course, is that most operating systems today do not provide appropriate support of object identity. There is no way to test whether two files refer to the same object; that is, whether the two files have been linked to the same file. Note that this is very different from the *compare* operation supported by most operating systems. The UNIX cmp command:

> cmp file1 file2

does not "complain" if file1 and file2 contain the *same* information. But (when we last checked) there is no built-in command to check if two files are actually the same file object. The distinction between same *content* versus same *object* is fundamental to understanding object identity.

■ 4.4 IDENTITY THROUGH IDENTIFIER KEYS

Another method for identifying objects is with *unique keys* (also called identifier keys). This mechanism is commonly used in database management systems. For example, for the database table storing Person, the key would be a person's name (last name, first name); for the database table storing items, the identifier key would be the item number.

In the relational model, a relation is a set of records (tuples, rows) of the same type or structure. A relation can be viewed as a two dimensional table of rows and columns, where all the elements in a column have the same base type (integer, character string, floating point number, and so on). Each row is a tuple or a record. The column values of a row are its attributes. An identifier key is some subset of the attributes of an

identifier Key

Last Name	First Name	Age	Address
Adams	Tim	23	"12 Sutton..."
Brown	Jim	32	"43 Doloney..."
Ripper	Jack	70	"1 London..."
Silverman	Leo	34	"55 H Street..."
Smith	John	32	"1212 Main..."
Smith	Mary	32	"1212 Main..."

Figure 4.3 The table Person.

object that is unique for all objects in the relation. Figure 4.3 presents the Person table, where the key is indicated as the concatenation of the last name and first name attributes of a person.

Using identifier keys for object identity confuses identity and data values (or object state). There are three main problems with this approach:

1. *Modifying Identifier Keys.* One problem is that identifier keys cannot (or should not) be allowed to change, even though they are user-defined descriptive data. For example, a sales manager's name may be used as the identifier key for the sales manager and replicated in salesperson objects to indicate for whom the employee works. But the sales manager name may need changing due to a change in marital status, or because the locals find the foreign name of the manager too hard to pronounce (let alone spell!). This would cause a discontinuity in the identity for the sales manager object.

2. *Non-Uniformity.* The main source of non-uniformity is that identifier keys in different tables have:
   a. Different types: integer, character string, floating point
   b. Different combinations of attributes

For example, the identifier key for the Item table is the ItemNumber, an integer; for *Person*, a string of characters (*LastName*, *FirstName*). Dealing with different collections/types of attributes for identification is inconsistent and gives added difficulty when working with several tables.

A second, more serious problem is that the attribute(s) to use for an identifier key may need to change. For example, RCA may use an employee number to identify employees, while General Electric may use Social Security numbers for the same purpose. A merger of these two companies would require one of these keys to change, causing a discontinuity in identity for the employees of one or both companies.

3. *"Unnatural" Joins.* A third problem is that the use of identifier keys causes joins to be used in retrievals instead of simpler and more direct object retrievals, as in GEM (Zaniolo, 1983), FAD (Bancilhon et al., 1987), and OPAL (Maier and Stein, 1986). For example, suppose we have an employee relation:

Employee(Name, Age, Address, Salary, DeptName)

and a department relation:

Department(Name, Budget, Location, . . .)

and the DeptName attribute establishes a relationship between an employee and a department. Using identifier keys, DeptName would have as its value the identifier key of the department. A retrieval involving both tuples would require a join between the two tuples.

Thus, in SQL to retrieve the name and the location in which the employee works for all employees, we would use

```
SELECT Employee.Name, Department.Location
FROM Employee, Department
WHERE Employee.DeptName = Department.Name
```

This is unnatural; in most cases what the user really wants instead of the *DeptName* is the actual department tuple. Tables in relational systems are in first normal form; they are *normalized* or flattened. With normalization the user is restricted to a fixed collection of base types and is not allowed to assign and manipulate tuples, relations, or other complex object types of the attributes. Hence, normalization loses the semantic connectives among the objects in the database. In fact, relational languages such as SQL incorporate additional capabilities like foreign key constraints to recapture the lost semantics. In Chapter 7, we describe several complex object and semantic data models that allow a more direct and intuitive representation of object spaces.

■ 4.5 THE TYPE/STATE/IDENTITY TRICHOTOMY

Each object is an instance of a class. A class implements a type. It describes both the structure and behavior of its instances. The structure is captured in the instance variables and the behavior is captured in the methods that are applicable to the instances. An object *O* can respond to the message:

O class

returning the name of its class.

The values of the instance variables of an object constitute the state of an object. Each instance variable value is an object.

Assume each *Employee* has the instance variables {*Name, Age, Address, Salary, Rank, Department, Manager*} with the following types:

Name:	NAME
Age:	INTEGER
Address:	ADDRESS
Salary:	DOLLAR
Rank:	INTEGER
Department:	DEPARTMENT
Manager:	MANAGER

where *NAME, ADDRESS, DEPARTMENT*, and *MANAGER* are also names of classes.

The class *NAME*, for example, contains the instance variables:

LastName:	String of Characters
FirstName:	String Of Characters

Similarly the class *DEPARTMENT* contains:

Name:	String of Characters
Budget:	DOLLAR
Location:	ADDRESS

Therefore, through each instance of *Employee* there actually is:

> an instance of *NAME* (the value of Name)
> two instances of *INTEGER* (the values of Age and Rank)
> an instance of *ADDRESS* (the value of Address)
> an instance of *DOLLAR* (the value of Salary)
> an instance of *MANAGER* (the value of Manager)
> an instance of *DEPARTMENT* (the value of Department)

Hence, each object

- is the instance of a class (its type)
- has a state, made up of the values of its instance variables.

In addition, each object

- has a *built-in* identity, which is independent of its class or state.

The identity of an object is generated when the object gets created. The state of an object (the values of its instance variables) can change arbitrarily: an employee's address, department, rank, scalar, manager, and even name can change, but the identity remains the same. Object-oriented systems supporting strong built-in identity also allow the object to undergo *structural* modifications (changing its class) without any changes in its identity.

As we said earlier, identity formalizes the notion of pointers used in more conventional languages. Without identity or another means of referencing objects independent of their state, it is impossible for the same object to be the value of the instance variable of more than one object.

Here are two examples:

> *Same Address:* Assume the employee Mary Smith is John's wife and lives at the same address. If there is no mechanism whereby the instance variable values of Address in both objects have as values the same address object, then it will be very hard if not outright impossible, to maintain consistency across all occurrences of this same address value.

> *Same Department:* In the above situation, the value of an instance variable was overridden by another object. In some cases, the state of the object which is the value of an instance variable is modified. For instance, assume Jim Brown, like John Smith, works in the same Hardware department. Then if we change the budget of John's department, we better make sure all copies of the budget of the hardware department instance occurring everywhere are updated consistently. With object identity, this is unnecessary. There is only *one* copy of the hardware department instance in the whole system.

An object's state is constructed from base or rock-bottom values, such as integers, character strings, and floating point numbers. Using just base or rock-bottom values of instance variables (integer, character strings, floats, and so on) *without identity or object references*, the following paragraphs give two solutions for sharing objects.

The first is object replication: This is illustrated in Figure 4.4. The instance JohnSmith and the instance MarySmith each replicate the address information. Besides being wasteful in space, the main problem with replication is consistency. Whenever an instance variable is updated, as in:

JohnSmith ChangeAddress: NewAddress

which changes the value of the *Address* instance variable to *NewAddress*, the user has to make sure *all* addresses that must be the same as John's address are updated accordingly. Thus the user has to create and maintain auxiliary structures in order to preserve the semantic consistency of two people having the same address.

The same is true when the budget of John Smith's department is changed through:

JohnSmith ChangeBudget: NewBudget

It is necessary to access and update the budgets of all employees who work in the hardware department.

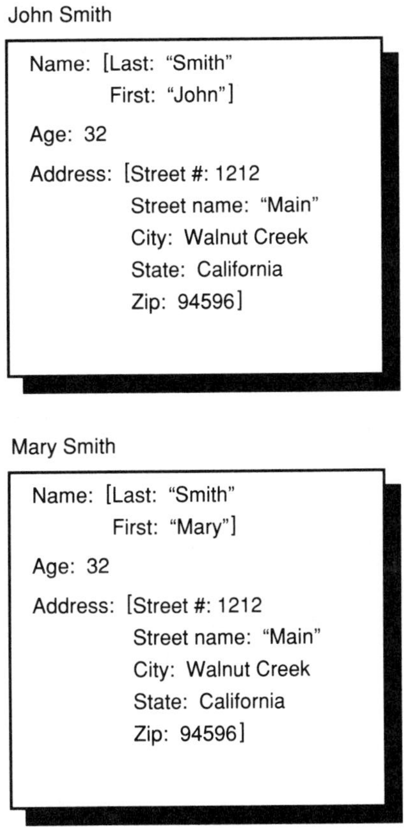

John Smith

Name: [Last: "Smith"
            First: "John"]

Age: 32

Address: [Street #: 1212
                Street name: "Main"
                City: Walnut Creek
                State: California
                Zip: 94596]

Mary Smith

Name: [Last: "Smith"
            First: "Mary"]

Age: 32

Address: [Street #: 1212
                Street name: "Main"
                City: Walnut Creek
                State: California
                Zip: 94596]

Figure 4.4 Replicating the same address.

The second solution is commonly used in identifier key systems, like relational databases. Here tables containing all addresses or all departments are constructed. A table must have an identifier key, such that each object has a unique key value. The key value is then stored in the referencing object. For instance, the department name can be used as the key value of a *Departments* table and store the same key value (the department name) in both John Smith's and Jim Brown's instances. There are several problems with this solution.

First of all, the *Department* instance variable is not storing an instance of class *Department* but rather a string of characters (the name of the department). Second, in order to retrieve or update any information for John's department, the user must perform a "join" operation matching the name of the department stored in John's *Department* instance variable with a key value in the *Departments* collection or table. In other words, this scheme needs a declarative database query/retrieval sub-language. This is *exactly* what happens in relational systems, where the model imposes normalization constraints that force the retrieval of objects by matching key values in different tables.

Object identity does not have the overhead of replication and identifier key solutions. With identity, a logical identifier (pointer) is associated with each and every object in the system (as will be shown, in Smalltalk identities are not allocated to the very basic objects such as the integers). The advantages of identity and the direct representation of complex object spaces through object identity are discussed in the next section.

4.5.1 Object Spaces with Identity

To clarify this exploration of object identity, some formalism will be introduced in the definition of objects or object spaces. The definition in this section will formalize the type/state/identity trichotomy of objects.

Object spaces are built on top of base or rock-bottom objects. The most common base object type or class is the integer. Other base types include floating point numbers, characters, booleans, and so on. Objects that are instances of these classes usually do not have instance variables. They are *built-in* object types or classes supported by the underlying system. In most cases, they map onto object types directly supported by the underlying hardware.

Many object-oriented systems treat these base objects differently; for instance, some do not assign identities to base objects. In Smalltalk we cannot have two different objects with the integer value of 5. There is just one integer *5* object!

As mentioned earlier (and detailed in Section 4.6.1) Smalltalk supports two equality predicates:

== to check for identical objects
= to check for equality of object states

However,

5 == 5
5 = 5

are both *true*. Furthermore,

Integer new

or

Float new

both generate errors. The *new* message typically generates an identifier and associates it with the newly created object. But base objects do not get an identifier; their value is their identifier (more or less).

Therefore, conceptually there is an infinite pool of identifiers I such that:

1. An identifier is associated with every non-base object.
2. The identifier gets associated with the object at object creation time and remains associated with the object irrespective of state or type modifications undergone by the object.
3. Each identifier can be associated with one and only one object. Furthermore, if there *is* an identifier in the system it *must* be associated with an object. In other words, an object and its identifiers are "indistinguishable": The identifier uniquely identifies the object and the object remains associated with an identifier throughout its lifetime.

Therefore, each object has three properties:

1. The object is an instance of a class: this indicates the object's type.
2. The object has an identity: an identifier in I is associated with the object.
3. The object has a state: the object values of its instance variables. More specifically if $A_{I1}, \ldots, A_{In}$ are the instance variables of an object O, then the state of the object is:

$$A_{I1} : i_1$$
$$A_{I2} : i_2$$
$$\cdot$$
$$\cdot$$
$$\cdot$$
$$A_{In} : i_n$$

where each i_j is either an object identifier or a base object. If the object is a collection object (for instance, a set), then its state is $\{i_1, \ldots, i_n\}$, where each i_j is the identifier of an object in the collection.

There are a number of alternative graphical representations that clarify this conceptual model of object spaces. In Figure 4.5, identifiers are associated with non-base objects. Each object is framed in a rectangular box. Note that the *Department* instance variable value of John is a non-base object. Furthermore, Jim and John *share* the same *Department* value.

Figure 4.6 gives an alternative graphical representation of objects, following the representation of set and tuple models as in (Bancilhon et al., 1987), (Bancilhon and Khoshafian, 1989) or (Khoshafian, 1989). Here each object is labeled by an identifier. Furthermore, for each instance variable (attribute in set and tuple models) there is a labeled and directed arc from the object to the value of the object. The label is the name of the instance variable. The target is the value of the instance variable.

The object space illustrated in Figure 4.6 is a directed acyclic graph. Actually, it is just as easy to represent arbitrary graph-structured object spaces with arbitrary cycles. For example, assume each person has an additional instance variable Spouse. Then, as

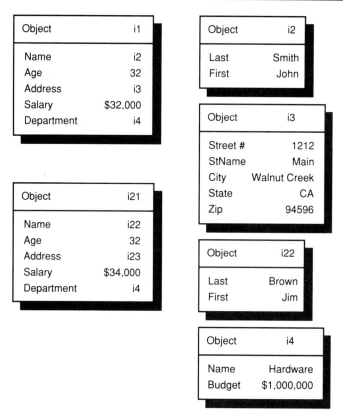

Figure 4.5 Objects in rectangular boxes.

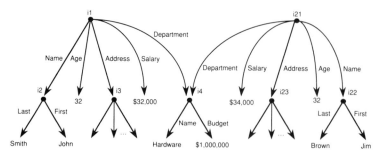

Figure 4.6 Graphical representation of objects.

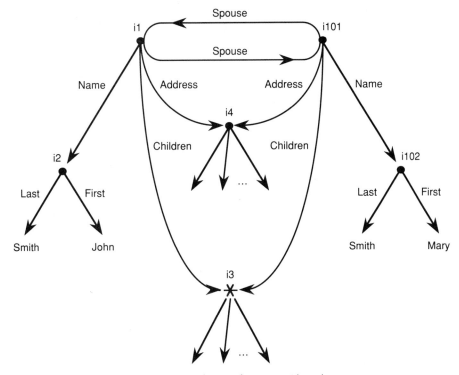

Figure 4.7 Object references with cycles.

illustrated in Figure 4.7, a person can "reference" his or her spouse and be referenced back without any constraints. In the figure, John and Mary also share their Address and Children. The star indicates a set of objects (the Children).

As mentioned earlier, programming languages achieve this object referencing ability and allow variables to "point" to the same object from multiple sources through virtual address pointers. In fact, pointers (or virtual memory addresses) can be used to *implement* object identity.

The fundamental difference between object identity and virtual addresses or pointers is that identity is a semantic concept associated with objects. Addresses represent memory locations of an underlying Von Neumann machine. Also there are other techniques that implement object identity.

4.5.2 Implementation Techniques

As described in (Khoshafian and Copeland, 1986), there are six basic techniques for implementing or supporting object identity. To comprehend some of the schemata proposed here, it is essential to have a rudimentary understanding of *persistence*. Chapter 7 presents a much more detailed description of persistence in the context of object-oriented databases, but an overview is given here.

4.5.2.1 *Persistence*

4.5.2.1.1 Persistence in Programming Languages

In most programming languages (conventional *and* object-oriented), the lifetime of objects is the duration of the program execution. Once the program terminates its execution, all objects that are still active become inaccessible. The program's environment is the only one that allows the access and manipulation of the objects created in the program.

To save and re-access objects between programs, most programming languages employ either or both of the following mechanisms to guarantee persistence:

Files. It is possible to create files of character strings or even records and subsequently read or write to these files. After the program terminates, the data stored in the file persists, and hence can be opened, read, or updated within other programs. Of course, these programs need to know the name and location of the file.

Images. In some languages, including Smalltalk and LISP, it is possible to save the entire execution environment of the program. These languages are more interpretive. Objects are created and manipulated interactively. The user can save the image of the session, come back at a later time, and continue where having left off.

A number of extensions of programming languages have attempted to provide a more seamless and elegant support of persistence. For example, although some programming languages such as Pascal support persistence through files of records, only *certain* types of objects are allowed to persist. Records that had pointer-valued fields in them could *not* be made persistent. For instance, a linked list where each element has a field that is a pointer to the next element of the list cannot be made persistent in Pascal or even an object-oriented language such as Eiffel. Machine-address memory pointers have no meaning outside of the current execution of the program.

There have been other attempts to add persistence to a programming language. A persistent extension of Algol, called PS-Algol (Atkinson et al., 1983), allowed any object to persist. In other words, PS-Algol made the heap of the dynamically allocatable memory persistent. In PS-Algol it became possible to make objects with reference or pointer-valued fields persistent.

Another interesting persistent language is the E programming language (Richardson et al., 1989). E is an extension of C++ that incorporates persistence and other constructs for developing database management systems. The language E allows the definition of database types in defining the schema of a persistent database. It also incorporates parameterized types and iterators over collections of objects. These features are very useful in database programming.

The support of persistence in programming is a useful add-on feature. Persistence allows the sharing of objects across multiple applications and users. It also allows the construction of much larger object spaces. For database management systems, the support of persistent objects is *central* to the DBMS.

4.5.2.1.2   Persistence in Databases

The main purpose of database management systems is the efficient storage and concurrent access of persistent objects. In database management systems, the structure of the object space is defined in a *schema*. The schema is itself persistent and all the objects that are instances of the types described by the schema are persistent.

Unlike persistent languages, database management systems support *transactions*. Persistent objects are created, updated, and retrieved under transaction control. A transaction is a program that is executed atomically; a transaction is executed entirely or not at all. Several transaction programs can execute concurrently, manipulating the same database.

Database management systems also incorporate the actions of an *integrity constraint*. Constraints such as the Age attribute must be greater than or equal to 0 but less than 200; the fact that an employee must not earn more than the manager; the total number of accounts assigned to a salesperson must not exceed 100: All of these are examples of integrity constraints on the persistent database. None of these constraints must be violated. It is acceptable to temporarily violate a constraint within a transaction, since no one else can see that value while the transaction is active. But once the transaction terminates, the integrity constraints must remain intact. Therefore, in addition to being atomic, transactions maintain consistency.

Database management systems store and manage the persistent databases on secondary storage media (hard disks). The persistence in a DBMS has a much stronger connotation dealing with *resiliency* of the data. A substantial portion of the complexity in a database management system comes from the support of different *recovery* strategies. A number of strategies have been developed for data lost in one of the three types of failures (Gray, 1978):

1. *Transaction failures:* usually caused by concurrent transactions conflicting in their accesses to the "shared" database. When such conflicts are detected, the DBMS aborts one or more of the conflicting transactions.
2. *System failures:* usually caused by software errors in the operating system, the DBMS, or by hardware failure other than the disk media.
3. *Media failures:* usually caused by hard disk crashes.

4.5.2.2   *The Implementation Strategies*

There are a number of alternative implementation strategies that can be used to support object identity. Included in these strategies are the use of identifier keys, or virtual or physical address as identity which we criticized. Our criticism concentrated primarily on the *modeling* or *conceptual* deficiencies. Yet these strategies can be used as the underlying implementation techniques supporting the more complete object identity concept.

There are two dimensions in implementing identity:

- Transient versus persistent object spaces
- Address versus indirection strategies

4.5.2.2.1 Transient versus Persistent Object Spaces

This dimension is included for completeness. As indicated in the previous section, programming languages are being extended with persistence. The dominant implementational strategy of identity is to support persistence. Nevertheless, there are still many implementations of object-oriented languages including Ada, C++, Smalltalk, and object orientation extensions of LISP that are based on transient or memory-resident object spaces.

The basic and obvious reason for having a persistent object space in the underlying implementation is to support persistent database or programming languages. Another reason for supporting persistent or secondary storage identifiers is for providing access to a much larger object space. For instance, an earlier implementation of the Smalltalk-80 virtual machine was a memory-resident transient system that could accommodate only 64 K objects (Goldberg and Robson 1983). Other implementations attempted to extend this limitation and allow a larger object space. One of the earliest such attempts was the LOOM (Large Object-Oriented Memory) virtual memory system (Kaehler and Krasner, 1983), which supported objects residing in secondary storage. LOOM provided support for a much larger number of objects in the object space. LOOM achieved this through implementing object identities using a 32-bit object pointer, versus the 16-bit object pointers of the memory resident implementations of Smalltalk-80. The basic idea underlying LOOM was to "trap" the object pointer references and transparently load referenced objects from secondary storage on demand.

4.5.2.2.2 Address Versus Indirection

The second dimension provides a more crucial categorization for distinguishing between the different implementation strategies: The use of an address versus an indirection.

The address could be a:

- Virtual memory address.
- Secondary storage address.
- Structured name in a distributed environment.

The indirection could be through:

- A memory-resident table.
- An index for secondary storage-resident objects.

A fundamental tradeoff between an address-based scheme and an indirection based scheme is between the ease and flexibility of object movements versus the overhead of accessing components of objects.

4.5.2.2.2.1   Indirection through an Object Table

This implementation strategy involves an object table (or array) of starting addresses of objects. Each object identifier is an index or pointer to an entry in this table. That entry contains the starting address of the object. Figure 4.8 illustrates this for a person.

Earlier Smalltalk implementations (Krasner, 1981; Goldberg and Robson, 1983) used an object table to implement object identity. The pointers to the table were called *oops* (object-oriented pointers) instead of identifiers.

An Object Table is used to map:

Object Pointer → Memory Address

Given the memory address, the rest of the indirection-based scheme is the same as the address-based scheme described below. Therefore, compared to the address-based schemes, the underlying system has to go through an extra level of indirection to access the object's state when using an object pointer.

Still, although this indirection through an object table strategy involves an extra memory access and some processing overhead, it has the advantage that the objects can be freely moved in memory without affecting its identity. Only the starting memory address of the object needs to be changed: it is stored in only *one* place, the object table. The *oop* implementing the object identity remains the same. Moving objects is extremely important in garbage collection (which was discussed in Section 2.2.3.2).

The indirection through an object table is used primarily for memory-resident objects. As with the LOOM implementation, the scheme could be combined with a virtual memory system to swap objects to and from secondary storage.

4.5.2.2.2.2   Identity through Address Schemes

Perhaps the simplest implementation of the identity of an object is to use the address of the object as its identity. As discussed earlier, this is the main option used to reference objects in conventional languages such as Pascal, as well as some object-oriented languages such as C++ or Eiffel. There have even been some implementations of Smalltalk that avoid the use of object tables and indirection. One example is the Tektronix 4044 Smalltalk implementation (Caudill and Wirfs-Brock, 1986). Here a

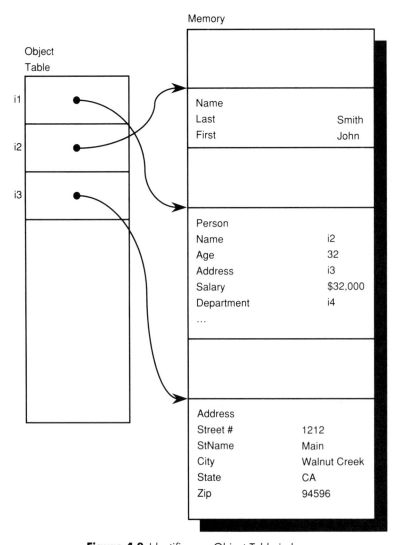

Figure 4.8 Identifiers as Object Table indexes.

much larger object space is supported through using object addresses directly as object pointers.

Using the virtual address as the identity of an object does not preclude persistence. There are two reasons for this:

1. *Dual representation.* It is possible to have an implementation of identity or object state representation for secondary storage-resident persistent objects and

have a different representation when the object is read into the primary memory. In other words, one scheme of identity is used to support disk-resident objects. When the object is read into primary memory it gets transformed to an *in-RAM* representation. The easiest way to do this is to look at each variable in the object's state and replace each secondary storage identity with its primary storage identity, reading it in if necessary. This is the strategy used in LOOM. Since many objects could be transitively reached from an object, it is more convenient to perform the transformations "greedily": in other words, access and transform *only if* the object is referenced.

2. *Persistent store.* It is possible to have a persistent store address space, and use the persistent address space like any other virtual address space. The persistent heap in PS-Algol (Atkinson et al., 1983) uses this approach. There is no difference in the usage, referencing, or access of objects that are stored in the persistent address space as compared to "normal" in-memory addresses.

Using the virtual address is just one identity-as-address alternative. With persistent collections there are two other strategies that have been used to implement identity:

1. *Identity through record identifiers.* In some database management systems, such as System R (Astrahan et al., 1976), and INGRES (Stonebraker et al., 1976), internal record or tuple identifiers are introduced to identify individual records in a relation. A relation in these models is a set of tuple objects. A tuple identifier is the secondary storage address of the tuple. It consists of the pair:

   [Disk Page Number, Slot/Line Number]

   The *Disk Page Number* identifies a unique secondary disk page on the (logical) hard disk. Each page contains a slot array that contains the pointers to the actual records or tuples in the page. The slot or line number indicates the particular entry for the tuple pointer in the page. Strictly speaking there is partial indirection in the record identifier strategies: The disk page number is direct and the slot array is indirect.

2. *Identity through structured identifier.* This strategy is very similar to the naming of conventions for paths in operating systems. Structured identifiers are very useful in multi-workstation environments that are managed by a distributed file system. In some distributed systems, such as the Cambridge File Server (Dion, 1980) and the LOCUS system (Popek et al., 1981), the identifiers of files (the objects of the systems) are structured, where part of the structure captures an aspect of the location of the object, such as a disk or server. More recent distributed file management systems such as Microsoft's LAN MAN use a similar strategy. Of course, the structured identifier strategy also relies on

naming conventions: the name of the workstation, the name of the drive, the name of the directory, the name of the file, and so on. However, each name is mapped onto a physical unit or device. Therefore, strictly speaking there is some indirection in mapping the name onto the actual physical entity when accessing the object. This scheme provides full data independence, in the sense that the structured identifier is unattached to the actual content of the object. Yet like any addressing strategy, it does not provide location independence; the identifier is a function of the object's storage location.

4.5.2.2.2.3 *Surrogates Are the Best!*

The most powerful technique for supporting identity is through "surrogates" (Abrial, 1974; Hall et al., 1976; Codd, 1979; Bancilhon et al., 1987). Surrogates are system-generated, globally unique identifiers, completely independent of object state or object address. Surrogates are persistent identifiers and they can be used to access objects that are stored in persistent store.

Conceptually an object identity associated with an object is independent of the object's name, state, type, or location address. The surrogate implementation strategy directly reflects the value, location, type, or name independence of object identity. With the surrogate strategy each object of any type is associated with a globally unique surrogate at the moment it is instantiated. This surrogate is used to internally represent the identity of its object throughout the lifetime of the object.

The surrogate implementation strategy uses *indirection*: given a surrogate we must still find the address of the object indicated by the surrogate. Unlike the identifier key approach, or the object table entry approach, a surrogate is unique throughout the system, even if it is distributed. A database identifier key is unique only within the set of tuples or relation.

As illustrated in Figure 4.9, a surrogate is attached to the object as a self-describing, special attribute. As long as the surrogate is stored together with the object, the object can be moved to a different location, copied, replicated, fragmented, and so on. Leach et al. (1982) discuss several implementation issues involved in the nontrivial task of generating globally unique surrogates in a distributed environment. We will not discuss them here.

| Surrogate | Name | | | Age | Address | | | | | ... |
	Surrogate	Last String	First String		Surrogate	Street #	StreetName	City	State	...
S1	S2	Smith	John	32	S4	1212	Main	Walnut Creek	CA	...

Figure 4.9 Identifiers through surrogates.

■ 4.6 OPERATIONS WITH IDENTITY

Identity is a property of an object that distinguishes the object from all other objects in the computational environment. The type/state/identity trichotomy implies several operations which are associated with object identity. The three most important categories of operations are:

- Equality predicates
- Copy operations
- Merge and swap operations

4.6.1   The Different Facets of Equality

The definition of equality among objects in an object-oriented system is fundamental for understanding the semantics of object states. Equality predicates partition the object space and determine when two objects can be treated as one or used interchangeably. As programming constructs, equality predicates are commonly used in loop structures (WHILE statements), IF. . .THEN. . .ELSE conditions, and CASE statements.

In conventional programming languages such as C or Pascal, two sorts of objects can be compared using the equality predicate (=):

- Base objects such as integers, floating point numbers, booleans, or characters
- References or pointers to records

Other languages have attempted to have a richer semantics of equality. The strongly typed language ML (Harper et al., 1986) supports an overloaded predicate " = " which provides identity with references (pointers), equality with base values, and recursive application of equality with record structures. The LISP family traditionally provides two kinds of equality: EQ, which tests addresses (pointers) and is hence implementation-dependent, and EQUAL, which tests for isomorphic structures.

With object-oriented systems that support object identity, a clean and rich collection of equality predicates can be supported. As described in (Khoshafian and Copeland, 1986) there are three genres of equality in object models:

1. *Identity predicate (identical).* The identity predicate corresponds to the equality of references or pointers in conventional languages: It checks whether the object identities are the same. With the semantics of object identity, if the object identities are the same then the objects are the same. Both Simula and Smalltalk support this predicate, which is indicated by " == ".

   Consider Figure 4.10. Here are three instances of Person, where for each instance the Name, Age, and Address is indicated. The object identifiers of only the structured person and address objects are indicated. Here the Address of John and Mary is the same, identical object. In other words,

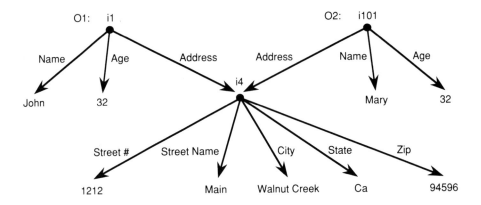

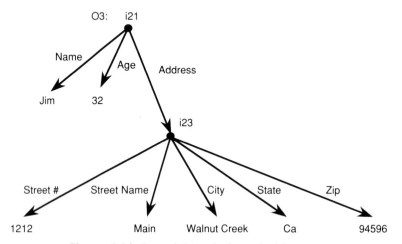

Figure 4.10 O1 and O2 with identical addresses.

O1.Address == O2.Address

is TRUE! Jim, who happens to live at the same physical address, has a different object value for O3.Address. Put another way, although the content of the *Addresss* attribute of Jim is the same as that of John and Mary, the Address instance variable or attribute value of Jim is a *different object* (identifier i23) than the *Address* of Mary or John (identifier i4). Therefore,

O3.Address == O1.Address
O3.Address == O2.Address

are both FALSE.

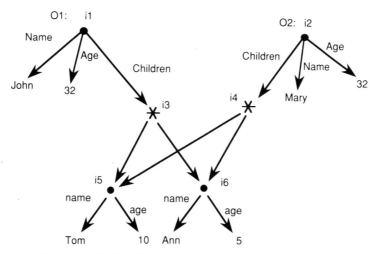

Figure 4.11 The Children of O1 and O2 are shallow equal.

2. *Shallow equality predicate (shallow-equal).* Two objects are shallow equal if their *states* or contents are identical. That is, two objects are shallow equal if they are instances of the same class and the values they take for every instance variable are identical—corresponding instance variables cannot merely have the same object contents but must be identical objects. Two objects could be different but yet be shallow equal. The syntax for shallow equal in Simula and Smalltalk is " =".

Figure 4.11 illustrates two objects that have different objects as the values of their *Children* instance variables. Therefore, in this case:

  O1.Children == O2.Children

is FALSE. However, the *content* of *O1.Children* is identical to the content of *O2.Children*: They have the same children objects. Thus,

  O1.Children = O2.Children

is TRUE.

To further demonstrate shallow equality with instance variables, consider the rectangles of Figure 4.12. Each rectangle has two instance variables representing their lower-left and upper-right vertices. In this example:

  REC1 = REC2

is TRUE, that is, *REC1* is shallow equal to *REC2*. This is because the values of the corresponding instance variables of *REC1* and *REC2* are identical.

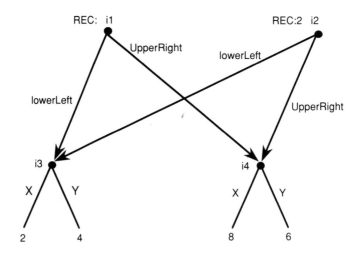

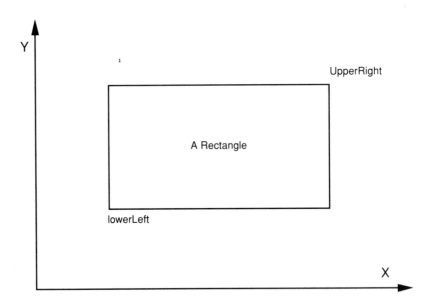

Figure 4.12 REC1 is shallow equal to REC2.

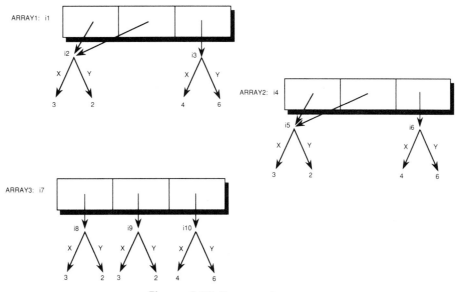

Figure 4.13 Deep equal arrays.

$$REC1.LowerLeft \quad == \quad REC2.LowerLeft$$
$$REC1.UpperRight == REC2.UpperRight$$

are both TRUE.

3. *Deep equality predicate (deep equal).* The third, and in a sense the weakest genre of equality is purely value-based deep equality. There are two flavors of deep equality, depending whether the predicate is checking for the isomorphism of the object graphs.

In its simplest form deep equality ignores object identities and checks whether:

a. two objects are instances of the same class (have the same structure or type), and

b. the values of corresponding base objects are the same.

Figure 4.13 illustrates three arrays that are deep equal to one another: All are one-dimensional arrays of three elements. Each element of each array is an instance of an XY Point. Furthermore, in all three arrays:

> the value of the X-axis of the first element is 3
> the value of the Y-axis of the first element is 2
> the value of the X-axis of the second element is 3
> the value of the Y-axis of the second element is 2
> the value of the X-axis of the third element is 4
> the value of the Y-axis of the third element is 6

Therefore,

ARRAY1 deep-equal ARRAY2
ARRAY2 deep-equal ARRAY3
ARRAY1 deep-equal ARRAY3

are all TRUE!

The observant reader will realize that *ARRAY1* and *ARRAY2* are more similar to each other: Both arrays contain two objects rather than three. Furthermore, the first and second elements in both arrays are the *same* object. This is not the case in *ARRAY3*, which contains three different objects.

Therefore it is possible to define a more restrictive form of deep equality (say, iso-deep-equal) and require that the graphs of the two objects be isomorphic, preserving the sharing of references or the cycles in their corresponding sub-objects. In this sense:

ARRAY1 iso-deep-equal ARRAY2

is TRUE, but

ARRAY1 iso-deep-equal ARRAY3
ARRAY2 iso-deep-equal ARRAY3

are both FALSE.

In summary, we have three flavors of equality:

1. Identical, which checks whether two objects are the same.
2. Shallow, which goes one level deep, comparing corresponding identities of the values of the instance variable or elements of the object.
3. Deep, which compares the contents of corresponding base objects. There are two flavors of deep equality: a weaker one that only checks for equality of a corresponding base object and a stronger one that also checks for the isomorphism of the graphs of the objects.

Each predicate defines an equivalence relation for the object space. This means:

1. Each object is (identical/shallow/deep) equal to itself: *reflexive*.
2. If O1 is (identical/shallow/deep) equal to O2 then O2 is (identical/shallow/deep) equal to O1: *symmetric*.
3. If O1 is (identical/shallow/deep) equal to O2 and O2 is (identical/shallow/deep) equal to O3 then O1 is(identical/shallow/deep) equal to O3: *transitive*.

The strongest form of equality is identical. Shallow equality is stronger than deep equality. In other words, two identical objects are always shallow equal and deep equal. Two shallow equal objects are always deep equal.

4.6.2 The Different Facets of Copying

The previous section presented several flavors of equivalence relationships between objects. The most powerful of these, namely the identical predicate, is used to check whether two variables are referring to the same object. For instance, in Smalltalk/V we can create a new *Complex* number object:

C1 := Complex new

and execute the variable assignment:

C2 := C1

then the value of *C2 == C1* will be TRUE: *C1* and *C2* will be two global variables referring to the same object.

Similarly, object-oriented systems supporting object identity promote two flavors of object copying: *shallow copy* and *deep copy*. Both operations create and return a new object.

1. *Shallow Copy*. The shallow-copy message will create a new object that will have instance variables with values *identical* to the instance variables of the target object. Hence if:

   O2 := O1 shallowCopy

   then *O1 = O2* (that is, *O1* is shallow-equal to *O2*) is true. However, *O1 == O2* is false: *O1* and *O2* are *different* objects. For example, either of the rectangle objects illustrated in Figure 4.12 could have been created through the *shallowCopy* operation. In other words:

   REC2 := REC1 shallowCopy

   would have yielded the *REC2* object sharing its instance variable values with *REC1*, as illustrated in the figure.

   If we have a collection object such as a set, shallow copy will create a new object whose content will be the same as the content of the target object. For example, either of the sets of children illustrated in Figure 4.11 could have been created through the *shallowCopy* operation. That is:

   O2.Children := O1.Children shallowCopy

would have generated the same sharing of children between John and Mary, as shown in Figure 4.13.

2. *Deep Copy*. Conceptually the deep-copy message will create a new object that will have instance variables with entirely new values such that the new object is deep equal to the target object. Every sub-object that is reachable from the root of the object which is created as a result of the deep-copy operation will be a *new* object. The newly created copy does not share any component (element, if it is a collection or the value of an instance variable) with the original target object.

As was said earlier there are two flavors of deep equality: One that checks for the isomorphism of the graphs of the objects and another weaker flavor of deep equality that just checks for the equality of corresponding base objects. Corresponding to these two types of deep equality are two forms as of deep copy. For example *ARRAY2* of Figure 4.13 could have been created through a *deepCopy* message:

> ARRAY2 := ARRAY1 deepCopy

which preserves the graph of the target object. In terms of implementation, it is easier to support the weaker form of deep copy, which just traverses the object and creates copies of each sub-object (values of instance variables or elements in collection objects). Thus:

> ARRAY3 := ARRAY1 deepCopy

In fact, in Smalltalk/V *deepCopy* is even weaker than this. The statement:

> O2 := O1 deepCopy

will create an object *O2 whose instance variables are shallow copies of the instance variables of O1*. If the object is a collection then every element of the new object will be a shallow copy of the corresponding element in the target.

4.6.3 Merging and Swapping

There are additional operators associated with object models that support identity. One of the more interesting operations is *merging*. For example, two objects with separate identity may later be discovered to be the same (the murderer is the butler!) and therefore need to be merged. Codd (1979) has argued for a "coalescing" operator in RM/T that merges identity. This operator basically checks if all the corresponding instance variables of two objects are equal (=) and if so, makes one object identical to the other, such that all references to either object are now to one and the same object. The support of object merging is very useful in statistical databases when an

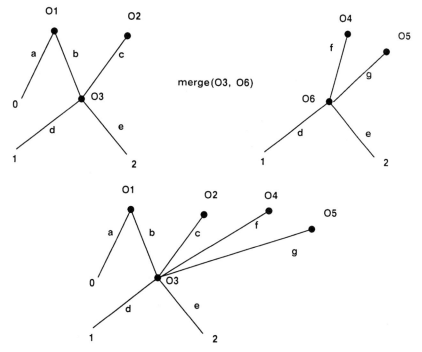

Figure 4.14 Merging O3 and O6.

attempt is made to merge information that was gathered by different sources. This is called record linking (Wrigley, 1973; Howe and Lindsay, 1981), where records that contain different sorts of information about the same objects are coalesced.

Note that this is an updating operation. The semantics and support of this operation can be tricky and difficult to implement. The simplest approach is to require that the two objects be:

- Instances of the same class (and hence the same type) and
- Deep equal.

Then all we need is to ensure that all the references to the old objects and their sub-components now refer to the merged object and its sub-components. It is possible to make merging more sophisticated and provide support for the merging of differently structured objects. Figure 4.14 illustrates the merge of two tuples O3 and O6. Before the merge O1.b and O2.c referenced the same object O3; similarly O4.f and O5.g referenced the same object O6. Objects O3 and O6 were different. After the merge, the object O1.b, O2.c, O4.f, and O5.g all reference the same object.

Smalltalk does not support the merge operation as described here but instead provides a **become:** method. When:

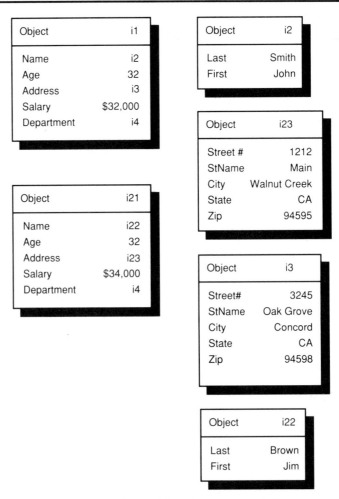

Figure 4.15 John's Address becomes Jim's Address.

O1 become: O2

is executed, the identifiers of *O1* and *O2* are interchanged. This means objects that were referencing or accessing *O1* (*O2*) will now be accessing *O2* (*O1*). For example, assume John is in office number OF1001 and Tim is in office OF2002. If John and Tim swap offices all we have to do is:

John getOffice become: Tim getOffice

If, for example, John is the assistant of his manager, Mary, and Mary has an instance variable, *officeOfAssistant*, then *before* John's office became Tim's office:

Mary getofficeOfAssistant officeName

would have returned: OF1001. *After* the swapping, the same message to Mary would return OF2002.

As another example, Figure 4.15 shows what happens when John's home address becomes Jim's home address (that is, John and Jim interchange houses). Then objects such as Jim's children, spouse, parents, or friends, which were referencing his old address will automatically reference his new address. The same holds for John. This scheme avoids all the headaches of address changes and forwarding addresses.

■ 4.7 SUMMARY

Object identity organizes the objects or instances of an application in arbitrary graph-structured object spaces. Identity is a property of an object that distinguishes the object from all other objects in the application. In conventional programming languages, identity is realized through memory addresses. In databases, identity is realized through identifier keys. User-specified names are used in both languages and databases to give unique names to objects. Each of these strategies compromises identity.

In a completely object-oriented system, each object will be given an identity that will be permanently associated with the object, immaterial of the object's structural or state transitions. The identity of an object is also independent of the location or address of the object. With object identity users can *referentially* share objects. Object identity provides the most natural modeling primitive, having the same object be a sub-object of multiple parent objects.

There are many techniques to implement identity. The best way is to assign each object a system-wide, unique object identifier, called a surrogate, which is independent of the object's type, address, or state. When a surrogate is stored with an object, it allows the object to be relocated without losing its identity (the object becomes self-describing).

There are many operations associated with identity. Since the state of an object is different from its identity, there are three types of equality predicates for comparing objects. The most obvious equality predicate is the identical predicate, which checks whether two objects are actually one and the same object. The two other equality predicates (shallow equal and deep equal) actually compare the states of objects. Shallow equal goes one level deep in comparing corresponding instance variables. Deep equal ignores identities and compares the values of corresponding base objects (integers, floats, characters, and so on.). As far as copying objects, the counterparts of deep and shallow equality are deep and shallow copy. Deep (shallow) copy produces a replica which is deep (shallow) equal to the original object. Other operations associated with identity include *merge* and *become*.

5

C++

■ 5.1 INTRODUCTION

In the past few years, several hybrid object-oriented languages have emanated from the computer industry. Most of these hybrid languages extend the definitions of popular languages such as Pascal, C or LISP. Among the extensions made to the C language, the C++ language has emerged as the leader. Almost all publishers are selling books on this language. Chapters 2, 3, and 4 concentrated on the presentation of object orientation concepts. This chapter presents C++ as one of the most popular object-oriented languages.

The C++ language was designed by Bjarne Stroustrup at AT&T in the early 80s (Stroustrup, 1986 and Weiskamp et al., 1990). Bjarne's early experience with Simula, the first object-oriented language, influenced his design of the C++. The language's acceptance spread from AT&T to major universities and to other computer industry firms.

The first implementation of the C++ language was released as a preprocessor for any C compiler. The decision to release the language as a preprocessor was intended to ease the adoption of C++. However, there is nothing inherent in the design of the language that demands a preprocessor approach. Currently there are many C++ compilers.

5.1.1 Chapter Organization

The rest of this chapter discusses C++ and its object orientation capabilities. Section 5.2 turns to a brief overview of object-oriented extensions of C++. Section 5.3 discusses pros and cons of the language. Section 5.4 explains class definition; Section

5.5, inheritance. Section 5.6 examines polymorphic capabilities of the language. Section 5.7 covers specification versus implementation of a class definition. Section 5.8 discusses the new concept of stream I/O. Finally, Section 5.9 presents a few case studies in C++.

C++ also introduces new features to the C language that are not related to object orientation. Within each section, these extensions are introduced and discussed.

■ 5.2 OBJECT ORIENTATION IN C++

This section presents an overview of object orientation features of C++. The language supports all object orientation concepts such as: abstract data type, inheritance, object identity, overloading/overriding, and dynamic binding.

1. *Abstract data types.* C++ provides two constructs for abstract data type definition. The first one is an extension of *struct* construct and the other is through the new *class* construct. Abstract data type was defined in Section 2.2.

    The *struct* construct in C allows structural definition of an object that is composed of several members. To this, C++ extends the ability of defining functions as attributes of an object's definition. All properties of a class declared through this construct are public. This last statement may be heresy to the object orientation purist, but it makes the C++ compiler backward-compatible with existing C code.

    To the above construct, C++ adds the new *class* construct. With it, the designer constructs classes conforming to the more traditional object orientation view that instance variables can be hidden. Refer to Section 5.4 for a detailed discussion of C++ support for class definition.

2. *Inheritance.* C++ allows the hierarchy of class definition to inherit both methods and instance variables from existing class definitions. Inheritance is discussed in Chapter 3. The first release of C++ only allowed tree hierarchy (single inheritance) to be defined. The new release of C++, Version 2.0, allows multiple inheritance. Section 5.5 presents C++ inheritance capabilities.

3. *Object identity.* C++ allows reference to objects either by name or address. The address of an object can be used as a reference in the definition of a complex object. For a user-defined class, the language provides copy constructors automatically. There are no operations provided to support the different types of equality (identical, shallow, or deep) with associated object identity. The only system-supported comparison (equality) of objects is by the value of their addresses. Users can develop both comparison or copy operations as part of class definition. For a more complete description of object identity refer to Chapter 4.

4. *Overloading/Overriding and dynamic binding.* The language allows overloading of function names and operators. Parametric polymorphism is not supported. Polymorphism is discussed in Section 2.3. Function names can be overloaded to have varied numbers of arguments of different types. System-defined operators such as +, −, *, and others can be overloaded for user-defined classes. One of the greatest benefits of operator overloading comes with stream I/O. With this new I/O method, users can overload the stream operators to support user-defined data types directly. C++ polymorphic capabilities are discussed in Section 5.6. Stream I/O is discussed in Section 5.8.

C++ also supports dynamic binding through virtual functions. (Refer to Section 2.4 for a complete discussion of dynamic binding in general.) See Section 5.5.5 for the in-depth discussion of dynamic binding in C++.

■ 5.3 PROS AND CONS OF C++

This section discusses the advantages and disadvantages of C++ as an object-oriented language. We examine both the major advantages of the language, and its disadvantages; real and potential.

5.3.1 Advantages

The major advantages of C++ are:

True Extension of the C Language. The language is designed as a super set of ANSI C (Kernighan and Ritchie, 1988). Any C++ compiler accepts most standard C programs. All language extensions guarantee backward compatibility to the existing C language with some minor incompatibilities. For example, to support class definition, C++ extends the definition of *struct* construct.

Good Performance. One of the original drawbacks of object-oriented technology was its performance. The earlier implementations of object-oriented languages such as Smalltalk had poor performance results. C++ does not suffer the performance problems associated with the earlier object-oriented language implementations. Some published results demonstrate the run-time performance of C++ code to be as good as that of standard C (Zortech, 1989). There is a slight performance hit with virtual functions, since most C++ compilers implement them with an extra level of indirection.

Popularity and Multivendor Support. C++ has become a popular object-oriented language. The popularity of the language has far exceeded Smalltalk or other object-oriented languages such as Objective C (Cox, 1986), Eiffel (Meyer, 1988) or Object Pascal (Schmucker, 1986). Several vendors have released C++ compilers, preprocessors and development environments including AT&T, Apple, Apollo, Sun, Zortech, Oasys, Glockenspiel, and Oregon Software.

5.3.2 Disadvantages

The disadvantages of C++ are:

Hybrid Object-Oriented Language. C++ is not a purely object-oriented language, since it allows the developer to fall back on traditional C coding habits. As demonstrated later in this chapter, the designer of a class can provide complete access to the instance variables of a class. In effect, this means C++ class definitions need not enforce information hiding. The developer bears this responsibility. Thus one of the fundamental object-oriented principles may be ignored.

Manual Garbage Collection. The language does not support automatic garbage collection, as discussed in Section 2.2. Some object-oriented languages such as CLOS and Smalltalk support automatic garbage collection.

Manual garbage collection shifts the burden of object management onto the shoulders of the developer rather than the system. Thus the developer must worry about managing memory for allocation/deallocation of objects at run time. This requires a certain amount of application code dedicated to this task. The underlying problem is the "dual semantics" of a high-level programming language with embedded low-level memory management constructs. This was discussed in Section 4.2.

Other languages provide garbage collection subsystems at run time to manage user- and system-created objects. However, while automatic garbage collection relieves the developer of this responsibility, the run-time code associated with it can be quite expensive. With some real-time applications the run-time cost can be unacceptable. For a related discussion on garbage collection refer to Sections 2.2.3 and 4.2.

Current Lack of Development Tools. Currently there are not many development environments (symbolic debugger, browsers, and the like) available. These tools should be available in the near future as more tool vendors supporting C++ finish development of such tools. As this book nears completion, some vendors are already advertising development environments for C++.

Also, unlike Smalltalk, C++ does not contain a predefined class hierarchy. Some vendors and universities are filling this gap by providing a library of class definitions including CommonView from Glockenspiel. CommonView provides a set of class definitions for Microsoft Windows and Presentation Manager application developers. Chapter 8 covers both Microsoft Windows and Apple MacApp.

■ 5.4 CLASS DEFINITION

This section explains C++ support for abstract data types. Chapter 2 presented abstract data types in detail. C++ provides two methods for class definition: a new *class* construct and extended C *struct* and *union* constructs. Section 5.4.1 discusses the new *class* construct. Section 5.4.1 explores the ability to define methods through member functions. Section 5.4.2 looks at how objects can be created and destroyed. Section 5.4.3 shows how friend functions can provide selective access to private instance variables and methods of a class. Section 5.4.4 discusses extensions made to existing *struct* and *union* constructs to support class definition. Section 5.4.5 delves into inline functions, one of the new features of C++. And finally, Section 5.4.6 presents static members.

5.4.1 *Class* Construct

The *class* construct is used to declare a new abstract data type. A class is declared using the following grammar rule:

```
class <class-name>
{
        <private-member-declarations>
    public:
        <public-member-declarations>
}
```

The construct <*class-name*> identifies the name of the new class definition. A member may be either an instance variable or a method. The above construct allows two types of member declaration: private and public. Both types of members are accessible within the boundaries of the class definition. Note that there is a third type of member called *protected* that will be presented in Section 5.5.4.

The private members are accessible only within the class definition. Both private and public members declared within the class definition can access private members. For example, a method defined as a public member can access instance variables and methods defined as private members.

The public members are accessible both inside and outside the class definition. Members declared within the class definitions can access all public members. Also, these members are directly accessible to the clients of the class definition.

The following example declares a class called *Person*.

```
class Person {
        int Age;
        char Sex;
    public:
        void Get(int *a, char *s) { a = Age; s = Sex;}
        void Set(int a, char s) { Age = a; Sex = s;}
        void Print()
            { printf("age = %d sex = %c ", Age, Sex);}
};
```

In this example, we have declared two private instance variables called *Age* and *Sex*. These private instance variables are accessible only through *Get* and *Set* methods. As stated previously, the private members are not accessible outside the class declaration. Thus the above members are hidden from the instantiating clients of the class. *Member* functions, discussed next, can be used to manipulate private instance variables and methods.

The following example illustrates how a *Person* object can be declared and used:

```
Person John;
. . . .
John.Set(26, "m");
John.Print();
```

The *Set* and *Print* functions provide access to the private data associated with the object *John*. These functions are called *member* functions and are discussed next.

5.4.1.1 Member Function

Member functions are the methods of the class. They have access to all instance variables and methods declared within the class declaration. Controlled access to private members can be provided via these functions. In the previous example, *Set* and *Get* member functions provided such access to *Person* objects.

The body of a member function can be defined either inside or outside the *class* construct. When defined within the class declaration, the member function is treated as an inline function. Inline functions do not have the time and space overhead associated with a function call. They are analogous to a macro definition (see Section 5.4.5). When a member function is defined outside the class construct, then the function is treated as a regular function definition.

For example, the above class declaration can be specified as:

```
class Person
{
        int Age;
        char Sex;
```

```
      public:
          Set(int a, char s)
          Get(int *a, char *s)
          Print() { printf("age = %d sex = %s", Age, Sex);}
};

Person::Set(int a, char s)
{
          Age = a > 0 ? a : 0;
          if (s == 'M' // s == 'F')
                Sex = s;
          else
                Sex = 'F';
}
```

Notice that *Set* function is declared inside the *Person* class and its function body defined later. During the function declaration the name of the function is declared as: *Person::Set*. The *operator (::)* is used to identify the class containing the definition of this *Set* function. This enables several classes to have member function with the same name but completely different purpose. Note that this operator *(::)* has other uses as well, which are discussed later in this Chapter.

A member function is invoked for a specific object; references to the class data and functions are made in regards to the specified object. For example, the following line:

```
    John.Set(12, 'm');
```

invokes the function called *Set* in *Person* class. And references to *Age* and *Sex* data are for the object called *John*.

5.4.1.2 The this Pointer

In a member function definition, the pseudovariable *this* contains the address of the instance for which the method was called. Most often, the *this* pointer is used to disambiguate reference (see Section 2.2). For example, given an instance variable called *Spouse* in the *Person* class, the *GotMarriedTo* method modifies this instance variable's point to the person identified as the spouse.

```
    class Person
    {
          Person *Spouse;
      public:
          GotMarriedTo(Person *p)
              { this -> Spouse = p};
    }
```

The pseudovariable *this* is also used with operator overloading. Section 5.6.2 contains additional examples of the pseudovariable *this* in operator overloading.

5.4.2 Constructors and Destructors

This section discusses constructors and destructors of a class. Instances of a class are created and destroyed via a constructor or destructor function. See Sections 2.2.3 and 4.2 for a complete discussion of object creation and destruction. Briefly, a constructor creates an instance for a class. In C++, the constructor of a class has the same name as the class name. A constructor can optionally accept parameters to use for initialization.

A destructor destroys an instance of a class. Given a class called X, the name of the destructor function for this class is $\sim X$. The destructor function never takes any argument and is usually called by the compiler only. The compiler provides a default destructor for a user-defined class.

Example:

```
class person
{
        int Age;
        char Sex;
    public:
        Person(int AnAge, char SomeSex)
            {Age = AnAge; Sex = SomeSex;}
        ~Person();
};

f()
{
        Person Bob (32, 'm');
        Person John = Person(26, 'm');
        . . . . .
}
```

Objects called *Bob* and *John* are created at the beginning of the function called *f*. During the function termination, the $\sim$*Person* destructor will dispose the *Bob* and *John* objects. In other words, the destructor function is invoked implicitly just before the return of the *f* function. This destructor function does not have to be defined since the default definition provided by the compiler is sufficient.

Any type of operation can be performed within a destructor or constructor. More specifically they are used to create/destroy complex or aggregate objects, or change the values of the static members (see Section 5.4.6 on static members).

Several constructors can be specified for a given class. All of these constructors have the same name but different types of arguments. For example, a class called *Furniture* can be defined with several constructors:

```
class Furniture
{
        int NumOfLegs;
        char *Fabric;
    public:
        Furniture(char *Style);
        Furniture(int num_legs, char *fabric);
};

Furniture::Furniture(char *style)
{
        if(strcmp(style, ".....")) 
        {
            NumOfLegs =...
            strcpy(Fabric, ....);
        }
        ...
}

Furniture::Furniture(int num_legs, char *fabric)
{
        NumOfLegs = num_legs;
        strcpy(Fabric, fabric);
}

f()
{
        My_Furniture chair ("Wooden Chair");
        My_Furniture chair son_ (3, "kid");
        ....
}
```

This code defined two constructors for the *Furniture* class. Both constructors have the same name as the class name but completely different types of arguments. C++ allows users to overload functions (as discussed later). Overloaded functions are distinguished by the number of arguments and their types.

5.4.2.1   When Are Constructors or Destructors Called?

The language allows objects to be created or destroyed as *automatic, static, free store*, or *member* objects.

1. *Automatic* objects are created during a declaration inside a function or a block of code. These objects disappear when the block of code containing the object declaration is terminated.

2. *Static* objects are created once at the beginning of the program and destroyed during program termination.

3. *Free store* objects are created and destroyed under the control of the application program. C++ provides the *new* operator to create a new object and *delete* to destroy an object. (For a more general discussion on allocation/disposal, see Sections 2.2 and 4.2.)

4. *Member* objects are created and destroyed by the containing objects. An object can be a member of another object. The member object's longevity depends on the lifespan of containing objects. The member object will be created by the constructor of the containing object. And the destructor of the containing object will be responsible for invoking the destructor of the member objects. In many cases, this is done automatically if each member object has a default constructor.

5.4.3 Friend Functions and Classes

A function declared as *friend* can have access to private instance variables and methods of a class. A friend function can itself be a member function of another class declaration. This feature is useful since without it all class declarations are "black boxes." A friend function provides a window to the private section of the class declaration. This violates the information hiding principle of object orientation. The grammar rule to declare a function as friend to a class declaration is:

```
class <class_name>
{
      . . . . . .
      friend f(. . . .);
}
f(. . . .)
{
      . . .
}
```

Unlike member functions, friend functions do not automatically pass the current object pointer (the pseudovariable *this*) to the function. Users of friend functions must pass it explicitly.

Example 1: Extend the class *Person* to support a friend function called *aging*.

```
class Person
{
          int Age;
          char Sex;
      public:
          friend void aging(Person* p, int years);
};
```

```
void aging(Person* p, int Years)
{
        p -> Age + = Years;
}
```

This function has access to both *age* and *sex* private instance variables of an object. To access these instance variables, the address of the object is passed as an argument. Thus the following C++ statement:

```
aging(&John, 1);
```

increments the *age* of the *Person* object called *John*.

Example 2: Two classes are declared with a friend function called *f1*. This function has access to private sections of both *X* and *Y* classes.

```
class X
{
        int x1;
        int x2;
        X(int , int);
    public:
        friend void f1 (X* x, Y* y);
};

class Y
{
        int y1, y2;
        int Y(int, int);
    public:
        friend void f1 (X* x, Y* y);
}

void f1 (X* x, Y* y)
{
        y -> y1 = x -> x1;
        y -> y2 = x -> x2;
}
 . . . .
```

Frequently some classes interact very closely with each other. The ability to provide access from one class to another is very useful. The C++ language provides a notation for two friendly classes:

```
class X
{...};

class Y
{
    . . .
    public:
    . . . .
    friend class X;
    . . .
};
```

This makes all private members of class *X* available to the object declared as class *Y*. To provide the private members of class *Y* access to *X*, the following declaration

```
friend class Y;
```

may be added to *X* class definition. Given an instance x of X in a method of Y, the instance variables of x could be accessed or updated directly in Y's methods.

5.4.4 Struct and Union

As stated previously, C++ class declaration is an extension of the C *struct* construct. This subsection discusses object-oriented extensions made to *struct* and *union* constructs. Both constructs are extended to support methods. The *struct* construct extensions are examined first, followed by *union* extensions.

5.4.4.1 Struct

The *struct* construct has been extended to support method definition. All instance variables and methods declared with the new revised *struct* construct are public by default. This approach causes *struct* construct to be upward-compatible. A class declaration with no private section is equivalent to a *struct* declaration. Thus

```
class X
{
    public:
    . . . .
}
```

is equivalent to

```
struct X
{
    . . .
}
```

Example: Redefine the *Person* class as a *struct*.

```
struct Person
{
    int Age;
    char Sex;
    print() { printf(" age = %d sex = %c", Age, Sex);} ;
};
```

Notice that since *Age* and *Sex* instance variables are available to the public, *Set* and *Get* methods are no longer needed. This feature can be helpful in some applications requiring direct access to instance variables. Conversely, however, this new definition of *Person* class makes instance variables available to the clients of the class. Thus information hiding or encapsulation has been completely sacrificed and left to the programmer.

To declare an instance of type *Person*, a programmer can still use the same notation as used previously such as:

```
Person Bob;
```

Note that this notation is different from ANSI C, where in order to define an instance of *Person struct* the following is used:

```
struct Person Bob;
```

This is one of the incompatibilities of C++ with ANSI C. In a sense, for a *struct* called *person*, C++ implicitly provides the following *typedef* for *struct* declarations:

```
typedef struct person Person;
```

Thus allowing the first object declaration.

5.4.4.2 Union

The *union* construct has also been extended to support method definition. For example, the following declaration:

```
union Share
{
    int x;
    char *y;
    Share (int AnInt) { x = AnInt;}
    Share(char *AString) { strcpy(y, AString)} ;
};
. . .
```

Share First (1); // declares a "Share" union with
// integer value
Share second ("nxvnzx"); // declares a "Share" union
// as string.

specifies a union with two data fields called *x, y* which share the same memory location and appropriate constructors for each field.

The above union declaration is very hard to manipulate. Given a *Share* object, it is impossible to determine the type of its data. In order to alleviate this problem, the above declaration can be redefined as:

```
class Share
{
        enum { INTG, STRG} tag;
        union
        {
            int x;
            char *y;
        }
    public:
        Share(int x) { tag = INTG; Share::x = x;} // constructor for integer.
        Share(char *y) { tag = STRG; strcpy(Share::y, y);} // constructor for
                                                        //character string.
};
```

Notice that there is a new operator (*::*) which is called the *scope resolution operator*. In the first constructor, the parameter name and private data share the same name: X. The scope resolution operator distinguishes the private data name from the parameter name. This operator has the following grammar rule:

[<class name>] :: <member name>

Given a class name, *<member name>* is either an instance variable or a method of the class declaration. When class name is missing, then *<member name>* refers to the name declared in the global scope. For example, given a class with a method called *printf*, the standard C library *printf* can still be accessed from this method. The C library *printf* function can be referenced as *::printf* without conflicting with the user-defined method.

5.4.5 Inline Functions

One of the new extensions to C exploited by C++ is the ability to define inline functions. When a call to an inline function is encountered, the C++ compiler replaces the function call with the body of the function. All parameters are substituted for the arguments. Inline functions do not have the run-time cost associated with usual function invocation.

Thus inline functions are analogous to *#define* macros. The advantage of using an inline function instead of a macro is that argument type checking is done by the compiler. In a macro definition, no type checking is performed.

We recommend use of inline functions for small functions only. Only functions with few lines should be declared as inline. If the function performs a simple (one- or two-line) computation then an inline function is preferred. For example, if a member function retrieves or updates the value of a private instance variable, an inline function is preferred.

5.4.5.1 *Declaring Inline Functions*

Previous examples demonstrated that member functions defined within a class construct are declared as inline functions. Standard C functions can also be declared as inline. To do so, the keyword *inline* must be specified with the function declaration.

The following function declares *squar* as an inline function:

```
inline int squar(int *num)
    { num *= num;}
```

Thus given a function call as:

```
squar(count)
```

the compiler will replace the function call with the following code:

```
count *= count;
```

Thus no run-time overhead is associated with the above function call. In addition, the compiler will do type checking before performing the substitution.

5.4.6 Static Members

In a class definition, an instance variable can be declared as *static*. C++ static members are like Smalltalk class variables (see Section 3.4). For a given class definition and all its instances, only one copy of each static member exists. A static member exists even if no instance exists. Static members can be used to hold information about the class and its instances such as number of instances created. Or they can be used to enforce integrity constraints, such as keeping an employee's salary within a range.

The following example keeps a count of the number of *Person* objects. The *NoPersonObjects* static member exists regardless of existence of any *Person* object. Note that it is incremented in the class constructor method and decremented in the destructor method; thus keeping a count of the number of *Person* objects in existence. As stated previously, constructor and destructor methods are typically used for the purpose of keeping track of objects of a class.

```
class Person
{
            static int NoPersonObjects;
            int Age;
            char Sex;
      public:
            Person (int AnAge, char SomeSex)
            {
                NoPersonObjects ++;
                . . . .
            }
            ~Person() { NoPersonObjects --;}
}
```

A static member is referenced outside the class definition by the following notation: *<class>::<member_name>*. Using the previous example, the following statement initializes the *NoPersonObjects* to zero:

```
Person::NoPersonObjects = 0;
```

The scope rules for static members are the same as for other members, except for initialization. Static members defined for a class definition can be initialized as a global variable outside any function definition.

■ 5.5 INHERITANCE IN C++

In Chapter 3, inheritance between classes and subclasses was explored. C++ supports inheritance and calls its subclasses *derived classes*. A derived class is used to define a subclass of an existing class, which is called the base class. A base class is any predefined class definition. A derived class inherits instance variables and methods from one or more base classes. The user may declare several derived classes for one base class. A derived class can in turn be a base class for other subclasses. This allows a hierarchy of class declaration. Version 1.0 of C++ only allows single inheritance; Version 2.0 lifts this limitation and supports multiple inheritance.

The general form of derived class declaration is as follows:

```
class <derived-class-name>
    : [public | private ] <base-class-name>
{
    <derived-class-members>
}
```

where *<derived-class-name>* is the name of the new class definition and *<base-class-name>* is the name of an existing class. Only the public members of the base class are inherited by the new class.

When the *public* keyword is specified, public members of the base class are inherited as public members of the derived class. When omitted or the *private* keyword specified, the public members are inherited as private members.

For example, to define *Student* as a subclass of *Person* class, it is possible to write:

```
class Person
{
    public:
        char Name[10];
        char Address[20];
        int Age;
};

class Student : public Person
{
    public:
        int StudentId;
        char CampusAddress[20];
};
```

Given the above class declaration, the following statements demonstrate the use of inheritance:

```
Student Joe;
. . .
strcpy(Joe.Name, "Joe Jackson");
strcpy(Joe.Address, "43 Main St. SF, CA");
Joe.Age = 21;
Joe.StudentId = 1011134;
```

Notice that the object called *Joe*, besides having instance variables called *StudentId* and *CampusAddress*, also inherits members from the *Person* base class.

In this example, the *public* keyword is used to define the *Student* class. This keyword is used so commonly that there is an equivalent, shorthand notation. Instead of declaring a derived class as:

```
class <derived-class-name>: public <base-class-name>
{
    public:
        <public_members_decl>
}
```

which inherits all the public members from a base class, the following notation can be used:

```
struct <derived-class-name>: <base-class-name>
{
    <public_members_decl>
}
```

The above declaration only allows definition of public members in the derived class. For instance, the following declares *GraduateStudent* as a subclass of *Student*:

```
struct GraduateStudent : Student
{
    AdvisorName : char[20];
};
```

which has access to all public members from both *Student* and *Person* classes.

5.5.1 Private Base Class

As stated previously, the *public* keyword may be omitted from the derived class declaration. This causes the base class public members to be inherited as private members for the newly derived class. Thus the instantiating clients of the derived class cannot access these members.

The private base class declaration can be used to provide an alternate view of the base class. The new derived class declaration can selectively allow access to some of the base class members.

For instance, to declare a *PrivatePerson* subclass that only allows access to the *Name* instance variable, the following is used:

```
class PrivatePerson : Person
{
    public:
        Person::Name;
};
```

The above class declaration gives access to the *Person* class's *Name* instance variable only. The notation *Person::Name* makes the *Name* instance variable of the *Person* class available as a public member of this new class.

Given the above declaration, the following statement can be written to access the *Name* instance variable:

```
PrivatePerson Mary;
. . . . .
strcpy(Mary.Name, "Mary Joe");
```

Whereas, the following code segment will cause the compiler to generate an error since the *Age* instance variable is not accessible to the clients of *PrivatePerson* class:

Mary. Age = 32; // This line is an error

5.5.2 Extending a Class Declaration

One of the advantages of class hierarchy is that a derived class declaration can extend or enhance the base class declaration. The newly derived class, in addition to inheriting members, can define additional members and restrict or override existing members.

A set of base classes can be part of the initial design of a software system. With the passing of time and changing requirements, additional members may become needed. The designer can take one of the following approaches:

1. *The base class declaration can be redefined with new members.* In some instances, this alternative may not be feasible. Imagine that an application is based on a library of classes supplied by a vendor. Most likely the client does not have access to the library source code.
2. *Newly derived classes can be declared with these additional members.* This approach allows design of new applications that apply the extended class declaration.

Sections 5.8 and 5.9.2 present examples of how class extension can be exploited. Section 5.8, demonstrates how the C++ stream I/O classes can be extended for user-defined types. And in Section 5.9.2, the *And3* class definition extends the *And2* superclass definition.

5.5.3 Inheritance and Constructors/Destructors

Occasionally a base class needs constructors or destructors to allocate, initialize, or deallocate base class objects. The derived class object must call the constructor or destructor of the base class. (In Version 2.0, this may be done automatically by the compiler.) Constructors first build the base class object, then the derived class. During destruction, the destructor destroys the derived class object first, then the base class.

Example: Redefine *Person* and *Student* class definitions with constructors to initialize the instance variables.

```
class Person
{
    public:
        char Name[10];
        int Age:
        Person(char *AName, int AnAge);
};
```

```
class Student : public Person
{
    public:
        int StudentId;
        Student (int AnId, char *AName, int AnAge)
            : (AName, AnAge)
            { StudentId = AnId; }
};
```

The *Student* constructor is declared as:

```
Student (int AnId, char *AName, int AnAge)
    : (AName, AnAge)
    { StudentId = AnId; }
```

The notation : (*AName*, *AnAge*) invokes the constructor for the *Person* class first. Thus *Name* and *Age* instance variables are initialized first before invoking the *Student* constructor to initialize *StudentId*.

5.5.4 Protected Members

Version 2.0 introduced protected members. As stated previously, a derived class inherits both public and protected members. A protected member is treated as a private member by instantiating clients of the class definition. But a friend and a method of a derived class can access the protected members of a base class. In this way, a protected member is different from a private member.

In the following example, class *Y* inherits both public and private members of class *X*. The protected instance variable *i* from class *X* is accessible to the *Y*'s *Afunc* member method.

```
class X
{
    protected:
        int i;
}

class Y: public X
{
        Afunc() { i++};
}
```

The protected member *i* is not accessible to the instantiating clients of the class *X*. Thus the following code is illegal:

```
X Anx;
Y Ay

. . .

Anx.i = 1;   // Error
Ay.i = 2;    // Error
```

5.5.5 Virtual Functions

C++ supports dynamic binding through virtual functions. A virtual function allows overriding of the same member function name for all classes within the hierarchy (see Section 3.3 for overriding). Each subclass within the hierarchy can choose a different implementation for this function. For example, in a hierarchy of different shapes (circle class, triangle class, and the like) we could define a member function called *Print*. This function displays the appropriate shape of each object. For each subclass, the appropriate shape will be drawn. For a complete discussion on dynamic binding and method overriding refer to Sections 2.4 and 3.3.2.

Each derived class may either inherit the virtual function from its base class or define its own. The resultant type and the arguments of a virtual function must remain the same for each derived class within the hierarchy.

In the following example, the *Person* and *Student* class hierarchy is redefined to include a display capability.

```
struct Person
{
    char Name[20];
    int Age;
    Person(char *AName, int AnAge);
    virtual void Print();
};


void Person::Print()
{
    printf("name = %s age = %d", Name, Age);
}


struct Student : Person
{
    int StudentId;
    Student(char* Name, int age, int id);
    void print();
};
```

```
void Student::Print()
{
    printf("Student ID = %d",StudentId);
    Person::Print();
}
```

The *Student::Print* function invokes the *Person::Print* function to display the instance variables of a *Person* object. Note that *virtual* is only used in the declaration of the base class.

Given the above declaration, the following function displays any object within the hierarchy:

```
void Display(Person* Aperson)
{
    Aperson -> Print();
    printf("\n");
}
```

Thus the following code segment:

```
Student Joe("Joe", 21, 12343);
Person Wanda("Wanda", 22);

Display(Joe);
Display(Wanda);
```

produces the following display:

```
Student ID = 12343 name = "Joe" age = 21
name = "Wanda" age = 22
```

Notice that the *Display* function invokes the *Print* function for an object of type *Person* or any of its subclasses. The *Student::Print* method of *Student* is invoked by the *Display* function. This function is not aware of the *existence* of the *Student* class. The decision of which *Print* method to invoke is done at run time, not compile time. This is the essence of dynamic binding (see Section 2.4 on dynamic binding). In fact, the *Student* class could be declared after the *Display* function is already developed and compiled.

5.5.6 Multiple Inheritance

Multiple inheritance is the most important feature of Version 2.0 of C++. See Section 3.6 for a complete coverage of multiple inheritance. Briefly, in C++ it allows a newly derived class definition to inherit public and protected members from more than one base class. The following syntax can be used to define a newly derived class definition that inherits from several base classes:

```
class <new-derived-class>:
    [virtual] [public | private] <base-class1>
        {, [virtual] [public | private] <base-class2>...}
{
...
}
```

where *<base-class1>*, *<base-class2>*, and so on are existing class definitions. A base class may not be specified more than once. The *virtual* keyword is explained later in this section.

In the following example, derived class *C* inherits members from both *A* and *B* classes. The public instance variables *a* from class *A* and *b* from *B* class are accessible to the class *C* definition.

```
class A
{
    public:
        int a;
}

class B
{
    public:
        int b;
}

class C: public A, public B
{
        int c;
        f() { a = 5; b = 6; c = 8;}
}
```

5.5.6.1 Construction/Destruction and Multiple Inheritance

When an object of a derived class is constructed, by default, the base classes are constructed first in the same order as their declaration. The user can override this default by specifying the order of construction explicitly. With single inheritance, the constructor of the derived class does not refer to the name of the base class, since there is only one direct base class. With multiple inheritance, the name of the class definition must be used to refer to the constructor of one of its base classes. The destructors of base classes are invoked in the reverse order of constructors.

In the previous example, if classes *A* and *B* both had constructors, then the class *C* constructor would invoke *A*'s constructor first, then *B*'s. The class *C* constructor can invoke *A* and *B* class constructors explicitly. To override the order of construction, the class *C* can be changed to the following:

```
class C: public A, public B
{
        int c;
    public:
        C (Ana, Ab, Ac)
            : B(Ab), A(Ana)
            {c = Ac};

}
```

Thus the class *B* constructor is called first, followed by *A*'s.

5.5.6.2   *Virtual Base Class*

In C++ multiple inheritance actually makes a copy of all members of its base classes (see Section 3.6). To illustrate this point, we will use the class hierarchy in Figure 5.1; where classes *B* and *C* inherit from *A*, and class *D* inherits from both *B* and *C*. Consequently, class *D* will have two copies of members from *A*: one through class *B* and the other through *C*.

In some cases, this behavior is wanted. But to avoid it, C++ provides virtual base classes. A virtual base class guarantees that only one copy of the base class members will be created for the derived class. In Figure 5.1, if both *B* and *C* define *A* as a virtual base class, then class *D* will have only a single copy of *A*'s members.

In the following example, class *Person* is defined as a virtual base class for both *Student* and *Staff* classes. Thus the *WorkStudy* derived class has only one copy of *Person* member (*name*).

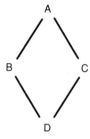

Figure 5.1 Typical class hierarchy.

```
class Person
{
    public:
        char *name;
};


class Student : virtual public Person
{
    public:
        char *ID;
};


class Staff : virtual public Person
{
    public:
        char *office;
};


class WorkStudy : public Student, public Staff
{
};
```

5.5.6.3 Resolving Ambiguity

With multiple inheritance, there is the possibility of inheriting multiple members with the same name (see Section 3.6). To resolve the conflict, the ambiguous member can be qualified by its class name.

In the following example, references to *ID* in method *GetID* are ambiguous. Two instance variables with the same name (*ID*) are inherited from *Student* and *Staff* classes.

```
class Student
{
    protected:
        int ID;
};


class Staff
{
    protected:
        int ID;
};
```

```
class WorkStudy : public Student, public Staff;
{
    public:
        GetId () { return ID; // error } ;
};
```

To resolve the ambiguity, the above *GetId* method can be redefined as:

```
GetId () { return Staff::ID} ;
```

With a shared virtual base class, no ambiguity exists when referencing the shared virtual base class members, since only one copy of its members are inherited. Thus, in the class hierarchy of the first *WorkStudy* example, the *name* instance variable of *Person* class definition can be referenced by *WorkStudy* objects without any conflict.

■ 5.6 OVERLOADING/OVERRIDING AND DYNAMIC BINDING IN C++

Most existing languages support overloading of system-defined operators and functions. For example, the arithmetic operators ($+,-,*$) are applied on both integers and floating point numbers. Or the same I/O function name, *printf* in C, can be used for different types of system-defined data types.

There are several advantages to overloading. One is notational convenience. Another is reducing the number of function names needed to support numerous data types. Yet a third is extending the use of language operators for user-defined types. Imagine the added complexity if one addition operator were required for integers and another for floating point numbers.

C++ lets the user provide several definitions for the same function or operator name. The following subsections discuss this type of overloading. First attention is given to function overloading, second to dynamic binding, and finally to operator overloading.

5.6.1 Function Overloading

Function overloading allows the same function name to be applied with different types and quantities of arguments (see Section 2.3). The same function name can be used to perform operations on different data types. Several functions can share a name but completely different implementations. C++ uses the following information to distinguish among different versions of the same overloaded function name:

- parameter types
- number of parameters

For example, the task is to define two doubler "functions" with the same name. One doubles the value of an integer variable. The second doubles the contents of a character string.

```
int Doubler(int a)
{
    return a * 2;
}

char *Doubler(char *ch)
{
    char *new = malloc(2 * strlen(ch));
    strcpy(new, ch);
    strcat(new, ch);
    return new;
}
```

Each one of the doubler functions has a different type of argument and returns a different type of result. Each accomplishes a completely different task. The first *Doubler* function computes the result by multiplying the input parameter by two. And the second one doubles the input string by concatenating the input string to itself.

5.6.2 Dynamic Binding

In Section 5.5.5, the virtual functions were discussed in detail. These functions allow dynamic binding of function names. (See Section 2.4 for a complete discussion of dynamic binding.) Remember, however, that virtual functions have subtle but significant differences from the function overloading just discussed. The major differences are:

1. Virtual function overloading can only be done within a class hierarchy. Therefore, virtual functions support *overriding* as discussed in Section 3.3.
2. When a function is virtually overloaded, the type and number of arguments, and the resultant type are the *same* for all overloaded functions.
3. Unlike function overloading, virtual functions bind at run time not compile time.

5.6.3 Operator Overloading

Operator overloading allows redefinition of the C operators for any user-defined class. This feature permits the user to redefine any one of the operators listed in Table 5.1. Operator overloading is essentially a sugar-coated member function that greatly

Table 5.1 C++ operators that can be overloaded.

+	−	*	/	%	^	&	|	~	!	=	<	>
+=	−=	*=	/=	%=	^=	&=	|=	->	->*,			
<<	>>	>>=	<<=	==	!=	<=	>=	&&	||	++	−−	
[]	()	*new delete*										

enhances the readability of the program. Instead of defining a member function with one or two arguments, the user may apply a language-defined operator. (See Section 2.2 for operator overloading in general and Section 3.3 for a discussion on overriding.)

The justification in favor of operator overloading is as strong as that for having operators for language-defined types like integer and character. Imagine how a program would look if the programmer could not use +, −, and other operators. Instead it would be necessary to resort to calling functions such as *add*, *minus*, and so on.

When overloading operators in C++, a few points must be kept in mind. First, the arity of an operator cannot be changed, binary operators remain binary and unary operators remain unary. Second, the precedence of operators cannot be altered. Therefore the user must keep in mind the precedence table when overloading operators for a user-defined class. Third, when ++ and −− operators are overloaded, it is not possible to distinguish between the postfix and prefix notation.

Binary or unary operators can be defined either as friend functions or as member functions. If defined as a friend function, all operands are specified as arguments.

If the operator is defined as a member function, then the left operand is automatically supplied. The hidden argument (pseudovariable), called *this*, points to the left operand. The only argument to the member function specifies the right operand.

To overload an operator the following function declaration syntax must be used:

<return-type>operator <op-type>(<operand(s)>)

For example, to overload the + operator for a class called complex, the following member function is declared:

Complex operator + (Complex &Right)

Note that only the right-hand operand is specified. As stated previously, the left-hand operand is supplied automatically if the operator is defined as a member function.

The class definition for complex numbers will be:

```
class Complex {
        int Real;
        int Imaginary;

    public:
        Complex(int rl = 0, int ig = 0)
            /* default parameters for constructor */
            { Real = rl; Imaginary = ig;} ;
        Complex operator + (Complex& Right);
        Complex operator + (int& Right);
        Complex operator = (Complex& Right);
```

```
        Complex operator = (int& Right);
        friend Complex operator - (Complex& Left,
                                        Complex& Right);
        friend Complex operator - (Complex& Left,
                                        int& Right);
};
```

There are overloaded + operators for two different types of right-hand side operands. The first one allows two complex numbers to be added, while the second adds an integer number to the real portion of a complex number.

Notice that the previous example introduced two new features of C++: default parameter values and reference parameters:

1. *Default Parameter Values*. Default parameters allow specification of a default value for missing arguments. In the above example, if either of the arguments to the constructor is missing, the default value *0* will be used.

   Note that in the previous example, all the following declarations are legal:

   ```
   Complex a;        /* Real = 0 and Imaginary = 0 */
   Complex b(2, 3);  /* Real = 2 and Imaginary = 3 */
   Complex c(2);     /* Real = 2 and Imaginary = 0 */
   Complex d(,3);    /* Real = 0 and Imaginary = 3 */
   ```

2. *Reference Parameters*. Reference parameters essentially provide true call by reference. Prior to C++, pointer parameters had to be passed to emulate call by reference parameters. With this new feature, the compiler handles call by reference directly.

   To use this feature, the parameter must be declared as:

   ```
   <type> & <parameter-name>
   ```

   In the previous example, all arguments of an overloaded operator are declared as reference parameters. In the case of the assignment operator, the contents of the left-hand side are modified at the end. Any use of the parameter in the function is implicitly dereferenced (unlike pointers).

The following example illustrates how complex number operators are used:

```
main()
{
    Complex a(1,3);
    Complex b;
    Complex c = Complex(4,3);
    Complex d;
```

```
        b = a + c;
        d = a - b;
        b = a - 1;
        a = b - Complex(0,1);
}
```

The example defines four complex number objects: *a*, *b*, *c*, and *d*. The first declaration defines complex number object *a* and initializes the real portion to *1* and imaginary portion to *3*. The next one defines complex number object *b*, initializing the real portion to *0* and imaginary portion to *0*. The last value is determined by the default parameters. The following line defines complex number object *c* and assigns the value of complex number constant *4 + 3i*.

After execution of *b = a + c*, complex number object *b* will have *5* as its real portion and *6* as its imaginary portion. (See next section for the implementation of +.)

Here, now is a display of the actual implementation of some of the overloaded operators. The entire complex number class definition is presented in Section 5.9.1.

```
Complex Complex::operator + (Complex &Right)
{
        Complex Res;

        Res.Real = this -> Real + Right.Real;
        Res.Imaginary = this -> Imaginary + Right.Imaginary;

        return Res;
}

Complex operator - (Complex& Left, Complex& Right)
{
        complex Res;

        Res.Real = Left.Real - Right.Real;
        Res.Imaginary = left.Imaginary - Right.Imaginary;
        return Res;
}
```

The first operator is declared as a member function. Therefore the left-hand operand is hidden and is represented by the object *this*. In C++, *this* is a predefined object that always points to the current object invoking the member function. In operator overloading *this* object is always the left operand.

The last operator defines the subtraction operator for complex numbers. Here, the operator has been declared as a friend function. Thus both the left- and the right-hand side operands are present as arguments.

Currently C++ does not support parametric polymorphism directly (see Section 2.5). Multiple inheritance can be used to incorporate generic types. For example, given the following class definitions called *Array* and *Person*, a newly derived class can be defined called *PersonArray* (Wiener and Pinson, 1989).

The *Array* class allows manipulation of a homogeneous collection. We have specified only a limited portion of the *Array* class definition to make the example manageable. This class definition can easily have a large collection of methods and overloaded operator definitions.

```
typedef void* elem;

class Array
{
    private:
        elem *val;
        unsigned size;

    public:
        Array (int ArraySize)
        {
            size = ArraySize;
            val = new elem[size];
        }

        ~Array(void) { delete val;}
        // Accessing Methods—only one specified here
        elem& operator[] (unsigned AnIndex);
        // other accessing methods ....
};

elem& Array::operator[] (unsigned AnIndex)
{
        // Warning: No limit checking done here
        return val [AnIndex – 1];
}
```

The following *PersonArray* class definition allows the user to define objects that are arrays of *Person* objects.

```
class PersonArray : public Array, public Person
{
    public:

    // Constructor
    PersonArray (int ArraySize) : Array (ArraySize) {}
```

```
// Accessing Methods
Person& operator [] (unsigned AnIndex)
{
      return
            (Person&) Array::operator[] (AnIndex);}
};
```

Given the above class definition and the *Person* class definition defined earlier in this chapter, the following code segment can be written:

```
PersonArray Class101 (50);
Person Wendy;
short i;
  . .

  . .

  . .
Class101 [i]  = Wendy;
  . .

  . .

  . .
for (int index  = 1; index  < = 50; index  ++)
      printf("%s", Class101 [index]  –> name);
```

▪ 5.7 SPECIFICATION VERSUS IMPLEMENTATION

One of the major advantages of object-oriented systems is that specification and implementation of a class declaration are separate from each other. Since the actual definition of a member does not change, the implementation of any member can be altered without affecting the clients or users of the class.

The actual class declaration can be specified in an *include* file, or *.hpp* file. The implementation of member and friend functions can be defined in a separate source program, or *.cpp* file. Clients of a class definition include the header file before instantiating and invoking methods of the class. In Section 5.9, both case studies presented demonstrate this capability.

▪ 5.8 STREAMS IN C++

C++ provides a new library for performing I/O: *<stream.h>*. Streams perform serial I/O on formatted and unformatted data. Besides supporting system-defined types (*int, short, char, float,* and so on) such streams can be extended to support user-defined classes. This capability exists because streams are defined as classes. As with all C++ operators, users can overload stream input and output operators with user-defined types.

This section introduces streams in C++. Section 5.8.1 examines general characteristics of streams. Section 5.8.2 explores the extension of streams' user-defined classes.

5.8.1 Streams in General

There are three standard streams defined in C++: *cout, cin*, and *cerr*. These three streams are equivalent to *stdout, stdin*, and *stderr* in standard C. The following syntax is used to *output* to a stream:

```
<stream-name> << <data1> << <data2>...
```

where *<stream-name>* is either system defined such as *cout* or a user-defined output stream. The *<data1>*, *<data2>* and others can be character strings, floating point numbers, or integers.

Example: Display the result of an integer variable.

```
#include <stream.h >
main()
{
    int AnIndex = 20;

    cout << "Value of Index = " << AnIndex;
}
```

The following syntax is used to *input* to a stream:

```
<stream-name> >> <data1> >> <data2>...
```

where *<stream-name>* is either system defined such as *cin* or a user-defined input stream. The *<data1>*, *<data2>* and others can be character strings, floating point numbers, or integers.

Example: Input an integer number to a variable called *Index* and display the result.

```
#include <stream.h >
main()
{
    int index;

    cout << "Please Input an integer number";
    cin >> index;
    cout << "Value of index = " << index;
}
```

To perform formatted output, the *form* function can be applied. This function has the following function prototype:

```
char *form(char *format, . . . . );
```

This function is similar to the *printf* function from the *stdio* library in standard C.

Example: Redo the previous example with formatted output.

```
#include <stream.h>
main()
{
    int i;

    cout << "Please Input an integer number";
    cin >> i;
    cout << form("Value of i = %d", i);
}
```

5.8.1.1   Stream States

An input or output stream has four states: *_good*, *_eof*, *_fail*, and *_bad*. After an I/O operation, the above states have the following meaning:

- *_good*, that previous I/O was successful and next input may succeed
- *_eof*, that previous I/O was successful and the end of file has been reached
- *_fail*, that previous I/O was not successful
- *_bad*, that previous I/O was not successful and data may be corrupted

After performing an I/O operation on a stream, the function *rdstate()* can be called to examine the value of the stream state:

```
cin >>. . . . . . . . . . .
while(cin.rdstate() ! = _bad)
{

    . . . . . . . . .
    cin >>. .

}
```

5.8.1.2   Streams Class Definition

As stated previously, a stream is defined as a class. Each stream is defined with two class definitions: one for input and the other for output.

For the input stream the *istream* class declaration has the following definition:

```
class istream
{
    public:
        istream &operator >> (char *);
        istream &operator >> (char &);
        istream &operator >> (short &);
        istream &operator >> (int &);
        istream &operator >> (long &);
        istream &operator >> (float &);
        istream &operator >> (double &);
        stream_state rdstate();
}
```

Notice that in input stream all the data operands are passed by reference. This is necessary since the contents of the operand may be modified if the input operation is successful.

Output streams are objects of the *ostream* class declaration which has the following definition:

```
class ostream
{
    public:
        ostream &operator << (char *);
        ostream &operator << (int i);
        ostream &operator << (long);
        ostream &operator << (double);
        ostream &put(char);
};
```

Notice that both classes define overloaded operators >> and <<. These two operators can also be overloaded with user-defined data types at any time.

5.8.2   Extending Stream I/O Definition

Notice that we have not shown the full definition of both class definitions. The reader is encouraged to examine contents of <*stream.h*> (Stroustrup, 1986) for more detail.

How to extend stream I/O for a user-defined class is now demonstrated with an example.

Example: Overload the output stream to display *Person* objects.

```
ostream& operator <<(ostream& s, Person p)
{
    return s << "(" << p.Name << ", "
        << p.Age << ", ";
}
```

Example: Overload the input stream for *Person* objects as (Name, Age).

```
const OpenParen = '(';
const CloseParen = ')';
const Comma = ',';

istream &operator >> (istream &s, Person &p)
{
    // Person objects are read in as (name, age)

    char ch;
    char name[20];
    int i = 0;
    int age = 0;

    name[0] = '/0';

    s >> ch;
    if (ch == OpenParen) {
        s >> ch;
        while(isalpha(ch)) {
            name[i++] =ch;
            s >> ch;
        }
        name[i] = '/0';
        if (ch == Comma)
            s >> age >> ch;
        if (ch != CloseParen)
            s.clear(_fail);
    }
    else
        s.clear(_eof);

    if (s) p = Person(name, age);
        return s;
}
```

Note that the code calls the member function *clear* in two places. This function sets the state of either an input or an output stream. In the first call, the value of output stream is set to *_fail* upon discovering an unexpected input character.

Example: This example demonstrates how the previously overloaded operators for *Person* class can be applied.

```
#include <stream>
#include <person.hpp>
main()
{
    Person Wanda("Wanda",22);
    Person Joe;

    cout << Wanda;
    cin >> Joe;
    cout << Joe;
}
```

We assume that *person.hpp* includes declaration for the *Person* class and the overloaded stream I/O operators defined earlier.

Given the following as the input on *cin* device:

```
(JOE, 32)
```

the following will be displayed on *cout* device:

```
(Wanda, 22)
(Joe, 32)
```

■ 5.9 CASE STUDIES

This section presents two case studies in C++. The first one presents the complete class definition for complex numbers. And the second case study presents an electronic design class hierarchy.

5.9.1 Case Study One—Complex Numbers

This section applies the overloading capabilities of C++ to deal with complex number arithmetic. Complex numbers are represented in the current generation of programming languages through indirect means demonstrated later in this section. Object orientation concepts such as operator overloading can be used to extend language constructs such as arithmetic operators to support complex numbers directly in the language.

Section 5.9.1.1 discusses the approach taken in the current generation of programming languages to represent a numbering system for complex numbers. Section 5.9.1.2 demonstrates the representation in C++ using object orientation concepts.

5.9.1.1 *Supporting a Complex Number System in C*

In order to represent complex number system support for both structural components (real and imaginary numbers) and the operational (addition, subtraction, and so on) components must be provided.

Complex numbers can be supported in C through the *struct* construct and a set of functions as:

```
struct complex
{
    int real;
    int imaginary;
};


typedef struct complex Complex;


AddComplex (Complex *Left, Complex *Right, Complex *Res)
{

    Res –> real = Left –> real + Right –> real;
    Res –> imaginary = Left –> imaginary + Right –> imaginary;

}
```

The *struct* construct supports the representation of the structural components. And the set of functions provides the operational support such as addition and subtraction. For example,

```
AddComplex(&a, &b, &c)
```

where *a*, *b*, and *c* are structures representing complex numbers and *AddComplex* is a function that computes addition of *a* and *b* and returns the result in *c*.

With input and output of complex numbers, we can use procedures that perform transformation between the file format of complex number, that is, (*a*, *b*) and the internal representation as a structure.

The problem with this solution is that complex numbers are supported through indirect means. The language should allow the application developer to extend the definition of language constructs and operators to support new user-defined types.

5.9.1.2 *Supporting a Complex Number System in C++*

Complex numbers can be represented directly in C++ since the language allows operators to be overloaded (refer to Section 5.6). To represent complex numbers directly in the language, a class called *complex* is defined to support the following:

I. Instance variables: *real* and *imaginary* integers to contain the real and imaginary portions of the complex number.

II. Methods:

   A. Constructor and destructor methods: Ability to create and destroy complex numbers as needed.

   B. Arithmetic operations: Ability to perform the Arithmetic on complex numbers. The following C++ operators are overloaded to perform arithmetic operations on two complex numbers:

      i. + for summation

      ii. − for subtraction

      iii. * for multiplication

      iv. / for division.

   C. Assignment operation: Ability to assign the value of one complex number to another. The C++ operator = is overloaded to assign the value of one complex number to another.

   D. I/O operations: Ability to overload input and output with direct representation of complex number as *(a, b)*.

   E. Retrieval and update operations: Ability to retrieve or update imaginary and the real portions of any complex number.

5.9.1.2.1 Complex Class definition

Figure 5.2 displays the definition of the class called *complex*. This class definition supports all the instance variables and methods of complex numbers discussed in the previous section. This figure contains a complete source for the module *complex.hpp*. The implementation of the smaller methods are included within the class definition. The implementation of remaining methods are defined in a separate module called *complex.cpp*.

Notice that instance variables *real* and *imaginary* are hidden from the user of the class. (Defined as private members.) Currently, *int* is used to represent both numbers. In the future, a user may choose to change the representation to *double*. To make this change happen, only the implementation of methods associated with the *complex* class will change. This technique localizes the changes, thus making the maintenance task much easier.

```
class complex
{
            // Instance variables used for complex number.
            int real;          // Real portion
            int imaginary;   // Imaginary portion
    public:
            // methods to construct a complex number
            /* Note that default values of 0 are set up
             * if no values are specified.
             */
            complex(int rl=0, int imag=0)
            {real=rl;
             imaginary=imag;
            }

            // methods to retrieve complex number values.
            GetImag() {return imaginary;}
            GetReal() {return real;}

            // methods to update complex number values.
            SetImag(int imag) {imaginary=imag;}
            SetReal(int rl) {real=rl;}

            /* overloaded operators(+,-,*,/) to perform
             * addition, subtraction,
             * multiplication, division of two
             * complex numbers.
             */
            complex operator+(complex &right);
            complex operator-(complex &right);
            complex operator*(complex &right);
            complex operator/(complex &right);

            /* overloaded operator(=) to assign value of
             * one complex number to another.
             */

            operator=(complex &expr);

            /* overloaded stream operators to allow input
             * and output of complex numbers.
             */
            friend ostream& operator<<(ostream&, complex&);
            friend istream& operator>>(istream&, complex&);
};
```

Figure 5.2 The module complex.hpp.

5.9.1.2.2   Complex Class Implementation

This section presents the implementation of methods (overloaded operators) used for complex numbers. Figure 5.3 displays the code for the entire module containing the implementation of these methods.

To demonstrate the coding techniques, we repeat the method used for the addition operation here.

```
// Overloaded arithmetic operators for complex numbers.
complex complex::operator + (complex &right)
{
    complex res;

    res.real = this -> real + right.real;
    res.imaginary = this -> imaginary + right.imaginary;

    return res;
}
```

Two complex numbers, left and right operand, are added together and the result is returned. Notice that only the right operand is represented in the argument list. The left operand is the object that the methods (overloaded operator) is invoked on. The *this* pointer refers to the left-hand side operand.

5.9.1.2.3   Using complex numbers

The program listed in Figure 5.4 demonstrates how the complex number representation can be applied. Notice that arithmetic operators are applied directly on complex numbers such as *a* and *b*. Also, the I/O stream overloading permits the direct transfer of complex objects between the program and file system.

5.9.2   Case Study Two—Electronic CAD

Computer-aided technologies ranging from mechanical, electrical and electronic CAD, to computer-aided software engineering (CASE) are apt to benefit from object orientation tremendously. These technologies require representation of complex objects. The example in this section demonstrates use of object orientation (inheritance and data hiding) to represent complex CAD entities.

Section 5.9.2.1 describes the design and implementation of the components and Section 5.9.2.2 demonstrates a sample program utilizing these components.

5.9.2.1   Design and Implementation of ECAD Components

A class hierarchy as depicted in Figure 1.17 models different types of ECAD objects. Members of ECAD class or its subclasses should be able to perform the operations listed in Chapter 1. In the class hierarchy, the top-level classes called *ECAD, Pads,*

```
#include <stream.hpp>
#include "complex.hpp"
/*********************************************************
   Definition of overloaded operators for complex numbers.
   ********************************************************/
// Overloaded arithmetic operators for complex numbers.
complex complex::operator+(complex &right)
{
        complex res;
        res.real = this->real + right.real;
        res.imaginary = this->imaginary + right.imaginary;
        return res;
}

complex complex::operator-(complex &right)
{
        complex res;
        res.real = this->real - right.real;
        res.imaginary = this->imaginary - right.imaginary;
        return res;
}

complex complex::operator*(complex &right)
{
        complex res;

        res.real = this->real * right.real
            - this->imaginary * right.imaginary;

        res.imaginary = this->real * right.imaginary
            + this->imaginary * right.real;

        return res;
}


complex::operator=(complex &expr)
{
        this->real = expr.real;
        this->imaginary = expr.imaginary;
}
```

Figure 5.3 The module complex.cpp.

```
// Overloaded operators for I/O stream operations.
/* Overload ostream << operator to display
 *          complex number as (real, imag)
 */
ostream& operator<<(ostream &strm, complex &OutNum)
{
        return
            strm << "(" << OutNum.real << ","
                 << OutNum.imaginary << ")";
}


/* Overload istream >> operator to a input complex number
 *          as (real, imag)
 */
istream& operator>>(istream &strm, complex &InNum)
{
        char InChar = 0;      // Input character
        int real=0, imag=0;
                              // Real and Imaginary input numbers.

        strm >> InChar;
        if (InChar == '(')
    {
                strm >> real >> InChar;
                if (InChar == ',') strm >> imag >> InChar;
                if (InChar != ')') strm.clear(_bad);
        }
        else
                strm.putback(InChar);


        if (strm) InNum = complex(real, imag);
        return strm;
}
```

Figure 5.3 (Continued)

and *Gates* are generic class definitions. There will never be an object that is a direct member of any of these classes. These classes serve as the hub of generic methods and instance variables for the entire class hierarchy.

Each one of the specialized subclass definitions such as *InPad*, *OutPad*, and *And2* have their own specialized instance variables and specialized methods.

```
#include <stream.hpp>
#include <stdio.h>
#include <complex.hpp>

main()
{
        complex a;
        complex b(3,4);
        complex c,d;

        cout << "Please input a complex number (real, imag)";
        cin >> a;

        cout << "\n" << " a = " << a;
        cout << "\n" << " b = " << b;
        cout << "\n" << " a - b =" << a - b;

        c = a + complex(2,7) - b;

        cout << "\n" << " c = " << c;

        d = c *(a + b) / b;

        cout << "\n" << " d = " << d;

        // Change Imaginary and Real values of b
        b.SetImag(3);
        b.SetReal(4);

        cout << "\n" << " b = " << b;
        cout << "\n" << " a + b = " << a + b;
}
```

Figure 5.4 The module complex_test.cpp.

Notice that the same function name should be used to evaluate, move, or draw any ECAD object. There should be no need to have a function called *eval_And2* and *eval_Or2*. One overloaded function called *eval* should be able to operate on any ECAD object. Figure 5.5a presents the implementation of the ECAD class definition.

This section presents the design and implementation of ECAD components. We present the general strategy followed throughout the design. Next the design and implementation of some of the major components such as ports, pads, and gates are demonstrated.

5.9.2.1.1   Design of Ports and Interconnections

Ports are used to interconnect two or more ECAD components. Anyone of these ports can be connected to one or more components. When the output port of a gate is connected to two or more components, the result obtained from this gate drives the input ports of all outgoing components. When two or more components are connected to a given input port, the result obtained from conjunction of the incoming ports drives the input port. In the *And2* gates, discussed later, two input ports and one output port are required.

The *Port* class definition must support the following:

1. *Instance variables* represent the list of connections. A linked list is used to provide multidirectional connections to a port. Each node on this list contains a pointer to the node connected and a pointer to the next point in this list.
2. *Methods*
   a. Connecting one or more ECAD objects to a port.
   b. Evaluating the result of a conjunction of connections.

Figure 5.5*b* displays the *Port* class definition and Figure 5.6 (see page 229) displays the code for the implementation of the methods specified above.

5.9.2.1.2   Design and Implementation of Pads

Pads are used to communicate data between a logic circuit and the outside world. Two kinds of pads are under consideration: input and output pads. Figure 5.5*c* displays the implementation of *Pad, InPad,* and *OutPad* class definitions.

Input pads are used to drive the circuit with binary states such as *on* or *off.* Since only 8-bit data are considered here, then an input pad can accept 8-bit data only. To support an input pad the following are needed:

1. *Instance variable:* 8-bit unsigned data, holds the current state of the input pad.
2. *Methods:* evaluate the result of the input pad.

Output pads are used to communicate the result of a logic circuit to the outside world. An output pad is connected to the output ports of one or more ECAD components. In order to support an output pad the following are needed:

1. *Instance variable:* a port allowing connection to one or more ECAD components.
2. *Methods*
   a. Connection to ECAD components, one or more ECAD components can be connected to an output pad.
   b. Evaluate the result of the output pad. This is done by evaluating the result of the logic circuit(s) connected to the port of this pad.

```
#define NULL 0
#define NULLPort (Port *) NULL

class ECAD {
    // No Instance variable used with ECAD objects.
    public:
    // Methods attached to all ECAD objects.

    // evaluate the ECAD  object.
       virtual unsigned char Eval() { return 0;}
    // draw the ECAD object.
       virtual Draw() {}

    // move the ECAD object.
       virtual Move() {}

    // check for loops within this ECAD object.
       virtual CheckForLoops() {}
};
```

Figure 5.5a The module cad.hpp.

```
/* this class is  used to connect several ECAD objects
   together.
*/
class  Port : public ECAD {
  protected:
    // Instance Variable used with port objects
    ECAD *connection;  // Connection to the port
    Port *next;        // next port connection.
  public:

    // Methods attached to the port objects.
    // define the constructor
    Port(ECAD *node = NULL)
    {
       connection=node;
          next = NULLPort;
    }
    // connect another node to the same junction
    AddConnection(ECAD *node);
    unsigned char Eval();
};
```

Figure 5.5b The module cad.hpp.

```
// Definition for pads
class Pad : public ECAD {
  protected:
    // Instance variables
    Port *APort;
  public:
    // Methods attached
    Pad() {APort = NULLPort;}
    Conn(ECAD *node) {APort->AddConnection(node);}
};

class InPad : public Pad {
  protected:
    unsigned char value;
  public:
    InPad(unsigned char val = 0) : () {value = val;}
    unsigned char Eval() { return value;}
};

class OutPad : public Pad {
  public:
    OutPad() : () {APort = new Port;}
    unsigned char Eval() { return APort->Eval();}
};
```

Figure 5.5c The module cad.hpp.

5.9.2.1.3 Design of Gates

This section concentrates on the design of **and** gates, only. The design of other gates is similar. First, the design of an **and** gate with two inputs (*And2*) is presented, followed by the design of an **and** gate with three inputs (*And3*). Figure 5.5*d* presents the implementation of the class definitions of all gates. The *And2* class definition needs to support the following:

1. *Instance variables:* represent the two input ports and the one output port.
2. *Methods:* evaluate the current **and** object.

The *And3* class definition inherits the input and output ports of *And2* class definition and adds a third input port. The methods required for this class are the same as its superclass with the added code required for the third input port, so the *And2* methods are invoked within the *And3* methods.

```
class Gates : public ECAD {};

// two input and gate
class And2 : public Gates {
  protected:
    Port *in1;
    Port *in2;
  public:

    // constructor for and gate
    And2(ECAD *i1 = NULL, ECAD *i2 = NULL)
      {in1 = new Port(i1);
       in2 = new Port(i2);
      }

    // evaluator for and gate
    unsigned char Eval()
            { return in1->Eval() & in2->Eval();}
};

// three input and gate
class And3 : public And2 {
  protected:
    Port *in3;
  public:


    // constructor for three input and gate
    And3(ECAD *i1 = NULL, ECAD *i2 = NULL, ECAD *i3 = NULL)
      :(i1, i2) {in3 = new Port(i3);}

    // evaluator for and gate
    unsigned char Eval()
            { return And2::Eval() & in3->Eval();}
};
```

Figure 5.5d The module cad.hpp.

5.9.2.2 An ECAD Sample Program

Figure 5.7 displays the C++ implementation of a logic circuit applying the library of ECAD components defined. The logic circuit implemented is presented in Figure 5.8. Notice that the same function *Eval* is used to evaluate the result of any ECAD component.

```
/* This module contains the implementation of methods used
 * for ECAD port components.
 */

#include "cad.hpp"

Port::AddConnection(ECAD *node)
{

    Port *last = this;
    if (last->connection == NULL)
    {
         last->connection = node;
       return;
    }
    while (last->next != NULLPort)
       last = last->next;
    last->next = new Port(node);
    return;
}

/* Evaluate the result of this ports. Its done by logical
        ORing all connected ports.
  */
unsigned char Port::Eval()
{
   unsigned char result = 0;

   Port *last = this;
   while (last != NULLPort)
   {

        result |= last->connection->Eval();
      last = last->next;
   }
        return result;
}
```

Figure 5.6 The module cad.cpp.

```
#include <stdio.h>
#include "cad.hpp"
main()
{
        // Allocate the input pads.
        ECAD *P1 = new InPad(7);
        ECAD *P2 = new InPad(129);

        // Declare the output pads.
        OutPad OP1;
        OutPad OP2;
        OutPad OP3;
        OutPad OP4;

        // Define the logic circuit and their interconnections.
        ECAD *G1 = new And2(P1, P2);
        ECAD *G2 = new Or2(P1, P2);
        ECAD *G3 = new And3(G1, G2, P1);
        ECAD *G4 = new Adder2(G1, G2);

    // Connect the output pads to their logic circuits.
        OP1.Conn(G1);
        OP3.Conn(G2);
        OP2.Conn(G3);
        OP4.Conn(G4);

        // Display the result of each output pad.

        printf("\nResult of and = %d ", OP1.Eval());
        printf("\nResult of or = %d ", OP2.Eval());
        printf("\nResult of and3 = %d ", OP3.Eval());
        printf("\nResult of adder2 = %d ", OP4.Eval());
}
```

Figure 5.7 The module cadtest.cpp.

■ 5.10 SUMMARY

C++ is emerging as the object-oriented language of the 90s. Already major computer vendors are rallying behind this language. This chapter presented a comprehensive discussion on the object orientation features of C++. The language provides constructs to define abstract data types. These constructs are the new *class* construct and extended C *struct* and *union* constructs. With numerous examples the authors have demonstrated the treatment of instance variables and methods in C++. The language also provides inheritance. Section 5.5 covered a wide variety of topics in inheritance:

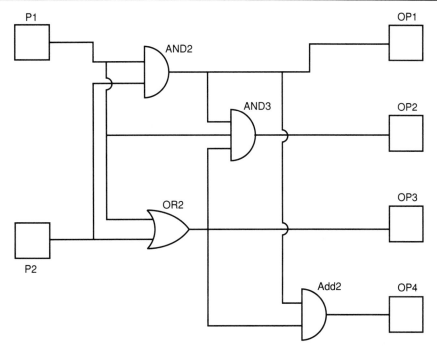

Figure 5.8 Logic circuit in ECAD case study.

The importance of base and derived classes in C++; construction and destruction of objects within a hierarchy; the role of protected members and virtual functions; and support of multiple inheritance. Polymorphism and dynamic binding were described in Section 5.6. This section examined function and operator overloading and dynamic binding.

The authors turned to stream I/O in Section 5.7 and demonstrated how the stream I/O subsystem can be extended to support any user-defined type. Finally, the chapter closed by presenting two complete examples in C++. After all, the best way to learn a new language is by experimentation. These two case studies can be used by the reader to learn object orientation features of C++. Complex numbers is a simple example, yet it illustrates much of the power of C++ (and other object-oriented languages). The CAD example gives a small sample of existing applications that use object orientation today. The next chapter turns to another popular object-oriented language, namely Ada.

6

ADA

■ 6.1 INTRODUCTION

Chapters 2, 3, and 4 provided a comprehensive coverage of abstract data types, inheritance, and object identity. Chapter 5 examined the C++ language, one of the most powerful and popular object-oriented languages. This chapter examines the object-oriented features of the Ada programming language. Ada is the result of a U.S. Department of Defense (DoD) effort to reduce the cost of software development. Currently the DoD, in its many different systems, has code from a few hundred different computer languages. The cost of maintaining software in such a large number of diverse languages is undoubtedly staggering. Ada is reputed to be the *last* language. The DoD intends Ada to be the language of choice for all future embedded system development.

Ada contains the usual control structures and the ability to define types and subprograms. It provides modular design via the *package* concept. Packages allow language components and constructs, types, data, and subprograms to be divided into logical design pieces. Modularity is also provided by allowing separate compilation units. Packages correspond to the notion of classes, as described in the previous chapters. Ada supports parametric polymorphism.

In addition to the object-oriented constructs, Ada provides constructs to aid development of real-time applications. These include models to handle parallel executing tasks and exceptions. These constructs are not discussed in this chapter. For a complete coverage of Ada refer to Booch (1986) or ANSI-MIL-STD-1815A-1983.

6.1.1 Chapter Organization

Section 6.2 discusses object-oriented features of Ada in brief. Section 6.3 explains type declaration via the subtype and derived type declarations. Overloading of functions and operators is covered in Section 6.4. Section 6.5 explores the powerful *package* constructs. Parametric polymorphism is examined in Section 6.6.

■ 6.2 OBJECT ORIENTATION IN ADA

This section provides a quick overview of the object orientation capabilities in Ada. Protracted debates continue over whether Ada can be considered an object-oriented language (Seidewitz, 1987; Booch 1986; and Colland 1989). Ada supports object orientation concepts such as abstract data types, overloading of functions and operators, parametric polymorphism, and even specialization of user-defined types (see Chapter 2). The only object-oriented concept lacking is inheritance (see Chapter 3).

Ada supports abstract data types via the notion of *packages*. Packages allow users to group logically related entities together as one unit. User-defined types can be defined based on specialization of existing system types or other user-defined types.

Function names and system-defined operators can be overloaded with user-defined definitions. Parametric polymorphism (see Section 2.5) is achieved via *generic units*. A generic unit is either a generic subprogram or package unit. Generic units are parameterized templates for design units. These templates can be developed with only limited knowledge of the actual objects or constructs to be defined when the templates are invoked.

In regard to object identity, like most conventional languages, Ada supports (virtual) pointers. Objects can be uniquely identified by name or (virtual) address. Objects can be referenced by subparts of another object. Chapter 4 covers object identity in detail.

■ 6.3 ADA TYPE CONSTRUCTS

Ada is a strongly typed language, which means that:

1. The only operations allowed on an object are those defined as valid for the type of which the object is a member; and
2. Objects are typed statically at compile time.

To illustrate the first point, consider an object that has been defined as an integer. The only valid operations that can be performed on it are those that are defined for integer types, such as arithmetic or relational operations. The second statement means that before an object is used, a type must be declared. Also, the type declared for this object cannot be modified at run time.

This section covers typing in Ada with concentration on the object-oriented features. The complete type system is covered in more detail in Booch (1986) and ANSI-MIL-STD-1815A-1983. The overall type system is briefly outlined first. Specific object-oriented features are then covered in more detail in the following subsections.

Ada supports scalar, homogeneous aggregate (array), and heterogeneous aggregate (record) type declarations. In addition, it allows enumerated types, types derived from other predefined types, record definitions with variant components, and objects referencing other objects.

New types can be defined based on predefined user or system types. For example, here a type *Positive* is defined, where only the subset of integers ranging from 1 to the largest integer are permitted:

```
type Positive is range 1. .INTEGER'LAST;
```

The notation *INTEGER'LAST* specifies the largest integer. This provides some support of inheritance or subtyping through restrictions (see Section 3.3). As discussed in Section 3.2, the *Positive* subtype of integers is not "closed" under all the integer operations. For example, the difference of two positive integers (10 − 100) could be a negative integer (−90).

To define *String* as an array of characters the following can be specified:

```
type String is array(Positive range <>) of CHARACTER;
```

Gates can be represented as a record that represents electronic gates such as:

1. Two- and three-input *and* gates
2. Two- and three-input *or* gates and
3. Two-input exclusive *or* gates.

The following defines *GateTypes* in Ada:

```
type GateTypes is (AND2, AND3, OR2, OR3, XOR2);

type Gates (GTypes: GateTypes) is
    record
        In1Port: INTEGER;
        In2Port: INTEGER;
        OutPort: INTEGER;
        case GTypes is
            when AND3 | OR3 => In3Port: INTEGER;
            when others => null;
        end case;
    end record;
```

This type of record definition, called a *variant record*, is the same as the one provided in Pascal. Thus, for gates of type *And3* or *Or3* an additional input port called *In3Port* is defined.

Finally, based on the previous *Gates* declaration it is possible to declare *G1* as a two-input *or* gate and *G2* as a three-input *and* gate:

```
G1 : Gates(OR2);
G2 : Gates(AND3);
```

G1 has two input fields *In1Port* and *In2Port* whereas *G2* has these input ports plus *In3Port*.

6.3.1 Enumeration Types

Enumerated types allow the user to define new types based on a set of enumerated literals. Each enumerated literal must be distinct. An enumerated literal can be either a character literal or an identifier. Each literal has a unique numeric value. This numeric value is based on the position number of the literal in the definition. The position number for the first enumerated literal is zero; the position number for each subsequent literal is one more than the position number of the previous one.

For example, a new enumerated type called *Languages* is defined which can take any one of the enumerated literals: *Chinese, English, French, Spanish, Italian, German, Farsi,* and *Armenian*.

```
type Languages is (Chinese, English, French, Spanish,
                   Italian, German, Farsi, Armenian);
```

These enumerated literals have values ranging from *Chinese*(0), *English*(1) to *Armenian*(7).

The same enumerated literal can be used in more than one enumerated type declaration. In this case, the same literal is overloaded for two distinct enumerated types. The next example, in which a new type for cars made in different countries is defined demonstrates this:

```
type Cars is (American, English, German, French);
```

Here the enumerated literal names: *English, German,* and *French* are overloaded for two different user-defined types: *Cars* and *Languages*. Thus the enumerated literal *English* is overloaded to have the value of 1 and the type of *Cars* in the last type definition, while in the first type declaration the same literal has the value of 2 and the type of *Languages*.

6.3.2 Subtype Definition

Subtype definition allows the user to define a constrained view of an existing system or user-defined type. In Ada, subtype declarations are not new type declarations. They simply provide a new name for a subset of a previously defined type. Subtypes can be defined based on other subtype declarations (see Section 3.2). For instance, we may define a subset of languages to represent *IndoEuropean* languages composed of: *French, English, Armenian, Spanish, Italian, German,* and *Farsi.*

```
subtype IndoEuropean is Languages
    range English .. Armenian;
```

Based on the previous subtype definition, we can define a new subtype called *European* languages where the enumerated literals are: *English, Spanish, French, Italian,* and *German:*

```
subtype European is IndoEuropean range
    English .. German;
```

Subtypes inherit all operations from the predefined type definition. In addition, all subtypes derived from one type definition are equivalent within the boundaries of new constraints. Objects of these subtypes can be mixed together without an explicit conversion, keeping in mind the constraints of the new subtype. For example, given the *IndoEuropean* and *European* subtype definitions, the following objects can be declared:

```
BookTranslated : European := French;
EuroAsian : IndoEuropean := Armenian;
European : European := German;
BookTranslated := EuroAsian;    -- Invalid conversion
EuroAsian := European;          -- Valid conversion
```

The first assignment statement is invalid since the *BookTranslated* is constrained to be the enumerated literals: *English, Spanish, French, Italian,* or *German.* The second assignment statement is valid since the *EuroAsian* enumerated literals include the *European* literals.

The constraint defined on subtypes can be a run-time constraint. For example, the following record definition with variant parts defines a computer type whose instances can be either analog or digital computers.

```
type ComputerTypes is (Analog, Digital);

type Computer(Type: ComputerTypes) is
    record
        FootPrint: FLOAT;   -- In Square footage
        Manufacturer: String(1 .. 20);
        case Type is
            when Analog => VoltageRange : INTEGER;
            when Digital => Base : INTEGER;
        end case;
    end record;
```

The following defines *DigitalComputers* as a subtype of Computer:

```
subtype DigitalComputers
    is Computer(Type => Digital);
```

6.3.3 Derived Type Definition

Another mechanism that provides some limited support of inheritance in Ada is the *derived type*. Unlike subtypes, derived types in Ada define a new type stemming from a predefined type. This new type inherits its characteristics from the parent type. All operations and constraints defined for the parent type are inherited by the derived type. A derived type definition can further constrain the parent type definition just as can a subtype, as discussed in the previous section.

Let us define two new types called *Money* and *Height* derived from the type *FLOAT*:

```
type Money is new FLOAT;
```

```
type Height is new FLOAT;
```

Both new types inherit all operations that can be performed on *FLOAT* type data (+, −, and ∗). Objects of type *Money* and *Height* cannot be mixed together without an explicit conversion. It does not make sense to add an object of type *Money* to an object of type *Height* unless the user explicitly means to do so for peculiar reasons. Unlike inheritance (as discussed in Chapter 3), derived types cannot *extend* or *specialize* the behavior (that is, the operations) of the parent type (the supertype). For example, there is no direct mechanism to define an operation Convert on *Money*.

Like inheritance, the derived type relation is transitive. A newly derived type can be defined based on an existing derived type. The newly derived type declaration can have additional constraints defined or can have the exact structure of the parent type. For example, given the *Money* derived type definition, the following derived type can be defined:

```
type Credit is new Money;
```

Credit now inherits all operations defined on the *Money* type.

Objects belonging to a derived type definition may use any subprogram or operators defined for the parent type prior to the derived type definition. Thus, any operator or subprograms defined for *Money* prior to the *Credit* derived type definition can be applied to objects of type *Credit*. All other operators and subprogram defined for *Money* type after the *Credit* definition will be invisible to objects of type *Credit*.

6.3.4 Type Discriminants

Discriminants permit the definition of parameterized user-defined types (see Section 2.5). Each discriminant acts as a parameter to the type definition. These parameters can specify array size constraints, initial values for type fields, variant record fields and so on.

The following grammar rule is used for type discriminants:

```
<discriminant_part> ::=
    {<discriminant_spec> {;
        <discriminant_spec>}...)
<discriminant_spec> ::=
    {<id_list> :<type_name> [:= <default_expr>]}
```

Each discriminant specification is an identifier of a certain type (or subtype) with an optional expression used as a default value. The next example defines a square matrix whose size is parameterized:

```
type Matrix is array(INTEGER range <>, INTEGER range <>) of REAL;
type SquareMatrix (Size : INTEGER := 4)
    record
        SQ_MT : Matrix(1..Size, 1..Size);
    end record;
```

In this example, *Size* is used to define the size of a square matrix. Thus the following statement declares *CoordMatrix* as 5 by 5 and *EigenMatrix* as 4 by 4.

```
CoordMatrix : SquareMatrix(5);
EigenMatrix : SquareMatrix;
```

Discriminants can be specified for a record type, a private type declaration, or in generic parameter declarations. Within a record type definition, a discriminant is treated as a field of the record definition. Record discriminants can be used for default expression for record components, as variant names, and in component subtype definition.

For instance, this example defines a record to represent a Cartesian coordinate system.

```
type Coordinates(XCoord, YCoord : INTEGER := 0) is
    record
        Name : String(80);
    end record;
```

Thus this type definition contains three fields: *XCoord*, *YCoord*, and *Name*.

■ 6.4 OVERLOADING

Section 2.3 covered operation or method overloading. Ada supports three types of overloading: name, function and subprogram, and operator overloading. Name overloading allows an enumerated literal or a character literal to be used in more than one definition. Subprogram and function overloading permit the overloading of the same subprogram or function name. Finally, operator overloading permits the developer to extend most of the Ada language operators for user-defined types. This section covers each one of these overloading capabilities in detail.

6.4.1 Name Overloading

An enumeration literal or character literal can be used in more than one enumeration type definition. Consider the following example:

```
type Color is (Red, Green, White, Brown);
type TrafficLight is (Red, Green, Yellow);

. . .

APaint : Color;
ATrafficLight : TrafficLight;
. . .

APaint : = Red;
ATrafficLight : = Red;
```

In this example, *Red* and *Green* literals are overloaded in *Color* and *TrafficLight* type declarations. Also, in the assignment statements both variables are assigned the value of *Red*. These statements are not ambiguous. The type of the variable in the assignment statement determines correct interpretation of the *Red* literal.

6.4.2 Functions and Subprograms

Both function and procedure subprograms can be overloaded in Ada. Consider the following example:

```
procedure Set (WallPaint : in Paint);

procedure Set (Light : in TrafficLight);

procedure Set (State : in BOOLEAN);
```

The identifier *Set* is used as a procedure name in three different subprogram declarations. Thus the following subprogram call can be made:

```
Set(White);
```

```
Set(TRUE);
```

A call to an overloaded subprogram can be ambiguous. In the previous subprogram declaration, the following subprogram call is ambiguous:

```
Set(Red);   -- Ambiguous
```

Table 6.1 List of Ada operators that can be overloaded.

+	−	*	/	*mod*	*rem*	**	
<	>	<=	>=	*and*	*or*	*xor*	&
=	*(unary)*+	*(unary)*−	*not*	*abs*			

From this subprogram call, the language compiler cannot determine which one of the overloaded subprograms should be invoked.

The compiler may use any of the following to disambiguate subprogram calls: number of arguments, the types and the order of the actual parameters, the names of formal parameters (if named-parameter association is used), and the result type (for functions). Thus to disambiguate the previous subprogram call, the call can be rewritten with named parameter association:

Set(Light => Red);

6.4.3 Operator Overloading

Ada allows most of the predefined language operators to be overloaded for user-defined types. Table 6.1 depicts the list of operators that can be redefined. Number of arguments and precedence of these operators cannot be changed.

Both unary and binary + and − operators can be overloaded. Equality (=) and inequality (/=) operators are automatically supplied for all non-limited private types. Notice that the inequality operator cannot be declared for a user-defined type. The defined equality operator implicitly defines the inequality operation. The assignment operation is implicitly defined for all types except limited private types. For these types, an identifier must be used to assign the value of one limited type to another. See Section 6.5.4 for private type declaration.

■ 6.5 PACKAGES

In Ada, abstract data types are implemented through packages. In addition to their use for defining abstract data types, packages have a much wider application. In general, packages are used to group logically related entities. For example, the definitions of a group of related constants can be assembled inside one package. This section demonstrates how packages can be used to construct abstract data types. First packages are defined in general terms and then it is shown how they can be used to construct abstract data type definitions. See Chapter 2 for an in-depth discussion of abstract data types.

A package is usually defined in two parts: a package specification and a package body. Every package must have a package specification but the body is optional. The next two subsections present each one of these parts in detail.

6.5.1 Package Specification

Package specification is the declarative part of a package structure. It identifies the components of the package that are visible to the user. Any component defined and available to the package's users must be placed in the specification section. A component is any Ada definition. These can include constant, type, subprogram, task, or even other package definitions.

Package specifications have the following grammatical rule:

```
package <package_name> is
        <declarative_items>
     [ private
        <declarative_items>]

end <package_name> ;
```

As far as information hiding (see Section 3.3) is concerned, a package specification has two parts:

1. *Visible*. The components defined in the visible part are accessible outside of the package specification.
2. *Private*. The private part of the package specification is not accessible to the clients of the package. The following two examples do not contain any private components of the package specification.

A package can only have instantiating clients (see Section 3.3). The package below defines a set of commonly used constants in mathematics:

```
package Mathematic is
     PI : constant := 3.14159;
     PIOver2 : constant := PI / 2;
     PIOver4 : constant := PI / 4;
     E : constant := 2.71828;   -- Euler's constant
end MATHEMATIC;
```

The next package defines types for the metric system:

```
package MetricSystem

     type Meter is new FLOAT;

     type Liter is new FLOAT;

     type Kilo is new FLOAT;

end MetricSystem;
```

6.5.2 Referencing Packages

Packages can be compiled separately as discrete modules. To access components defined in a package from another program unit, the *with* clause is used. For example, imagine we wish to access the types defined in the metric system package from a procedure:

```
with MetricSystem;
procedure ComputeMeasurements is
A, B, C : MetricSystem.Meter;
D, E, F : MetricSystem.Liter;

begin
. . . . . . .
. . . . . . .
end ComputeMeasurements;
```

In this code segment the procedure is commonly referred to as *importing* the *MetricSystem* unit. The *with* construct allows the components defined in the visible part of our *MetricSystem* package specification to be *imported* to *ComputeMeasurements*.

Visible components of a package specification can be identified using the following notation, called *selected component notation*:

```
<package_name>.<component_name>
```

In the previous example, we referred to types declared in *MetricSystem* as: *MetricSystem.Meter* and *MetricSystem.Liter*. The selected component notation allows sharing of the same identifier among several packages. Thus another package specification can use the identifier *Meter* to have a completely different meaning.

Prefixing package names to identify visible components of a package can be tedious. The *use* clause provides a way to identify these components directly. For example, the code fragment introduced above can take advantage of the *use* clause as follows:

```
with MetricSystem; use MetricSystem;
procedure ComputeMeasurements is
A, B, C : Meter;
D, E, F : Liter;

begin
. . . . .
. . . . .
end ComputeMeasurements;
```

Notice that the *use* clause can generate ambiguity if the same component name is defined in more than one package. Thus, to alleviate the ambiguity, it may be necessary to revert to the selected component notation.

However the *use* clause plays a more important role than seen in the examples so far. When operators are overloaded in a package specification without the *use* clause, they can only be applied using prefix notation. Imagine the following partial package specification:

```
package ComplexSystem is
    type Complex . . .
    function " + " (Left, Right : in Complex)
                                return Complex;
    function " - " (Left, Right : in Complex)
                                return Complex;

    . . .
end ComplexSystem;
```

In this example, two functions have been defined for complex numbers as "+" and "−" which overload the definition of the corresponding system-defined operators.

It is possible to take advantage of these operators without resorting to the *use* clause by prefixing them:

```
with ComplexSystem;
procedure ComplexTest is
    A, B, C: ComplexSystem.Complex;

begin

    . . .
    C := Complex." + "(A, B);
    . . .
end ComplexTest;
```

With the addition of the *use* clause to the above code segment, the code can be specified more concisely:

```
with ComplexSystem; use ComplexSystem;
procedure ComplexTest is
    A, B, C: ComplexSystem.Complex;

begin

    . . .
    C := A + B:
    . . .
end ComplexTest;
```

Notice that infix notation is used instead of prefix for the "+" operator and the *Complex* type is used directly to define complex numbers: *A*, *B*, and *C*.

6.5.3 Package Body

The package body contains definitions of components that are hidden from the package clients. These definitions are used only within the package structure. Any valid Ada programming construct can be specified in a package body. Generally, it contains subprogram declarations and data declarations hidden from the user of the package. A package body can be defined in a separate module from the package specification. The grammar rule for defining a package body is as follows:

```
package body <package_name> is
. . .
end <package_name>;
```

A partial definition of the body for our *ComplexSystem* package with "+" and "−" function definitions will look like this:

```
package body ComplexSystem is
. . . .
    function "+" (Left, Right: in Complex)
                            return Complex is
    begin
        return (Left.RealPart + Right.RealPart,
                Left.ImagPart + Right.ImagPart);
    end "+";

    function "−" (Left, Right: in Complex)
                            return Complex is
    begin
        return (Left.RealPart − Right.RealPart,
                Left.ImagPart − Right.ImagPart);
    end "−"
. . . .
end ComplexSystem;
```

Section 6.5.5 presents the complete package body for this example.

6.5.4 Private Type Declaration

Previous sections explained how data hiding is accomplished in Ada. However, in the specification of our *ComplexSystem* package we skipped over the actual definition of *Complex* type. Private types are used for this purpose.

Private types allow new data types to be defined while hiding their actual implementation. Like other types, private types are declared within a package specification. A private type is declared (named) in the visible part of a package, but the actual definition of its internal structure is specified in the private part of package specification.

Together, the visible and private parts of a package specification define the operations allowed on this new data type for the clients of the package. The structure of the type, defined in the private part, is accessible only within the package body.

Here is the complete definition for the *Complex* type:

```
package ComplexSystem is
    type Complex is private;
    function " + " (Left, Right : in Complex)
                                return Complex;
    function "–" (Left, Right : in Complex)
                                return Complex;

    . . .

    private
        type Complex is
            record
                RealPart : FLOAT;
                ImagPart : FLOAT;
            end record;
    end ComplexSystem;
```

The operations allowed on private types are assignment, tests for equality and inequality, and any additional operations explicitly defined within the package specification. For the *Complex* type definition above, + , –, = , NOT = , and : = are the operations allowed.

Ada also provides a more limited private type definition called *limited private*. The major difference is that limited private type does not automatically inherit operators for assignment and tests for equality and inequality. Suppose, for a moment, that a new file system is being defined. A package definition will be used for this purpose. To define a file handle, a limited private type definition would most likely be used. This type is chosen here since it does not make sense to perform assignment and comparison operations on file handles.

Each private type will specify the structure of the instances of the type. This corresponds to the instance variable declarations of a class, as discussed in Section 2.2. The operations associated with a private type capture the behavior of the type and correspond to the methods of a class, as discussed in Section 2.2. Therefore, through a package and private type declarations, Ada programmers can cluster a collection of encapsulated abstract data types that are semantically related to one another.

6.5.5 A Complete Example

We now give a detailed example: The complete definition for the *ComplexSystem* package discussed in previous sections. The purpose is to demonstrate how Ada packages can be exploited as classes.

```
package ComplexSystem is

    type Complex is private;

    function "+" (Left, Right : in Complex)
                        return Complex;

    function "-" (Left, Right : in Complex)
                        return Complex;

    function "*" (Left, Right : in Complex)
                        return Complex;

    function "/" (Left, Right : in Complex)
                        return Complex;

    function GetReal (A_Complex: in Complex)
                        return FLOAT;

    function GetImag (A_Complex: in Complex)
                        return FLOAT;

    procedure SetReal (A_Complex: in out Complex;
                            A_RealPart: in FLOAT);


    procedure SetImag (A_Complex: in out Complex;
                            AnImagPart: in FLOAT);

    procedure Set (A_Complex: in out Complex;
                        A_RealPart: in FLOAT;
                        AnImagPart: in FLOAT);

    private
            type Complex is
              record
                    RealPart : FLOAT;
                    ImagPart : FLOAT;
              end record;
end ComplexSystem;
```

Figure 6.1 Complex package specification.

```
package body ComplexSystem is

        function "+" (Left, Right: in Complex)
                                            return Complex is
        begin
                return (Left.RealPart + Right.RealPart,
                        Left.ImagPart + Right.ImagPart);
        end "+";

        function "-" (Left, Right: in Complex)
                                            return Complex is
        begin
                return (Left.RealPart - Right.RealPart,
                        Left.ImagPart - Right.ImagPart);
        end "-";


        function "*" (Left, Right: in Complex)
                                            return Complex is
        begin
                return (Left.RealPart * Right.RealPart -
                        Left.ImagPart * Right.ImagPart,
                        Left.RealPart * Right.ImagPart +
                        Left.ImagPart * Right.RealPart);
        end "*";
```

Figure 6.2 Complex package body.

Since the *Complex* type is defined as a *private* type, Ada automatically provides assignment and tests for equality and inequality. In previous examples, we defined the addition and subtraction operators. Now, we will also provide operators for multiplication and division. Finally, in addition to the above operators, we will provide two additional subprograms to retrieve and alter the imaginary and real parts of a complex number. Figures 6.1 and 6.2 display the complete Ada source for the package specification and body. Figure 6.3 displays an example application program utilizing the *ComplexSystem* package.

■ 6.6 GENERIC UNITS

This section introduces generic units in Ada. Generic units are parameterized polymorphic subprograms or packages. Section 2.5 provided a complete discussion on parametric polymorphism. The designer can develop templates for generic program units that can be applied to a wide range of system- or user-defined types or constraints.

```
function GetReal (A_Complex: in Complex)
                                    return FLOAT is
begin
        return A_Complex.RealPart;
end GetReal;

function GetImag (A_Complex: in Complex)
                                    return FLOAT is
begin
        return A_Complex.ImagPart;
end GetReal;


procedure SetReal (A_Complex: in out Complex;
                          A_RealPart: in FLOAT) is
begin
        A_Complex.REAL := A_RealPart;
end SetReal;

procedure SetImag (A_Complex: in out Complex;
                          AnImagPart: in FLOAT) is
begin
        A_Complex.ImagPart := AnImagPart;
end SetImag;

procedure Set (A_Complex: in out Complex;
                      A_RealPart: in FLOAT;
                      AnImagPart: in FLOAT) is
begin
        A_Complex.ImagPart := AnImagPart;
        A_Complex.RealPart := A_RealPart;
end SetImag;


end ComplexSystem;
```

Figure 6.2 (Continued)

```
with ComplexSystem; use ComplexSystem;
procedure Main is
A, B, C, D: Complex;

begin

        Set (A, 3, 4);
        Set (B, 4, 5);

        C := A + B;

        D := A - B;


end Main;
```

Figure 6.3 An example of *Complex Numbers*.

Generic units enable the user to develop reusable code. Once a software component applicable to a variety of data types is developed, a copy of it can be kept as a generic unit. In this generic unit certain objects can be left typeless. Then this generic software component is instantiated for a specific data type when it is needed.

Subsection 6.6.1 turns first to a broad overview of generic units. Generic unit definition and instantiation are discussed in the next two subsections and finally, Subsections 6.6.4 and 6.6.5 conclude this chapter with a closer examination of generic subprograms and packages.

6.6.1 Generic Unit Concept

Generic units allow the programmer to develop templates for generic packages or subprograms. During large-scale software system development, certain parallel operations required for different types of data are routinely found. For instance, within the same application, the developer may use stacks for integers, strings, and other user-defined data types. In a conventional language the same operation is usually redefined for different kinds of data types. Ada's generic units allow the user to define a template for a generic stack and a set of push and pop operations that operate on this generic stack. So when a specific type of stack is needed, a stack of *Employee* record type for example, the user can instantiate the template. Likewise the push and pop operations that can operate on this type are instantiated.

Generic units are polymorphic software units with parameters. To define stacks, the stack size and type of each element are passed as parameters, during instantiation of the stack generic unit.

Generic subprograms or packages cannot be called; their only purpose is to serve as generic templates. The only operation allowed on generic units is instantiation. Instantiation materializes the generic unit with all parameters specified. After instantiation, the materialized unit (subprogram or package) can be treated as a regular program unit.

6.6.2 Definition

The following grammatical rule is used to define a generic program unit:

```
generic
    <generic_parameter_declaration>
    {<subprogram_specification>
    | <package_specification>}
```

The next example defines a generic subprogram unit to swap entities of any type:

```
generic
       type Element is private;

procedure Swap(First, Second : in out Element);
```

Next, the body of this generic subprogram:

```
procedure Swap (First, Second : in out Element) is
     Temp : Element;
begin
     Temp := First;
     First := Second;
     Second := Temp;
end Swap;
```

Note that the body of the subprogram exchanges the contents of two parameters without knowing the actual type of data used at the time of generic subprogram definition. In a sense, this offers a safe escape from the strong type checking constraints of Ada. The developer can freely design generic subprograms or packages that can be applied to any system- or user-defined data type.

In <generic_parameter_declaration>, three types of generic parameters can be defined:

1. **Generic formal objects** can be used to provide global constants or variables to the instantiating program unit. A user might want to provide different limits to

each instance of a generic subprogram. Thus a generic hash table subprogram with varying hash table sizes could be defined as follows:

```
generic
    Size : in INTEGER := 100;
    type HashTable is array (INTEGER range 1..Size)
        of INTEGER;
package HashTable is . . .
```

During the instantiation, *Size* can be given a value. Notice that a default value of 100 is assigned to *Size*. This permits the table size to be optional. If not specified, the default value will be assigned during instantiation.

Generic formal objects are defined either with *in* or *in out* keywords. When defined with *in*, an object is used as a constant, and a value is either supplied during instantiation or a default value is specified within the generic definition. When defined with the *in out* keywords, the object is treated as a global variable and a variable name is passed during instantiation.

2. **Generic formal types** can be used to pass a system- or user-defined type as a parameter during instantiation of a generic program unit. Generic types can be either a generic type definition or a private type declaration. Using generic formal types, the previous example can be extended to support hash tables of any type:

```
generic
    Size : in INTEGER := 100;
    type Item is private;
    type HashTable is array (INTEGER range 1..Size)
        of Item;
package HashTable is . . .
```

3. **Generic formal subprograms** can be used to pass a function or subprogram as a parameter to a generic unit during instantiation. For the hash table example, different hashing functions can be specified during instantiation:

```
generic
    Size : in INTEGER := 100;
    type Item is private;
    type HashTable is array (INTEGER range 1..Size)
        of Item;
    with function Hash(AnItem : Item) return INTEGER;
package HashTable is . . .
```

The line starting with the keyword *with* defines a generic function called *Hash*. The actual name is specified during instantiation and the arguments must conform to the *with* statement.

6.6.3 Instantiation

Instantiating a generic unit creates a copy of the generic unit. Generic parameters are matched against the actual parameters during instantiation. A program unit is materialized by substituting all occurrences of generic parameters with actual parameters throughout the specification and the body of the generic unit. A generic subprogram unit becomes a regular subprogram unit. A generic package unit becomes a regular package unit.

Actual types are specified for all generic formal types. A variable or a constant is specified for all generic formal objects. An actual function or subprogram name is given for any generic formal subprogram.

To instantiate the generic subprogram *Swap*, for example, the following statement can be specified:

```
procedure INTEGER_Swap is new Swap(INTEGER);
```

Now, there exists a subprogram called *INTEGER_Swap* that exchanges two integer variables.

Suppose we have the following *Employee* record definition:

```
type Employee is
    record
        Age : INTEGER range 0 .. 150;
        Name : String(1 .. Size);
        OfficeNo : INTEGER range 1 .. 200;
    end record;
```

We can easily instantiate a procedure called *EmployeeSwap* that exchanges two employee records:

```
procedure EmployeeSwap is new Swap(Employee);
```

When a package is instantiated, all subprograms defined within the generic package definition become available with the same names given in the generic definition. Thus subprogram names are overloaded when instantiation occurs for more than one data type.

Assume the *HashTable* generic package is as follows:

```
generic
        Size : in Positive := 100;
        type Elem is private;
package Stack is
        procedure Push(AnElem : in Elem);
        procedure Pop(AnElem : out Elem);
end Stack;

package body Stack is
    type StackTable is array (Positive range <>) of Elem;
    StackTable : StackTable(1..Size);
    Top : Natural :=0;

    procedure Push(AnElem : in Elem) is
    begin
        if Top >= Size then
                -- report an overflow error
        end if;

        Top := Top + 1;
        StackTable(Top) := AnElem;
    end Push;

    procedure Pop(AnElem : out Elem) is
    begin
        if Top = 0 then
                -- report stack is empty
        end if;
        AnElem := StackTable(Top);
        Top = Top - 1;
    end Pop;
end Stack;
```

Figure 6.4 A generic stack in Ada.

```
generic
    Size : in INTEGER := 100;
    type Item is private;
    type HashTable is array (INTEGER range 1. . Size)
        of Item;
    with function Hash(AnItem : Item) return INTEGER;
package HashTable is . . .
```

Given a function called *KnuthHash*, the hash table package with 1000 integer elements can be instantiated as follows:

```
package NewTable is new HashTable(1000, INTEGER,
                                      KnuthHash);
```

We can take advantage of the keyword argument and default value for the size and define a new hash table of 100 elements:

```
package SmallerTable is new HashTable(Item => INTEGER,
                                         Hash => KnuthHash);
```

6.6.4   Generic Packages Example

This section presents a complete example using generic packages. The example chosen is a generic stack with push and pop operators that can be applied to any system- or user-defined type. To simplify the example, the code has not been specified for exception handling.

Figure 6.4 displays the complete Ada software for this generic stack package. Given the code in this figure, an integer stack big enough to hold 1000 elements can be instantiated:

```
package INTEGERStack is new (1000, INTEGER);
```

Given the *Employee* record defined previously, an employee stack big enough to hold 1200 elements can be instantiated:

```
package EmployeeStack is new Stack(1200, Employee);
```

Subprograms *Push* and *Pop* will be overloaded for both *Employee* and *INTEGER* data types, as stated previously.

■ 6.7 SUMMARY

This chapter discussed the object orientation features of Ada. The language has many data typing capabilities, including subtypes and derived types. Then the authors proceeded to the discussion of *name*, subprogram and function, and operator overloading. Ada has a powerful *package* construct. Abstract data types can be defined using this construct. A presentation of a complete example of packages was included. Finally, the authors concentrated on parametric polymorphism in Ada using generic units with a complete example.

7

OBJECT-ORIENTED DATABASES

■ 7.1 INTRODUCTION

The first four chapters presented the fundamental concepts of object orientation. Chapter 2 was dedicated to abstract data typing. Classes implement abstract data types, which describe sets of objects with the same structure and behavior. The sharing of code and structure is the major advantage of the second object orientation concept: inheritance, discussed in Chapter 3. Chapter 4 focused on the third fundamental concept of object orientation, namely object identity. While inheritance organizes the classes of objects, object identity organizes the instances or the individual objects in the object space.

Abstract data typing, inheritance, and object identity are the basic building blocks for the specification of object-oriented languages. Throughout Chapters 2, 3, and 4, the authors presented the capabilities of some popular object-oriented languages, including Smalltalk, CLOS, Eiffel, and Trellis/Owl. Chapters 5 and 6 gave detailed descriptions of the languages C++ and Ada.

These languages form powerful environments for building large, complex software. Yet there are desirable features missing, features that have to be added by a programmer when needed. These features include persistence, support of transactions, simple querying of bulk data, concurrent access, resilience, and security. Database management systems offer these features, and more.

How can object orientation concepts be combined with database capabilities? The solution is the object-oriented database (OODB). In this chapter the authors describe the essential features of object-oriented database management systems, and present several examples.

257

Also discussed are *intelligent databases*, which are fast becoming *the* foundation of all future database management systems. Intelligent databases incorporate object orientation capabilities, and are thus a superset of object-oriented databases. In addition, intelligent databases tightly integrate inferencing, information management, multimedia data types, and distributed database capabilities.

7.1.1 Introduction to Object-Oriented Databases

There is an exciting and irreversible trend toward sharing and integration in the computer industry: Integration of different environments and products in an attempt to have the same "look and feel" on multiple platforms. Tighter or seamless integration of operating systems, databases, and programming languages is leading to the development of applications that use these environments. Tighter integration of databases, spreadsheets, word processors, AI expert system shells, and full-text retrieval products is leading to the sharing of data among these different products. In the past it has been necessary to deal with diverse languages, environments, and command sequences. With each new product, new ways to implement even simple actions had to be learned. The diversity and complexity of different products and computational environments has amounted to considerable loss of effort and time.

In the integrated environment of the 90s, database management systems (DBMS) will become the single most important component in a computing environment. Integration requires sharing of data and information across components, products, and computing environments. There are two aspects of sharing: One is *referential sharing* where multiple applications, products, or objects share a common sub-object. For instance, the same database's tabular material is part of a spreadsheet and is displayed with a word processor terminal. With referential sharing, hypermedia links are used to "navigate" from one object to another. Object-oriented databases allow structuring and referential sharing of objects through the support of object identity and inheritance.

The other type of sharing is *concurrent sharing* of objects. The bulk of the functionality of database management systems (especially on minicomputers and mainframes) is dedicated to controlling concurrent access to persistent database objects by multiple users or applications. Like most conventional database management systems, object-oriented databases support atomic transactions. These transactions update or retrieve from persistent database objects. Object-oriented databases can recover from system or even media failures, consistent "snapshots" of persistent objects. Additional database functionalities of object-oriented databases include security, integrity, and *versioning* of persistent objects.

Therefore through combining database functionality with object orientation concepts, object-oriented databases become the *ideal repository* of the information that is shared by multiple users, multiple products, and multiple applications on different platforms. In addition, object-oriented databases solve the following problems:

1. *The semantic gap*. Object-oriented databases remove the so-called "semantic gap" between an application domain and its representation in persistent storage.

Since the real world is modeled as closely as possible, the links and relationships among entities in the complex real world are represented and manipulated directly. Object-oriented databases achieve their modeling capability through the object-oriented concepts of abstract data typing, inheritance, and object identity.

2. *Impedance mismatch*. Object-oriented databases also alleviate the "impedance mismatch" between the programming language and the database management system. In complex applications, the data is retrieved from a database management system using a database query language such as SQL and then manipulated through routines written in a conventional programming language such as C or PL/1. Conventional languages are procedural. Database query languages are higher-level and more declarative. Therefore applications involving both languages mix (mismatch) these different programming paradigms. Furthermore, the data types in the different languages (SQL and C, for instance) are not the same and have to be mapped onto one another. The reason for accessing the data through a database language and then processing it through a conventional language is because the database language is limited to querying. Typically, database languages provide little support for complex computations. The computations are done in the programming language. Object oriented databases are more *complete* in the sense that they typically provide expressivity.

The data manipulation language (DML) of an OODB typically incorporates general purpose programming constructs:

   a. control structures (IF-THEN-ELSE, WHILE Loops, CASE statements, and so on).

   b. variables and assignment statements.

   c. a rich collection of data types or classes.

   d. constructs to define methods, functions, abstract data types (classes), and so on.

To be thorough, it should be noted that some conventional databases also incorporate more general programming constructs through fourth-generation languages or dialects of SQL. For instance, both TransactSQL from Sybase and dBASE/SQL from Ashton-Tate include control structures, variables, procedures, and other general programming constructs.

3. *Engineering and office automation application requirements*. The main markets of object-oriented databases have been for engineering: Computer-Aided Design (CAD), Computer-Aided Manufacturing (CAM), Computer-Aided Software Engineering (CASE), along with those for office automation. These applications have characteristics that are different from traditional business or accounting applications. In the engineering and office automation applications the amount of information stored in the database is much larger and the informational correlations are more complex. The size and complexity of the data makes

it nearly impossible to cluster all possible permutations of related data. Thus, a considerable amount of maneuvering is necessary to access and update objects in the database. Accessing the numerous parts of an automobile transmission, for example, could take a very long time. Associative and ad hoc queries are common, with queries such as: *retrieve all parts heavier than 2 lbs*. The structures of databases in these applications are heterogeneous and multifaceted; there are many object types corresponding to each individual component and composite object. Imagine all the different parts of a jet aircraft! A database for the plane would need a different object type for each different kind of part. Furthermore, in typical design applications each piece will undergo refinements and have multiple versions or alternatives. Many of the features of object-oriented databases are attempts to satisfy these requirements.

Therefore object-oriented databases (OODBs) combine object-oriented concepts, programming constructs, and database management capabilities. OODBs support the concurrent and referential sharing of objects and alleviate the impedance mismatch between programming languages and databases. They satisfy most of the database requirements of engineering and office automation applications. In any case, with all these advantages, it is difficult to identify a sole originator of the object-oriented database terminology or concepts (contrast this with the relational model, whose origin and standardization could be accredited to Ted Codd). Examples of the early use of the object-oriented database concepts include: (Maier and Copeland, 1984), which describes the origins of the GemStone object-oriented database system; the collection of papers in the first international workshop on object-oriented databases in Pacific Grove, California (Dittrich and Dayal, 1986); and the PhD thesis of Dr. Mohammad Ketabchi (1985). In his thesis Ketabchi performed an analysis of the requirements of CAD databases. Besides complex/composite object representation capabilities, Ketabchi illustrated that CAD databases require information hiding and object/message paradigms (see Chapter 2) for manipulating design data. Object-oriented data models integrate these primitives to simplify the organization of and access to design databases.

7.1.2 Chapter Organization

The rest of the chapter is organized as follows. Section 7.2 presents the post-relational complex object and semantic data modeling alternatives. Object-oriented databases were influenced by the modeling features of these advanced data models. Section 7.3 discusses the database capabilities of OODBs and surveys the OODBs in research and industry. Each of the nine database capabilities of object-oriented databases are discussed in Section 7.4. Finally, Section 7.5 describes the emerging, next-generation intelligent databases.

■ 7.2 DATA MODELING ALTERNATIVES

Databases have generally provided efficient support for atomic transactions, concurrency control, recovery, and querying of persistent object spaces. However, the traditional database management systems (hierarchical, network, and relational) lack the necessary modeling primitives to represent real-world applications easily and naturally. Consider the relational model (Codd, 1970). Relational systems impose the first normal form constraint. This means the object space must be mapped onto a collection of flat relations (tables). With this approach much of the inherent semantic eloquence of complex object composition is lost. Foreign key joins must be performed to reconstruct complex objects.

There have been several attempts to address this issue and introduce semantically richer data models. With regard to post-relational models, there have been two interrelated data modeling approaches:

- complex object models
- semantic data models

The complex object models attempt to incrementally extend the relational model to allow more expressiveness while maintaining a solid theoretical foundation. Complex object modeling alternatives are discussed in Section 7.2.1.

Semantic data models (Chen, 1976; Smith and Smith, 1977; Hammer and McLeod, 1981) represent another approach in database modeling, and provide the capability for conceptually encompassing complex objects, object identities, and inter-object relationships. Semantic data modeling strategies are discussed in Section 7.2.2.

7.2.1 Complex Object Data Models

With the attempts to extend incrementally the relational data model was the attempt to relax the first normal form restriction of the relational model. Complex object models are also called *non-first normal form data models, set and tuple models*, or *logic-based data models with complex terms*. They allow/contain one or more of the following extensions:

1. Sets of atomic values (set of character strings, integers, floating points, . . .)
2. Tuple-valued attributes
3. Sets of tuples (nested relations)
4. General set and tuple constructors
5. Object identity

Sets of atomic values can be very useful. For example, if a table contains information about books, in one field the names of all the authors can be stored. In fact, (Jaeschke and Schek, 1982) present an algebra for a non-first normal form model that allows attributes to be sets of atomic values. Note that with a relational (first normal form) representation it is necessary to either store all the authors in a single character string or in a separate table: The former does not allow a direct representation of the set of authors and the latter would involve joins.

Now consider the example of a person's address. An address consists of a street number, street name, city, state, and zip code. This cannot be thought of as a set of atomic values; each piece has a different meaning. Still, there are several ways to store an address in the relational model. Minimally, the address can be stored as a long string of characters. But the structure of the address is lost. The user then has to worry about the different fields and attributes within the long field. Qualification on the different fields of addresses becomes either difficult or impossible.

Another possibility is to capture the different fields of address in the name of the attribute, such as different fields for *AddressNumber*, *AddressName*, *AddressCity*, *AddressState*, and *AddressZipCode*. This option loses the logical *aggregation* of the address fields. The table definition looks strange and the association of the different fields to the same logical object must be done by the user.

A third alternative is to store addresses in a separate table and perform *joins* to retrieve the different fields of address. Although this option avoids some of the pitfalls of the other two alternatives, it incurs the extra overhead of joins in the retrieval of the fields of a person's address. Moreover, the table of addresses is not an interesting grouping, since in most cases users retrieve addresses through a person's record.

But the most natural representation for an address is to allow tuple-valued attributes. With this alternative, the address will be a tuple and exist as a single logical entity, instead of being spread across multiple fields or tables. Yet the user will be able to access and update each field separately (see Figures 4.4 and 4.10 in Chapter 4).

Although a set of atomic values and tuple valued attributes allow us to have more direct representations in the persistent object space, there are a number of cases where it is desirable to have a *relation nested* within another relation. For example assume each person has an education. The education consists of a set of tuples (that is, relations) where each tuple contains the degree, the year of graduation, the title of a thesis (if applicable), and the school or university. In a non-first normal form all degrees are stored in a separate table. With each degree the *key* of a person's tuple is stored. To retrieve a degree the user must perform a join. With a nested relational model, the user will be able to have a relation (set-of-tuples) valued attribute and hence represent, store, and retrieve the set of tuples directly. There have been a number of nested relational models, including VERSO (Bancilhon et al., 1983), one by Schek and Scholl (1986), and others.

More general complex object models can be built on top of a collection of base atomic types using two object constructors—sets and tuples; (Lecluse et al., 1988; Abitboul et al., 1990; Carey et al., 1988; Bancilhon and Khoshafian, 1989; Khoshafian, 1989) and others have presented general complex object data models that allow the representation of arbitrary complex objects using set and tuple object constructors.

In these models the object space is defined as follows. We have a set of attribute names N, and atomic values A. Atomic values include integers, floats, character strings, and so on. Objects are defined as follows:

1. Every atomic value in A is an object.

2. If $a_1, \ldots, a_n$ are distinct attribute names in N and $O_1, \ldots, O_n$ are objects, then $T = [a_1: O_1, a_2: O_2, \ldots, a_n: O_n]$ is a tuple object. The object O_i is the value of attribute a_i of T. The "." (dot) notation is used to retrieve object O_i: $T.a_i$.

3. If $O_1, \ldots, O_n$ are distinct objects then:

$S = \{O1, \ldots, O_n\}$ is a set object. We say each O_i is an element of S.

For example:

[Name: John, Age: 30, Salary: 600000]

is a tuple object, and

{ [Name: John, Age: 30, Salary: 600000],
[Name: Mary, Age: 32, Salary: 700000]}

is a set of tuples. Finally,

{ [Name: John, Age: 30, Salary: 600000, Children:
{ [Name: Jim, Age: 3],
[Name: Ann, Age: 5]},
Friends: { Marlene, Vivian}],
[Name: Mary, Age: 32, Salary: 700000, Children:
{ [Name: Joey, Age: 2],
[Name: Agatha, Age: 5]},
Friends: { Mark, Vicki}]}

is a complex object that includes a nested relation and a nested set of atomic objects. In each tuple *Children* stores a relation (set of tuples) and *Friends* stores a set of names. Note that unlike the identity-based object model of Chapter 4, the objects in these examples do not have an identity independent of their state or value.

Although these extensions add considerable flexibility to object representation capabilities of the relational model, they do not have the direct support of referential sharing of objects (Khoshafian and Valduriez, 1987*a*). Referential sharing allows the same object to be owned by multiple parent objects. Object sharing becomes feasible when a model supports object identity. An entire chapter (Chapter 4) was dedicated to describing the merits of object identity. Chapter 4 gave many examples of the advantages and applications of object identity. Database data models that support a strong notion of identity include the Logical Data Model (LDM) (Kuper and Vardi, 1984 and 1985), FAD (Bancilhon et al., 1987), O_2 (Lecluse et al., 1988), ENCORE (Zdonik and Wegner, 1986), TEDM (Anderson et al., 1986), OPAL (Maier et al., 1986), and others.

7.2.2   Semantic Data Models

The motivation of semantic data models (and most data models for that matter) is very similar to the goal of object orientation: model the real world as closely as possible. Yet there is one fundamental difference between semantic data models and other models. Semantic data models do not incorporate behavioral abstraction (or abstract data typing); the goal of semantic data models is to model structural abstractions. This is similar to AI knowledge representation. Semantic data models attempt to capture the semantics of the objects (entities) and relationships of an underlying object space. They are primarily used as design tools for underlying relational or network databases.

Semantic data models are not semantic networks. However, there are common elements. Semantic data models use the node and link representational schema of semantic networks. Each node is an entity type. Similar to types in programming languages, an entity type represents a set of objects (entities), all having the same attributes. An attribute is a function that can apply to an entity in the entity type. The name of an entity type also identifies the extension (set of all instances) of the entity type. Entity types are analogous to classes and entities to instances. Attributes are analogous to instance variables.

Semantic data models also capture inheritance and incorporate various sorts of attributes (or *slots* in semantic networks). The fundamental difference, however, is that while semantic networks are used as an associative memory for the entire knowledge base, semantic data models are used to represent the structure of an underlying extensional database.

Examples of early introductions to semantic models include Abrial's model (1974), (Hall et al., 1976), and the famous entity-relationship (ER) model introduced by Chen (1976). The ER model is considerably simpler than the more generalized semantic data model described in the following paragraphs. It (the original ER model) does *not* incorporate the notion of inheritance. In particular, nodes in an ER diagram are either entity type nodes, printable attribute nodes, or relationship (aggregate) nodes. The ER approach is a widely accepted technique for data modeling.

To illustrate the different node and link types of semantic data models the authors present a portion of the office automation database using the Generalized Semantic Model (GSM) of Hull and King (1987). The GSM is a representative semantic model that incorporates concepts from many alternative semantic modeling strategies. The different node (entity) and link (relationship) types in GSM are illustrated in Figures 7.1 and 7.2.

For node types, an oval represents printable base types, such as integers, character strings, and floating point numbers. A triangle is used to represent an abstract entity type. Each instance of an abstract entity type will have an object identity. The set of all instances of an abstract entity type is its extension. Entity types can inherit from one another. A circle represents an entity type that has an IS-A relationship (that is, it is a subtype) to another entity type. Figure 7.1 also illustrates two very commonly used constructor types: the aggregation node type and the set or grouping

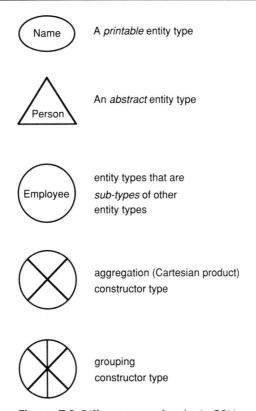

Figure 7.1 Different types of nodes in GSM.

node type. These roughly correspond to tuple and set object types in complex object models. The instances of an aggregation node type are elements of the Cartesian product of its children: The Cartesian product of sets $S_1, \ldots, S_n$ is

$$\{(e_1, \ldots, e_n) \mid e_1 \text{ is in } S_1, \ldots, e_n \text{ is in } S_n\}$$

Grouping node types have one child. An instance of a grouping node type is a set whose elements are instances of the node type's child.

Figure 7.2 shows the different types of links or relationships that can exist between the nodes of a semantic model. Entity types have attributes that can be single or multivalued functions. Single valued functions are indicated by single arrow heads; multivalued functions are indicated by double arrow heads. These arrows map instances of one entity type to instances of another type. Another important relationship is the IS-A inheritance relationship, which is represented by a thick white arrow. Finally, constructed types point to their children through dashed arrows.

Using these node and link types Figure 7.3 illustrates a portion of the sales office automation example in GSM. As the figure illustrates, SalesPerson inherits from

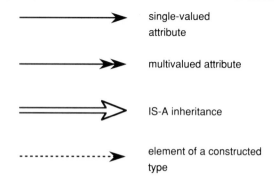

Figure 7.2 Different types of links (relationships) in GSM.

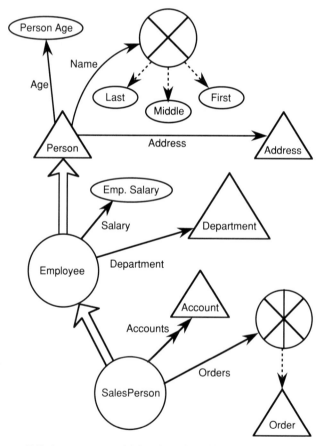

Figure 7.3 A semantic model for the sales office automation example.

Employee and Employee inherits from Person. Name is an aggregate. Age, Name, Salary, and Address are single valued attributes of Person. A specific set of accounts is assigned to each salesperson. Also each salesperson has a set of pending orders. So both Accounts and Orders are sets. To illustrate two alternative representational choices for representing sets, we have used different constructs for Accounts and Orders. Accounts is a multivalued attribute (or function) of SalesPerson. Orders, on the other hand, is a single valued attribute of SalesPerson. However, the value is a group (set) of Orders. If the value of an attribute is a set, set operations can be performed on it.

Figure 7.3 shows the use of different constructs for Name and Address. For Name an aggregate was used and for Address an entity type was used. The basic difference is that only abstract entity types (or subtypes) have distinguishable object identities. In other words, if an aggregate or grouping object is the attribute value of an entity, and the entity is deleted, the aggregate object is also deleted. On the other hand, if an entity (object) is the attribute value of another entity, it will not be deleted when the entity referencing it is deleted. It has an existence (object identity) of its own. Entities can be shared among entities (be the attribute value of more than one entity). For example, the same address could be referenced by the Address attribute value of each Person living in the same house.

Some semantic data models emphasize constructor types while others emphasize attributes (functions). The Functional Data Model (Kerschberg and Pacheco, 1976) is attribute based. Attribute values are entities and attributes can be single or multivalued. The data language DAPLEX (Shipman, 1981) was one of the earliest languages that

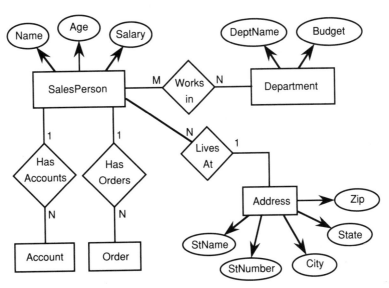

Figure 7.4 An entity-relationship model for the sales office automation example.

supported the Functional Data Model. It provided both a data definition language and a data manipulation language based on attributes (functions).

At the other end of the spectrum is the aggregation based entity-relationship model that was mentioned earlier. A schema in an ER diagram consists of:

> *rectangles* representing entity types,
>
> *ovals* representing ranges of attributes, and
>
> *diamonds* representing relationships (that is, aggregations).

Relationships can be one-to-one (such as each person having one spouse), many-to-one (a person having many children), many-to-many (employees can work in different departments and many employees work in the same department). Figure 7.4 illustrates a portion of the sales office automation example using an ER diagram.

■ 7.3 OBJECT-ORIENTED DATABASES

The complex object models and the semantic data models laid a strong foundation for the development of a number of object-oriented databases, both in research and in industry. Concepts such as complex objects, object identity, inheritance, and set and tuple valued attributes propagated into these powerful object-oriented database systems. Each object-oriented database was influenced by one or more of the complex and semantic data modeling alternatives. In addition, they were influenced by the encapsulation, inheritance, and object identity concepts of object-oriented languages such as Smalltalk.

In the rest of the chapter the term "object-oriented database" is used in its most comprehensive sense, combining the object orientation features with "traditional" database capabilities. More specifically from Chapters 2 through 4 we know:

Object Orientation =
Abstract Data Types + Inheritance + Object Identity

In addition to these elements, (ideally) object-oriented databases support the following interrelated database concepts:

Database Capabilities:

1. Persistence
2. Transactions
3. Concurrency control
4. Recovery
5. Querying

6. Versioning
7. Integrity
8. Security
9. Performance issues

Each of these elements will be discussed in detail in the following sections of this chapter.

We define the ideal object-oriented database by:

Object-Oriented Database =
        Object Orientation + Database Capabilities

Those databases that *partially* support the object orientation and database features shall still be labeled "object-oriented." The formula represents the ideal target of all database management systems as they become more object oriented.

The following subsections briefly discuss some object-oriented databases in research and in the industry. Six alternative strategies for object-oriented databases are described. These alternatives are used to incorporate object orientation features in databases.

Then Section 7.4 concentrates on each of the nine database capabilities and demonstrates how they are included in different object-oriented databases.

7.3.1 Research Prototypes

There are several research prototypes of object-oriented databases. Some of these have made significant contributions to the field. Here is a very brief overview of some of the research prototypes.

FAD. One of the earliest such prototypes was based on the FAD (Bancilhon et al., 1987) object-oriented data language. FAD stands for the Franco-Armenian Database language. The first prototype was built at the MCC (Microelectronic and Computer Corporation) consortium and completed in 1987. FAD provided a very clean support of object identity. The language was based on lambda calculus. FAD was implemented in a distributed environment. The underlying implementation supported complex object storage and indexing. More details about the implementational architecture can be found in (Khoshafian and Valduriez, 1987a) and (Khoshafian and Valduriez, 1987b). The strategies used in storage architecture can be found in ((Khoshafian et al., 1988) and (Khoshafian et al., 1990a). Implementation techniques for complex object comparisons are presented in (Khoshafian and Frank, 1988).

ORION. Another research prototype also developed at MCC was the ORION (Banerjee et al., 1987) object-oriented database. ORION is a LISP-based system that ran on the Symbolics. The ORION project dealt with some interesting object-oriented database issues such as schema evolution and complex object *locking* (Kim et al., 1987).

IRIS. Iris (Fishman et al., 1987, 1989; Beech 1988) is a next-generation database management system prototype developed at Hewlett-Packard laboratories. The Iris data model supports inheritance and abstract data typing. It is based on functional data models. Referential sharing of objects is supported. One of the interfaces of Iris is an object-oriented extension of SQL called Object SQL. Iris also incorporates a version control mechanism.

Galileo. The Galileo strongly typed language (Albano et al., 1985) was developed at the Universite di Pisa, in Pisa, Italy. Galileo incorporates inheritance of types and support of complex objects. It is one of the few database languages that attempts to distinguish between the notions of a type and a class.

Other Systems. Besides these research prototypes there are many others both in universities and in industry. Some of these include the PROBE data model, developed at Computer Corporation of America (Manola and Dayal, 1986); the ENCORE object-oriented database system developed at Brown University (Zdonik and Wegner, 1986); the EXODUS extensible database management system from the University of Wisconsin, Madison (Carey et al., 1990); the ADAPTABLE environment for specifying and implementing database systems (Stemple et al., 1990); the POSTGRES database system from the University of California, Berkeley (Stonebraker and Rowe, 1986; Stonebraker et al., 1990); the O_2 object-oriented database system of the Altaïr project (Deux et al., 1990); and others.

7.3.2 Commercial Object-Oriented Databases

As stated earlier, commercial object-oriented databases started to appear in the mid-80s. The creators of these earlier systems did pioneering work in defining the components of object-oriented databases and tested the market for the applications of this novel technology.

G-Base. One of the earliest object-oriented database products was G-Base from Graphael, which was introduced in 1987. G-Base is a LISP-based system; it is written in LISP and the entities and methods are defined using LISP syntax. G-Base supports abstract data typing and multiple inheritance of classes. The G-Base environment also includes an interactive graphical object browser, an interactive report generator, and a declarative query language. The database model is comprised of entities and relationships. Abstract data typing is supported by allowing users to define methods for entities. G-Base can also interface with relational databases. Another important G-Base tool is G-Logis, which integrates inferencing (via an extension of Prolog) in the G-Base environment. Thus G-Base provides elegant modeling, browsing, and querying capabilities for bulk data.

GemStone. The GemStone (Servio Logic, 1987; 1989) object-oriented DBMS is also one of the earlier, influential, next-generation systems. The GemStone is from

Servio Logic Corporation of Beaverton, Oregon. The GemStone system is significant in many ways. It was one of the earliest object-oriented database management systems that provided strong support of object identity, inheritance, and encapsulation, coupled with many database capabilities such as persistence, transactions, and ad-hoc querying. GemStone's data definition and manipulation language is called OPAL. The basis of OPAL is Smalltalk. Therefore the syntax of OPAL is very similar to Smalltalk. Yet, as will be shown, OPAL incorporates many database-specific constructs and operations.

Ontos.   The Ontos object-oriented database system (Ontologic 1988, 1989) is from Ontologic, Burlington, Massachusetts. Ontos is a C++ based system, and offers a C++ client library that serves as the interface between an application program and the persistent database. The Ontos system has a predecessor product called Vbase, also from Ontologic, which supported an extension of C for defining methods and a type definition language to create the entity types and the schema. Many of the concepts in Ontos come from Vbase. The Ontos C++ library includes classes for defining collection objects such as sets and other aggregate types. The Ontos model supports encapsulation, inheritance, and the ability to construct complex objects. In terms of database capabilities Ontos supports concurrent and even nested transactions on persistent objects.

Statice.   Statice (Symbolics, 1988) is an object-oriented DBMS from Symbolics. It supports inheritance of entity types and methods that can be associated with entity types. Statice supports both entity and set valued attributes. The syntax of the Statice data definition and manipulation language is similar to LISP. In terms of database capabilities Statice supports concurrent transactions, recovery, associative access, and querying. Statice is designed to support the Genera integrated environment of Symbolics. This environment allows the construction of complex systems and incorporates many interactive tools such as debuggers and editors.

SIM.   SIM (Jagannathan et al., 1988; UNISYS, 1987) stands for Semantic Information Manager and is a commercial database management system based on the semantic data model, from UNISYS Corporation. SIM is the core system of the InfoExec Environment of UNISYS. Other products in InfoExec include a data dictionary system, an interactive querying facility, and language interface components.

The data model in SIM is based on Hammer and McLeod's (1981) Semantic Data Model. In SIM, users can define entity types (classes) that can inherit from one another. Attributes of entities are like functions from one entity to another. Thus, complex objects and complex relationships between entities can be modeled very easily. The attribute functions can be single or multiple valued. SIM also allows the specification of various forms of integrity constraints.

Other Systems.   There are many other object-oriented database products that offer users a wide variety of capabilities. Some of the industry trends are described in the September 1989 issue of *Release 1.0* by Esther Dyson (1989). Another comprehensive analysis of object-oriented products in general and object-oriented databases in particular is presented in a 1989 Ovum report (Jeffcoate et al., 1989). Some systems provide class hierarchies for the storage, versioning, and concurrent access of persistent objects. Other products emphasize browsers and user-interface tools for visual database programming, using object-oriented paradigms. Besides the "pure" object-oriented database products, there are some relational systems that are evolving toward object orientation incrementally. In fact, in the 90s most relational database vendors are incorporating increasingly richer object orientation features in their next generation products. The object orientation features being integrated in relational systems can be categorized as follows:

1. *User-defined functions.* Relational systems come with a built-in collection of aggregate functions (AVERAGE, COUNT, SUM, trigonometric functions, and so on). Many relational systems allow the users to define their own functions using a fourth-generation language, a general purpose programming language, or a dialect of SQL that incorporates control structures. For instance dBASE IV from Ashton-Tate allows the definition and usage of user-defined functions in dBASE statements. Another database product that incorporates user-defined functions is the relational DBMS of the Empress corporation.

2. *User-defined abstract data types.* In most relational systems the base types provided to the user are fixed. Usually these types are INTEGER, FLOAT, CHAR, and in some cases DATE and LOGICAL (boolean). All column values must be one of these types. The next logical step is to allow the users to define their own data types, as in POSTGRES (Stonebraker and Rowe, 1986) or FAD (Bancilhon et al., 1987). In these systems the user can define the data type and the operations/functions on the type. The operation of the abstract data type is typically written in a lower-level language (such as C). Examples of user-defined types include stacks, arrays, points, complex numbers, and so on. Once a type is defined, it can be used in table declarations to indicate that a column in a table is of a given user-defined type.

3. *Very long multimedia fields.* Another term used to describe long fields storing multimedia data is *blob* (binary large object). Multimedia data types (text, images, voice, video, and so on) are becoming increasingly important in many applications. Some relational systems support multimedia data types that can be (within reason) arbitrarily large. Of course, long fields can be stored in operating systems files. Storing them in the database allows the multimedia data to be concurrently shared by many users, under transaction control. The fields that store multimedia data are alternatively called: BLOB, LONG VARCHAR, TEXT, IMAGE, and so on. In some cases long fields are allowed to grow to two gigabytes! Relational systems that support long fields include DB2 from IBM, the SQL server from Sybase, Informix, and Interbase. The user-defined function or abstract data type capability can be combined with the support of long fields to define operations or abstract data types on multimedia objects.

For instance, in Interbase users can define blob filters to convert the type of a blob.

4. *Other extensions.* In addition to these three extensions, it is possible to incorporate table inheritance, tuple (record type) inheritance, object identity, and abstract data types for tables and tuples as discussed in Section 7.5.

7.3.3 Alternative Object-Oriented Database Strategies

There are at least six approaches for incorporating object orientation capabilities in databases:

1. *Novel database data model/data language approach.* The most aggressive approach is to develop an entirely new database language and database management system with object orientation capabilities. Most of the research projects in object-oriented databases have pursued this approach. In the industry, SIM introduces novel DML (Data Manipulation Language) and DDL (Data Definition Language) constructs for a data model based on semantic and functional data models.

2. *Extending an existing database language with object orientation capabilities.* A number of programming languages have been extended with object-oriented constructs. C++, Flavors (an extension of LISP), and Object Pascal are a few examples of this approach in programming languages. It is conceivable to follow a similar strategy with database languages. Since SQL is a standard, and by far the most popular database language, the most reasonable solution is to extend this language with object-oriented constructs, reflecting the object orientation capabilities of the underlying database management system. This approach is being pursued by most vendors of relational systems, as they evolve their next generation products. There have been many such attempts incorporating inheritance, function composition for nested entities, and even some support of encapsulation in an SQL framework. Both Iris and Vbase/Ontos have their own object-oriented dialects of SQL. Section 7.5 discusses the capabilities of a powerful object-oriented dialect of SQL called Intelligent SQL.

3. *Extending an existing object-oriented programming language with database capabilities.* Another approach is to introduce database capabilities to an existing object-oriented language. The object orientation features (abstract data typing, inheritance, object identity) will already be supported by the object-oriented language. The extensions will incorporate database features (querying, transaction support, persistence, and so on). GemStone's OPAL language extended Smalltalk with database management classes and primitives. OPAL introduced constrained collection objects to store bulk data of the same structure, as well as selection blocks to have quantified queries on the constrained collection objects.

4. *Providing extendable object-oriented DBMS libraries.* Whereas Servio Logic introduced new language constructs to an existing object-oriented language,

Ontologic's Ontos product introduced a C++ client library for database management. These libraries include classes for aggregates (sets, lists, arrays), and types. There are methods for start/commit/abort transactions, exception handling, and object clustering. Other companies such as Object Design and Object Sciences also provide C++ interfaces and support for object-oriented database application development.

5. *Embedding object-oriented database language constructs in a host (conventional) language.* Database languages can be embedded in host programming languages. For example SQL statements can be embedded in PL/1, C, FORTRAN, and Ada. The types of SQL (that is, relations and rows in relations) are quite different from the type systems of these host languages. Some object-oriented databases have taken a similar approach with a host language and an object-oriented database language. For example, O_2 (Bancilhon et al, 1988) provides embedded extensions for C (called CO_2!) and Basic. The extensions include special type constructors and different embedded escapes to the object-oriented message passing environment of O_2.

6. *Application-specific products with an underlying object-oriented database management system.* Another interesting approach is the development of a number of application/domain specific tools and environments that either use object-oriented database technologies or provide an object-oriented database view for the application domain. The intention in application/domain specific solutions is not to provide a general-purpose environment. Only useful or application-specific constructs, possibly with some object orientation features, are made visible to the user. For example, TeamOne is a configuration management system from TeamOne Systems, Inc. It provides a logical extension of the Unix file system and an object-oriented view of an object repository for project design files. Access and modifications of objects in the repository are accomplished through manipulating encapsulated objects. The main target application area of TeamOne is configuration management for engineering applications (including software engineering).

■ 7.4 DATABASE CAPABILITIES OF OBJECT-ORIENTED DATABASES

In this section the authors define each of the database capabilities of object-oriented databases and illustrate how existing object-oriented database management systems support them.

7.4.1 Persistence

The data manipulated by an object-oriented database can be either *transient* or *persistent*. Transient data is only valid inside a program or transaction; it is lost once the program or transaction terminates (transactions are discussed in the next section). Persistent data is stored outside of a transaction context, and so survives transaction updates. There are several levels of persistence. Usually the term persistent data is used to indicate the *databases* that are shared, accessed, and updated across transactions. For example, the personnel database, the inventory database; or the different database on salespeople, accounts, or items, all contain persistent data. But there is a continuum of persistence. The least persistent objects are those that are created and destroyed in procedures data (*local data*). Next are objects that persist within the workspace of a transaction, but that are invalidated when the transaction terminates (aborts or commits). Transactions are typically executed within a session. The user establishes the login and sets different environmental parameters within a session, such as paths, display options, windows, and so on. If the system supports multiprocessing, several transactions could be active within the same user session at the same time. These transactions will all share the session objects (that is, the objects that persist for the duration of the session). When the user terminates the session, however, the session objects are invalidated. The *only* type of objects that persist across transactions (and sessions for that matter) are permanent objects that typically are shared by multiple users.

These objects (databases) persist across transactions, system crashes, and even media crashes (such as, magnetic disk head crashes). Technically these are the *recoverable* objects of the database. Still, we will use the term *persistent* to identify this most persistent category of objects, with the understanding that there are actually several levels of persistence.

There are several alternative strategies to indicate which objects should become persistent. The two main strategies used to create and identify persistent objects are:

- persistence extensions, and
- persistence through reachability.

7.4.1.1 Persistent Extensions

In conventional database management systems (such as relational), when the user defines a schema using a DDL (data definition language), both a structure *and* an extension are defined. For example, when a table is created in SQL through:

```
CREATE TABLE Person(
    Name       CHAR(20),
    Age        INTEGER,
    Address    CHAR(100))
```

we are defining:

1. A *type:* A person has three attributes, *Name*, *Age*, and *Address*. Names are character strings that are 20 bytes long, *Age* of persons are integers, *Address* of persons are also character strings.
2. And defining an *extension*: the collection of all persons. Every time we do an SQL INSERT, DELETE, or UPDATE for *Person*, we are affecting this

collection. Thus INSERT populates *Person*, DELETE removes rows from *Person*, and UPDATE modifies the state of one or more rows in *Person*.

To retrieve rows from *Person*, a SELECT statement is used. For example, to retrieve the *Name* and *Address* of all persons 21 years or older:

```
SELECT Name, Address
FROM Person
WHERE Age > = 21
```

All the persons in the persistent database are contained in *Person*.

In object-oriented languages, users define the structure of objects through the *class* construct. A class is like a type in a conventional programming language such as Pascal, *except* that the class specifies the behavior (or operations) of objects as well as their structure.

Most object-oriented database systems also use classes to define the structure of objects and the operations associated with the object type. Database management systems are used to store, manipulate, and iterate over *bulk* data. Therefore it is useful to have class extensions and treat the class both as an abstract data type constructor *and* as the container of all its instances. This extension then becomes a persistent collection of objects, very similar to persistent databases and tables in SQL.

Note that in object-oriented languages such as Smalltalk, Eiffel, or C++ classes do not have extensions. In these languages there are no built-in methods with which to traverse all the instances of a class. But these languages (especially Smalltalk) do support numerous collection classes such as arrays, sets, and bags. Thus if the user wants to cluster, traverse, and/or manipulate sets of objects, an instance of such a collection object can be created and named.

Several object-oriented databases incorporate the notion of a class extension to make the instances of a class persistent. With class extensions, the class also serves as a set object. As will be shown, object-oriented database languages supporting class extensions typically provide different selection or iteration language primitives to associatively retrieve or update instances of the class collection. By "associative retrieval" we mean the user quantifies on one or more values of attributes and asks the system to search a collection based on these values. Section 7.4.5 gives several examples.

Strictly speaking, persistence and class extensions are orthogonal in the sense that one can have an object-oriented system that has class extensions, but uses a different mechanism (that is, reachability) for persistence. However, the object-oriented database languages that support class extensions usually make the extensions persistent. Next are some examples of object-oriented database languages that support class extensions: Galileo, SIM, and O_2.

Galileo (Albano et al., 1985) is a strongly typed programming language for database applications. In Galileo the notions of a type and a class are different. A type represents a (perhaps infinite) set of values. There are a number of operations that apply to a given type. The language has a number of type constructors. The most important of these is the tuple constructor:

```
Type TPerson <—>
    (Name:       string and
     Age:        integer and
     Address:    string)
```

A class in Galileo has a name and a type. The type gives the structure of the elements of the class (such as each element is a tuple with attributes *Name*, *Age*, *Address*, and so on). The name of the class is a handle for all the elements of the class currently existing in the database. This collection of elements is the extension of the class.

So in order to create the class *Person* the user defines:

```
Person class TPerson <—>(
    Name:       string and
    Age:        integer and
    Address:    string)
```

With this class declaration, *Person* will contain all the instances of type *TPerson*. Associated with the class is an object constructor **mkPerson**, which is used to create new objects of the named type. These objects are placed in the collection of *Person*. Similarly, objects are removed from *Person* through a destructor function **remove.**

In SIM, each class contains all the elements of an entity type. The class declaration for *Person* is:

```
Class Person(
    Name:      string[10],
    Age:       number,
    Address:   string[20])
```

This also defines the extension of the class, namely the set of all existing instances of the class. Objects are explicitly inserted and deleted from the class extension. For example, to insert the *person* John in class *Person*:

```
INSERT Person(
    Name      := "John Smith",
    Age       := 32,
    Address   := "1234 Main ...")
```

The user can inquire about particular persons through querying the set of all persons accessible through *Person*. For example, to retrieve the name and address of all persons older than 21:

FROM Person
RETRIEVE Name, Address
WHERE Age > 21

Querying is discussed in more detail in Section 7.4.5.

To provide more flexibility, the O_2 (Lecluse and Richard, 1989; Deux et al., 1990) object-oriented database management system for Altaïr allows the users to explicitly specify whether they want the extension of a class to be maintained. Thus a user can define a class with an extension through:

add class Person **with extension**
    type tuple   (Name: string,
                   Age: integer,
                   Address: address)

The **with extension** clause indicates that every time a new *Person* is created, it becomes an element of the set of all persons. As with Galileo or SIM, this set can be accessed and queried. The set that contains all the instances is, of course, *Person*. In O_2, objects that are instances of classes without extensions will persist *only if* they are reachable from a persistent root object. Persistence through reachability is discussed in the next section.

7.4.1.2 *Persistence through Reachability*

An alternative approach is to have one or more persistent database roots and to make every object that is reachable from these, persistent. This was the approach used in one of the earliest persistent programming languages, namely PS-ALGOL (Atkinson et al., 1983).

Programming or database languages typically incorporate different type constructors for tuple (record, aggregate, and so on) and collection objects (set, extension, group, and so on). Reachability can be defined transitively using the set-and-tuple model, as in FAD.

The persistent object space has a root called **database** and every object reachable from this database root is persistent. More specifically, the persistent object space is defined as follows:

1. database is a persistent tuple object:
   database = [S1: { . . . }, S2: { . . .}, . . . , Sn:{ . . .}]

2. If pT is a persistent tuple object, then pT.a (the attribute a of pT) is a persistent object.

3. If pS is a persistent set object then every element e of pS is persistent.

Every database or programming language that provides persistence through reachability uses a similar definition.

Figure 7.5 illustrates the transient and persistent object spaces accessible in a transaction. Note that persistent objects can be sub-objects of transient objects. But, by the definition above, the converse cannot happen (any sub-object of a persistent object is persistent). In other words, a persistent object can have multiple parents, some of which may be transient. The objects in the transient object space are visible only within the current transaction. When the transaction terminates, the transient objects on the right-hand side of Figure 7.5 disappear.

7.4.2 Transactions

A transaction (Eswaran et al., 1976) is a program that is either executed entirely or not executed at all. This is called atomicity; transactions are atomic. If the user

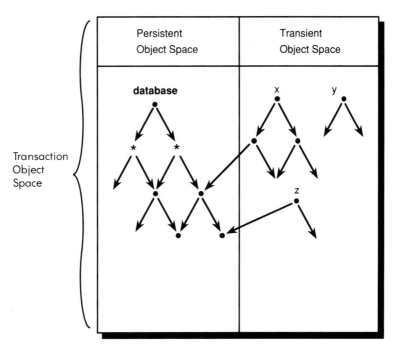

Figure 7.5 Persistent and transient object spaces.

performs updates to the persistent database within a transaction, then either *all* of the updates must be visible to the outside world or *none* of the updates must be seen. In the former case, it is said that the transaction has been committed. In the latter case we say the transaction has been aborted.

Database languages typically provide primitives to identify the sections of code that should be run as transactions. More specifically, many database management systems support most of the following constructs:

> *Begin transaction* indicates the start of a transaction. In some database management systems the *Begin Transaction* is implicit: a transaction is automatically started when the user starts executing a database statement. The section of code between this statement (implicit or explicit) and *End Transaction* will be executed atomically.

> *End transaction* indicates the end of the transaction. When this statement is executed successfully, all the statements (especially the updates) between *Begin Transaction* and *End Transaction* are committed. All updates become committed and programs which execute afterwards can see the updates performed by the transaction.

> *Abort transaction* is used on the occasion when the user decides to *undo* all work and terminate the transaction without committing its updates. To this end database languages provide a transaction abort mechanism. This is also known as transaction *rollback* or transaction *undo*.

Consider the following simple transactions:

```
Begin Transaction
     -- give Joe a 10% raise
     -- promote Joe to Sales Manager
End Transaction
```

The atomicity of the transaction guarantees that either Joe gets the raise *and* the promotion or he gets *neither*. Since the transaction is atomic "partial" executions are not possible. For example, Joe cannot be given a 10% raise and nothing more, even if there is a power failure or a system crash. The database system must ensure that the transaction is continued to the end *or* undo the 10% raise when power is restored.

Of course, in different database systems the actual syntax of the transaction begin, commit, and abort mechanisms differ. But the overall intention and semantics are the same. For example, GemStone's OPAL language provides some primitives for committing and aborting transactions. When logging in, a user is given a new workspace and a "copy" of the current committed database. All updates to the database are done in this workspace, transparent to all other users. Therefore, only that user sees updates, unless the user commits. Committing a transaction is achieved through sending a commit message to the system. In OPAL, the syntax is:

System commitTransaction

which asks the underlying system to commit the transaction. The user might choose to continue the session after the commit. This will start a new transaction and create a new workspace. Alternatively, the user might decide to undo all the updates to the database and abort the current transaction. This is achieved through the message

System abortTransaction

which tells the underlying system the transaction must be aborted.

One important concept associated with object-oriented databases is the notion of a nested transaction (Moss, 1981). With a nested transaction model, each transaction itself consists of atomic subtransactions. The subtransactions are also nested transactions. For a transaction to commit, each of its sub-transactions must either commit or be aborted.

As was said earlier, the main application domain of many of today's object-oriented database management systems is design or engineering applications, such as computer-aided design. As described in (Korth et al., 1990), the transaction management environment in computer-aided design projects is different from more traditional accounting transactions (which typically read and update a few records at a time).

A design object, such as a CAD object, is maintained and updated through a number of *project transactions*. Each project includes a number of individual designers who cooperate for the completion of the project. Thus a project transaction in turn consists of one or more *cooperating transactions*. Cooperating transactions include the transactions of the individual designers. The *designer transactions* are nested within the cooperating transactions and cooperate for the completion of the common task. Figure 7.6 demonstrates the different types of nested transactions in a design environment.

With nested transactions there is always a *top-level transaction*. Each top-level transaction can have a number of child transactions. For example, the top-level transaction that releases the design object has a number of child project transactions nested within it. These children can also have nested transactions within them. The updates of the transaction tree become visible to the outside world *only after* the top-level transaction commits. The updates of the committed transactions at the intermediate levels become visible only within the scope of their immediate predecessors. In the example, assume T1 starts T2 and T2 updates Joe's salary, gives him a promotion, and commits. Before committing T1, Joe's raise and promotion is only visible *within* T1. Transactions that are nested in T1 and that start after T2 will see these updates. But Joe's raise and promotion will not be visible outside T1, until T1 commits. Some object-oriented databases such as Statice and Ontos support nested transactions.

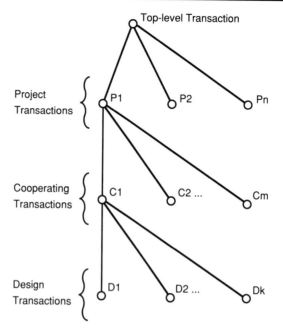

Figure 7.6 Nested transactions in a design environment.

In summary, database management systems must support atomic transactions. Object-oriented databases are geared toward engineering and design applications. Nested transactions provide a more direct support of project development for these applications.

7.4.3 Concurrency Control

In the typical execution environment of a DBMS, transactions run concurrently. In other words, multiple transactions will be active at the same time. These transactions can access and update the same persistent databases and/or the same persistent data objects. The DBMS must guarantee the consistency of the persistent database and the transaction results.

If transactions are allowed to run concurrently without any conflict resolution, anomalies can occur both in the persistent database and in the transaction executions. For example, assume T_1 and T_2 are executing concurrently, and T_1 reads an item I_1. Subsequently T_2 updates the same item I_1. Now assume T_1 reads I_1 again. If the DBMS does not have a concurrency control mechanism, T_1 will read a T_2's update. If T_2 aborts and its change to I_1 is rolled back, T_1 would have read a value that does not exist anymore! Even if T_2 commits, T_1 would have performed two identical read operations and obtained different values!

To guarantee database and transaction consistency, DBMSs impose a *serializable* order of execution. Serializable order means the results of the transactions are the same as if the transactions were executed one after another (in a series). When a DBMS enforces a serializable order, any order of execution of concurrent transactions can be reduced to an equivalent serialized execution schedule. A serializable execution schedule of concurrent transactions $\{T_1, \ldots, T_n\}$ is a sequential order of execution of the transactions in some permutation.

To guarantee serializability of transactions, DBMSs employ concurrency control strategies. There are three basic concurrency control algorithms:

1. *Time-stamp ordering* (Bernstein and Goodman, 1980). With this strategy, each transaction is given a time stamp (in most cases the transaction start time), and the system attempts to order the execution of transactions based on their time stamps. For example, assume transaction T_i has a time stamp i and transaction T_j has a time stamp j with i < j. The system will attempt to impose $< T_i$ *before* $T_j >$ serialization order. Assume T_j updates an object O and commits. Later, T_i attempts to read O (which has been updated by a younger transaction, T_j, which committed). This is a conflict, and the system will abort T_i. Executing transactions in their time stamp order always guarantees serializability.

2. *Optimistic algorithms* (Kung and Robinson, 1981). These algorithms allow transactions to continue executing until they are done. The transactions update the persistent data in private workspaces. This approach is optimistic because if the transaction aborts (such as due to conflict) all its work will be wasted. When the transaction is done with updating or retrieving from the persistent database, it enters a certification phase and attempts to commit. If the data it had read or updated does not conflict with reads or updates of other transactions, it is allowed to commit. Optimistic algorithms are best in applications where there is little contention for data objects (that is, transactions usually manipulate different objects of the persistent database).

3. *Pessimistic or locking algorithms* (Eswaran et al., 1976). Locking algorithms assume the worst and acquire locks on every persistent object that a transaction accesses. If a transaction reads an object, it must acquire a read lock. If a transaction wants to write an object, it must first acquire a write lock on the object. If an object is already locked, the transaction must wait until the lock is released. Thus there is the potential of deadlocks and the system must use some mechanism to either detect deadlocks and abort a transaction or prevent deadlock from occurring in the first place.

With locking algorithms to guarantee serializability, transactions must follow the *two-phase locking protocol* (Gray, 1978):

1. Before performing any read (write) operations on an object, the transaction must first acquire a read (write) lock on the object.

2. After releasing a lock, the transaction must never acquire any more locks.

Which objects are locked by a transaction? In relational systems locks are associated with tables, individual rows of tables (or records), or physical data pages. In object-oriented databases, users manipulate classes, instances, sets, and composite (complex) objects. Some objects are members or sub-objects of other (parent/container) objects. Therefore several object-oriented databases—and most notably, ORION (Kim et al., 1990)—have used *multigranule* locking. The main motivation for multigranule locking is to minimize the number of locks and, subsequently, maximize the concurrency. This enhances the overall throughput of the system. For example, when most of the instances of the class are to be accessed, it is wiser to lock the entire class (versus each instance of the class). However, when a few instances of a class are accessed, it is better to only lock the individual instances. This would allow concurrent transactions to access other instances. Therefore, when a lockable unit is at a finer granule level (for example, instances) there is more overhead. However, the concurrency is increased. By the same token, when locking is at the coarser granule level (for example, classes or container/composite objects) there is less overhead but also less concurrency.

For a more flexible approach to concurrency control it is possible to have hybrid schemata that combine the optimistic and pessimistic approaches. GemStone, for instance, supports both optimistic and pessimistic (locking) concurrency control mechanisms. With the optimistic approach the system allows the user to continue updating a copy of the database in his or her own workspace. When the user attempts to commit the transaction, the system might refuse to commit due to conflicts. A conflict would arise if, for example, while an object was read and updated in the user's workspace, it got modified and committed by another transaction.

The pessimistic concurrency mechanism in GemStone is an add-on to the optimistic scheme. Users are given the option to lock individual objects. A transaction can lock some objects, while accessing others optimistically (without locking). There are three types of locks:

> Read (Shared) Locks
>
> Write Locks
>
> Exclusive Locks

Multiple transactions can hold read locks on the same object. But only one transaction can hold a write lock or an exclusive lock on an object. If a transaction holds a read lock on an object, it prevents other transactions from updating or writing the object. For example, if T_1 gets a read lock on Joe's personnel record, no other transaction can update an attribute of Joe (such as his age or salary) and commit. With a read or a write lock, other transactions can still read the object. With an exclusive lock however, other transactions cannot even read the object and commit.

Locking does not have to be explicit and under the control of the user or the application. In many database management systems, locking is automatic and under the system's control. For instance, the Statice object-oriented DBMS uses a pessimistic concurrency control mechanism. Statice locks individual data pages on behalf of transactions, as these transactions access or update the data objects on the pages. When a transaction request attempts to read or write a page, the underlying system attempts to lock the page. If there are no conflicts the lock is granted. Otherwise the request must wait. If transactions cyclically wait for each other (they are *deadlocked*) one of the transactions is aborted, the deadlock chain is broken, and the other transactions are allowed to proceed.

7.4.4 Recovery

As described earlier, transactions are atomic. This means the DBMS must guarantee that *partial* results or partial updates of transactions that fail are not propagated to the persistent database. There are three types of failures from which a system must recover. To discuss the implications of each failure type we assume an underlying two-level memory system: a volatile main memory and a stable secondary memory (such as a magnetic or optical disk). The persistent data is always propagated to the secondary storage.

The three failure types are (Gray, 1978):

1. *Transaction failures:* Usually caused by the concurrent transactions conflicting in their access to the shared database. When such conflicts are detected, the DBMS aborts one or more of the conflicting transactions. Failures can also occur from user aborts.

2. *Systems failures:* Usually caused by software errors in the operating system, the DBMS, or power failure. This corresponds to a system crash in an operating system. When a system failure occurs, the content of the main memory is lost. However, the secondary disk storage remains intact. After a system failure the system must be rebooted and restarted.

3. *Media failures:* Usually caused by hard disk crashes or other nonrecoverable errors on the hard disk. A portion (possibly all) of the data on the hard disk is lost. Media failures are the hardest failures to recover from.

Reliability and the graceful recovery from these types of failures is an important feature of a database management system. The *recovery manager* is the module that handles the techniques for recovering from these failures. There are a number of data structures and strategies that are used to implement the recovery manager.

One of the most commonly used data structures for recovery management is the *log*. The log is used to record and store the *before* and *after images* of updated objects. The *before image* is the state of the object before the transaction update. The *after image* is the state of the object after the transaction update. Depending on the particular recovery algorithms used, one or both types of images must be stored on the log. The before and/or after images are recorded on the log during the normal execution of transactions. When a failure occurs and the system is restarted, the recovery manager is invoked to reconstruct a consistent database from the log and the existing data in secondary storage (the hard disk, assuming the failure was not a media failure).

Logging is used primarily to recover from transaction or system failures. It is more difficult to handle media failures. One simple technique often used to handle any kind of failure is *data mirroring* or *data replication*. If the persistent database is replicated or mirrored, there will actually be two or more copies of each persistent object. The copies will be stored on different media (different magnetic or optical disks), so if one of the disks crashes, the database can easily be recovered from the other disk. The underlying assumption, of course, is that the possibility of both (or all) hard disks crashing at the same time or within the same interval is negligible.

The GemStone object-oriented DBMS allows the user (actually, the system administrator) to create replicas or mirrors of the persistent database. The replica is created through a system command such as:

SystemRepository replicateWith: <file name>

where *<file name>* specifies the location of the replica. The replica can reside in the same disk as the original persistent database or on an entirely different disk volume. A different disk volume must be used if protection from media failures is desirable.

When a transaction performs an update, all replicas are updated before the transaction commits. Maintaining these replicas incurs execution time and storage overhead. Yet many critical applications require fault tolerance from any kind of failure. Examples include medical, military, and real-time transaction systems. In these situations, users are willing to live with the extra overhead, as long as they are guaranteed fast recovery and access to their databases.

7.4.5 Querying

Database management systems are used to process, store, update, and access bulk data. The persistent data objects are partitioned into collections or sets of objects with the same structure. For instance, the sales office automation example contains sets of persons (the salespeople), items, orders, accounts, warehouses, and so on. Queries are used to select subsets and sub-objects from database collection objects or sets. Here are some example queries:

> retrieve the name and age of all salespeople whose total sale in March 1990 was at least $50,000
>
> retrieve the name and address of all the salespeople who report to John Smith
>
> retrieve all warehouses that are within 1 mile of 1212 Main Street and contain at least 500 screwdrivers

Queries are extremely useful since they provide a high-level declarative style of programming to restrict and retrieve sub-objects from a large database. Declarative means the user specifies *what* is wanted from the database, without worrying *how* the data is stored or actually retrieved from the underlying system.

Query languages were introduced by relational systems. In previous chapters and sections we have already seen some examples of SQL queries. Most object-oriented database management systems provide some capability for querying collections, class extensions, or other set objects. For instance, both Ontos from Ontologic and Iris from Hewlett-Packard have a query language that is an object-oriented extension of SQL.

In Iris, the object-oriented extension of SQL is called Object SQL or OSQL (Fishman et al., 1989; Beech, 1988). The underlying data model in Iris is based on the functional data model (Shipman, 1981). Entity types are used to classify objects. Each entity type specifies one or more properties, which are functions that apply to the instances of the type. Entity types have extensions and can inherit from one another.

For example, the type *Person* can be created by:

```
Create Type Person (
    Name        char(20),
    Age         integer
    Address     address)
```

where *address* is another type. In Iris, *Name*, *Age* and *Address* are called properties (functions), and apply to instances of type *Person*.

Assume the address has a property called "State." With Object SQL a user can retrieve the name and state of all people who are older than 21:

```
Select Name(p), State(Address(p))
for each Person p
where Age(p) > 21
```

If type T_i has a property P_i which returns an object of type T_{i-1}, a user can compose the function application:

$$P_n(P_{n-1}(\ldots P_1(P)))$$

in the *Select* statements. For example, assume *Employee* is a subtype of *Person* and *SalesPerson* is a subtype of *Employee*. Furthermore, assume addresses have street names, salespeople have sales managers, and sales managers have secretaries. Secretaries are also employees. A user can then retrieve: the street name of the address of the secretary of the manager of each salesperson whose salary is more than $50,000 with:

Select
> *StreetName(Address(Secretary(Manager(p))))*
> *for each SalesPerson p*
> *where Salary(p) > $50,000*

As these examples illustrate, users can declaratively express queries for the persistent object-oriented databases, using an extension of SQL. There are several advantages to extending SQL:

- SQL is the most popular relational query language and is endorsed by almost all the major developers of relational systems. Therefore, an extended and upward-compatible SQL can easily support the application programs developed in SQL, and users can maintain their investment in these programs.
- It is the only relational language that has a standard developed for it.
- SQL is being promoted as the interface language of database engines and database servers. Therefore, new applications developed in SQL extensions can easily call these database servers for remote data access.

Still, some object-oriented databases have introduced new languages and language constructs for querying collections or sets of objects in persistent databases. One example is GemStone's OPAL, which introduces a special *selection block* construct for querying collections or sets of objects. A selection block specifies a query that associatively filters the qualifying elements in a collection, very similar to a SELECT clause in SQL. Selection blocks are delimited with braces ({}) and sent through a "select:" selector.

Assume *Emps* contains a set of employees. To obtain the subset of all employees in *Emps* who earn more than $60,000 the query is:

> *richEmps := Emps select:*
> *{ :anEmployee | anEmployee.salary > 60000}*

The predicate in the selection block can be more complex and involve conjunctions. For example to retrieve the employees whose last name is Jones and whose age is greater than 21:

> *Jones := Emps select:*
> *{ :anEmployee | (anEmployee.age > 21) &*
> *(anEmployee.name.last = 'Jones')}*

Whether through an extension of SQL or through new (querying) constructs, most OODBs offer some form of querying capability to retrieve sub-objects from the persistent databases.

7.4.6 Versioning

Access to previous states or alternate states of objects is an inherent part of many applications. Application domains that require access to the evolution of object states include engineering design applications (such as CAD, CAM, or CASE), office automation (for document management), as well as more traditional financial or accounting applications.

In these applications, the *same* object undergoes multiple changes or state transitions, and it is desirable to access or investigate specific previous states of the object. For example, each of the chapters of this book underwent an evolution. For some of the chapters we explicitly kept different versions. Versions of a chapter differed in organization (sections or sub-sections) and many times in content or emphasis. For some chapters the final version was constructed through mixing and integrating different components of previous versions. We found it extremely useful to keep the previous versions around and access or use parts of them in subsequent versions. This happens often in document management, and over much more complex document systems.

Version management in an object-oriented database consists of a number of tools and constructs to automate or simplify the construction and organization of versions or configurations. Otherwise it would be up to the user to organize and maintain the versions. For this book, we did not have access to any version management tools in the DOS environment, so we had to use a naming convention to keep track of the different versions of the same chapter, and the relationship (the derivation tree) of the versions with one another. This proved to be quite laborious and subject to error. In complex design applications, automatic version management is an extremely useful and powerful utility.

Many engineering and design applications use versioning to create progressively more enhanced versions of the design object. In these applications, the design objects are typically stored in a central (persistent) repository. Designers *check out* a persistent object from the database, work on it for a while and, when they are satisfied they have a better implementation, they *check in* their object as a different version of the object.

When a versioned object gets created, it is initially the root of a version set that eventually contains all the versions of the object. Designers create new versions of existing versions of objects. The main property that is common to all the versions of the *same* object is the *identity* of the object. Throughout its versioned history, the object may undergo multiple state and even structural modifications.

If all the versions of an object are created sequentially, we get a linear version set. But in general versioning, multiple designers can create alternative versions of an object. This is illustrated in Figure 7.7 for the object O1. The version set of O1 is {V1, V2, V3, V4, V5, V6, V7}. The version V1 was the original version and V7 the final released version. V2 and V3 are alternatives of V1. V4 and V5 are alternatives

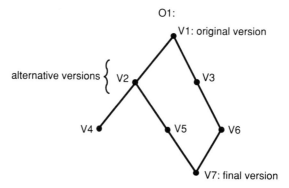

Figure 7.7 Version set of O1.

of V2. The path V1–V3–V6–V7 is a linear versioning path from V1 to V7. As the figure illustrates the versions are partially ordered. Each version has successors and predecessors.

Some object-oriented languages that support versioning provide language constructs to:

> check-out and check-in object versions
> retrieve successors or predecessors of versions

To create a version in Iris a user must first name and check out a successor version of an existing version:

> *checkout V1 as V2*

This command creates a new version V2 of V1. To actually commit V2 as a version the user must:

> *checkin V2*

This command inserts V2 in the version set of V1's object and makes it a successor of V1. Iris provides special functions for retrieving all predecessors, immediate predecessors, all successors, and immediate successors of a version. For example, using the versions in Figure 7.7:

> *Successor(V2)*

will return all the successors of V2: {V4, V5, V7}. Similarly:

> *Predecessor(V6)*

will return all the predecessors of V6: {V3, V1}.

The Ontos object-oriented DBMS also provides a versioning and alternatives mechanism for objects. Users can create *configuration* objects, which contain all the objects of the same version. The configuration hierarchy is actually a tree. Thus, Ontos also supports both linear versions and alternatives of the same version. Only the configurations that are at the leaves of the tree are updatable. Inner configurations can only be deleted.

In summary, versioning is a convenient and powerful functionality offered by many OODBs. Versioning facilitates the configuration management of large and complex persistent object spaces.

7.4.7 Integrity Constraints

Through transactions, database management systems map one consistent database state onto another. The consistency of the database is typically expressible through predicates or conditions on the current state of the database. Predicates can also apply to objects or attribute values in the database. The predicates that capture the consistency of a database are called *integrity constraints*. Generally, there are a number of integrity constraints that must be enforced on a database state to guarantee its consistency. Here are some simple examples:

1. The age of a person cannot be a negative number.
2. An account balance must be less or equal to the sum of the deposits.
3. If an employee works for a particular department, a record for that department must exist in the database.
4. The social security number of each employee must be unique in the set of all employees.
5. A person must have a name; the Name attribute cannot be empty or null.

As these examples suggest, there are many types of integrity constraints that must be imposed on a database to maintain its consistency. The integrity constraint types can be categorized in the following ways:

a. Unique key constraints
b. Referential or foreign key constraints
c. Non-null constraints
d. Domain constraints
e. General integrity constraints

Unique key constraints are illustrated in the social security example (number **4.** above). Object-oriented databases support object identity; each object is unique, independent of its state or attribute values. Yet the user or designer of the database might still like to specify and enforce unique attribute value constraints on collection or set objects. In SIM, for instance, we can express a unique option on an attribute of a class with:

```
Class Person(
    Name:      char[20];
    Age:       integer;
    Address:   Address);

Subclass Employee of Person(
    SocSecNum:   integer, unique;
    Salary:      dollar;
    Rank:        char[1];
    Works-In:    Department);
```

The second type of constraints are referential or foreign key constraints. The following example illustrates this type of constraint. As indicated before, the relational model is value based (versus object or identity based). This means all attribute values are base values (integers, floating point, or character strings). Column or attribute values cannot be objects. For instance, a common way of defining the *Department* table and the *Employee* table in SQL is:

```
CREATE TABLE Department(
        DepartmentNumber      INTEGER,
        DepartmentName        CHAR(20),
        Budget                FLOAT,
        . . .
        PRIMARY KEY (DepartmentNumber))

CREATE TABLE Employee(
        Name                CHAR(20),
        Age                 INTEGER,
        Address             CHAR(100),
        Salary              FLOAT,
        Rank                CHAR(1),
        DepartmentNumber    INTEGER)
```

Here the WorksIn attribute (see Figure 7.4) is an integer valued *DepartmentNumber* in the relational model. Each *DepartmentNumber* in *Employee* indicates a department in *Department*. The integer value is used to retrieve information pertaining to an employee's department by joining the *DepartmentNumber* column in *Employee* with the *DepartmentNumber* column in *Department*. A *DepartmentNumber* in *Employee* that does not correspond to *DepartmentNumber* in *Department* is a meaningless *dangling reference* to a nonexisting object. To protect against such erroneous references, some relational systems (including the SQL standard) have introduced an explicit referential or foreign key constraint. Thus the CREATE TABLE declaration for *Employee* would also contain:

```
FOREIGN KEY (DepartmentNumber)
REFERENCES Department
```

and an attempt to insert a *DepartmentNumber* in *Employee* that does not exist in *Department* would cause an error.

As mentioned in Chapter 4, most of the joins or complex queries in relational systems are foreign key joins. In the example, each value of the *DepartmentNumber* column in *Employee* is matched with a value in *Department* to retrieve attributes of an employee's department. For instance:

```
SELECT Department.Budget
FROM Employee, Department
WHERE Employee.Name = "Joe" AND
    Employee.DepartmentNumber
        = Department.DepartmentNumber
```

retrieves the budget of Joe's department.

In object-oriented databases such as FAD, GemStone, SIM, or Iris, object identity solves the problem of dangling references and the need for referential integrity constraints. This is a very powerful and important quality of object identity: The ability to reference objects or entities directly. In object-oriented databases the department of an employee is referenced and accessed directly by its (tuple) identity, instead of by an indirect and semantically void number such as *DepartmentNumber*. Therefore, in object-oriented databases supporting object identity, *there is no need* for referential integrity constraints (with the guarantee that objects pointed to or referenced by other objects are not deleted by the system).

Consider the *Employee* class as defined earlier in SIM. The WorksIn attribute references an object or entity in *Department* directly. So there cannot be a WorksIn attribute value that references an object that does not exist! Of course it *could* be the case that an employee is currently unemployed or in transition, and is not working in any department. In this case the WorksIn attribute value will be null.

In retrieving an attribute of a referenced object, it is not necessary to perform joins. As mentioned in Chapter 4 joins are actually quite *unnatural*, and they are needed in relational systems because of the lack of support for object identity. The WorksIn attribute value is actually a department whose attributes can be accessed directly in a query. For instance, using the SIM data manipulation language and assuming a class *Department* with a *Budget* attribute, the above query ("retrieve the budget of Joe's department") can be expressed as:

```
FROM Employee
RETRIEVE Budget of WorksIn
WHERE Name of Employee = "Joe"
```

Another type of constraint is the non-null constraint. The fifth example, given at the beginning of this section, indicated that a person must have a name. This means the *Name* attribute value of a person *must* be initialized or have a value. Without a value in the *Name* attribute, it will be impossible (or meaningless) to retrieve information about that tuple. So, when a user creates an instance of a person, a character string constant must be provided as a value for *Name*. *Name* cannot be empty or null.

Some database management systems, including some dialects of SQL, have an explicit construct to impose non-null integrity constraints. The SIM object-oriented DBMS also supports non-null integrity constraints through a REQUIRED specification. Therefore to indicate that the *Name* of a person is not null, the *Person* class declaration becomes:

```
Class Person(
        Name:      char[20], REQUIRED;
        Age:       integer;
        Address:   Address);
```

The domain of an attribute may also be limited. This is known as a *domain constraint*. An example is that *Age* must be restricted to a nonnegative integer. Object-oriented systems can easily support domain constraints using specialization through restriction (see Chapter 3). For example, a user can create a class NON_NEGATIVE_INTEGER as a specialization of the INTEGER class, restricting its domain to integers greater than or equal to 0. Then a user can specify the *Age* attribute to be of type NON_NEGATIVE_INTEGER, and achieve the desired domain constraint.

A domain constraint is just a specification that attribute values must satisfy certain constraints. The most natural way to achieve this is to create a domain or a class whose instances are only those objects that satisfy the constraints. Even some relational systems have this capability. Some dialects of SQL provide a CREATE DOMAIN construct that allows the user to create new domains restricting the values of existing base types (integers, floating point numbers, and character strings) to be within a certain range. This provides a limited support of specialization (through restriction).

But object-oriented databases can allow *more general* integrity constraints because of their ability to create subclasses and often through separate constraint constructs. The integrity constraints discussed so far deal mainly with individual attribute values. Yet it is possible to define much more general integrity constraints, involving multiple attribute values or aggregates of attribute values. Arbitrary constraints on persistent objects can be expressed! A simple example is given at the beginning of this section: The summing of deposits and the evaluation of a balance.

In many cases the constraints are expressed in terms of aggregate functions. Some examples of aggregate functions include *sum*, *average*, and *count*. Here are some integrity constraints involving aggregate functions:

1. The total number of accounts allocated to a salesperson should not exceed 100.
2. There should be an inventory of at least 50 sledgehammers in warehouse 3.
3. The total amount of salesmanaged by a sales manager should exceed $100,000 per year.

The SIM object-oriented DBMS has a *Verify/Assert* mechanism that can be used to define general integrity constraints. For example, in the office automation example, there is the multivalued (*mv*) attribute *Accounts* in the *SalesPerson* subclass:

> *Subclass SalesPerson of Employee(*
> *Accounts: Account mv;*
> *...)*

Integrity constraint (i) can be expressed with:

> *Verify account-restriction on SalesPerson*
> *assert count(Accounts) <= 100*
> *else "too many accounts"*

Note that the *Verify/Assert* construct can also be used to indicate the domain constraint that *Age* must be nonnegative:

> *Verify age-restriction on Person*
> *assert Age >= 0*
> *else "negative age value: error"*

Integrity constraints are declarative constructs that are used to define consistent databases. When a transaction terminates successfully (that is, commits), it must guarantee database consistency (although during the execution of the transaction some of the integrity constraints might be violated). Object-oriented databases provide richer data semantics. Therefore some integrity constraints (for instance, referential integrity constraints) are handled automatically by the model. However, OODBs can still support key, non-null, and more general integrity constraints to maintain the integrity of the persistent databases.

7.4.8 Security

When a user logs into a multiuser operating system, a password must be provided to gain access to the system. Furthermore, even after the user is logged in, each file or directory in the system has access privileges. Some files/directories cannot be accessed at all; others can be read but not updated; other files can just be executed.

Database management systems also incorporate security primitives for accessing or updating persistent objects. Some relational systems require that the user have certain privileges for a table to perform retrieval or update operations. SQL, for instance, has a GRANT operation that is used to grant SELECT (read), INSERT, DELETE, and UPDATE privileges. For example to allow the user John read from the *Employee* table, he must first be granted the SELECT privilege:

> *GRANT SELECT ON Employee TO John*

To allow user Mary to INSERT and UPDATE records in the *Employee* table, the declaration is:

GRANT INSERT, UPDATE On Employee TO Mary

In the GemStone object-oriented DBMS, every user owns at least one *segment* in which to create objects. A segment is similar to an operating system directory. It contains a group of objects and all objects in a segment have the same access privileges. If a user has permission to read one object in a segment, the user has permission to read *all* the objects in the segment. A user who owns a segment can grant read or write permission to other users or groups of users. Objects can be moved from one segment to another. Thus if a user wishes to protect an object that is stored in a segment accessible by many users, the object can be moved to a *protect* segment accessible only to that user.

A security mechanism and the protection of persistent databases from adverse access is an integral part of any DBMS. Object-oriented databases are no exception.

7.4.9 Performance Issues

Performance in database management systems, as in many other applications, is extremely important. If two DBMSs provide similar functionalities, choosing between them is often based on their performance on standardized "benchmarks." Benchmarks are programs that are used to measure the performance of some critical properties of a DBMS: How is the response time for some complex queries; how fast can the database perform updates; how many users can be accessing the database concurrently; and so forth.

Object-oriented databases have developed the reputation of being "rich in functionality but poor in performance." So, for object-oriented databases, the need to excel in performance is even more critical than for other applications.

Database management systems employ three main strategies to enhance the overall performance of the system:

1. Indexes or accelerators
2. Storage management techniques
3. Query optimization

The following paragraphs explain these techniques, and demonstrate some object-oriented database languages that let users provide hints for creating indexes or controlling the storage management.

7.4.9.1 Indexes

In many applications, users restrict their queries based on a fixed subset of attributes. The access to the qualifying objects will be much faster if the system has indexed those attributes. If users retrieve information about *Persons* based on *Name*, then it makes sense to have an index for attribute *Name* of *Person*. An index stores attribute values in a specified order (say alphabetical), so that the entire table does not have to be searched during a query like "retrieve the age of all persons named Smith." All Smiths will be stored in one place in the index, and once a person with a name after Smith (like Snail) is found, the search can be stopped.

Most database data definition languages allow the user or designer of the database to create an index. The user specifies which attributes in a collection or set object must be indexed. When the user submits a query based on these attributes, the underlying system uses the index to accelerate the query execution time. It should be emphasized that indexes do not represent new information. Their purpose is to make some programs or queries run faster. The DBMS will return the same query results independent of the existence of indexes.

Indexes can be created in many ways. In Statice, users can specify different indexes on attributes when *defining* an entity type. For example:

```
(define-entity-type person()
    ((name string
        :inverse person-named
        :inverse-index t)
    (age integer)
    (soc-sec-num integer)
    (address address-type)))
```

This data definition construct creates a person entity with attributes name, age, social security number, and address. The *:inverse-index* declaration indicates that an index must be created from values of name to entities of person. The name entries in the index will be hashed or sorted in some order.

Figure 7.8 illustrates a possible index, sorted on last name. Each entry is of the form:

Name Value	Entity
Adams, Tim	e100
Jones, Mary	e50
Ripper, Jack	e200
Silverman, Leo	e75
Smith, John	e300
...	...

Figure 7.8 An index sorted on name.

> *<last-first name string> <entity>*

The *<entity>* corresponds to a logical pointer to the object. When given a name, the system can quickly retrieve the corresponding person object (entity) using this index.

Statice also supports what it calls regular indexes (versus the inverse indexes above). For set valued attributes, regular indexes associate the entity of a parent object with the list of entities that correspond to the set elements. For instance, salespeople have the *Accounts* and *Orders* set valued attributes. Assume the salespeople entity type is created through:

```
(define-entity-type sales-person(employee)
  ((quota integer)
   (accounts (set-of account) :index t)
   (orders (set-of order) :index t)
   . . .
)
```

The *:index* for *accounts* and *orders* indicates that an index will be created that accelerates the access from a salesperson entity to the accounts. Therefore, regular indexes accelerate access from an entity to the values of a set valued attribute. Inverse indexes accelerate accesses from values of attributes to the entity.

GemStone's OPAL allows the specification of indexes explicitly on instance variables or paths to expedite associative retrievals. A path is a concatenation of instance variable names separated by periods ("."). The path traverses values of the instance variables of composite objects. For example, if the instance variable *Name* is an object with instance variables *Last* and *First* then to obtain the last name and first name of John we have:

> *John.name.last*
> *John.name.first*

where John is an instance of *Person*. If John is an employee, we can obtain the budget of his department through:

> *John.department.budget*

We can obtain the last name of his manager through:

> *John.manager.name.last*

Paths can be used in selection blocks to qualify instance variable values. Without an index, the search in a selection block will traverse and consider every single element in the collection instance. Indexes restrict these exhaustive searches and hence drastically improve the performance.

As pointed out earlier, OPAL supports both the equality (=) and identical (==) predicates. Accordingly, OPAL allows the creation of two types of indexes: identity indexes and equality indexes. Identity indexes are useful when the predicate in the selection block involves an (==) on the indexed instance variable.

Equality indexes are useful in value based comparisons such as = and >=. Equality indexes can be created only on base types such as booleans, numbers, strings, and so on. Assume *LocalEmps* is a set of employees. An equality index on the last names of employees could be created through:

> *LocalEmps CreateEqualityIndexOn: 'name.last'*

This latter index will be created on a path. As a "side effect" an identity index will be created on *name*. In general, indexes on paths will create identity indexes on every instance variable in the path except the last instance variable, which could have an equality index as in this example.

An identity index is always automatically created on the elements of the set. Therefore, if the predicate in the selection block is

> *anEmp.name.last = 'Jones'*

then

1. The equality index on *last* will be used to retrieve identities of qualifying *name* objects.
2. The identity index on *name* will be used to retrieve identities on employees. Note that the identity index on *name* associates identities of *name* with identities of corresponding employees.
3. The identity index on the *employee* collection instance will be used to retrieve the qualifying employees.

Another important usage of identity indexes is in predicates involving ==. For example, if *hardDept* indicates a particular hardware department object, then

> *EmpsInrichDept := myEmps select:*
>   *{ :anEmp | :anEmp.dept == hardDept }*

will retrieve all employees that are in that particular hardware department. An identity index on the *'dept'* instance variable will greatly accelerate the search.

7.4.9.2 *Storage Management*

Indexing is one element of a much larger issue in object-oriented databases, namely the storage management of the persistent object spaces. Storage management deals with the efficient organization, storage, and access of the persistent objects. Random access memory (RAM) or the main memory of a computer system is volatile; when the power is turned off, the memory content is lost. In order to be persistent, the objects have to be stored in a persistent medium, such as a magnetic or an optical disk.

Also, the object spaces in object-oriented databases are large and complex. But the underlying physical spaces of the persistent media are linear address spaces, in many cases partitioned into fixed-size segments or pages. Figure 7.9 gives a schematic diagram of the difference between an object space and physical storage mediums. This difference causes many difficult storage management issues in object-oriented databases. On the left-hand side is a complex object of sets (collection objects) and tuples (entities). On the right-hand side is a collection of data pages. The complex object is a graph, since objects can arbitrarily reference other objects or be components of other objects.

Here are some of the problems that must be resolved by an object manager:

1. How should the object space on the left-hand side be mapped onto the data pages on the right?
2. What auxiliary structures, accelerators, or indexes should be used to enhance the accesses of nested sub-objects?

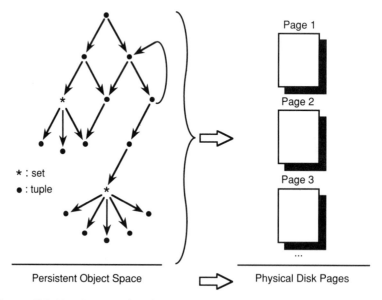

★ : set
● : tuple

Persistent Object Space   Physical Disk Pages

Figure 7.9 Mapping complex object spaces onto secondary-storage disk pages.

For the latter enhancement problems it has been shown how object-oriented databases allow users to create different kinds of indexes. The underlying storage manager of an object-oriented database builds and maintains physical indexes. These indexes map attribute values onto the disk pages of the objects containing these attribute values. For example, if the instance variables of John Smith are stored on page 3, the index will indicate that "Smith, John" is stored on page 3.

Storage management in object-oriented databases is rather complex. In more conventional hierarchical, network, or relational systems, the structure of the database is more regular. A relational database, for example, consists of a collection of flat tables. Each table is a set of tuples. The tuples are all of the same type and typically of manageable size. Objects are not nested in one another and do not reference each other.

Besides indexing, the main issue in storage management is *clustering*. Clustering tries to group or organize objects that are most frequently accessed together on the same storage pages. The idea of "most frequently accessed together" is problematic. The authors illustrate this with a simple example.

Assume classes have extensions. Consider the *SalesPerson* and *Account* classes. In order to store the accounts of salespeople there are at least two choices:

1. To cluster (store together) the accounts of each salesperson with that salesperson's own storage record; or
2. To store all the accounts of all salespeople together, and maintain the association between a salesperson and the account through auxiliary structures.

If the accounts are accessed through a salesperson most of the time, then it is better to use the first option. The storage manager can just go to where the salesperson object is stored, and all the accounts are there on one page. If the second option is chosen, the storage manager would have to locate the salesperson object, and then traverse the auxiliary structures to find out where each account is stored. If most of the time the users are accessing all the accounts (without caring about the salespeople), then the second option is better. There can be many different access patterns, each of which implies a different optimal storage organization.

How can these access patterns or the storage organizations be specified? Whether discussing indexing or clustering there are two fundamental strategies in choosing between different storage organization options:

1. *Automatic (Dynamic) strategies.* If the system can keep track of the different access patterns used, it can decide how to place or organize the objects. If certain objects are accessed together very frequently, the object manager places these objects on the same storage page. If certain attributes are accessed associatively very frequently, then the storage manager creates an index automatically.

2. *User-Specified (Static) strategies.* The simpler strategy is to let the user or database designer specify which indexes or clustering strategies should be used. The system merely follows the user's design.

For static strategies, the data definition language must include special language constructs for creating indexes and/or specifying clustering. Earlier it was shown how the user can create indexes in object-oriented databases such as Statice and GemStone. In GemStone, users can also specify how objects should be clustered on disk. GemStone supports a basic cluster method; whenever the user sends the message:

MyObject cluster

the underlying system assigns *MyObject* to a disk page. Through repeated application of the clustering method the user can specify for the system how the instance variables of objects should be clustered together on disk. The disk pages which are used by the *cluster* method belong to a *bucket*. A bucket is a sequence of disk pages. When the user repeatedly applies *cluster* to objects, the pages from the bucket sequence are allocated one after the other, to store the objects on disk.

To cluster an instance of *Person* in breadth-first order, the user can specify a method:

```
clusterPersonBreadthFirst
        self cluster.
        name cluster.
        age cluster.
        address cluster.
                name first cluster.
                name middle cluster.
                name last cluster.
                address streetNum cluster
                address streetName cluster
                address State cluster
                . . .
```

GemStone also provides a built-in method, *clusterDepthFirst*. The user can invoke this method to store the instance variables of an object in a depth-first order. Figure 7.10 illustrates the breadth-first and depth-first storage of the same person. The illustration is much simpler than what would actually be stored on disk by GemStone. However, it illustrates the general intent of breadth-first versus depth-first clustering.

To minimize the I/O overhead of database accesses it is desirable to cluster in secondary storage the objects that are most often accessed together. Clustering becomes much more significant in object-oriented databases, since the object spaces are much more complex (than flat tables in relational databases).

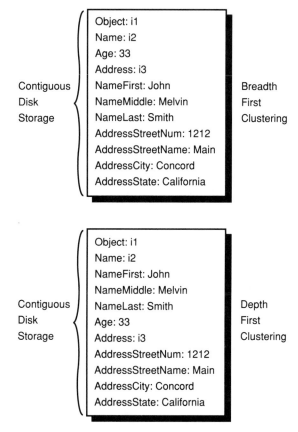

Figure 7.10 Breadth- and depth-first clusterings of the same person.

7.4.9.3 *Query Optimization*

As shown, some object-oriented languages allow the users to provide indexing and clustering hints to the system. These hints have no effect on the semantics of the operations or the returned results. They are used to improve the overall performance of some frequently used queries or operations.

Given a query, the underlying system uses the indexes and clustering strategies to come up with an optimal execution plan: The plan that will return the results of the query in the shortest time. In a database management system, the *query optimizer* is the module that is responsible for finding this optimal plan. Query optimization is completely hidden from the users. A query optimizer attempts to reduce the:

1. Number of I/O or disk page accesses.
2. Computation (CPU) overhead for executing the query.

Similar to relational database optimization techniques, the query optimizer in an object-oriented database management system can use the following information to generate an optimal execution plan:

1. *Statistics on the classes or collection objects:* These include the cardinality of the number of instances of a class or number of elements in a collection, the distribution of values, the correlation of values, and so on.

2. *Information on the clustering of values of instance variables in the class heirar-chy:* These include the type of clustering (for instance, breadth- or depth-first), information on the secondary storage segments that store instances of different classes, and so on.

3. *Information on accelerators:* In other words, information on the indexes of classes or collection objects.

Besides these kinds of statistical information, the query optimizer chooses between different algorithms for evaluating query results. For instance, relational query optimizers chose between alternative *join* algorithms: sort-merge, nested loop join (Selinger et al., 1979), hash join (Kitsuregawa et al., 1983; DeWitt and Gerber, 1985), join indexes (Valduriez, 1987), and so on. In many cases the components of complex objects are *decomposed* or fragmented (Copeland and Khoshafian, 1985). Object-oriented databases can choose a particular surrogate-join algorithm to correlate or *reconstruct* fragmented complex objects.

Besides indexing, clustering, and query optimization there are other techniques that enhance the overall performance of object-oriented databases. For example, *buffering* (caching) of frequently accessed persistent objects can be used to reduce the secondary storage accesses. Another implementation/performance issue related to buffering deals with the translation of secondary storage object references to (virtual) main memory addresses (Maier and Stein, 1990; Kim et al., 1990; Deux et al., 1990).

As this brief discussion illustrates, query optimization in object-oriented databases is *at least* as complex as optimization in relational systems. As pointed out by Zdonik and Maier (1990) there are many characteristics of object-oriented databases that compound the difficulty of query optimization. Some of the problems include the diversity of the data types, the richness and generality of the data manipulation language, data hiding, and so on. Optimization will remain a crucial issue for object-oriented databases.

■ 7.5 INTELLIGENT DATABASES

There have been several proposals, prototypes, and systems that have interfaced database management systems with AI (artificial intelligence) engines, multimedia data types, and object-oriented capabilities. Some examples include TAXIS (Mylopoulos et al., 1980; Wong, 1983), which allowed relational systems to specify semantic integrity constraints and exception handling through classes and inheritance heirarchies; PROSQL (Chang and Walker, 1986), which interfaced Prolog to SQL/DS; and POSTGRES (Stonebraker and Rowe, 1986; Stonebraker et al., 1990), mentioned earlier. POSTGRES integrates abstract data types, constructed types and a rule system with a relational database management system.

In the evolution of databases and data models, object-oriented databases form an important and necessary phase. The future of databases, however, is with intelligent databases. Intelligent databases include object-oriented databases as a subset. A comprehensive definition and exposition of intelligent databases is given in the book *Intelligent Databases* (Parsaye et al., 1989). As defined there, intelligent databases are:

> Databases that manage information in a natural way, making that information easy to store, access, and use.

The emphasis in intelligent databases is on *information* rather than *data*, because intelligent databases incorporate not only traditional applications such as inventory management, but also knowledge bases, automatic discovery systems, imaging applications, and so on. Intelligent databases represent a new technology for information management that has evolved as a result of the integration of traditional approaches to databases with more recent fields such as:

- Object orientation concepts
- Expert systems
- Multimedia information retrieval

This is illustrated in Figure 7.11. Therefore, intelligent databases represent the merging of a number of distinct paths of technological development. Until recently, these technologies were treated in isolation, with each technology being only weakly linked to others. For instance, expert systems have relied on little more than file-transfer protocols to gather data from databases. Due to the phenomenal growth in each field, the connections to the other fields did not have time to form. Now that these technologies have reached a stage of maturity, it is possible to define an overall unifying structure for viewing all these fields. Intelligent databases provide a common approach to the access and use of information for analysis and decision making.

The top-level architecture of the intelligent database consists of three levels:

- High-level tools
- High-level user interface
- Intelligent database engine

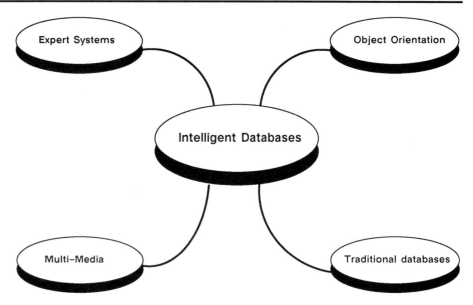

Figure 7.11 Intelligent databases.

As Figure 7.12 shows, this resembles a staircase architecture. Users and developers may independently access different layers at different times. The details and functionality of each level is given in (Parsaye et al., 1989). Here is a brief overview.

The first of these levels is the high-level tools level. These tools provide the user with a number of facilities: Intelligent search capabilities, data quality and integrity control, and automated discovery. These high-level tools represent an external library of powerful tools. Most of these tools may be broadly classified as information management techniques, similar to spreadsheets and graphic representation tools. They look and work much as their stand-alone equivalents, but are modified so as to be compatible with the intelligent database model. They are object-oriented, and their basic structure mirrors the object representation methods of the intelligent database model.

The second level is the high-level user interface. This level creates the model of the task and the database environment that users interact with. It has to deal as much with how the *user* wants to think about databases and information management as with how the database *engine* actually operates. Associated with this level is a set of representation tools that enhance the functionality of the intelligent database.

The user interface is presented in two aspects. First, there is a core model that is presented to the user. This core model consists of the object-oriented representation of information, along with a set of integrated tools for creating new object types, browsing among objects, searching, and asking questions. In addition, there is a set of high-level tools that enhances the functionality of the intelligent database system for certain classes of user.

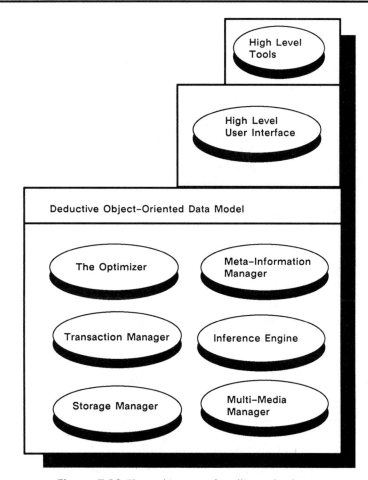

Figure 7.12 The architecture of intelligent databases.

The base level of the system is the intelligent database engine and its data model. This model allows for a deductive object-oriented representation of information, which can be expressed and operated on in a variety of ways. The engine includes backward- and forward-chaining inference procedures, as well as optimizing compilers, drivers for the external media devices, and storage managers.

The intelligent database engine, with its deductive object-oriented data model, is the underlying repository for integrated applications and products using the high-level tools and the high-level user interfaces. The engine is the *core* and the most important component of future systems. The intelligent database engine provides the functionality and the performance for supporting integrated applications. In addition, access to other databases, distributed inferencing, and database management systems can be achieved through the intelligent database engine.

Therefore, intelligent database engines consist of two components:

1. *The Deductive Object-Oriented Data (DOOD) Model.* This provides the interface with the layers above. DOOD is basically the core intelligent database language. Applications that intend to use the intelligent database engine submit programs written in DOOD. As its name suggests, DOOD incorporates object-oriented modeling capabilities.

2. *The intelligent database engine.* It compiles, optimizes, and executes DOOD programs. Figure 7.12 indicates some of the components of the architecture: The Optimizer, the Inference Engine, the Meta-Information Manager, the Transaction Manager, the Multimedia Data Manager, and the Storage Manager.

In the next two sections, a more detailed description of the data model and architectural components of the intelligent database engine is provided.

7.5.1 The Deductive Object-Oriented Data Model

The intelligent database strategy is to capture and represent the deductive, object-oriented, and multimedia capabilities of intelligent databases. One option is to create an entirely new language with these capabilities. Another alternative is to extend an existing database language with these features. As discussed in the previous sections, object-oriented database products have chosen one or the other approach. Some have introduced new languages whereas others have extended the most popular relational language standard, namely SQL. As discussed in Section 7.4.5, the second option has several advantages. Therefore we present the integrated intelligent database capabilities in DOOD as a dialect of SQL called *Intelligent SQL.* Here only a brief overview of Intelligent SQL is presented. For more details see (Khoshafian et al., 1990*b*) and (Khoshafian, 1990).

Intelligent SQL introduces three main categories of extensions to SQL:

1. *Deductive rules* to allow inferencing or proving goals from within database queries.

2. *Object-oriented features* to model the real world as closely as possible using abstract data typing, inheritance, and object identity.

3. *Multimedia data types* to allow more direct access to multimedia objects through the database data manipulation language.

7.5.1.1 Deductive Rules and SQL

The integration of expert systems (rule-based systems) and databases is becoming increasingly important to a larger class of users and applications. Expert systems have proliferated diverse applications such as in medicine, mathematics, business, and configuration of complex systems. Additional application areas include office automation, surveillance systems, manufacturing, oil refining, and battlefield management. However, although most of these applications use large data/knowledge bases, the integration of rule-based systems and database management systems remains "loosely" coupled.

There are two commonly used loose coupling strategies for AI/DBMS interconnection:

1. The inference engine submits queries (for example, in SQL) to the database engine as illustrated in Figure 7.13*a*. Besides the lack of integration of the two languages (the rule-based language and SQL), the performance penalty of this schema is severe. Furthermore it is very difficult to perform inferences and prove goals under a consistent transaction model of computation, since typically only the database management system is under transaction control. Thus the same goal in the same expert system shell session could generate different proofs because of modifications in the underlying databases. In addition to the query and data "traffic," in many cases the inference engine replicates the functionality of the database engine in its search, optimization, and storage strategies.

2. Alternatively, a rule-based system (expert system shell) could read data files generated by databases (such as a dBASE .dbf file) and then process the data locally, as illustrated in Figure 7.13*b*. There are numerous problems with this approach. For one thing, the integrity and concurrency control of the database files could easily be violated since accesses and updates are performed through a "foreign" application without going through the database management system. Moreover, the rule-based system must understand and manipulate different file formats generated by different database management systems. Sometimes the internal structures of these file formats are proprietary.

The intelligent database approach is to have a "tight" coupling of the engines and the languages. This is illustrated in Figure 7.13*c*. As discussed in Section 7.5.2, the databases and intelligent engines are integrated into one intelligent database engine. This means proving goals, database queries, and database updates are all under the same transaction control mechanism. It also means the intelligent database engine has a single optimizer and the data traffic between the two engines is minimized.

As for the languages, the integration of rules with SQL will allow the user to have:

1. SQL SELECT statements in the premise of *if-then* rules.
2. Logical predicates in the WHERE clauses of SQL statements.

The general form of *if-then* rules is:

        \<Conclusion clause and arguments\>

If

        \<Condition clauses and their arguments\>

The syntax of the rules follows (Parsaye and Chignell, 1988). To add SQL to rules, the concept of a condition clause is extended to include the concept of an SQL clause. An SQL clause is thus a statement of the form:

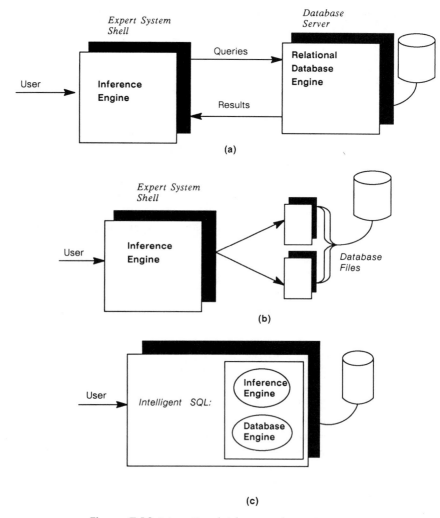

Figure 7.13 Integrating databases and expert systems.

SELECT A1 [as X1], A2 [as X2],..., An [as Xn]
FROM R1,..., Rm
WHERE <search condition>

which may appear within a rule. Therefore a rule can be of the form:

    Predicate X1,..., Xn
If
    SELECT A1 [as X1], A2 [as X2],..., An [as Xn]
    FROM R1,..., Rm
    WHERE <search condition>

where *<search condition>* may be a combination of pure SQL search conditions and goals that are to be proven by rules. Thus rule-based inferencing and SQL search conditions may be combined.

To illustrate the use of rules with SQL consider the schema:

```
CREATE TABLE Employee(
    Name            CHAR(20),
    Age             INTEGER,
    Address         CHAR(40),
    Rank            CHAR(1),
    Salary          INTEGER)

CREATE TABLE Manages(
    ManagerName     INTEGER,
    EmployeeName    INTEGER,
    Duration        INTEGER)
```

We define three rules to find all direct and indirect subordinates of a manager. First we have the *SubordinateOf* predicate which is defined through two rules:

> Employee *SubordinateOf* Manager
>
> IF
>
> Employee *ReportsTo* Manager

and the second rule:

> Employee *SubordinateOf* Manager
>
> IF
>
> Employee *ReportsTo* ImmediateManager
>
> AND
>
> ImmediateManager *SubordinateOf* Manager

The *ReportsTo* predicate is defined through a rule involving an SQL statement:

> Employee *ReportsTo* Manager
>
> IF
>
> SELECT EmployeeName AS Employee, ManagerName AS Manager
> FROM Manages

With these rules we can ask the intelligent database management system to tell us who are the subordinates of John:

> ?X *SubordinateOf* John

where *?X* will bind *X* to the names of John's subordinates. Similarly we can determine who are the supervisors of Mary:

Mary *SubordinateOf* ?S

where *?S* will bind *S* to the names of supervisors of Mary.

To find the names and address names of young supervisors as well as names and ranks of employees who would report to them:

```
SELECT S.Name, S.Address, E.Name, E.Rank
FROM Employees S, Employees E
WHERE E.Name SubordinateOf S.Name AND
      S.Age <= 30
```

7.5.1.2 The Object-Oriented Constructs in Intelligent SQL

As discussed throughout the book, the three main concepts of object orientation are *encapsulation*, *inheritance*, and *object identity*. All three concepts are integrated in Intelligent SQL.

7.5.1.2.1 Abstract Data Types

For abstract data typing, methods and operations can be associated with tables or other object types, such as user-defined abstract data types for base objects or tuple types.

The operations or methods associated with table or tuple types are very similar to the operations or methods defined for classes. We have given numerous examples of operations such as EvaluateBonus, ChangeAddress, or TotalOrders that were defined for employees and salespeople.

Here we show a simple generic stack type that can be used in Intelligent SQL tables. The generic Stack class has Push and Pop methods. The type parameter will allow the creation of stacks of different types of objects.

```
CREATE CLASS Stack[T] (
INSTANCE VARIABLES (
        ARRAY     StArr[M] of T,
        Top       INTEGER);

    METHODS (
    Push
    Stack X T –> Stack
    (St Stack, Value Integer
    St.Top = St.Top + 1
    St.StArr[St.Top] = Value
    RETURN St);
```

```
          Pop
          Stack -> T
          (St Stack
          St.Top = St.Top - 1
RETURN StArr[St.Top + 1]); ))
```

Once the data type stack is defined, it can be used in Intelligent SQL tables:

```
CREATE TABLE Account(
    AccountNumber       INTEGER,
    Location            CHAR(20)
    Payables            Stack[DOLLAR])
```

and Intelligent SQL queries:

```
SELECT AccountNumber, Pop(Payables)
FROM Account
WHERE Location = "New York"
```

7.5.1.2.2 Inheritance

In Intelligent SQL inheritance can be used with user-defined abstract data types, tuple types (discussed in the next section), or tables. Here is an example of table inheritance involving persons, employees, and students:

```
CREATE TABLE Person(
    Name     CHAR(20),
    Age      INTEGER,
    Address  CHAR(40))

CREATE TABLE Employee
    SUB-TABLE OF Person(
          Salary   FLOAT,
          Rank     INTEGER)

CREATE TABLE Student
    SUB-TABLE OF Person(
          GPA      FLOAT,
          Major    CHAR 10)

CREATE TABLE StudentEmployee
    SUB-TABLE OF Employee, Student
```

Each table definition defines a structure and an extension (the set of all existing instances). The underlying semantics of table inheritance is set inclusion. This means when we retrieve elements of a super-table we also retrieve qualifying elements of all its subtables. For instance,

SELECT * FROM Person

retrieves all persons, all employees, all students, and all student-employees.

To retrieve the age and address of all employees who earn more than 50k ($50,000):

SELECT Age, Address
FROM Employees
WHERE Salary > 50k

The table *Employee* inherits the columns *Name*, *Age*, and *Address* from *Person*.

Similarly to obtain the name, GPA, and salary of all student-employees who are more than 30 years old:

SELECT Name, Salary, GPA
FROM StudentEmployee
WHERE Age > 30

7.5.1.2.3 Object Identity

Intelligent SQL supports tuple types as in:

TUPLE (Str #   INTEGER,
        StName   CHAR(20),
        Zip   INTEGER,
        State   CHAR(20))

which represents an address. These tuples can be used in column or attribute values in Intelligent SQL tables. Since it is natural to *share* tuple values (such as addresses), Intelligent SQL also supports object identity for tuples and other types. As discussed in the previous sections, object identity in Intelligent SQL will practically remove the need for having referential integrity constraints.

Using the extended "dot" notation the attributes of tuple valued fields can be accessed. Object identity can also be associated with atomic valued attributes (that is, base types). This makes a lot of sense for fields that store multimedia data types. For example if an image is shared in current database engines, it must be normalized in a separate table and subsequently joined with the referencing table. With object identities all the rows accessing the long field can have direct references to the object.

Consider the example of employees and departments, where departments can share the picture of the building in which they are located:

```
CREATE TABLE Department (
    DeptName    CHAR(20),
    Budget      FLOAT,
    Building    REF TUPLE (
        Str #      INTEGER,
        StName     CHAR(20),
        Zip        INTEGER,
        State      CHAR(20),
        Picture    IMAGE ))
```

Here the TUPLE constructor is used to create tuple objects. We use the REF TUPLE to indicate that the tuple can be accessed by multiple rows (that is, the tuple has an identity).

With object identity it is possible to have the *Dept* attribute and a *Manager* attribute in an *Employee* table reference the corresponding table entry directly:

```
CREATE TABLE Employee
    SUB-TABLE OF Person(
        Salary     FLOAT,
        Dept       REF ROW Department
        Manager    REF ROW Employee)
```

To retrieve the salary, the manager's name, and the picture of the departmental building of employee Joe's department:

```
SELECT Salary, Manager.Name, Dept.Building.Picture
FROM Employee
WHERE Name = "Joe"
```

7.5.1.3 Multimedia Data Types

Intelligent SQL provides special operators and predicates to query and retrieve multimedia objects. These object types could be assigned to table columns without any restrictions on their sizes. Furthermore, for efficiency, special access methods such as grid files and inverted files are supported in the underlying database engine.

7.5.1.3.1 Text Data

Intelligent databases integrate information and record/database management. Intelligent SQL allows users to create, update, and retrieve text fields based on full-text boolean expressions. The boolean expressions can appear in SQL WHERE clauses, in conjunction with the usual search expressions. Thus retrieval operations can be associative. In other words a user can retrieve all records that cover a collection of topics ("keywords"), or all fields that contain a boolean combination of words. There are no restrictions on the size of a text field.

The support will incorporate boolean expressions to perform full-text searches. If T is a text valued field then an expression of the form:

["Term1" AND "Term2" ... AND "Termn"] IN T

can appear in an SQL WHERE clause. This expression is a predicate that is true if and only if all of the terms *Term1, . . . , Term n* are in T. Of course, other kinds of boolean expressions involving OR and NOT are also allowed.

The following query retrieves the author and publisher of all books that cover either "object orientation" and "databases" or "semantic data models," which were published before 1986.

```
SELECT Author, Publisher
FROM Books
WHERE
    ["Object Orientation" AND "Databases" OR
    "Semantic data models"] IN BookText
    AND Year <= 1986.
```

The schema of *Books* is:

```
CREATE TABLE Books (
    Author      CHAR(20),
    Publisher   CHAR(20),
    BookText    TEXT,
    Year        INTEGER )
```

7.5.1.3.2   Image Data

Image data can correspond to graphs, charts, moving video images, two-dimensional bitmaps, or groups of shapes. Images can be generated by scanners, or imported from external .PCX, TIFF or other image files. Images can also be used to represent spatial or geographic data.

Images can be represented and stored in vector format as groups of shapes at specific positions and with specific sizes, shades, and colors. In general the memory requirements using vector format is less than the bit-mapped storage of the same image. However, vector format is not as general as bitmaps.

Since each of these formats has relative advantages and functionalities, Intelligent SQL supports both raster and a number of vector images such as points, rectangles, and polygons.

Supporting tuple valued attributes as in the object-oriented extension of SQL, will help cluster the media-specific information with the multimedia field.

For spatial (vector image) data types, Intelligent SQL has built-in data types such as RECTANGLE and POINT. Each of these data types is a tuple type that can further be specialized by the user. More specifically, RECTANGLE is given by:

```
TUPLE (
      LOW-LEFT        XY-POINT,
      UP-RIGHT        XY-POINT,
      SCALE           FLOAT,
      ORIGIN          POINT,
      IMAGE           REF IMAGE)
```

Here LOW-LEFT and UP-RIGHT indicate the lower left-hand and upper right-hand corners of a rectangle; the scale and origin provide the necessary information to place the rectangle on the IMAGE. The (optional) IMAGE field stores either the image contained in the rectangle or the image of the environment in which the rectangle is contained (such as the rectangle contains a map and the IMAGE is the map of Madison, Wisconsin).

Similarly POINT is a built-in data type given by:

```
TUPLE (
      POINT           XY-POINT,
      SCALE           FLOAT,
      ORIGIN          FLOAT,
      IMAGE           REF IMAGE )
```

where SCALE, ORIGIN, and IMAGE are as before and XY-POINT is a tuple giving the X and Y coordinates of a point:

```
TUPLE (
      X-COORD         FLOAT,
      Y-COORD         FLOAT )
```

Following the Pictorial SQL (PSQL) (Roussopoulos et al., 1988) proposal, associated with the spatial data types RECTANGLE and POINT, Intelligent SQL has a number of built-in operations such as COVERED-BY, OVERLAPS, CLOSEST, PERIMETER, AREA, and so on (Güting, 1988). For example to retrieve the city name, state, and population of all cities a unit distance from the point [4,9] with a population greater than 1,000,000:

```
SELECT City, State, Population
FROM Cities
WHERE Location COVERED-BY [4  +/− 1, 9  +/− 1]
      AND Population > 1,000,000
```

Here the schema of *Cities* is:

```
CREATE TABLE Cities (
    City        CHAR(20),
    State       CHAR(20),
    Location    POINT )
```

7.5.2   The Integrated Intelligent Database Engines

The intelligent database engine implements the features of the deductive object-oriented intelligent database model, Intelligent SQL. A query or a request is submitted to the intelligent database interface. The query is compiled, optimized, and executed through the different architectural components discussed here.

The extended Intelligent SQL is compiled to an intelligent database virtual machine code. Many inference and database engines use a similar strategy. For instance the Warren (1977) engine has its own virtual machine instruction set that gets interpreted by the underlying system. The instruction set that corresponds to the functionality of the intelligent database engine is much richer than the instruction set of any existing inference or database engines. It incorporates instructions for the deductive, object-oriented, and multimedia data types supported by the engine.

The following are the fundamental components of the intelligent database engines:

The Optimizer—One of the most important modules of the engine is the optimizer. The Intelligent SQL submitted to the database engine is compiled and *globally* optimized. In other words, the optimization takes into account the whole query or program. This is in sharp contrast to the piecemeal optimization of loosely coupled database, information retrieval, and inference engines. Global optimization greatly improves upon the performance of loosely coupled systems, which could be prohibitive for large or serious applications.

The Inference Engine—Although some of the functionality of a traditional inference engine is handled by other modules of the intelligent database engine, there are some specific tasks that are performed by an inference engine embedded in the intelligent database engine. The inference engine handles the flow of control over the forward- or backward-chained inferencing during execution of the programs. The inference engine also keeps track of the *explanations* to provide the user reasons, and the flow of control on goals that succeed or fail. Another responsibility of the inference engine is the uncertainty algorithm. Since rules can be asserted with associated certainty factors, goals are proven with certainties. The deduction and evaluation of certainty factors for rules are handled by the inference engine.

The Transaction Manager—The transaction manager encapsulates all the algorithms that are needed to perform concurrency control on concurrently executing transactions.

Some intelligent database applications such as CAD/CAM or CASE have long duration transactions. To provide intermediate save points in long duration transactions the transaction manager of intelligent databases supports nested transactions, as discussed in section 7.4.2.

The Meta-Information Manager—The meta-information manager handles all the meta-data information associated with the persistent database. This includes schemata, the persistent class inheritance heirarchies, the user-defined abstract data types, information on different indexes for different collections or sets of objects. In addition, information on data placement is also indicated to the meta-information manager. For instance, the information that certain objects are clustered with other objects in the same storage bucket is recorded in the meta-information manager. Both the inference engine and the optimizer of the intelligent database engine interact with the meta-information manager to obtain different types of meta-data information during either optimization or inferencing.

The Storage Manager—This is one of the most important and complex modules of the intelligent database engine. Section 7.4.9 described techniques that are used to enhance the performance of databases: indexing, clustering, and query optimization. Another strategy is caching or buffer management.

The storage manager manages both the primary (RAM) and secondary storage of the databases.

> *The indexes* include single-key indexes, such as B-tree and multidimensional indexes. Multidimensional indexes are very useful in spatial data accesses. Intersection of regions or rectangles will use multidimensional indexes to accelerate the searches, much the same way single-key indexes are used in associative single-key retrievals.
>
> *Clustering* is an extremely important performance-sensitive strategy for intelligent databases. Section 7.4.9.2 demonstrated the importance of clusters in object-oriented databases. The support of complex objects and object identity allows the creation of nested objects. With clustering, these sub-objects can be stored in the same storage blocks as their parents. This means fewer I/O accesses when the object is retrieved or stored back to disk.
>
> Finally the cache or buffer manager sub-module of the storage manager is used to stage the objects from (to) primary memory to slower secondary memory (hard disk) modules. Actually, since optical disks are also supported, the memory hierarchy uses the hard disk as a cache for the slower optical disk systems. Some commercial optical file systems such as Epoch System's Epoch-1 Infinite Storage Server, use a similar multistaging hierarchical storage strategy.

The Multi-Media Manager—Intelligent database engines will handle information from many diverse sources: on-line databases, CD-ROMS, FAX cards, LANs, scanners, digitizers, optical disks, and so on. The multimedia manager incorporates routines to handle peripherals such as scanners and digitizers as well as efficient management of multimedia devices such as write-once optical disks, CD-ROMS, and so on. For instance, write-once optical disks would need special algorithms to allocate sectors in order to have more efficient storage utilization. (Magnetic media do not have this feature). The two main components of a multimedia manager include:

> The ability to connect and access peripheral multimedia devices.
>
> The use of software access, buffering, and placement techniques to efficiently manage these peripheral devices.

The access and storage of objects on (from) peripherals is at a much lower physical level in the multimedia manager than the storage (buffer) manager. Thus the storage manager invokes the multimedia manager to perform its efficient storage management of the persistent databases.

As this brief description testifies, the internal workings and architecture of intelligent database engines is rather complex. Intelligent database engines provide a functionality which is a superset of:

> object-oriented database engines
>
> inference engines of expert system shells
>
> traditional database engines
>
> multimedia data access (such as full-text) engines

However, *without* the tightly integrated intelligent database engines of the 90s, the performance of the loosely coupled solutions will not be acceptable. Furthermore mapping the complex integrated products and objects onto relational databases of the 80s and attempting to support multimedia data types in these archaic environments will be a monumental task. The increase in complexity of the development of the intelligent database or integrated products and objects, on top of loosely coupled technologies, will be inversely proportional to the elegance and ease of use of the next generation integrated environments. In other words, as the trend towards integration and sharing continues, tightly coupled intelligent database engines become a *must*.

■ 7.6 SUMMARY

This chapter discussed object-oriented databases, which merge traditional database capabilities with object-oriented concepts: Abstract data typing, inheritance, and object identity. We showed how complex object and semantic data models incorporated some of these object-oriented primitives. These models laid the foundation for the post-relational object-oriented database management systems.

The databases capabilities in object-oriented databases are:

- persistence
- transactions
- concurrency control
- recovery
- querying
- versioning
- integrity
- security
- performance issues

The chapter discussed and explained each of these features and showed how they are manifested in existing object-oriented databases. Object-oriented databases have become the dominant post-relational database management systems.

In fact, object-oriented databases are a necessary evolutionary step toward the more powerful intelligent databases. Object-oriented databases do not have inferencing capabilities. Inferencing is important both as a declarative style of programming and as a base technology to perform inductive reasoning about databases. Object orientation, augmented with inferencing, provides a powerful model to support complex applications in the 90s. Also the native support of more natural multimedia is crucial in next generation databases.

The last section discussed intelligent databases and intelligent database engines. It was shown how SQL can be extended to incorporate rules, object-oriented features, and multimedia data type operations. The dialect of SQL that incorporates all these features is called Intelligent SQL.

8

USER INTERFACES

■ 8.1 INTRODUCTION

Previous chapters dealt with object-oriented concepts, languages, and databases. This chapter turns the attention to the impact of object orientation on user interfaces.

The modern user interfaces are revolutionizing the application of computers by users with diverse needs and backgrounds. The popularity of the Macintosh, the "computer for the rest of us," is due to its intuitive interface which allows the user to perform complex tasks with little knowledge of operating systems, programs, or memorized commands. The mouse as a pointing device has simplified activities such as procedure and command invocation and data movement within the system. Without it, users had to memorize commands necessary to perform such tasks. Concepts such as the desktop metaphor make computers available to the majority of people who are either novices or nonprogrammers. The personal computer was invented for these users.

One of the main goals of modern user interfaces is to simplify and reduce commands required to perform tasks. For example, systems like Xerox Star or Macintosh provide generic commands such as cut, paste, and delete which are applied to different types of objects. The user uses the mouse to select a word, paragraph or whole sections of a document or a graph, then invokes the delete menu option causing the selected object to be deleted.

Computer giants such as IBM, Microsoft, Digital, and Hewlett-Packard (HP) in recent years have placed greater emphasis in migrating toward more friendly user interfaces. Command-driven user interfaces are being replaced with windows, menu bars, pull-down menus, and dialog boxes. The mouse is used as the primary pointing device to select commands from a list of menu choices.

IBM has directed its efforts toward a common user interface throughout its architectures based on Systems Application Architecture—Common User Access (IBM, 1988*b*). The CUA defines user interface components that are the same across all applications running on any IBM-SAA compliant architectures including System/370, AS/400, and OS/2 platforms. Along with IBM, large independent software vendors such as Lotus, Microsoft, and Computer Associate are adapting their tools to be compatible with SAA.

With the introduction of Microsoft Windows and Presentation Manager, Microsoft is changing the landscape of user interfaces for personal computers. Minicomputer and workstation vendors are busy adopting user-interface standards such as X-windows. HP's recent announcement of NewWave, as an easy-to-use computing environment for PCs, has caused tremendous interest among software vendors and end-users.

The ability to integrate different types of information such as text, graphics, spreadsheet data, images, and voice has become a necessity (Parsaye et al., 1989). In some companies, spreadsheet data is analyzed and interpreted by an analyst. Then the result of the analysis is presented in a document displayed as a pie chart or a histogram. Tools such as Metaphor DIS or HP NewWave present a modern way of providing dynamic linkages between different types of applications so they can share information.

8.1.1 Chapter Organization

This chapter presents the impact of object orientation on the design and presentation of the modern user interfaces. Section 8.2 discusses the major concepts in most user interfaces. Section 8.3 presents the influence of object orientation. Section 8.4 covers graphical user interfaces by concentrating on popular Microsoft Windows and Macintosh Toolbox. Section 8.5 discusses commercially available object-oriented user-interface tools such as MacApp, Actor, NextStep, NewWave, and Metaphor DIS.

■ 8.2 COMMON USER-INTERFACE TERMS

This section presents a list of terms used commonly with the graphical user interface (GUI). For more in-depth discussions of GUIs refer to: Johnson et al., 1989; Pertzold, 1988; Perry and Voelcker, 1989; Pfaff, 1985; and Schneiderman, 1987.

1. *Pointing devices.* Pointing devices allow users to point at different parts of the screen. Pointing devices can be used to invoke a command from a list of commands presented in a menu. They can also be used to manipulate objects on the screen by:

   a. selecting objects on the screen,

   b. moving objects around the screen, or

   c. merging several objects into another object.

Since 1960, a diverse set of tools have been used as pointing devices. These include the light pen, joystick, touch sensitive screen, and the mouse. The popularity of the mouse is due to optimal coordination of hand and eye and easier tracking of the cursor on the screen.

2. *Bit-mapped displays*. As memory chips get denser and cheaper, bit-mapped displays are replacing character-based display screens. Bit-mapped displays are made up of tiny dots (pixels) that are independently addressable, and so have much finer resolution than character displays. Bit-mapped displays have several advantages over character displays. One of the major advantages includes graphic manipulation capabilities for vector and raster graphics, which allow presentation of information as it would appear in the final form on paper. (Also called WYSIWYG: What You See Is What You Get.)

3. *Windows*. When a screen is split into several independent regions, each region is called a window. Several applications can display results simultaneously in different windows. Figure 8.1a presents a screen with two windows; one from Microsoft Paint and the other from Microsoft Write utilities. The end-user can switch from one application to another or share data between applications. Windowing systems have capabilities to display windows either tiled or over-lapped, Figure 8.1b. Users can organize the screen by resizing the windows, or moving related windows closer, or iconifying selected windows.

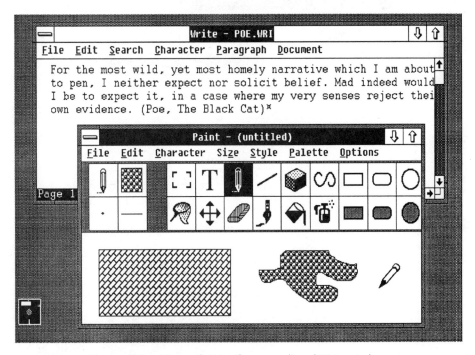

Figure 8.1a Microsoft Paint (foreground) and Write windows.

Tiled Windows

Overlapped Windows

Figure 8.1b Tiled and overlapped windows.

4. *Menus*. A menu displays a list of commands available within an application. Figure 8.2*a* presents the Microsoft Write with its menu bar. From this menu, the end-user can select operations such as *File*, *Edit*, or *Search*. Menus rely on the recognition memory of the user rather than recall. Instead of remembering commands at each stage, a menu can be used to provide a list. The menu bar contains a list of words or icons called menu items. Each menu item can be either a word or an icon representing a command or a function. Menu items can be invoked by moving the cursor on the menu item and selecting the item by clicking the mouse.

When a menu item is invoked it could cause other menus, called pulldown menus, to appear. Pulldown menus are used to present a group of related commands or options for a menu item. Figure 8.2*b* presents the *File* pulldown menu for the Microsoft Write. The end-user can select file operations such as opening a file or saving the existing file.

5. *Dialog boxes*. Dialog boxes are used to collect information from the user or to present information to the user. For example, when printing a file, Figure 8.3*a*, a dialog box is displayed to get additional information. Some of the information obtained are the number of copies and page numbers to be printed. Dialog boxes are also used to indicate error messages in the form of alert boxes. In Figure 8.3*b*, the end-user is given one more chance to save the changes before exiting from the Microsoft Write. Dialog boxes use a wide range of screen control elements to communicate with the user. Figure 8.4 displays some of these control elements. A group of radio buttons permit selection of an item from a list of mutually exclusive choices. For example, a group of radio buttons can be used to select the quality of the output (Draft or Final). An edit box is used to specify the magnification (100%). Two pushbuttons are used either to Print the result or Cancel the print operation.

6. *Icons*. Icons are used to provide a symbolic representation of any system or user-defined object such as file, folder, address book, applications, and so on. Different types of objects are represented by a specific type of icon. On a Macintosh, documents representing folders are represented by a folder icon, Figure 8.5. A folder icon contains a group of files or other folder icons. Double clicking on the folder icon causes a window to be opened displaying a list of file and folder icons representing the folder's contents. To delete a folder, simply drag its icon into the garbage can icon.

7. *Direct manipulation*. In today's computers, most of the applications provide a large set of commands to manipulate their objects. Direct manipulation simplifies the interface greatly by allowing object manipulation without the need to memorize a large collection of commands. Also, direct manipulation relies on recognition versus recall memory. Instead of memorizing commands to accomplish tasks, direct manipulation allows objects to be manipulated directly. For example, in the Macintosh, when a list of icons symbolizing a group of files are

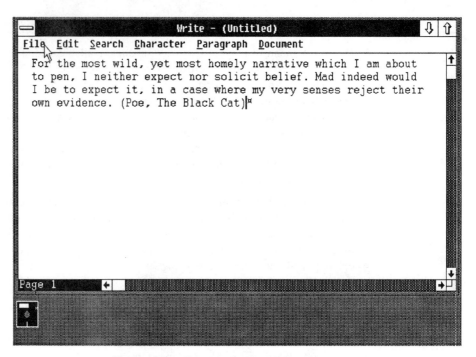

Figure 8.2a An example of a MS Windows menu.

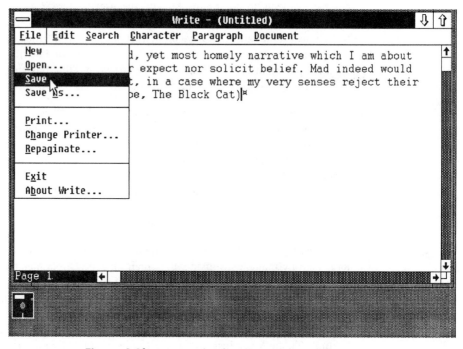

Figure 8.2b An example of a MS Windows pulldown menu.

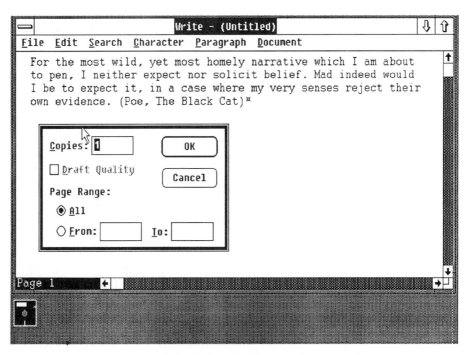

Figure 8.3a Typical MS Windows dialog box.

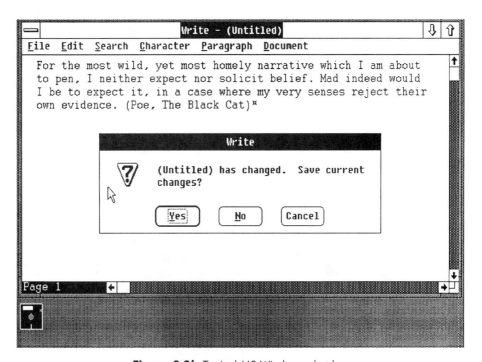

Figure 8.3b Typical MS Windows alert box.

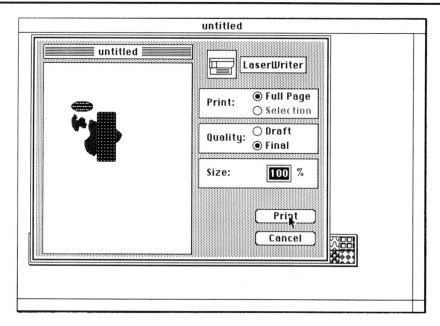

Figure 8.4 Control elements in a Macintosh dialog box (Ashton-Tate FullPaint).

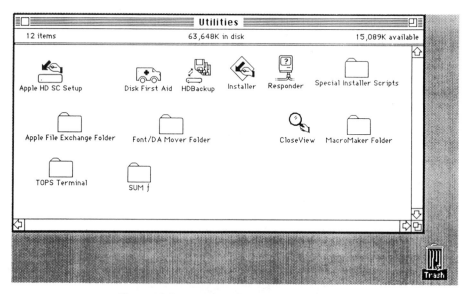

Figure 8.5 Examples of Macintosh folder icons.

presented, users can manipulate the files using the icons directly. To move one or more files, the user simply drags the file icons from one folder to another.

8. *Desktop metaphor*. In the desktop metaphor, users are not aware of programs or applications. Users deal with files, folders, drawers, a clipboard, an in-box, and an out-box. Instead of starting the word processor and loading a report file, users merely open the report document, which implicitly invokes the word processor. Clicking the mouse on an icon representing the *report* causes the word processor to get started and to load the *report* file implicitly. The Xerox Star was one of the first systems that introduced this concept (Johnson et al., 1989). Today, Macintosh, Metaphor DIS, and HP's NewWave are some of the computing environments that provide this capability. Sections 8.5.4 and 8.5.5 discuss HP's NewWave and Metaphor DIS in more depth.

9. *Graphic user interfaces*. GUIs are systems that allow creation and manipulation of user interfaces employing windows, menus, icons, dialog boxes, mouse and keyboard event handling. Smalltalk MVC, Macintosh Toolbox, Microsoft Windows, and X-windows are some examples of GUIs. Sections 8.4.1 and 8.4.2 cover Microsoft Windows and Macintosh Toolbox in more depth.

■ 8.3 INFLUENCE OF OBJECT ORIENTATION ON UI

User interfaces exploit object orientation in several ways. Designers apply object-oriented concepts to the design, presentation and integration of user interfaces.

1. *Design*. Designing modern user interfaces using the GUIs mentioned earlier is a difficult task. Most of the GUIs present an object-oriented layer on top of an application programming interface (API) to simplify design and the development of user interfaces. Examples of these layers are MacApp for Macintosh Toolbox or Actor for Windows. MacApp and Actor are covered in Sections 8.5.1 and 8.5.2.

The object-oriented layer provides a hierarchy of predefined classes. These classes encapsulate the behavior of screen objects such as windows, menus, and icons. Each class definition handles events such as drawing screen elements or clicking and dragging the mouse. For example, MacApp provides a predefined window design, see Figure 8.6, with a set of controls such as a resize box or vertical and horizontal scroll bars. An application developer can write a program to instantiate a window object and the resize box will automatically be there. Methods attached to a class definition allow the application developer to:

a. Specify which control options should be present, set, or reset

b. Draw the screen objects

c. Handle the events such as mouse click

d. Communicate with the GUI

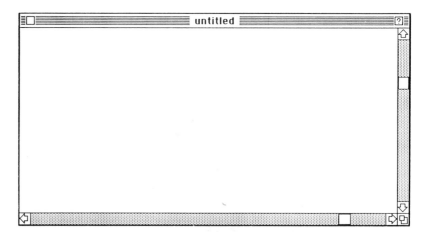

Figure 8.6 Predefined MacApp window design.

Subclasses within a hierarchy inherit behavior and structure from their super-classes (see Chapter 3). In addition, they can override, refine, or extend both behavior and structure. A developer can create a text window subclass for editing files and the resizing function will be inherited from the general windows class. A new subclass definition may specify a new dialog box or a new type of window.

2. *Presentation*. Direct manipulation of the computer is more intuitive than traditional command-based interfaces. Users perform their-day-to-day work on the computer by simply selecting or moving the icons and objects on the screen. In such systems, files and folders are dealt with as objects. Messages are used to manipulate objects. To delete an object, a *delete* message is sent to the corresponding object.

OfficeVision from IBM relies heavily on graphic user interfaces and desktop metaphor. It provides a desktop metaphor for office users such as secretaries and executives. It provides e-mail support, a phone list with automatic dialer, and text processing (Seymour, 1989b). Icons are used to represent and manipulate office objects such as files, folders, and a telephone. It provides common user interface regardless of the underlying platform. Platforms supported include OS/2, OS/400, VM, and MVS operating system.

3. *Integration*. Object-oriented concepts such as complex objects and object identity can be employed to enhance the capabilities of a user interface (see Chapter 4). Users develop complex applications by integrating information from a set of applications. An end-user can develop a document with information drawn from a set of applications such as database, spreadsheet, and word processor. HP's NewWave and Metaphor's DIS employ object-oriented technology for integration.

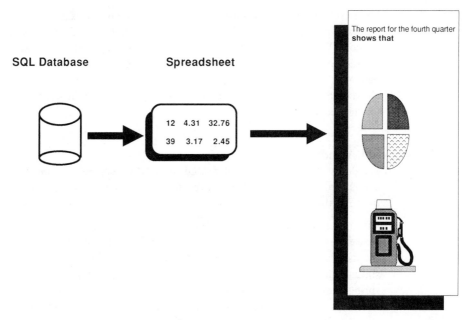

Figure 8.7 Typical compound document.

A financial report, for example, can contain diverse types of data, including multifont text and graphics, see Figure 8.7. A pie chart in the report can be drawn based on results obtained from analysis of a spreadsheet. The spreadsheet data could have been surmised from database tables. In HP's NewWave, links between the different data portions of a complex document are not static. The data is not simply copied from one application to another. Change in one object causes the corresponding change in the compound object.

■ 8.4 GRAPHICAL USER INTERFACES

This section presents Graphical User Interfaces (GUIs). Two popular GUIs, Microsoft Windows and Macintosh Toolbox, will be covered to provide a broad picture of the subject. There are a great many popular GUIs around including X-windows, Smalltalk MVC, NeXT NeXTStep, and others. Several books and many articles are completely dedicated to this topic. Some of these include Brown and Cunningham (1989); Hayes and Baran (1989); Pfaff (1985); and Schneiderman (1987).

The GUIs provide an Application Programming Interface (API) that allows users to:

• create screen objects
• draw screen objects
• monitor mouse activations

Most GUIs use an object-oriented approach to deal with screen object manipulation. For example, a template (class definition) is used to introduce a new type of window or icon. To display a screen object, an object is first instantiated and then drawn on the screen. Communication about the state of screen objects is accomplished through messages sent between the application and the user-interface engine. When a mouse is clicked on a menu bar, for example, a message is sent to the event handler responsible for the menu bar.

8.4.1 Microsoft Windows

Windows is the most popular GUI for IBM personal computers. Windows was announced November, 1983 and released November, 1985. According to Microsoft, over 2 million copies of Windows have been sold (Seymour, 1989b).

IBM and Microsoft announced OS/2 as a new operating system for 80286 and 80386 personal computers. The OS/2 Standard Edition 1.1 adds Presentation Manager (PM) for its graphical user interface. The user interfaces of Windows and PM are very similar but their APIs are different. Microsoft's strategy is to use Windows as a springboard for PM. Although the continued popularity of MS-DOS could make Windows application extremely successful; the popularity and acceptance of OS/2 still remains to be seen. If the tide shifts in favor of MS-DOS, then Windows will be here for a long time.

The next section gives further details about Microsoft Windows. Section 8.4.1.1 presents an overview of functionality. Section 8.4.1.2 examines the object-oriented features of MS Windows. Section 8.4.1.3 discusses how windows are created and manipulated. Section 8.4.1.4 explains pop-up and child windows. Section 8.4.1.5 covers resources. And finally, Section 8.4.1.6 discusses Graphics Device Interface.

8.4.1.1 Feature Overview

Windows provides an environment that enhances DOS in many ways. The major benefits of Windows are:

1. *Common Look and Feel*. All Windows applications have the same basic look and feel. Once you know one or two Windows applications, it is easy to learn another one.

2. *Device independence*. Windows presents a device-independent interface to applications. Unlike most of today's DOS applications, a Windows application is not bound to the underlying hardware such as mouse, keyboard, or display. Windows shields the application from this responsibility. The application deals with the Windows API to manipulate any underlying devices.

3. *Multitasking*. Windows provides non-preemptive multitasking support. Users can have several applications in progress at the same time. Each application can be active in a separate window.

4. *Memory management.* Windows also provides memory management to break the 640K limitation of MS-DOS. An application has the ability to use the extended memory, share data segments with other applications and swap unwanted segments to disk.

5. *Support for existing DOS applications.* Windows allows most standard MS-DOS applications to run under it directly. Any application that does not directly control the PC's hardware, use the PC BIOS, or MS-DOS software interrupts, can run in its own window.

6. *Data sharing.* Windows allows data transfer between applications using the Clipboard. Any type of data can be transferred from one window to another with the Clipboard. The Dynamic Data Exchange (DDE) protocol defines how two applications can share information. Information such as bitmap, metafile, character strings, and other data formats can be shared.

8.4.1.2   Support for Object Orientation

In order to create screen objects such as windows, the application developer defines a class specifying the necessary properties (see Chapter 2). Instances of the window class can then be created. Several applications can share the same window definitions simultaneously. To communicate with instances of a window class, messages are sent and received by a special function called the *window function.* The window function handles all messages such as redrawing the screen, displaying icons or pop-up menus, and changing the contents of the client area.

8.4.1.3   Creation and Manipulation of a Window

MS Windows presents a predefined style for user-defined windows. This section presents the structure of a window, followed by a discussion of window creation and manipulation.

1. *Structure of a window.* Figure 8.8 displays possible elements for a Microsoft window. The caption bar (or title bar) displays the name of application within the window. The system menu box contains names of commands available in all applications, such as minimize, maximize, resize, and close. The minimize box clicked once reduces the window to an icon. The maximize box enlarges the window to the full screen. The menu bar contains a list of commands used in the application. The client area is the area inside the window which is under the application control.

   Scroll bars can be used to control vertical and horizontal scrolling. Scrolling is achieved by clicking on the arrows or dragging the scroll thumb.

2. *Creating windows.* MS Windows is object-oriented to some extent. To create a window, a class is defined specifying the properties desired. Each window created on the screen is a member of some user-defined window class. Window

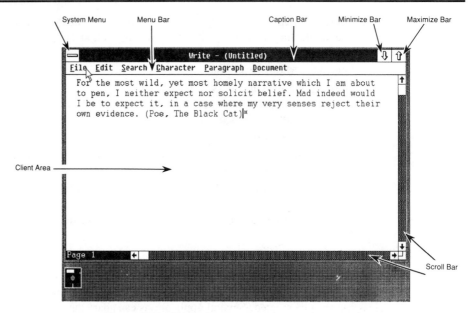

Figure 8.8 MS Windows screen element, for a window.

classes are created by application programs. Several window classes can be active simultaneously. Each window class in turn can have several instances active at the same time. There are no predefined generic window classes that come with MS windows.

To create a window the following steps must be taken:

a. *Setup a window class structure:* which defines the attributes of the window class. Attributes that can be defined include:

    i. the *window function*, which handles all messages for this class

    ii. the icon and the cursor used for this class of windows

    iii. the background color of the client area

    iv. the window class menu

    v. the redrawing function used when resizing horizontally or vertically

b. *Define the window class:* MS Windows refers to this process as registering the window class. Once a window class is registered, it is accessible to all Windows applications

c. *Create instances:* After a window class is registered then several instances can be generated by one or more applications

3. *Manipulating windows.* An application can choose to display the window, resize the window, display additional information in the client area, and so on. As stated previously, most of these actions are taken by sending messages from the application to the Windows runtime.

8.4.1.4 *Pop-Up and Child Windows*

Pop-up and child windows are special types of windows, and are used to communicate information between the application and the end-user. Pop-up windows are used to communicate information such as help, warning, and error messages from the application to the user. They remain on the screen for a short period of time. Figure 8.9 displays an example of a pop-up window. In this example, the pop-up window displays information about a given file such as date and time of creation and the file's size. Later, this section describes dialog boxes, which are more sophisticated forms of pop-up windows.

Child windows, as the name implies, are offsprings of other windows. They are commonly used as part of a dialog box. Most often child windows are used to allow the end-user to control the application and input data to the application. For example, buttons and option lists within a dialog box are represented via child windows.

Child windows are defined as a separate window class by themselves. They have their own *window function* to handle messages from Windows. For example, a mouse event within the boundaries of a child window causes Windows to send a message to *its window function* for processing.

A child window can communicate with its parent window by transmitting messages. Through messages, the parent window can either change the state of the child window, or the child window can inform the parent window of its current state.

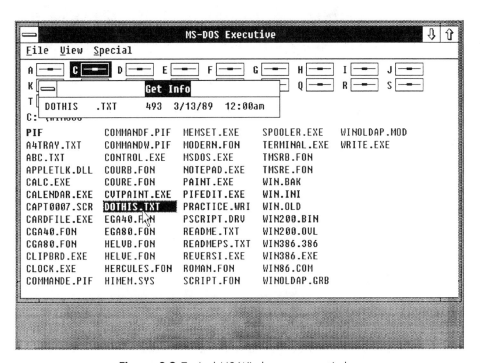

Figure 8.9 Typical MS Windows pop-up window.

MS Windows provides a collection of predefined child windows. These are the most common usage of child windows. These predefined classes are buttons, scroll bars, listbox, edit and static class. A developer can also define child windows that can be controlled by any user-defined operation. For example, Figure 8.10 shows the *MS-DOS Executive* menu. The drives "A" and "C" are examples of user-defined child windows. Figure 8.11 displays the Windows predefined controls and they are:

1. *Button class*—Windows provides eleven styles of predefined buttons. Once a button is clicked, it will inform its parent window on its current status. A user-defined text string can be associated with each button to provide a description of the functionality provided. For example: "OK" or "Cancel" buttons, or time zone buttons with "PDT," or "EDT" text.

   Some of the more popular styles of buttons, depicted in Figure 8.11*a*, are the following:

   a. *pushbutton*—used to initiate an action such as canceling a command or computing a result. The text used to identify the pushbutton appears inside the button and represents the action taken when the button is clicked.

   b. *radiobutton*—behaves very much like the buttons for preset stations on the radio in your car. Once clicked, it stays pressed, indicating that it is "on."

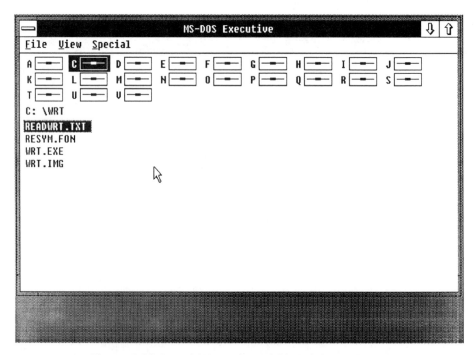

Figure 8.10 Typical MS Windows child windows (A, C, . . .).

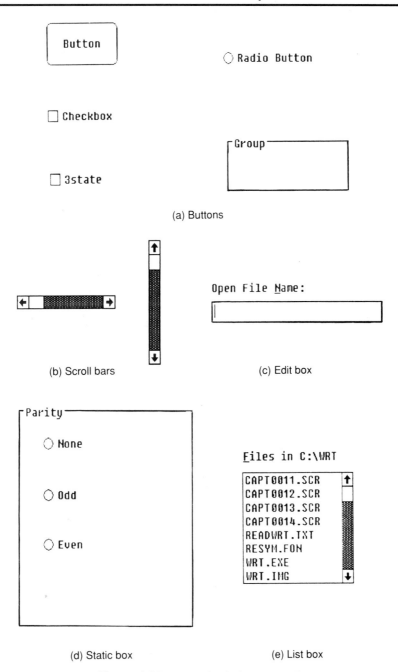

Figure 8.11 Microsoft Windows Controls.

A set of radio buttons can be used to represent a set of mutually exclusive conditions. For example, three radio buttons can be used to represent parity information: Even, Odd, and None.

c. *checkbox*—used as binary switches. They can be used to set or reset the state of a switch. Once the switch is turned on, an "X" appears indicating the switch has been turned on. Turning the switch off causes the "X" to disappear.

d. *3state*—very much like checkbox buttons except they can represent a three-state switch (on, off, disabled).

e. *group box*—used to encapsulate other buttons into a group.

2. *Scrollbar class*—provides horizontal and vertical scroll bars, Figure 8.11*b*. This type of control is useful for showing data that is too large to fit on the screen, or data that you do not want to show all at once.

3. *Edit class*—allows textual information to be entered. For example, an edit box can be used to type in a new file name, Figure 8.11*c*. The text in edit control can be left or right justified, centered, and can have multiple line input. A scrolling option is provided to scroll left, right, up, and down the edit window. Cut, copy, or paste operations using the mouse are also supported.

4. *Static class*—displays a box with associated text. This class of child window does not handle any message from the mouse or keyboard. They are most often used to contain a group of other child windows. Figure 8.11*d* displays a static control object containing a group of radio buttons.

5. *Listbox class*—allows a list of strings to be displayed and one or more of these strings selected. For example, a listbox can be used to display a list of file names, and allow one or more of these files to be selected, Figure 8.11*e*.

8.4.1.5 *Resources*

Resources are used to manage windows and user-defined objects. MS Windows provides nine kinds of resources to application developers. These resources are: icons, cursors, menus, dialog boxes, fonts, bitmaps, char strings, user-defined resources, and keyboard accelerators.

1. *Icons and cursors.* Windows defines a few types of icons and cursors. An icon or a cursor is essentially a bit-mapped region that is used to represent and symbolize a window or cursor. A developer can also define an original icon or cursor using the ICONEDIT utility.

2. *Menus.* Each window can have its own menu bar. A menu item can be a character string or a bitmap. Each item of a menu bar in turn can have a pop-up menu presenting a list of options. Currently, Windows does not support nesting of pop-up menus within other pop-up menus. (Windows 3.0 provides this functionality.) But a pop-up menu can invoke a dialog box. When a menu item is selected, Windows sends one or more messages to the *Window*

function of the window containing the menu bar. These messages can be interpreted to perform the function corresponding to that menu item.

3. *Dialog boxes*. These provide another mechanism besides pop-up menus and the menu bar to obtain information from the end-user. Dialog boxes are much more flexible than menu bars or pop-up menus. The end-user can type in a string as input to a dialog box option. Dialog boxes usually contain a group of child windows such as buttons, scroll bars, and editable fields. Just like windows, dialog boxes have a function that is used to process messages received from the user upon selection of options. Generally, dialog boxes appear as pop-up windows. The user selects the option needed from the dialog box and then the dialog box disappears. Figure 8.12 depicts an example of a dialog box that contains an edit box, a list box, and *open* and *cancel* buttons. The end-user can specify the name of a file either by selecting from the list box or by typing the name of the file in the edit box. By clicking on the *open* button, the application will open the selected file.

4. *Fonts*. Windows provides a few families of fonts with different sizes and shapes: modern, swiss, roman, helvetica, and script. Applications such as word processors and desktop publishing can define additional fonts as needed.

5. *Bitmaps*. They are used to represent icons, cursors, or draw pictures on the screen. Both mono and color bitmaps can be defined.

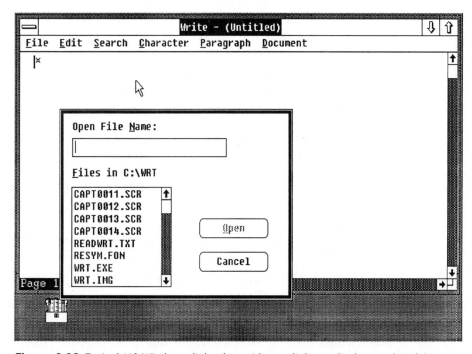

Figure 8.12 Typical MS Windows dialog box with an edit box, a list box, and push buttons.

6. *Character strings*. Character strings are handled as resources mainly to provide a manageable solution to internationalization of a window application. Instead of including a character string as part of the code, it can be placed in a resource file and handled as a resource. Once in a resource file, different versions of the same character string resource file can exist for different languages. This separation of the character strings from the code makes internationalizing the application much easier, and also makes maintaining the application much simpler.

7. *User-Defined Resources*. These can be used for any purpose and support any user-defined data type. Any arbitrary data can be managed as a user-defined resource.

8. *Keyboard accelerators*. They are a combination of keys that can generate a Windows message. These key combinations can represent a menu item or any action chosen by the application.

Resources are defined in a text file called a *resource script*. They are compiled through a utility called the *Resource Compiler* and linked with the Windows application. Resources are read-only data. Once a resource script is compiled, it can be shared with other window applications.

8.4.1.6 Graphics Device Interface

Graphics in Windows are handled by the Graphics Device Interface (GDI). Both vector and raster color graphics are supported by GDI. GDI supports only two-dimensional graphics. Vector graphics are supported by a set of vector drawing functions such as drawing a line, point, polygon, arc, or pie chart.

Raster graphics are supported by pixel manipulation. Raster graphics can be stored or manipulated either as a bitmap or as a metafile. A bit-mapped representation of the graph can be manipulated using utilities such as *BitBlt*, *PatBlt* and *StretchBlt*. A metafile provides binary encoding of GDI functions such as to draw vectors and to fill a region with a bitmap. Metafiles take up less disk space than a bit-mapped representation since they do not represent each pixel directly on disk. When metafiles are played, they execute the function encoding and perform the necessary graphics operations to display the graphics output.

8.4.2 Macintosh Toolbox

The tremendous success of the Macintosh computer popularized the window-style menu-driven user interface. Macintosh got its early start from Apple's Lisa.

The Macintosh GUI is called the Toolbox. The Toolbox presents a collection of utilities to manipulate Macintosh's resources. Section 8.4.2.1 presents an overview of Toolbox functionality. Section 8.4.2.2 examines the object-oriented features of the Toolbox. Sections 8.4.2.3 through 8.4.2.9 discuss major components of the Toolbox's user interface features. Section 8.4.2.10 briefly discusses the capabilities of Apple HyperCard.

8.4.2.1 Functional Overview

The Toolbox provides a collection of utilities to access and manipulate Macintosh's hardware and software resources. It provides a set of utilities to manipulate user-interface components such as windows, menu bar, and dialog boxes. These utilities are discussed in the following sections. Some of the other utilities provided are:

1. *Fonts manager*—allows manipulation of system and user-defined fonts
2. *Event manager*—provides monitoring of events generated by keyboard, mouse, and keypad
3. *Desk manager*—provides access to desk utilities such as the calculator
4. *Text edit*—provides simple text editing capabilities such as cut and paste
5. *Memory manager*—provides a set of routines to manipulate dynamic memory
6. *File manager*—provides a set of routines to manipulate files and transfer data between files and applications
7. *Sound driver*—provides access to sound and music capabilities
8. *Toolbox utilities*—provides a set of general routines to manipulate icons, patterns, strings, fixed-point arithmetic, and so forth.

The Toolbox can be manipulated either from the assembly language or from any Macintosh Programmer's Workshop (MPW) language (Pascal, C, C++). Also, the Toolbox can be accessed from non-MPW languages including Think C, Think Pascal, and Allegro Common LISP. One of the major features of the Toolbox is that most of the Toolbox utilities reside in ROM. This provides a very responsive user interface. The original Macintosh had 64K ROM, and the newer Mac II and SE have 256 K ROM (Brown and Cunningham, 1989).

A large portion of a Toolbox application code is dedicated to detecting and handling events. MacApp, presented in Section 8.5.1, presents a simpler approach to developing Macintosh applications.

For a more complete description of Toolbox, refer to (*Inside Macintosh* 1985–87; and Seymour 1989*a*). From this point on, we will concentrate on the user-interface components of the Macintosh Toolbox such as the Window Manager, the Control Manager, the Menu Manager, the Dialog Manager, the Scrap Manager, the Quick-Draw, and the Resource Manager.

8.4.2.2 Object-Oriented Features of Toolbox

Just like Microsoft Windows, the Macintosh Toolbox has object-oriented features. For example, the application developer defines a new type of window by defining a template for a new class of windows. Messages are sent between Toolbox and the application to change the behavior of screen objects such as windows and cursors. For each class of windows defined by the system or the user, there exists a function called the *window definition function*. When a window needs to be drawn or resized, a message is sent to the *window definition function* to perform the appropriate action.

8.4.2.3 The Window Manager

The Window Manager allows the application developer to manipulate windows on the screen. It deals with issues such as overlapping windows, resizing windows, moving windows around the screen, or changing a window from a foreground to a background window. Developers can create and manipulate predefined Toolbox windows or define their own windows. Macintosh allows the developer to create windows with any desired shape and form. For example, the user can create a circular or a hexagonal window.

Toolbox comes with a series of predefined windows. The most popular of these windows is the *document window*. The document window, depicted in Figure 8.13, has the following regions: Title bar, Close Box, Scroll bar(s), Size Box and Content region. The Title bar contains the title of the window. By clicking and holding the mouse within this region, the window can be dragged to a different part of the screen. The Close box is used to shut the window. Clicking inside this box will cause the window to disappear. The Size box is used to resize the window. The horizontal or vertical Scroll bars can be used to scroll the contents of the window. The Content region is the area that is controlled by the application.

When creating a document window any one of the components described above can be omitted. For example, any one of the Scroll bars can be absent from the document window.

New types of windows can be created through either the Window Manager or the Resource Manager. The Resource Editor can be used to create a window template. A window template essentially defines a class of windows that can be instantiated

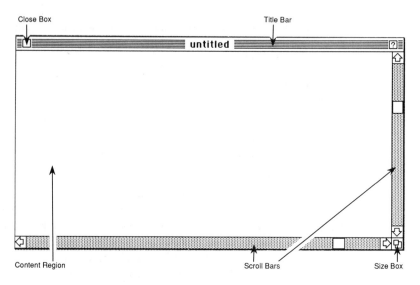

Figure 8.13 Macintosh Toolbox document window.

by an application. For each class of windows defined by the system or the user, there exists a function called the *window definition function*. This function is used to handle the behavior and appearance of the window. When a window needs to be drawn or resized a message is sent to the *window definition function* to perform the appropriate action for that type of window.

The Window Manager provides a large collection of routines to create, display, resize, hide, and activate/deactivate windows on the screen. The protocol used to draw a window on the screen is as follows:

1. *Create the window*—An application can create either a system-defined window or a user-defined window. This step returns a window pointer that later can be used to resize, hide, deactivate, or close the window.

2. *Manipulate the window*—The Toolbox Event Manager reports all events, including mouse and keyboard activities. For example, clicking the mouse inside the horizontal Scroll bar causes the Event Manager to report an event. The application code then calls the appropriate Window Manager routines to decide what region of window should handle the event. And, finally the appropriate action for the Scroll bar is taken, that is, the window is scrolled horizontally.

3. *Close the window*—When a window is no longer needed it can be closed by calling the close window function.

8.4.2.4 The Resource Manager

The Resource Manager provides access to various resources such as icons, menus, windows, and fonts. A user-defined resource such as a window is defined using the Resource Editor. The template of the window and the *window definition function* is stored in a file called the *resource file*. A unique resource identifier is used to access a predefined resource. A resource identifier can be used to recognize the type of the resource and the actual resource file to be read.

8.4.2.5 The Menu Manager

The Menu Manager provides a set of routines to create and manipulate menus. A menu bar, depicted in Figure 8.14, can contain a list of one or more menu items. Each menu item highlights itself when clicked with the mouse; this indicates the item is selected. The developer can define a menu using the standard apple menu bar, or define a menu of any shape or form using QuickDraw. Menus can be stored as a resource and managed by the Resource Manager. Once given to the Resource Manager, a unique identifier is used to reference the menu.

A menu item can even invoke a pull-down menu which can be used to set attributes or choose additional selections, see Figure 8.15. A menu item in a pull-down menu can then invoke a dialog or an alert box. A menu item can be a textual item or any icon. Unlike MS Windows, menus in ToolBox cannot be part of a window definition. Menus are only used to define the menu bar which is associated with one Macintosh screen.

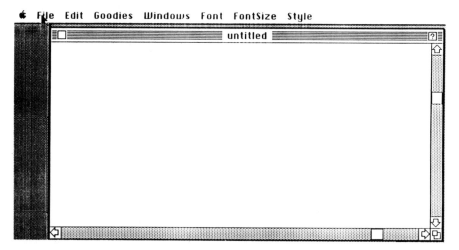

Figure 8.14 An example of Macintosh menu bar.

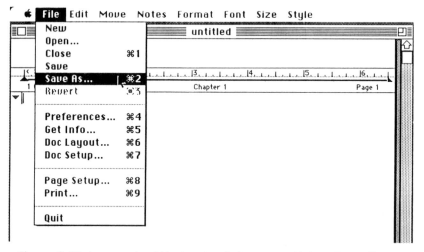

Figure 8.15 An example of Macintosh pull-down menu (Ashton-Tate FullWrite).

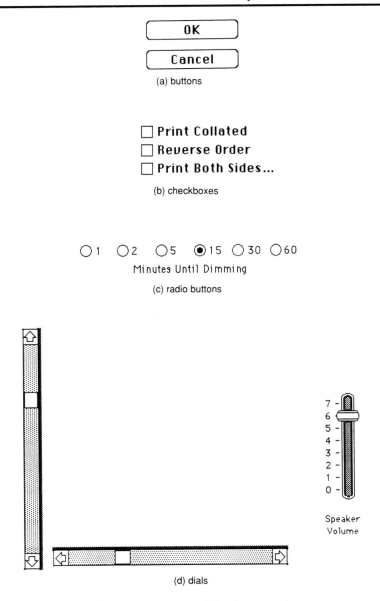

(a) buttons

(b) checkboxes

(c) radio buttons

(d) dials

Figure 8.16 Macintosh Toolbox controls.

8.4.2.6   The Control Manager

The Control Manager provides a set of routines to define and manipulate control objects like buttons, check boxes and scroll bars. Controls are usually defined within a window. For example, the scroll bars can be defined as part of a document window. Most often controls are defined as part of a dialog or an alert box. The Toolbox defines a set of controls, depicted in Figure 8.16, which are:

1. *Buttons*—cause an action to take place once the mouse is clicked inside the region of the button (see Figure 8.16a).

2. *Check box*—is used to indicate a binary option (see Figure 8.16b). A mouse click inside the check box is used to set or reset the check box. An "X" appears inside the box to indicate that the check box is set.

3. *Radio buttons*—are similar to check boxes. They are used for binary or on/off decisions. Normally, a group of radio buttons are used in conjunction. They are similar to MS Windows' radio buttons. (See Figure 8.16c.)

4. *Dials*—"These display a quantitative setting or value, typically in some pseudoanalog form such as the position a sliding switch, the reading on a thermometer scale, or the angle of a needle on a gauge; the setting may be displayed digitally as well." (Apple, 1985–87) The scroll bar is the only standard dial control object defined by the Control Manager. Both horizontal and vertical scroll bars can be defined. (See Figure 8.16d.)

An application can define its own control objects. For example, user-defined dials can be defined to represent a thermometer or a three-way check box. To define a control type, a developer uses the QuickDraw utility to build the graphic representation. The actual control object is managed by the Resource Manager. The actual behavior of a user-defined control is defined by the application developer via a routine called the *control definition function*. This function is used to perform all necessary actions on the control. For example, in a user-defined control representing a thermometer, a mouse click inside the thermometer can be used to change the temperature setting.

8.4.2.7   The Dialog Manager

The Dialog Manager provides a set of routines and data structures to manipulate dialogs and alert boxes. Dialog boxes are used to get additional information from the end-user of an application. An alert box is used to provide information such as a warning or a cautionary message. Figure 8.17a and b display an example of each.

A dialog box or an alert box is very much like a window. So, most of the actions performed on windows (such as moving or resizing) can be performed on dialog boxes. A dialog box can contain all control types such as dials, scroll bars, and check boxes. It can even contain one or more textual regions where the user can provide a response by typing-in characters. Icons can be placed in a dialog box and used as a control object.

A dialog or alert box can be defined with the Resource Editor. The template for the dialog or the alert box is stored in a resource file. To create a dialog box, the resource identifier is used to access the dialog template stored in the resource file.

8.4.2.8   The Scrap Manager

The Scrap Manager allows the user to move data from one application to another. A portion of one window can be cut from one window and placed in the scrap manager and then pasted into another window. Once a portion of a window is cut, it is placed in the *Clipboard*. Then the user can paste the contents of the *Clipboard* into another window.

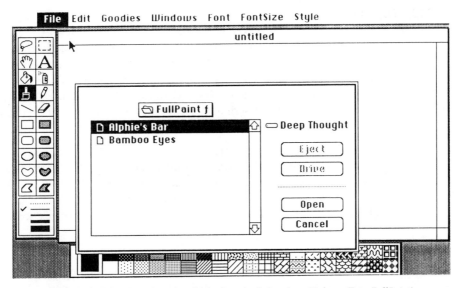

Figure 8.17a An example of Macintosh dialog box (Ashton-Tate FullPaint).

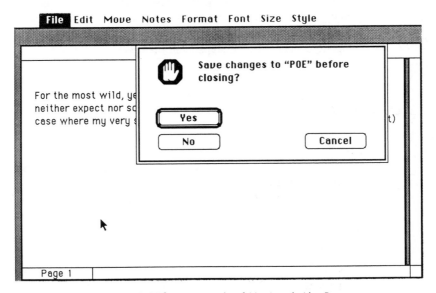

Figure 8.17b An example of Macintosh AlertBox.

8.4.2.9 *QuickDraw*

QuickDraw provides capabilities to draw and manipulate a large collection of graphic shapes such as lines, rectangles, ovals, wedges, and even arbitrary regions and text. The graphic objects can be defined with different shapes and forms. The text can be drawn in different fonts and sizes. QuickDraw also handles cursors and patterns.

8.4.2.10 HyperCard

Apple HyperCard is a popular product providing an easy to use application development environment. HyperCard comes free with any Macintosh computer. It was designed by Bill Atkinson in 1987. Since its introduction, it has created tremendous interest among Macintosh users. This chapter will not cover HyperCard in detail. What follows is a brief description of HyperCard capabilities and its object-oriented features. For a more complete description, please refer to Goodman (1987) and Chignell and Hancock (1988).

HyperCard allows nonprogrammers and programmers to develop hypermedia applications. It comes with an English-like language called HyperTalk. With Hyper-Talk scripts (programs), the user can develop HyperCard stacks and create links between various HyperCard objects such as buttons, fields, and stacks. For example, clicking on a button labeled *Next* can be linked to a HyperTalk script to display the next stack on the screen.

Although HyperCard and HyperTalk are not fully object-oriented, they do support some aspects of object orientation such as objects, methods, messages, and hierarchy. HyperCard supports five system-defined objects: stacks, backgrounds, cards, buttons, and fields. Each one of these objects can be attached to a user-defined method (HyperTalk scripts). In addition, these objects communicate with each other by sending and receiving messages. HyperCard has a system-defined hierarchy. This hierarchy is used for message handling. See Chapter 19 of Goodman (1987) for a complete coverage of the HyperCard hierarchy.

■ 8.5 OBJECT-ORIENTED USER INTERFACES

8.5.1 MacApp

MacApp is an object-oriented layer on top of the Macintosh Toolbox. MacApp is a library providing a large collection of classes in Object Pascal and MPW Assembly Language. (Object Pascal is an object-oriented extension of standard Pascal (Apple, 1987).) This large collection of classes provides services for creating windows, handling file I/O, handling icons and cursors, and control components such as button, dials, and scroll bars.

Without MacApp, programming a Macintosh application requires the ghastly task of writing code directly in the Toolbox utilities. The simple task of creating a window with a simple resize box requires a great amount of code to handle the events for handling the mouse, and controlling the display window and the scroll bars.

This section concentrates only on the user-interface capabilities of the MacApp. Other components will not be discussed here. To get more information refer to (Apple Computer, 1988) and (Schmucker, 1986).

8.5.1.1   *Overview of MacApp Capabilities*

To program directly in Toolbox, a large body of code is necessary just to manipulate user-interface objects. One function of MacApp is that it provides prebuilt class definitions that simplify creation and manipulation of user interfaces for Macintosh. Some of the operations automatically handled by these predefined classes are:

- managing windows, menus, and mouse
- handling errors
- editing text within windows
- and filing documents

Besides managing screen objects, event handling for each class definition is a major feature of MacApp. For example, in Figure 8.17a, when the mouse is clicked in the scroll bar region, the MacApp's predefined event handlers perform the necessary action to deal with the scroll bar. Also, these event handlers can be directed to invoke an application-specific event handler before returning control.

MacApp also provides powerful debugging tools such as:

1. *Inspector window:* used to view instance variables of any object present in the system.
2. *Interactive debugger:* used to debug methods attached to a class. Execution can be interrupted at the beginning or the end of a method.
3. *Debug menu:* during application development, the menu bar can contain a debug menu command. This allows examination of objects or data from the application.

MacApp can be used from any MPW language. If the user chooses to extend the class definition, then the new class definition must be defined in an object-oriented language. Among the MPW languages, Object Pascal or C++ can be used to define new MacApp subclasses.

8.5.1.2   *User-Interface Class Hierarchy*

This section presents the user-interface pieces of MacApp class hierarchy. Figure 8.18 displays the entire class hierarchy for MacApp. This section discusses the behavior and functionality provided by *TApplication*, *TDocument*, *TCommand*, *TList*, and *TView* classes.

1. *TApplication.* This class is responsible for the opening and closing of an application. When the user chooses an application by double clicking on the application icon, the application is opened and its menu bar is displayed.
2. *TDocument.* This class is responsible for the management of application files including opening, saving, or specifying the I/O format. *View* objects discussed next can be used to display objects of *TDocument* class.

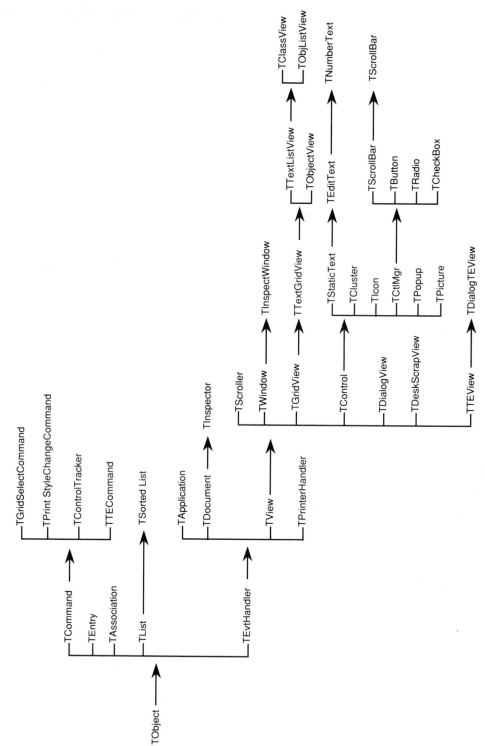

Figure 8.18 MacApp class hierarchy.

352

3. *TView*. A view is a rectangular display object with a given size and position. Every screen object such as a window, scroll bar, or control is an instance belonging to one of the *TView* subclasses. *TView* class definition itself is usually not instantiated directly. It provides an abstraction used by all subclasses including methods for event handling. Figure 8.19 displays the subclasses of *TView*. Some of the important subclasses of *TView* are *TWindow*, *TControl*, *TDialogView*, *TTEView*, and *TScroller*.

a. *TWindow*—Toolbox predefined windows are created by instantiating objects of this class. MacApp predefined methods handle events such as closing, resizing, moving the window around the screen. When creating a window, little work is done by the developer except to instantiate a *TWindow* object and specify regions required. For example, the developer can instantiate a *TWindow* object and request only a size box and a zoom box for the window. The developer does not need to write code for window event manipulation such as close and resize boxes. All the developer has to do is to manipulate the contents of the window.

b. *TControl*—objects of this class are used to manipulate Toolbox defined controls such as scroll bar, push buttons, editable text items, simple pop-up menus, and user-defined controls. Certain attributes such as whether the control is dimmed or highlighted can be set or reset by sending a message. Controls are usually grouped together in a dialog or an alert box. *TControl* subclasses also provide a mechanism to create a grouping of control boxes.

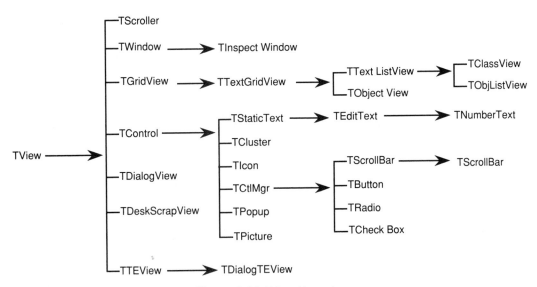

Figure 8.19 TView hierarchy.

c. *TDialogView*—objects of this class are used to manipulate dialog box windows. The developer can create both modal and modeless dialog boxes. A modal dialog box requests input from the user before the application can continue. A modeless dialog does not interrupt the execution of the application.

d. *TTEView*—objects of this class provide text views with the ability to handle the mouse for cut and paste editing, inserting, and modifying textual data via the keyboard.

e. *TScroller*—is used to manage any scrollable collection of views. *TScroller* objects automatically take care of all the scrolling tasks such as translating coordinates with the scroller bar movements.

One common feature of all view objects is that instances of view subclasses can be nested. Each view instance can be a superview of another view. And each view object can contain one or more subviews. This hierarchy of views can be displayed either as tiled or layered views. Tiled views are used to subdivide a window into several sections. Layered views are used to make one view act as the background for one or more other views. Any view can serve as a background for another view. Figure 8.20 depicts an example of both tiled and layered views. In this figure, we layered an object of *TScroller* and *TEView* and tiled these layers with two *TScrollbar* objects. Figure 8.21 depicts the superview/subview hierarchy relationship of these view objects.

The nested view mechanism is extremely handy when designing a dialog box. Every dialog view is made of a list of *TControl* subviews. These subviews use a *TDialogView* instance as their superview. When the mouse is clicked inside one of these subviews, the subview will handle the appropriate action.

During the display of a hierarchy of views, a view draws itself and then requests each of its subviews to draw themselves. Then, each subview draws itself and requests its subviews to draw themselves. These processes continue until there are no more views in the hierarchy to be drawn. Similarly, event handling is handled from the top layer down to the leaf views.

4. *TCommand.* Menu, mouse and keyboard commands are handled by objects of this class. If desired, a developer can define a subclass of *TCommand* and override the definition of its methods such as *DoIt*, *UnDoIt*, *RedoIt*, and *Commit*. When the menu item is chosen, the *DoIt* method will be invoked to perform the appropriate action. If the user chooses to *Undo* and selects this item from the menu bar then the *UnDoIt* method will be called.

5. *TList.* Objects instantiated by this class definition are used to form a list of objects. For example, a *TList* object can be used to keep a list of direct subviews of a view object.

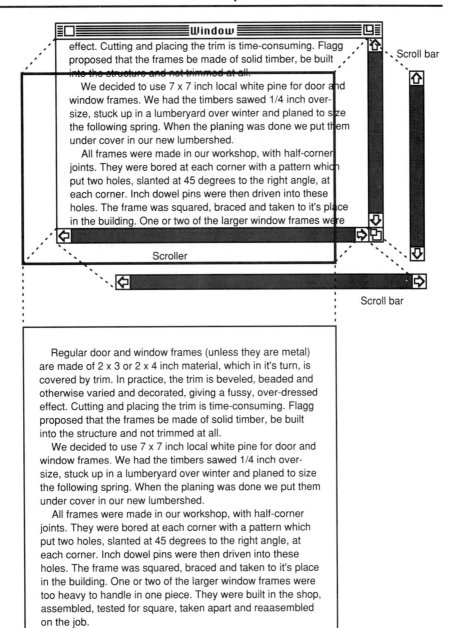

effect. Cutting and placing the trim is time-consuming. Flagg
proposed that the frames be made of solid timber, be built
into the structure and not trimmed at all.

We decided to use 7 x 7 inch local white pine for door and
window frames. We had the timbers sawed 1/4 inch over-
size, stuck up in a lumberyard over winter and planed to size
the following spring. When the planing was done we put them
under cover in our new lumbershed.

All frames were made in our workshop, with half-corner
joints. They were bored at each corner with a pattern which
put two holes, slanted at 45 degrees to the right angle, at
each corner. Inch dowel pins were then driven into these
holes. The frame was squared, braced and taken to it's place
in the building. One or two of the larger window frames were

Window

Scroll bar

Scroller

Scroll bar

Regular door and window frames (unless they are metal)
are made of 2 x 3 or 2 x 4 inch material, which in it's turn, is
covered by trim. In practice, the trim is beveled, beaded and
otherwise varied and decorated, giving a fussy, over-dressed
effect. Cutting and placing the trim is time-consuming. Flagg
proposed that the frames be made of solid timber, be built
into the structure and not trimmed at all.

We decided to use 7 x 7 inch local white pine for door and
window frames. We had the timbers sawed 1/4 inch over-
size, stuck up in a lumberyard over winter and planed to size
the following spring. When the planing was done we put them
under cover in our new lumbershed.

All frames were made in our workshop, with half-corner
joints. They were bored at each corner with a pattern which
put two holes, slanted at 45 degrees to the right angle, at
each corner. Inch dowel pins were then driven into these
holes. The frame was squared, braced and taken to it's place
in the building. One or two of the larger window frames were
too heavy to handle in one piece. They were built in the shop,
assembled, tested for square, taken apart and reaasembled
on the job.

Main Content View

Figure 8.20 Tiled + layered views example.

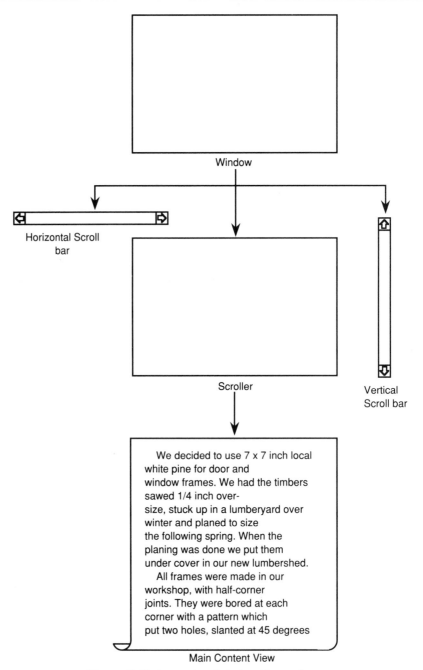

We decided to use 7 x 7 inch local white pine for door and window frames. We had the timbers sawed 1/4 inch over-size, stuck up in a lumberyard over winter and planed to size the following spring. When the planing was done we put them under cover in our new lumbershed.

All frames were made in our workshop, with half-corner joints. They were bored at each corner with a pattern which put two holes, slanted at 45 degrees

Figure 8.21 Hierarchy of tiled and layered views.

8.5.1.3 *Extensibility*

The user can add any new subclass to the MacApp class hierarchy, provided that the user writes the extensions using an object-oriented language such as Object Pascal. The MacApp class hierarchy can be extended to define a brand new class definition or a more specialized subclass definition.

To create a brand new class, a class definition must be added to the hierarchy. A class called TPalette can be added to support palettes. Each palette is a table of icons where each icon enables certain types of features. For example, the palette displayed in Figure 8.22 is used in a graphics editor. When the mouse in clicked inside the pencil icon, the cursor shape and behavior changes.

The TPalette class definition can be added as a subclass of *TView* since it is a display object. The developer must define appropriate methods and instance variables to fully implement palettes.

A developer can specialize a class by creating a new subclass definition. For example, a class definition can be added to support windows with built-in horizontal and vertical scroll bars. The new subclass definition will be added to the hierarchy as a subclass of *TWindow* with horizontal and vertical scroll bars built-in to the subclass.

8.5.2 Actor

MacApp is an object-oriented layer for the Macintosh Toolbox; for the IBM PC, Actor serves as an object-oriented layer on top of MS Windows. Actor, by Whitewater

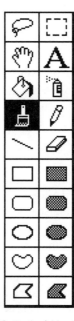

Figure 8.22 Typical Macintosh palette.

Group, is a complete object-oriented language specifically designed for developing Microsoft Windows applications. It provides a library containing a collection of classes to perform a wide variety of functions. Most of these classes deal with Windows objects such as windows, menus, dialog boxes, graphics, and so on. Actor currently runs on MS-DOS and MS Windows. Future versions of Actor are expected to run on OS/2, Unix, and other platforms.

The following sections discuss Actor in detail. Section 8.5.2.1 gives an overview of Actor. Section 8.5.2.2 presents the class hierarchy, concentrating on the user interface components. Section 8.5.2.3 talks about some extensions to the class hierarchy.

8.5.2.1 Overview

Actor is an object-oriented environment tailored for designing MS Windows application (Whitewater Group, 1987). The major components of the Actor environment are the Actor language, its development environment, and the class hierarchy.

Actor, just like Smalltalk, is a novel object-oriented language. The language supports abstract data typing, data hiding, inheritance, and polymorphism (overriding of methods within the hierarchy). The language comes with a predefined hierarchy of classes which is discussed in Section 8.5.2.2. Everything in Actor is an object: such as numbers, windows, and even classes. Just like instances of a class, a class object has instance variables and methods.

The language is a procedural language like C or Pascal. Some of the language constructs and features include if-then-else, case statement, while loop, and calling outside the Actor.

The language supports automatic garbage collection and incremental compilation. Even though Actor seems like a simple language at first, its power becomes quite apparent after a few trials with the system. Whitewater Group recently announced a product entirely built in Actor called the *Whitewater Resource Toolkit* (Whitewater Group, 1989*b*). This product provides an interactive environment to build Windows resources such as cursors, dialog boxes, icons, and menus.

In addition to the language, Actor comes with a powerful development environment consisting of:

1. *Inspector*—lets the user examine the contents of an object. It also allows the user to change the state of any attributes of this object. Figure 8.23 displays the Inspector Window.

2. *Browser*—allows the developer to view and edit the Actor system and the class hierarchy. Figure 8.24 displays the Browser Window. The developer can extend the class hierarchy with the *Browser*. Methods and instance variables attached to a class definition can be examined and modified. The class hierarchy can be traversed and new subclasses can be added very easily. It is also a powerful file editor, and the user can cut and paste code from one method to another. The developer can add or remove a method or an instance variable to a class

```
┌─────────────────────────────────────────────────────────────────────┐
│ ▄▄                    Browser: Dialog                        ⇩ │⇩⇩│ │
├─────────────────────────────────────────────────────────────────────┤
│ Accept!  Edit  Doit!  Inspect!  Options  Utility  Templates           │
├──────────────────────┬───────────────────┬──────────────────────────┤
│ WindowsObject      ↑ │ ▌hWnd          ↑ │ ▌runModal            ↑ ↑ │
│  Control             │ ▌defProc         │ ▌runModeless           │   │
│   ListBox            │ ▌parent          │ ▌sendDlgItemMessage    │   │
│    ClassList         │ ▌cRect           │ ▌setDialog             │   │
│ ███Dialog██████████  │ ▌                │ ▌setItemFocus          │   │
│  ClassDialog         │ ▌                │ ▌setItemText           │   │
│  DebugDialog       ↓ │ ▌              ↓ │ ▌toggle              ↓ ↓ │
├──────────────────────┴───────────────────┴──────────────────────────┤
│ /* Create and run a modal dialog box with the given resource id and   │
│    parent in ↑                                                        │
│    MS-Windows.  This method does not return until after the dialog    │
│    has ended. *                                                       │
│ Def  runModal(self, resID, par)                                       │
│ { parent := par;                                                      │
│   setDialog(self);                                                    │
│   ^Call DialogBox(HInstance, resID, handle(par), LpDFunc);            │
│ }                                                                     │
│                                                                    ↓ │
├──────────────────────────────────────────────────────────────────── │
│ ←│███████████████████████████████████████████████████████████████│→ │
└─────────────────────────────────────────────────────────────────────┘
```

Figure 8.23 Actor's Inspector.

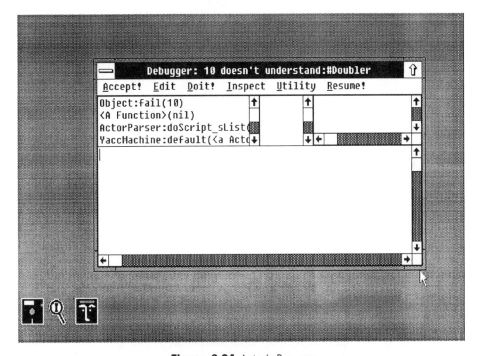

Figure 8.24 Actor's Browser.

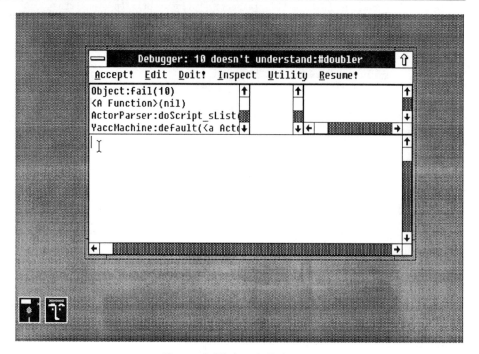

Figure 8.25 Actor's Debugger.

definition. Methods for both classes and objects of a particular class can be examined.

3. *Debugger*—is a combination of the *Browser* and the *Inspector*. Figure 8.25 displays the *Debugger* window. A *Debug Dialog* is produced when an error is encountered. It can be used to enter the *Debug* window to change either the value of an attribute such as a method or an instance variable.

Actor also provides an extensive library of class definitions. Some of the functions supported with this library include easy manipulation of MS Windows, set and collection objects, File I/O, parsing, and string handling. The next section concentrates on the user-interface capabilities of the class hierarchy. In addition, the class hierarchy can be extended to support any user-defined object.

8.5.2.2 Class Hierarchy

Most of the power of Actor resides in functionality provided by the class library. Figure 8.26 displays the entire class hierarchy of the library. In this section, only classes related to user-interface development are discussed.

Actor makes Windows application creation quite easy. Methods provided and inherited by the *WindowsObject* hierarchy automatically deal with mouse actions such as dragging and clicking, keyboard actions, and others. Invoking a method causes a

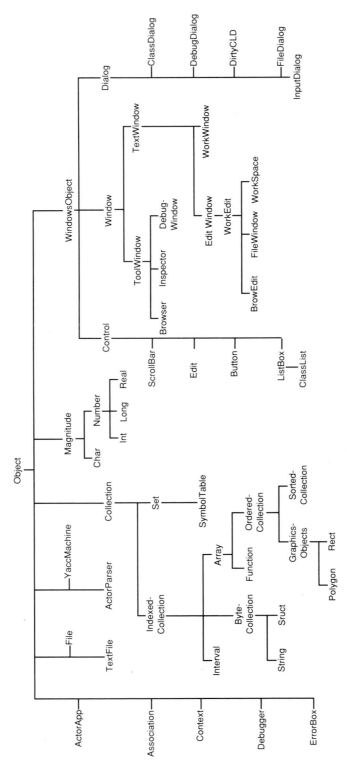

Figure 8.26 Actor class hierarchy.

message to be transmitted between Actor and MS Windows. These messages initiate actions such as resizing, closing, overlapping, and dealing with control objects such as scroll bars and buttons. For example, if the radio dial is turned off, a message is sent from MS Windows to the control object. Or to close a window, Actor sends a message to MS Windows to perform this action.

The user can add a new class definition to the hierarchy with more specialized Windows features. If this new class definition requires a special treatment of events such as different mouse handling, then the existing mouse handling methods can be overridden or extended.

To create an editable window, as in Figure 8.27, all the code required in Actor is:

```
Wind :=
    new(EditWindow, ThePort, "editmenu",
                            "Easy Edit", nil);
show(Wind, 1);
```

The equivalent code in Microsoft Windows is a few pages long. This simple program provides all the capabilities required in an editable window such as cut, paste, and backspace deleting.

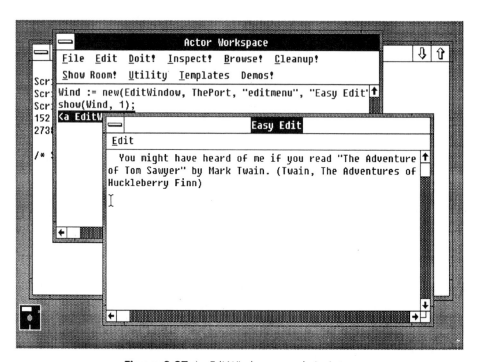

Figure 8.27 An EditWindow example in Actor.

The above code works as follows. The method *new* instantiates an object called *Wind* as member of an *EditWindow* class. Then the *show* message sent to the *Wind* object causes the new window object to appear on the screen.

Besides instantiating a new object, the method *new* specifies additional parameters for the object. For each class definition, the *new* method is overloaded with a different set of parameters specific to that class. For example, parameters specified for the *new* method of *EditWindow* in this example are:

1. Parent of the new object — *ThePort*, containing the window object that has the current input focus
2. Title of the new window — "Easy Edit,"
3. window style used–"editmenu"

The rest of this section presents the major user-interface classes which include the *Window*, *Control*, and *Dialog* classes. Figure 8.28 displays the *WindowsObject* class hierarchy.

1. *Window classes*. To create an instance of a window class, the user specifies the type of window (such as whether it is editable), the parent window, the menu used, the window title, and the location. All the events affecting that window

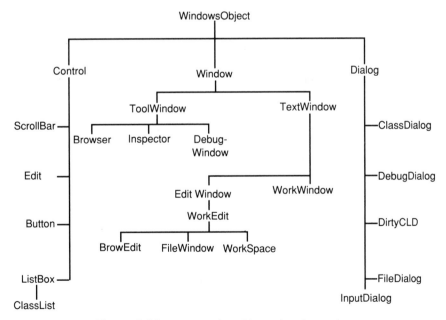

Figure 8.28 Actor WindowsObject class hierarchy.

are handled by the methods defined for the windows. Events handled include mouse, keyboard, and screen events.

A window's menu can be defined either with a resource file or created dynamically. Menus created dynamically can be easily manipulated with methods attached to *Window* classes. These methods are used to append a new item, removing or changing an existing one. But menus stored in a resource file are preferred over dynamic windows, as they are more efficient and shareable by several applications.

One of the most useful *Window* subclasses is the *EditWindow*. It allows windows to be created with built-in text editing capabilities such as cut, paste and backspace. Objects of this class are defined with the *"editmenu"* option which supplies a pulldown menu. This option allows cutting, copying, and pasting of textual data inside the window region. In a sense, the window contents appears as a simple text editor. Text scrolling, both horizontal and vertical, are also supported. The vertical and horizontal scroll bars are active and fully controlled by the methods attached to this class. All complicated MS Windows events are handled automatically, even editing capabilities.

2. *Control classes*. Figure 8.28 depicts the class hierarchy used for control objects such as buttons, scroll bars, edit string boxes, and list boxes. All control windows are child windows of the window containing them. This means that events such as moving and closing the parent window are also carried to child windows. Most of the time the control objects are created as part of a dialog window, which is discussed in the next section.

A special subclass of control objects is *ListBoxes*. To use it, an instance of *ListBoxes* is created and then the *insertString* method is called to add strings as items. Other methods defined for the *Listboxes* handle moving the scroll bar through the list and highlighting the selected item. Also, when a selection is made the actual text of the selection can be returned with the *getSelString* method.

3. *Dialog classes*. These allow creation of both modal and modeless dialog boxes. A modal dialog box appears when user input is required. All user input (keyboard, and so on) is directed to the dialog box until the box is closed. The modeless dialog boxes, on the other hand, do not take control of user input and behave more like pop-up windows.

To program a dialog in Actor, first a *Dialog* object is created, and then it is displayed on the screen.

A *dialog* object, like any object, is created with the *new* method:

```
D1 :== new(Dialog);
```

Then, the dialog must be displayed and initiated with either the *runModal* or *runModeless* method. These two methods have the following definition:

runModal(dialogObject, resourceID, parentObject);

runModeless(dailogObject, resourceID, parentObject);

The first parameter is the dialog object that receives this message. The second parameter is a constant identifying the resource used for this dialog. This *resourceID* is used by MS Windows to find the dialog resource file on disk. Most likely a given type of dialog class will have several dialog styles (resources) associated with the dialog definition. The last parameter is the parent object that the dialog belongs to. If the parent object is ever closed, a message is sent to the dialog box causing it to be closed, too.

Methods attached to the dialog classes handle a variety of events for dialog objects. Until the dialog box or window is terminated, Actor and MS Windows communicate with each other through messages. Actor sends messages to change the input focus from one control to another or to change the current value of a control. Windows sends messages back to Actor to communicate information such as the current state of a button. Some of the events handled include creating the controls within the dialog box, changing focus among control objects, and terminating the dialog box.

The developer does not have to create the controls within the dialog window. This is done automatically by the methods attached to the dialog's class definition. When the dialog is initialized, MS Windows can be directed to change the screen focus from one control to another. By default, the first control object has the screen focus. In addition, default values for all the controls can be defined by messages sent when the dialog object is created. For example, if a control is present to display a list of file names in a file list box, then a method is used to load the list of files in this control.

A dialog can be ended by changing the state of a button such as an "OK" or "CANCEL" button, or by pressing carriage return. This activity is handled by MS Windows sending a message to the dialog object to close the window. In turn, the corresponding object recognizes the message and terminates the dialog box.

8.5.2.2.1 Existing Dialog Class Hierarchy

Actor provides some predefined classes for dialog boxes. Figure 8.28 displays the class hierarchy for the dialogs. Even though dialog classes are few in number, they provide the general mechanism to handle dialog box events between Microsoft Windows and Actor for all predefined and user-defined dialog classes. Among the classes provided are *Dialog*, *ErrorBox*, *InputDialog*, and *FileDialog*:

1. *Dialog*—is the center focus of all dialog classes defined either by the system or by the user. The methods attached to this class allow the user to perform a wide range of functions. Some of these functions include:

   a. Sending a message to a specific dialog item

   b. Changing focus from one item to another

   c. Retrieving an item from a list

   d. Retrieving or specifying the text from an edit box

2. *ErrorBox*—is used to display an error message on the screen in an error box and wait for the user acknowledgment by clicking the OK or hitting carriage return. The *ErrorBox* is not a direct descendant of the *Dialog* class hierarchy. It is a descendant of the *Object* class.

   The developer can choose to display several styles of error messages and icons within an *ErrorBox* object. For example, to create an error window displayed in Figure 8.29 with the hand icon, and OK and CANCEL buttons, the following message is sent:

   new(ErrorBox, ThePort,
   "Do you really want to override READ.ME? ",
   "Save As ", MB_ OKCANCEL + MB_ ICONQUESTION);

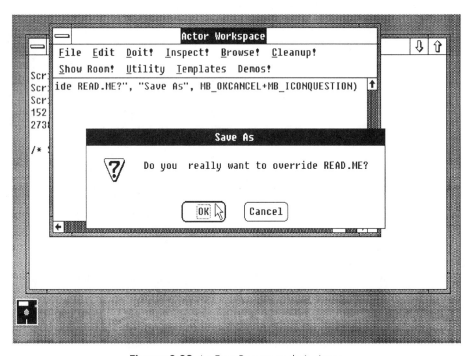

Figure 8.29 An ErrorBox example in Actor.

The parameters to this method specify the class name *ErrorBox*, the parent object *ThePort*, strings representing the error message and title, and the styles of the button and the icon. Objects of type *ErrorBox* are automatically displayed during creation.

3. *InputDialog*—provides a class definition with one editable text control box, plus OK and Cancel buttons. The input dialog box in Figure 8.30 is the result of a request to save a database. It is created by the following *new* message:

> S1 := new(InputDialog, "Save As",
>   "Save Database As:", ".sql");

The parameters specify the name of the class *InputDialog*, the title of the dialog box, the message inside the box, and the default string displayed in the edit box.

Dialog box *S1* can be displayed either as a modal or modeless box. To display it as modal, the following message is sent to *S1* object:

> runModal(S1, INPUT_BOX, ThePort);

which causes Figure 8.30 to be displayed. At this point, the input is focused on

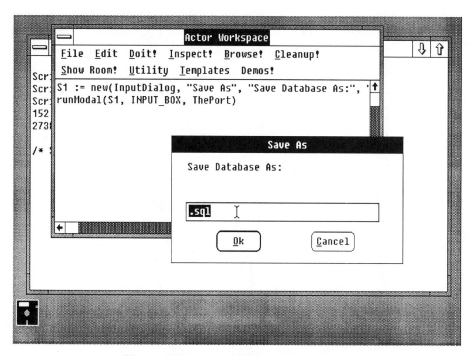

Figure 8.30 An InputDialog example in Actor.

the edit control box. The end-user can type in the name of the file in the edit control box and click on the OK, or the Cancel button to terminate the dialog box.

If the OK button is clicked the developer can access the text by invoking the following method:

fileName := getText(S1)

which returns the text. If the CANCEL is clicked or ESC is pressed, then the above message returns the previous value of the edit control box before the user types in the new value.

InputDialog objects can be used repeatedly once they are created. When used again the object remembers the last value of the input control box. For example, if the user makes a mistake by typing *PAYROL.RPT* instead of *PAYROLL.RPT*, the string is displayed again and can be corrected.

4. *FileDialog*—is used to load a file from a list of file names. This class is by far the most complex dialog class definition provided. For example, to load a database from a list of databases the dialog depicted in Figure 8.31 can be used. The File Name edit area can specify a wild card file name as in ∗. SQL

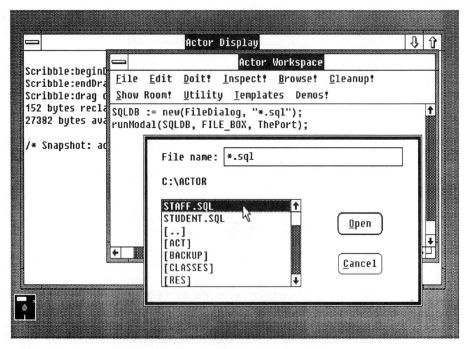

Figure 8.31 A FileDialog example in Actor.

to display the list of all files with extension .SQL. The user can also provide a directory specification, instead of the directory used as the default. When the dialog window is displayed, the end-user can type in a new search pattern in this box or type in any existing file name.

The file list box displays a list of files that satisfies the search pattern in File Name and the subdirectories [..]. Double clicking on a file will cause that file to be selected. Double clicking on a directory entry or [..] item causes the current directory or even the disk to be changed. Open and Cancel buttons can be used to terminate the dialog box.

To create an object of this class the following message can be sent:

SQLDB :== new(FileDialog, "∗.sql");

which defines the *SQLDB* object and specifies the search pattern used for the FileName edit box.

Then to display the dialog box as modal, the following message is sent to the *SQLDB* object:

runModal(SQLDB, FILE_ BOX, ThePort);

When a file is selected and the dialog box is terminated, the developer can retrieve the file name by invoking the following message:

getFile(SQLDB);

This method returns a string representing the current file name OPENed or double clicked, or the last file name if CANCELed.

8.5.2.3   *Extending the Class Hierarchy*

Users can extend the class hierarchy by defining new subclasses. The user-interface hierarchy can be extended to support additional styles of windows and dialogs. The developer can define a new window class definition with specialized attributes. For example, to create a new class of windows without a resize box, a subclass can be added to the *Window* class hierarchy with the resize box disabled.

The *WindowsObject* hierarchy is most often extended to support new types of dialog boxes. To create a new dialog box requires two major steps:

1. *Define the dialog box resource.* First define the dialog box resource. This resource specifies features of the dialog box such as the types of controls used and their position inside the dialog box. This task can be accomplished in two ways. Either write an original resource script in MS Windows, or use the Dialog Editor that comes with the Windows Software Development Kit.

2. *Define the new dialog subclass.* The second step is to create the class definition using the Actor language. This class is created as a subclass of Actor *Dialog* class, thereby inheriting the methods attached to the *Dialog* class definition. In addition, the designer can override existing methods or attach new methods to handle messages for the new features of the subclass.

8.5.3 NeXT

The NeXT computer, with its three-dimensional user interface, was introduced in 1988, Figures 8.32*a* and *b*. It has grabbed the attention of the computer industry. The machine has been hailed as the most innovative computer invented in recent times. The computer was initially intended for the educational market. But the NeXT Corporation decided to widen the market for its machine to the commercial arena.

We provide a brief overview of the NeXT software tools and capabilities, followed by a discussion of the capabilities of the user-interface design. To learn more about this machine please refer to (Webster, 1989) and (Knor, 1990).

8.5.3.1 Overview of NeXT Software

The NeXT computer is designed to reach a wide range of users from nontechnical to power users. The nontechnical users can deal with the graphic user interface to

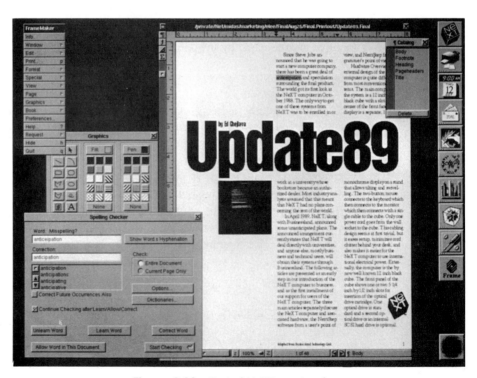

Figure 8.32a Typical NeXT user interface.

perform tasks by manipulating menus, icons, and dialog boxes. The power user can directly interact with its Mach operating system.

The NeXT system software is comprised of three major pieces: the Mach operating system, applications, and the NeXT user interface. The Mach operating system, developed at Carnegie Mellon University is a redesigned UNIX. Mach redesigns the UNIX kernel to reduce the size.

NeXT also comes with a set of bundled applications. Currently, there are new applications being developed that take advantage of NeXT hardware and software capabilities. Some of the applications supported on NeXT are NeXT SQL Database Server, Mathematica (symbolic mathematics package), WYSIWYG editors and word processors, and more.

8.5.3.2 NeXT User Interface

The third and last component, the NeXT user interface, is the most impressive piece of NeXT technology. The NeXT user interface draws heavily on direct manipulation and modern graphic user interfaces. The NeXT user interface is composed of four components: Workspace Manager, Interface Builder, Application Kit, and NeXT Window Server.

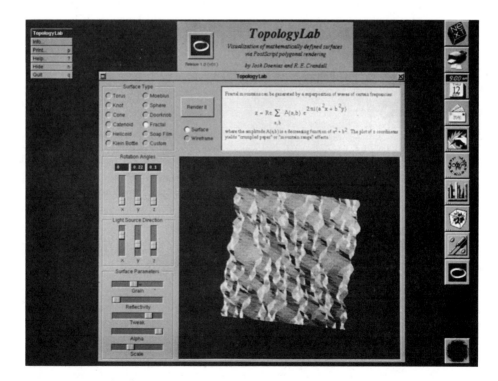

Figure 8.32b Typical NeXT user interface.

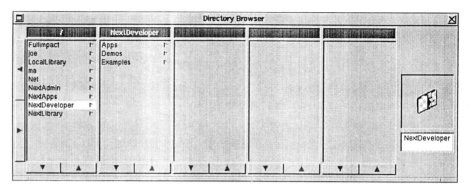

Figure 8.32c NeXT Workspace Manager Directory Browser.

The Workspace Manager allows the user to manage files and directories and to execute programs. When a user logs into a NeXT machine, the Workspace Manager is started, Figure 8.32c. The Directory Browser window is used to navigate through the files on disk.

The Interface Builder lets the user create interfaces on the screen without writing a single line of code. Users simply select the menu, control and screen objects from a palette, then move the controls to the desired location. It is also possible to resize the controls to the desired dimension. The Interface Builder is discussed in Section 8.5.3.4.

The Application Kit is a library of user-interface objects. It is used in conjunction with the Interface Builder to design user interfaces. The Application Kit is discussed in the next section.

The Window Server handles all screen activities, such as drawing windows and handling events such as mouse clicks. The Window Server itself does not perform the drawing and screen I/O commands. Display PostScript, designed by Adobe and NeXT, handles all such activities. Up to now, PostScript has been used only as a language for printer engines. With the advent of the Display PostScript, both screen and printer share the same protocol. Therefore one drawing method is used to display objects on the screen and the printer.

8 MS.5.3.3 Application Kit

The Application Kit provides an extensive library of predefined classes. The hierarchy of classes is shown in Figure 8.33. These classes provide functionality to define user interfaces composed of menus, windows, buttons, slide bars, and sound. Each class within the hierarchy defines the behavior of its objects. For example, a menu knows how to handle mouse events, when clicking on a menu item. Window objects know how to resize the window.

The Application Kit can be extended by adding new subclasses to the hierarchy. To add a new subclass, the class definition is written using the Objective C language. Each

NeXT machine comes with a copy of Objective C. Objective C is an object-oriented extension of C (Cox, 1987). The language is a superset of C incorporating object orientation features from Smalltalk. Just like Smalltalk, it comes with a large collection of predefined classes to simplify the software development task. The language supports abstract data types, inheritance, and operator overloading. Unlike C++, Objective C does not extend the definition of any existing C language constructs. It relies totally on the introduction of new constructs and operators to perform tasks such as class definition or message passing.

To develop user interfaces, designers can use Application Kit from Objective C, directly. This would be very much like developing an application using MacApp. They can create instances of objects from the Application Kit hierarchy and modify the attributes by calling the methods attached to the class definition. But the other method of defining user interface, using the Interface Builder, is much easier than coding it entirely in Objective C.

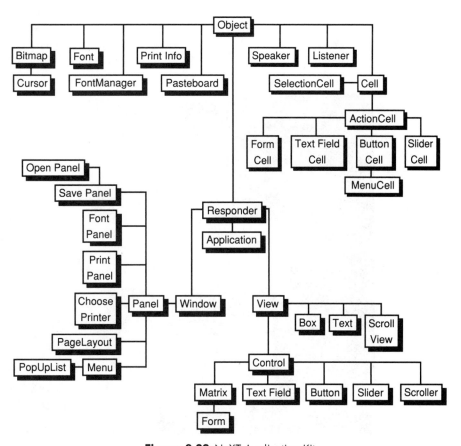

Figure 8.33 NeXT Application Kit.

8.5.3.4 Designing User Interfaces with Interface Builder

The Interface Builder provides an easy to use utility to design a user interface using the mouse and the screen. The Interface Builder is similar to an icon editor or screen painter, Figure 8.34. Designers can define the screen layout by selecting the screen objects from the Interface Builder palettes. The Interface Builder also helps to define the user-defined class and make connections between objects. Not all of the coding is automatic; the Application Kit and the Objective C language are also needed.

Defining a user interface using the Interface Builder requires the following steps:

1. *Define layout of screen.* The interface designer defines a user interface by simply selecting screen objects from the Interface Builder palettes, see Figure 8.35. After picking an object from a palette using the mouse, the object can be dragged into the destination window and resized as desired.

   The Interface Builder palettes include objects such as windows, menus, buttons, fields, radio buttons, and more. At the top of the palettes window, three buttons allow the interface developer to select a wide array of user-interface objects. Clicking the left button, displays the view objects such as radio buttons, switches, text fields, horizontal, and vertical scroll bars, Figure 8.35a. The middle button displays the window palette, which allows the user to define

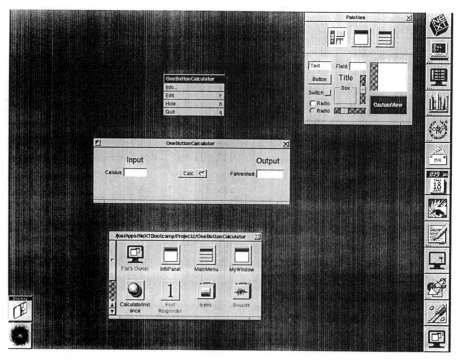

Figure 8.34 NeXT Interface Builder.

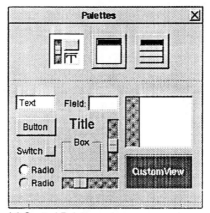

(a) Control Palette

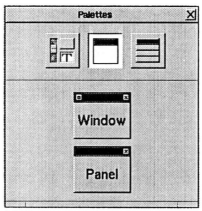

(b) Window Palette

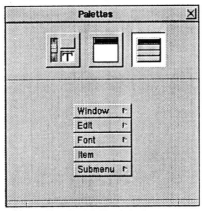

(c) Menu Palette

Figure 8.35 NeXT Interface Builder palettes.

new windows and panels, Figure 8.35*b*. Clicking the right-most button, Figure 8.35*c*, displays the palette for menus. Application menus can be defined by selecting menu objects from this palette.

Attributes of objects such as the title or text associated with a button are specified using the Interface Builder Inspector. For example, the developer can select a window object and drag it to a new area on the screen. Using the Inspector, the title of the window is defined. To enable or disable any controls (such as miniaturize) or close options, simply click on the controls buttons.

2. *Define the user-defined classes.* The developer defines a new class definition using the Classes Window. The Classes Window allows the developer to extend the Application Kit class hierarchy. The developer navigates through the class hierarchy and creates a new subclass within the hierarchy. Methods and *outlets* (see next step) are defined for this new class definition. When a class is defined this way, only the template of the class is created. The actual implementation of each method is defined later by writing the code in Objective C.

3. *Making connections.* Up to this point we have defined the layout of the user interface. At this step, the developer needs to make connections among application objects. For example, when a scroller's slide bar is moved, a message is sent to an application object to perform certain actions like shifting the text. Again the Inspector is used to connect user interface objects with methods of classes within the application.

The other form of interconnection is via *outlets*. An object's *outlet* contains the object identity of another application object. Thus, an object can send messages to the object connected by its outlets. An object can have many *outlets* allowing connections to several objects simultaneously.

4. *Actual application code.* The previous steps are handled by Interface Builder directly. The last step is accomplished by writing the application code in Objective C. When the developer is done with the first two steps, the Interface Builder defines the source files necessary to build the application. These files contain the templates for the class definitions and the connections made among objects. At this stage, the developer needs to extend these source files. Extensions are made to specify the logic of the program and the code for method definitions.

8.5.4 NewWave

Hewlett-Packard introduced NewWave into the market in 1989. It is a layer on top of Microsoft Windows. It enhances and extends the capabilities provided by Windows in several ways including communication, abstraction, ease of use, control, and others. In the future, it is expected that the NewWave environment will be offered on top of Unix and OS/2 machines.

Section 8.5.4.1 presents an overview of NewWave software capabilities. Section 8.5.4.2 examines the architecture of NewWave. And finally, Section 8.5.4.3 presents the Object Management Facility.

8.5.4.1 *Overview of NewWave Software*

NewWave comes with a set of utilities including the NewWave Office (Hewlett-Packard, 1988). NewWave allows end-users to create compound documents composed of text, graphics, images, and voice. NewWave applies the desktop metaphor and object orientation throughout its environment. NewWave and its tools such as NewWave Office provide an end-user environment that is easier to use than DOS. Existing tools such as Lotus 1-2-3 or dBASE can run within the environment with no change. To take full advantage of NewWave, the application must be retrofitted to work within the NewWave environment. Several software companies such as Microsoft, Adobe, Gupta Technologies, Neuron Data, Samna, and others have committed to writing new applications or rewriting existing applications.

Starting NewWave causes the NewWave Office window to be displayed on the screen, as depicted in Figure 8.36. NewWave Office provides a desktop metaphor environment for office end-users. It includes tools such as a Printer icon, an electronic mail utility (Mail), and WYSIWYG word processor (Write), supporting the full capabilities of the NewWave environment.

One of the strengths of NewWave is the ability to create compound documents composed of varied types of data. An end-user can create a document and type some text into this new document. Then, the user can drag the icon representing a

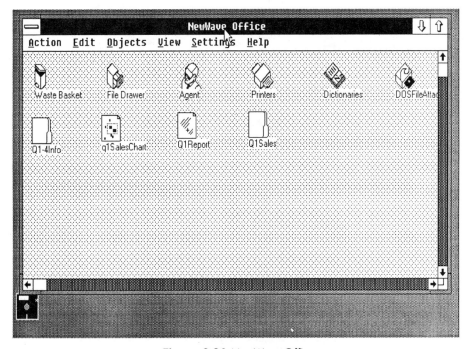

Figure 8.36 NewWave Office.

spreadsheet object into this newly created document. This causes NewWave to move the data object to the desired location within the document. The capability of creating compound objects will be discussed in more depth later.

In terms of ease of use, one of the advantages of NewWave is providing a desktop metaphor for DOS machines. NewWave Office displays every tool, utility, end-user files, and documents as icons on a desk. The end-user manipulates the system by manipulating these icons. To delete a document, for example, move its icon on top of the Waste Basket icon. Or to print a document, drag its icon onto the Printer icon.

NewWave views everything as an object. For example, spreadsheet data is treated as an object. Upon clicking on the spreadsheet icon, NewWave automatically loads the spreadsheet tool with the end-user data in that object.

In addition, the end-user can share an object among several compound documents or provide a limited portion of an object within another compound object. For example, given a spreadsheet the end-user may choose to include a section from the spreadsheet or a bar chart representation of the spreadsheet within a compound document.

8.5.4.2 NewWave Architecture

The architecture underlying the NewWave utilities is composed of two major components: the Object Management Facility (OMF) and the Application Programming Interface (API). Figure 8.37 displays the relationship of these components to Microsoft Windows and the end-user.

1. The *Object Management Facility* (OMF) manages the interrelationship of objects created in NewWave. An object can be any type of data or application—a spreadsheet utility, a database tool, an image, or a text file. The OMF allows data created by different applications to be combined to form a compound document. Each application still remains responsible for maintenance of its own piece of data. The OMF allows these pieces of data to be treated as objects. It keeps track of links created from one data object to another one. The OMF allows the user to create different types of links between objects. The OMF objects and links are covered in more detail in Section 8.5.4.3.

    For example, a financial report is an example of a compound document. A report usually contains diverse types of data such as a pie chart, a spreadsheet, and a scanned image, see Figure 8.38. Each data type can be created and maintained by a separate tool, such as a spreadsheet tool or a graph generation tool. The entire compound document representing the financial report and all components such as the spreadsheet data is seen as an object by the OMF. When it is time to print or update the report, each one of the data objects will be printed or updated by the corresponding utility that understands it.

2. The *Application Programming Interface* provides a set of system-wide services such as Agent Facility, Computer-Based Training (CBT), and context sensitive help.

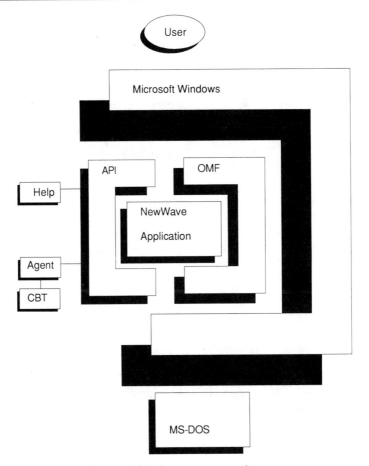

Figure 8.37 The NewWave architecture.

The Agent facility provides a batch facility for MS Windows applications. Users can record, save, and playback a set of MS Windows activities. The playback can be activated either at a specified time or by user demand.

The NewWave CBT facility allows the user to develop on-line tutorials for new tools. It is an application of the Agent facility. The developer can create lessons to teach different features of their NewWave tool. The CBT author can easily monitor, record, playback, and get responses from the student users. The CBT facility allows an author to create on-line tutorials without extensive knowledge of NewWave or Windows programming.

A NewWave application developer applies the context-sensitive help facility to catalog and link help messages to the application commands. The help subsystem for the NewWave application can be developed in parallel with the development of the application.

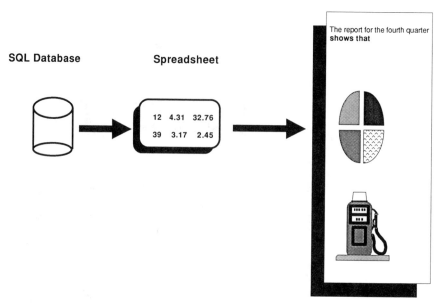

SQL Database   Spreadsheet

The report for the fourth quarter
shows that

12 4.31 32.76

39 3.17 2.45

Figure 8.38 Typical compound document.

8.5.4.3 Object Management Facility

NewWave OMF manages objects created by the system and the end-user. It also manages the relationship of objects with each other. The following section discusses different types of objects and links that can be created in OMF.

The NewWave Object Management Facility provides an object-based file system. It manages all relationships between user data and applications. Different types of information ranging from user data to applications are treated as objects. Users can create links among several types of objects. These links can group several objects into a folder object, or link an application and data together as a single object. This new object can be manipulated as a single entity. But even though it is part of a compound object, the user can still double click on the simple object and bring up the application to manipulate the original data file.

For example, an icon representing a spreadsheet can be dragged into a report document. Though inside the report document, clicking on the spreadsheet icon loads only the spreadsheet, not the report.

In addition, objects can communicate with each other using messages. For example, when displaying an entire compound document, a message is sent to each child object to display its own view of the data.

    1. *Objects.* As stated previously, objects can be created by the user or the system. Figure 8.39 demonstrates different types of objects managed by OMF. Different types of objects permitted are user objects, office tools and systems objects, container objects and compound objects.

a. *User objects*—these objects are created by the user. User objects are used to manage data such as databases, spreadsheets, charts, images, voice, and so on. User objects are linked to their applications. For example, double clicking on the Payroll icon automatically starts the database application and loads the user data corresponding to the payroll database. In addition, user objects can easily be moved, copied, and destroyed by the user. To destroy a user object, for example, the user drags the object icon onto the Waste Basket icon.

b. *Office tools and system objects*—NewWave treats all tools and system services as objects. Tools such as Waste Basket, File Drawer, printer, and calculator are treated as objects.

c. *Container objects*—are used to hold one or more objects. A file folder or the Waste Basket are perfect examples of container objects. When a file folder is opened, it displays icons and/or titles representing lists of contained objects.

d. *Compound objects*—provide the ability to handle objects that are composed of simple objects or other compound objects. They can be printed, copied, and moved as a single object. Compound objects communicate with container objects via messages. For example, to print a business report composed of graphics, spreadsheet, and text objects, the compound object sends

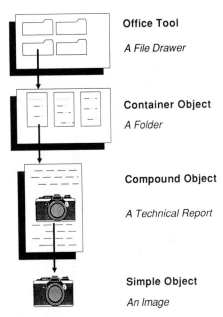

Figure 8.39 Typical NewWave objects.

messages to the individual objects to print themselves. Thus, the graphic tool is invoked to print the graphics.

2. *Links and views.* Links and views allow connections between OMF objects. The links in OMF form a directed acyclic graph. This means that any object can have multiple parents and children. An object can be included in one or more compound documents, as depicted in Figure 8.40.

Objects can share and pass information through links. For example, multiple links to a single object allow an object to be shared by several compound objects. Suppose an object is shared among several other objects. If the source object is modified, OMF automatically notifies the destination objects and updates the compound objects.

All links created are persistent and dynamic. For example, an object is part of several compound objects. A user updates the object by accessing the application directly. The new changes affect all references of the child object in the compound documents.

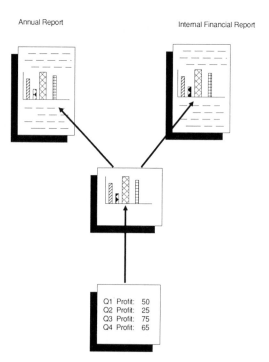

Figure 8.40 Typical NewWave object sharing.

Figure 8.41 displays an example of different types of OMF links. Three types of links are allowed:

a. *Simple links*—are used mainly by container objects to connect to other objects. For example, a file folder is connected with its individual files using simple links.

b. *Visual links*—allow one object to be projected inside another object. For example, a pie chart graph is included in the financial report using a visual link.

c. *Data passing links*—allow data to be passed from one object to another one, thus allowing interpretation of the data by the destination object. For example, a portion of a spreadsheet's cells can be passed into a graphic tool to draw a pie chart representing the spreadsheet data.

8.5.5 Metaphor

Metaphor's Data Interpretation System (DIS) provides a manager or corporate executive a computing environment tailored for their needs. It enables them to manipulate

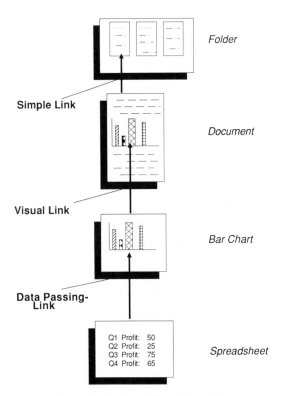

Figure 8.41 Typical NewWave links.

data and even develop applications without the help of their Management Information Systems (MIS) department. Metaphor DIS is supported either on Metaphor's own workstations or on top of PC-DOS or OS/2 workstations.

8.5.5.1 *Metaphor Software Overview*

The DIS (Metaphor, 1988) provides an end-user environment with emphasis on the desktop metaphor paradigm, see Figure 8.42. The end-user simply sees the entire tools collection as a set of icons. By manipulating these icons and a set of graphically oriented tools, the end-user can develop applications for their own needs. For example, the Query tool supports visual SQL see Figure 8.43. An end-user with no knowledge of SQL can create and manipulate databases stored on the workstation or any remote servers with this tool. DIS comes with a host of tools: Electronic mail, data query and reporting, spreadsheet, plotting, and even connection to databases on mainframe and minicomputers.

8.5.5.2 *Container Objects*

The DIS supports the concept of a container object. A container object encapsulates a group of other objects such as files. It allows users to organize data stored on their

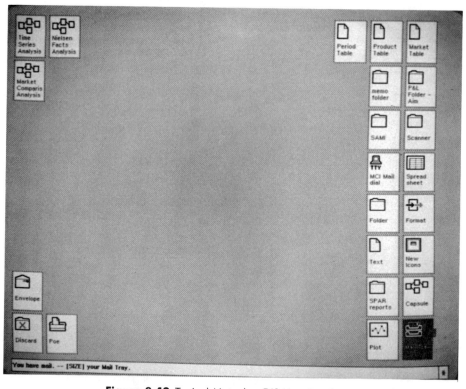

Figure 8.42 Typical Metaphor DIS User Interface.

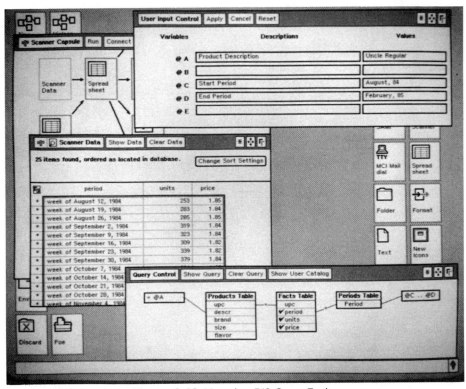

Figure 8.43 Metaphor DIS Query Tool.

workstations into groups of related objects. Each one of these objects can be either a simple data object or another container. A file folder is a good example of container object. Container objects are also used to develop user applications using the concept of *capsules*.

8.5.5.3 Capsules

Capsules allow a nonprogrammer to develop an application. A capsule encloses a group of interconnected icons. Each icon represents an individual tool such as the Query facility or yet another capsule. The end-user executes a capsule simply by selecting the capsule icon with the mouse. At this time, capsule starts executing the contents of capsule from left to right.

Essentially, a capsule allows the end-user to create an application through interconnected icons, each representing a tool performing a specific task, see Figure 8.44. Tools connected to each other pass their result from one tool to another until the application achieves its result. For example, a capsule can be used to generate a financial report containing a pie chart displaying the result of analysis from the corporate database. The Query facility can be used to extract the appropriate data from the corporate database. Then the Query facility results are sent to the Spreadsheet

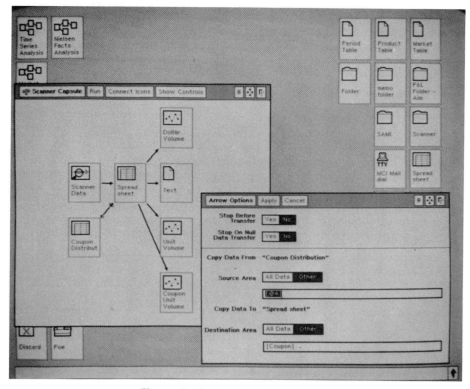

Figure 8.44 Metaphor DIS Capsules.

facility to perform an analysis. And the final analyzed result is sent to the Plot utility to generate a pie chart.

To develop the above application, users simply construct a capsule, as depicted in Figure 8.44. This capsule contains a set of icons representing the tools such as Query, Spreadsheet and the Plot facilities. The links, between the icons, indicate the flow of data from one tool to another tool. Data is transferred from one tool to another tool in the form of a matrix of information very much as does a set of spreadsheet cells. Links can also be modified to filter the result data as necessary.

■ 8.6 SUMMARY

This chapter covered user interfaces as the third area of computer science impacted by object orientation. The major areas of impact are in the design and presentation of user interfaces, and in the integration of diverse types of objects. We examined the impact on the design of user interfaces by covering graphical user interfaces first. Most GUIs do incorporate some object-oriented features, such as treating windows and resources as objects. We concentrated on two popular GUIs: Microsoft Windows and Apple Macintosh Toolbox, giving detailed examples of their object orientation features. There are also object-oriented layers defined on top of these GUIs, such as Apple MacApp and Whitewater Actor. Compared to the GUIs, MacApp and Actor present a higher level environment for the application developer. Both of these layers provide a large collection of predefined class hierarchies to simplify the task of user-interface development. In addition, these hierarchies can be extended to support any user-defined object.

Section 8.5.3 presented the NeXT user-interface development environment. This section demonstrated how direct manipulation can come to the rescue of programmers and application developers. The tools presented in the NeXT environment clearly show the future of user-interface design. Tools such as the NeXT Interface Builder will be incorporated in other platforms in the near future.

In Sections 8.5.4 and 8.5.5, attention was turned to user-interface environments and tools available to the end-user. In these two sections, we covered HP NewWave and Metaphor DIS. Both of these environments permit the end-user to directly manipulate objects that are familiar. Also, NewWave Object Management Facility allows creation and manipulation of objects composed of a variety of user-defined types, including text, graphics, and images. In addition, Metaphor DIS allows the end-user to graphically construct applications by connecting predefined components. This puts broad flexibility and power in the hands of the end-user.

9

SUMMARY

The preceding eight chapters described object-oriented technologies in programming languages, databases, and user interfaces. In the first four chapters of the book, the authors tried to explain the *concepts* and the *techniques* of object-oriented software development, independent of the idiosyncrasies of a particular object-oriented language, database, or user interface. Object orientation was defined through:

Object Orientation =
    Abstract Data Types + Inheritance + Object Identity

Although some of our examples were encoded using object-oriented languages (in most cases, Smalltalk/V from Digitalk), our aim in these four chapters was primarily to clarify each concept or feature through a real example. Illustrating and explaining all the object orientation features of particular object-oriented languages was accomplished in Chapters 5 and 6. We devoted an entire chapter for each of the most popular object-oriented languages, namely C++ and Ada. Although Smalltalk was very influential in shaping the object orientation concepts and terminology, we believe C++ and Ada will be the most dominant object-oriented languages in the 90s. Products that emphasize high performance, portability, and extensibility will use C++ (instead of C). Ada will remain popular because of its inertia and the backing of the Department of Defense.

Chapter 7 showed how object-oriented concepts could be integrated with database capabilities. This integration results in powerful systems called *object-oriented databases*. Object-oriented databases are the next generation post-relational database management systems of the 90s. We believe many applications that need object-oriented technologies to encode and manage complex systems will also need the *database* capabilities of object-oriented databases. These capabilities include persistent object spaces, transactions, querying, integrity, security, recovery, and versioning.

Chapter 8 was devoted to object-oriented graphical user interfaces. In these interactive environments, the object/message paradigm is expressed through physical metaphors. Users interact with icons, menus, and dialogs. An object's icon provides a physical metaphor for another underlying object. The underlying object performs a task analogous to the object depicted by the icon. In the 90s, almost all interaction with computers will be through picture or visual programming. Pictures and visual objects representing familiar "real world" objects facilitate the human/computer interaction. They provide friendlier user interfaces. Through the more natural object-oriented representation, user interfaces mirror the characteristics and interaction of objects in a problem domain.

This final chapter summarizes the characteristics of the object-oriented languages, databases, and user interfaces. In the last section, we describe the next generation integrated environments that will encapsulate object-oriented languages, databases, and user interfaces.

■ 9.1 ABSTRACT DATA TYPES

The first fundamental concept of object orientation is *abstract data typing*. Abstract data types describe a set of objects (data) with the same representation and behavior. In conventional programming languages, a program is a sequence of procedure calls. In object-oriented languages that support abstract data types, the dominant components are the objects or the data. Abstract data types describe the representation and behavior of objects.

With abstract data types there is a clear separation between the external interface of a data type and its internal implementation. The implementation of an abstract data type is *hidden*. Hence, alternative implementations could be used for the same abstract data type without changing its interface.

In most object-oriented programming languages, abstract data types are implemented through *classes*. A class is like a factory that produces *instances*, each with the same structure and behavior. A class has a name, a collection of operations for manipulating its instances, and a representation. The operations that manipulate the instances of a class are called *methods*. The state or representation of an instance is stored in *instance variables*. The methods are invoked through sending *messages* to the instances. Sending messages to objects (instances) is similar to calling procedures in conventional programming languages, but message sending is more dynamic.

Some object-oriented languages support classes but allow the instance variables of objects to be manipulated directly (rather than through methods). This is the case with Simula. This violates information hiding. Operations and object types are still *clustered* or grouped together in classes, such that operations associated with the type are part of the interface of the class. However, clients of the class know or "see" the representation (instance variables) of the class.

The same method name in a class can be *overloaded* with different semantics and implementations; the method Print can apply to integers, arrays, and character strings. Operation overloading allows programs to be extended gracefully. Because of overloading, the binding of a message to the code implementing the message is done at run time. This is called *dynamic binding*. The particular methods invoked when binding message names to methods depend on the recipient object's class.

Methods whose purpose is to access or update a particular instance variable are called *accessor* or *update* methods (functions, operations), respectively. With accessor functions the interface of a class remains the same. The representation of instance variables can be added or dropped without affecting existing clients of the class. Some object-oriented languages generate accessor or update methods automatically. This is the case with Trellis/Owl.

In some systems, classes can be created with parametric types. *Parametric polymorphism* allows the construction of abstract classes with type parameters: for example, Set[T] represents a parametric class that can be instantiated to Set[integer] or Set[Person]. Both sets share the code that is implemented in Set[T]. Code sharing is the most important advantage of parametric polymorphism.

Abstract data typing allows the construction of complex software systems through reusable components: the classes. Thus programming becomes modularized and extensible. Abstract data typing supports a much more natural representation of real world problems; the dominant components are the *objects* rather than the procedures. Abstract data typing allows objects of the same structure and behavior to *share* representation (instance variables) and code (methods).

■ 9.2 INHERITANCE

The second fundamental concept of object orientation is *inheritance*. Inheritance allows a class to inherit the behavior (operations, methods, and so on.) and the representation (instance variables, attributes, and so on.) from existing classes. Inheriting behavior enables *code sharing* (and hence *reusability*) among software modules. Inheriting representation enables *structure* sharing among data objects. The combination of these two types of inheritance provides a very powerful strategy for software modeling and development.

Inheritance is achieved by *specializing* existing classes. Classes can be specialized by extending their representation (instance variables) or behavior (operations). Alternatively, classes can also be specialized through *restricting* the representation or operations of existing classes. When a class C2 inherits from a class C1, the instance variables *and* the methods of C2 are a superset of the instance variables and methods of C1. The subclass C2 can override the implementation of an inherited method or instance variable, by providing an alternative definition or implementation.

Inheritance introduces some complexities, however, especially when integrated with other object orientation concepts such as encapsulation, typing, visibility, and object states. There are several areas of inheritance that characterize most of the different approaches used by existing object-oriented languages:

1. **Inheritance and Subtyping:** In most object-oriented languages the two concepts are used interchangeably. Yet it is useful to distinguish these two notions. A few languages even provide different constructs to support each concept.

2. **Visibility of Inherited Variables and Methods:** Some object-oriented languages such as Simula allow the direct manipulation of instance variables. Other languages such as C++ distinguish between public and private. With inheritance there is yet a third alternative, namely subclass visible.

3. **Inheritance and Encapsulation:** The visibility of instance variables violates information hiding (class encapsulation). In fact, there is a conflict between inheritance and encapsulation if the instance variables of superclasses are accessed directly. Furthermore, encapsulation and overloading could be used to support some of the functionality of inheritance. However, inheritance is a much more direct and natural mechanism to share code and structure.

4. **How to Specialize:** Inheritance is achieved by specializing existing classes. Classes can be specialized by extending their representation (instance variables) or behavior (operations). Alternatively, classes can also be specialized through restricting the representation or operations of existing classes.

5. **Object Inheritance:** Most object-oriented languages support *class* inheritance (that is, the ability of one class to inherit representation and methods from another class). An alternative approach is to allow *objects* to inherit from one another. Object inheritance allows an object to inherit the *state* of another object. There are models of computation that even incorporate operations with objects and use *only* object inheritance for organizing object spaces. These are called *prototype* systems. In these models, objects *delegate* messages to one another, thereby inheriting methods or values stored in other objects.

6. **Multiple Inheritance:** In many situations it is desirable to inherit from more than one class. This is called *multiple inheritance*. When a class inherits from more than one parent there is the possibility of *conflicts*: methods or instance variables with the same name, inherited from different superclasses, but with different or unrelated semantics.

Inheritance is perhaps the most useful object-oriented concept. Inheritance achieves software reusability and extensibility. Inheritance provides a very natural mechanism for code sharing. The methods in one class (the superclass) are shared by all its subclasses. If class hierarchies are maintained across multiple applications, the software development cycle will be greatly enhanced: More reliable code bases, more consistent systems, shorter development time, and more robust maintainable systems. In a very real sense, *programming* in an object-oriented environment becomes *specializing* existing class hierarchies.

■ 9.3 OBJECT IDENTITY

The third fundamental concept of object orientation is *object identity*. The inheritance hierarchies organize the object-oriented *code* and support extensibility and code reusability. Object identity organizes the objects or instances of an application in arbitrary graph-structured object spaces.

Identity is a property of an object that distinguishes the object from all other objects in the application. In programming languages, identity is realized through memory addresses. In databases, identity is realized through identifier keys. User-specified names are used in both languages and databases to give unique names to objects. Each of these schemata compromises identity.

In a completely object-oriented system, each object will be given an identity that will be permanently associated with the object, immaterial of the object's *structural* or *state* transitions. The identity of an object is also independent of the *location* or address of the object. Object identity provides the most natural modeling primitive for allowing the same object be a sub-object of multiple parent objects.

With object identity, objects can contain or refer to other objects. Object identity clarifies, enhances, and extends the notions of pointers in conventional programming languages, foreign keys in databases, and file names in operating systems. Using object identity, programmers can dynamically construct arbitrary graph-structured composite or complex objects, objects which are constructed from sub-objects. Objects can be created and disposed of at run time. In some cases, objects can even become persistent and be re-accessed in subsequent programs.

There are many techniques to implement identity. The best way is to assign each object a system-wide unique identifier, called a *surrogate*, which is independent of the object's type, address, or state. When surrogates are stored with an object, they allow the object to be relocated without losing its identity (the object becomes self-describing).

There are many operations associated with identity. Since the state of an object is different from its identity, there are three types of equality predicates for comparing objects. The most obvious equality predicate is the *identical* predicate, which checks whether two objects are actually one and the same object. The two other equality predicates, *shallow equal* and *deep equal* actually compare the state of objects. Shallow equal goes one level deep comparing the identifiers of corresponding instance variables. Deep equal ignores identities and compares the values of corresponding base objects (integers, floats, characters, and so forth.). As far as copying objects, the counterparts of deep and shallow equality are *deep* and *shallow* copy. Deep (shallow) copy produces a replica that is deep (shallow) equal to the original object. Other operations associated with identity include *merge* and *become*.

Object identity allows the creation of complex or composite objects. The value of an instance variable is an object. An object identity identifies a unique object in the user's object space. Therefore, values of instance variables are actually object identities. The identity of an object is immutable. The object can undergo state and even structural modifications or transitions without losing its identity. Object identity is the perfect paradigm for creating and maintaining multiple versions of an object. The only common property of multiple versions of the same object is the identity of the object.

■ 9.4 PROGRAMMING LANGUAGES

In 1982 it was predicted that " . . . object-oriented programming will be in the 1980s what structured programming was in the 1970s . . . " (Rentsch, 1982). The 1980s will probably be known as the decade that launched the object-oriented era of computation.

In the early 60s, the designers of the language Simula introduced the concept of an *object*. Conceptually an object contained both data and the operations that manipulated its data. Simula also incorporated the notion of *classes* which are used to describe the structure and behavior of a set of objects. Class inheritance was also supported by Simula. Simula also distinguished between two types of equality: identical and shallow equal, reflecting the distinction between *reference* (identity) based versus *value* (content) based interpretations of objects. Therefore, Simula laid the foundation of object-oriented languages and some of the object-oriented terminology.

During the 70s and 80s, the object-oriented concepts from Simula and other earlier prototypes were embodied in Smalltalk, one of the most influential object-oriented languages. This language incorporates many of the object-oriented features of Simula, including classes, inheritance, and support of object identity.

In fact, Smalltalk is not just a language. It also incorporates a whole programming environment and a menu-based interactive user interface. The Smalltalk environment includes an extensive initial class hierarchy. Programming in Smalltalk entails opening a working window, browsing, and extending the class hierarchy through another window, and so on. The programmer interacts with the system through dialogs and pop-up or pull-down windows, depending on the particular implementation of the environment.

Smalltalk is extremely rich in object-oriented concepts. In Smalltalk, everything is an object, including classes and base types (integers, floating point numbers, and so on.) This means that throughout the entire Smalltalk environment, programming consists of sending messages to objects. A message can add a number to another number, create a new instance of a class, or introduce a new method in a given class.

Smalltalk will remain a powerful influence in object-oriented programming. There is continuous design and development of different variations and dialects of Smalltalk, implemented on a host of different hardware platforms.

Throughout the 80s, object-oriented concepts (abstract data types, inheritance, and object identity), along with Smalltalk, Simula, and other languages began to merge and give birth to a number of object-oriented languages, extensions, and dialects. Figure 9.1 depicts the influence of Simula and Smalltalk on more recent object-oriented languages. As demonstrated throughout this book, object-oriented languages will evolve in the following four categories:

1. *Extensions, dialects, and versions of Smalltalk.* There have been several proposals (and prototypes) to extend Smalltalk with typing, multiple inheritance, or *concurrent programming* constructs. These are primarily research projects or prototypes.

    In terms of actual products, several vendors such as Xerox, Tektronix, Parc-Place systems, and Digitalk offer Smalltalk environment on several platforms.

2. *Object-oriented extensions of conventional languages.* One of the most popular object-oriented languages is C++. It provides two constructs for class definitions. The first method is an extension of *struct* construct and the other method is through the new *class* construct. C++ allows hierarchies of classes and permits subclasses to access methods and instance variables from other classes in their hierarchy. The language permits ad hoc polymorphism by allowing overloading of function names and operators.

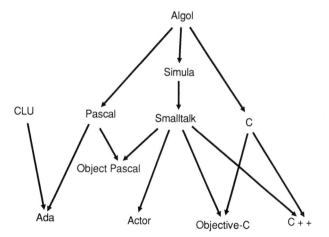

Figure 9.1 Evolution of object-oriented languages.

Another popular dialect of C is Objective C. This language is a superset of C incorporating object-oriented features from Smalltalk. Like Smalltalk, it comes with a large collection of predefined classes to simplify the software development process. Objective C supports abstract data types, inheritance, and operator overloading.

For Pascal, popular object-oriented extensions include Object Pascal for the Macintosh from Apple Computer and Turbo Pascal from Borland for IBM personal computers.

3. *Strongly typed object-oriented languages.* A very interesting and commercially available language is Eiffel, from Interactive Software Engineering, Inc. In addition to encapsulation and inheritance, Eiffel integrates a number of powerful object-oriented capabilities such as *parametric types*, and *pre-* and *post-conditions* for methods. Both concepts are described in detail in Chapter 2.

Other strongly typed object-oriented languages include Trellis/Owl (Schaffert et al., 1986) from DEC. One of the most important programming languages to support abstract data typing is *Ada* (Booch, 1986). The U.S. Department of Defense (DoD) commissioned the design of Ada to reduce and control the cost of software development. The DoD intended Ada to be the language of choice for the development of new embedded systems. Object-oriented constructs in Ada include packages and generic units, discussed in detail in Chapter 6.

4. *Object-oriented extensions of LISP* such as CLOS, Flavors, and Common Objects.

In the 90s, object-oriented languages, techniques, databases, and user interfaces will be even more popular. Most software development will be affected by object orientation in one way or another. The 90s will be the decade of the proliferation of object-oriented languages and technologies.

9.4.1 C++

Chapter 5 presented C++ as one of the most popular hybrid object-oriented languages. As stated, C++ is an object-oriented extension of C. We demonstrated how some of the C constructs are extended to support object orientation. The language supports object-oriented concepts such as abstract data type, inheritance, polymorphism, and dynamic binding.

As presented in Chapter 5, C++ provides two constructs for abstract data type definition. The first one is an extension of *struct* construct and the other is through the new *class* construct. The *struct* construct in C allows structural definition of an object that is composed of several members. To this, C++ extends the ability of defining functions as attributes of an object definition. C++ also adds the new *class* construct. With it, the designer constructs classes conforming to the more traditional object-oriented view that instance variables can be hidden.

C++ allows class definitions to inherit both methods and instance variables from existing class definitions. The first release of C++ only allowed tree hierarchy (single inheritance) to be defined. The new release of C++ Version 2.0, allows multiple inheritance.

In terms of object identity, C++ allows reference to objects either by name or address. Address of an object can be used as reference in the definition of a complex object. For a user-defined class, the language provides copy constructors automatically. There are no operations provided to compare user-defined objects. The only system-supported comparison of objects is by the value of their addresses. Users can develop both comparison or copy operations as part of their class definitions.

The language allows ad hoc polymorphism by permitting overloading of function names and operators. Function names can be overloaded to have varied numbers of arguments of different types. System defined operators such as $+$, $-$, $*$, and others can be overloaded for user-defined classes. C++ also supports dynamic binding through virtual functions.

One of the greatest benefits of operator overloading comes with stream I/O. With this new I/O method, users can overload the stream operators to support user-defined data types directly.

Briefly, the major advantages of C++ are:

1. *True extension of the C language*. The language is designed as a super set of ANSI C (Kernighan and Ritchie, 1988). Any C++ compiler accepts most standard C programs.
2. *Good performance*. C++ does not suffer the performance problems associated with the earlier object-oriented language implementations. There is a slight performance degradation with virtual functions, since most C++ compilers implement them with an extra level of indirection.
3. *Popularity and multi-vendor support*. C++ has become a popular object-oriented language. The popularity of the language has far exceeded other object-oriented languages such as Smalltalk, Objective C, Eiffel, or Object Pascal. Several vendors have released C++ compilers, preprocessors and development environments including AT&T, Apple, Apollo, Sun, Zortech, Oasys, Glockenspiel, and Oregon Software.

And, the major disadvantages of C++ are:

1. *Hybrid object-oriented language*. C++ is not a purely object-oriented language, since it allows the developer to fall back on traditional C coding habits. As demonstrated in Chapter 5, the designer of a class can provide complete access to the instance variables of a class. This violates the data hiding principle.

2. *Manual garbage collection.* The language does not support automatic garbage collection. Manual garbage collection shifts the burden of object management onto the shoulders of the developer rather than the system.

3. *Current lack of development tools.* Currently there are not many development environments (symbolic debugger, browsers, and the like) available. These tools should be available in the near future as more tool vendors supporting C++ finish development of such tools.

Also, unlike Smalltalk, C++ does not contain a predefined class hierarchy.

9.4.2 Ada

Chapter 6 examined the object-oriented features of the Ada programming language. Persistent debates continue over whether Ada can be considered as an object-oriented language. Ada supports object-oriented concepts such as abstract data types, overloading of functions and operators, parametric polymorphism, and even specialization of user-defined types. The only object-oriented concept lacking is inheritance. Ada is the result of a DoD effort to reduce the cost of software development. Ada contains the usual control structures and the ability to define types and subprograms.

Chapter 6 demonstrated type definition via the subtype and derived type declarations. We presented a few examples in this chapter to demonstrate how user-defined types can be defined. Even though Ada does not support inheritance, subtypes and derived types allow a new type definition to be defined as a more specialized or constrained definition of preexisting user- or system-defined type.

Packages allow users to group logically related entities together as one unit. With packages, user-defined types can be defined. Packages allow language components and constructs: types, data, and subprograms to be divided into logical design pieces.

Ada also allows operator and function overloading and has parametric polymorphism features. Function names and system-defined operators can be overloaded with user-defined definitions. Parametric polymorphism is achieved via *generic units*. A generic unit is either a generic subprogram or package unit. Generic units are parameterized templates for design units. These templates can be developed with only limited knowledge of the actual objects or constructs to be defined when the templates are invoked.

In regard to object identity, Ada allows objects to be identified by address and name. Objects can be referenced by subparts of another object. This is done by defining an object subpart that serves as a pointer to the second object.

■ 9.5 OBJECT-ORIENTED DATABASES

The object-oriented languages form powerful environments for building large, complex software. Yet there are desirable features missing. These features include persistence, support of transactions, simple querying of bulk data, concurrent access, resilience, and security. Database management systems offer these features, and more.

How can the object-oriented concepts be combined with database capabilities? The solution is object-oriented databases, which integrate the fundamental object-oriented concepts (abstract data typing, inheritance, and object identity) with database capabilities.

The databases capabilities in object-oriented databases are:

1. *Persistence:* the ability of objects to *persist* through different program invocations
2. *Transactions:* execution units that are executed either entirely or not at all
3. *Concurrency control:* the algorithms that control the concurrent execution of transactions to guarantee serializability
4. *Recovery:* the ability of the database management system to recover from transaction, system, or media errors
5. *Querying:* high-level declarative constructs that allow users to qualify *what* they want to retrieve from the persistent databases
6. *Versioning:* the ability to store and retrieve multiple versions of the *same* persistent database object
7. *Integrity:* the predicates that specify and define *consistent* states of the persistent databases
8. *Security:* the mechanisms that control the user access rights of persistent databases
9. *Performance issues:* the constructs and strategies that are used to enhance the response time and the throughput of database management systems.

Object-oriented databases can thus be defined through:

Object-Oriented Databases =
        Object Orientation + Database Capabilities

Figure 9.2 illustrates the evolution of database management systems. The forerunners of database management systems were "generalized" file routines. In the 1950s and 1960s, *data definition* products were developed by large companies. This laid the foundation for *network* database management systems. The underlying data model of these databases presented the user with a network view of the database. A network view consists of record types and one-to-many relationships among the record types. The network model allows a record type to be involved in more than one relationship. A less general model is a tree-structured hierarchical relationship among record types, which is the basis of the *hierarchical data model*. The hierarchical data model allows a record type to be involved in *only one* relationship as a parent and also *only one* relationship as a child.

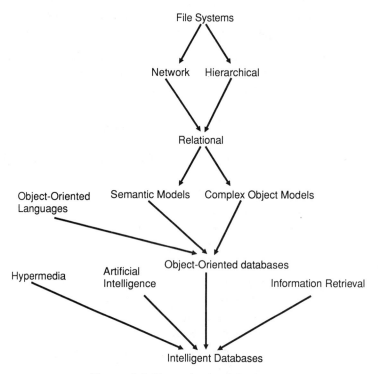

Figure 9.2 The evolution of databases.

Both the hierarchical and network data models were primarily *navigational*. Furthermore, the owner/member relationship (for the network model) or parent/child relationship (for the hierarchical model) were explicitly stored in the database records. In order to provide more flexibility in organizing large databases and alleviate some of the problems of the earlier models, Ted Codd introduced the *relational data model* in early 70s. Relational database management systems became increasingly popular in the 80s and their use and popularity is steadily increasing in the 90s. The relational model is simple and elegant. The underlying theory is based on the mathematically well-founded and well-understood concepts of relational algebra and first-order predicate calculus. Relational algebra consists of only a few operations: Set operations (union, intersection, difference, Cartesian product) and the relational operations (selection, projection, join).

In the late 80s, almost all the commercial database management systems were based either on the hierarchical, network, or the relational model. Still, there were several alternative database modeling proposals. One of the earliest alternative database data modeling proposals was the *semantic data models*. Semantic data models used the *node* and *link* representation schema of semantic networks. Each node is an *entity type*. Similar to types in programming languages, an entity type represents a set of objects (entities), all having the same attributes. An attribute is a function which can apply to an entity in the entity type. The name of an entity type also identifies the *extension* (set of all instances) of the entity type. Entity types are analogous to classes and entities to instances. Attributes are analogous to instance variables.

Semantic data models are primarily used as design tools for underlying relational or network databases. The forerunner of the semantic models was the famous entity-relationship model, introduced by Chen (1976). The semantic data modeling approach was not the only one that tried to add more semantics to the more traditional data models. There were a number of data models that attempted to *incrementally* extend the relational data model, to allow more flexibility while maintaining a solid theoretical foundation.

The object space in the relational model consists of a collection of flat tables. Each table is a set of rows (or tuples). The column values in each row (attributes of tuples) can only be instances of base atomic types such as integers, floats, or character strings. The flat-table representation is known as the *first normal form*. Complex object models attempted to relax the first normal form restrictions, while maintaining the strong theoretical foundation of the relational model. With nested and more general complex object models, more general object spaces could be constructed using *set* and *tuple* object constructors. The "column" values could thus be tuples, sets of base values, or sets of tuples (that is, relations). If the model supports object identity, the sets and tuples could be referentially shared. Thus users can construct arbitrary graph-structured object spaces and avoid the "unnatural" foreign key joins of the relational model.

The complex object models and the semantic data models laid a strong foundation for the development of a number of object-oriented databases, both in research and in industry. Concepts such as complex objects, object identity, inheritance, and set and tuple valued attributes propagated into these powerful object-oriented database systems. Each object-oriented database was influenced by one or more of the complex and semantic data modeling alternatives. Perhaps through an eagerness to explore, novel and emerging technologies took quick notice of the opportunities and potential of the integration of object-oriented concepts with database capabilities (that is, concurrency, persistence, access methods, querying, and so on).

The next evolutionary step after object-oriented databases are *intelligent databases*. In addition to object-oriented features, intelligent databases incorporate inferencing. Inferencing is important both as a declarative style of programming and as a base technology to perform inductive reasoning about databases. Object orientation, augmented with inferencing, provides a powerful model to support complex applications in the 90s. Intelligent databases also incorporate direct support of multimedia data types such as text, images, and voice. The intelligent database user interface provides a high-level hypermedia programming environment for the user. Intelligent database tools allow the users to discover intricate relationships in their persistent object spaces, automatically.

■ 9.6 USER INTERFACES

Chapter 8 turned the attention to the impact of object orientation on the design and presentation of the modern user interfaces. The modern user interfaces are revolutionizing the application of computers by users with diverse needs and backgrounds. One of the main goals of modern user interfaces is to simplify and reduce commands required to perform tasks. Command-driven user interfaces are being replaced with windows, menu bars, pull-down menus, and dialog boxes. The mouse is used as the primary pointing device to select commands from a list of menu choices.

In the 1960s, projects at SRI International, MIT, and other universities led to the invention of pointing devices and windowing systems. In the 70s, researchers at Xerox PARC were busy designing powerful new workstations armed with graphical user interfaces. Their experiments concentrated on applying the associative memory of the end-user combined with direct manipulation capabilities. The basic assumption of these new workstations was that one user could have a powerful desktop computer totally dedicated to that user's personal task. Thus, the computer is not only used to perform the user task, but can also provide a much more intuitive and easy-to-use environment. For user interfaces both the Star workstation (also developed at PARC) and its predecessor prototype the Alto, influenced the design and look-and-feel of Apple's Macintosh, Aldus' PageMaker desktop publishing software, Microsoft's Windows, and Metaphor's DIS software environment. Figure 9.3 depicts the influence of research effort in 60s and Xerox PARC projects on the user interface of modern computing systems.

In the 90s, computer systems will include much more powerful processor(s), higher resolution displays, and more memory. A larger portion of the computing power of the future machines will be used to make computers more aesthetically pleasing. The user interfaces in the 90s will be characterized by being more intuitive, by handling diverse types of objects, and by providing visual programming environments.

Emerging technologies such as Digital Video Interactive (DVI), optical disk drives, and digital signal processors will permit the end-user to interact with multimedia applications. Object-orientation will be exploited to integrate diverse sets of objects ranging from text and voice, to images and video. Apple HyperCard and other hypermedia tools will be used more often to interconnect these disparate objects.

Visual programming will help both nonprogrammers and programmers develop applications. Iconic and visual languages will allow programmers to create object types and quickly design the flow of control for the application. Visual SQL and QBE (Zloof, 1977) will allow an executive to generate a report or navigate through corporate databases on mini and mainframe computers without being computer literate.

As stated in Chapter 8, user interfaces exploit object orientation in several ways.

1. *Design.* Designing modern user interfaces using the GUIs mentioned earlier is a difficult task. Most of the GUIs present an object-oriented layer on top

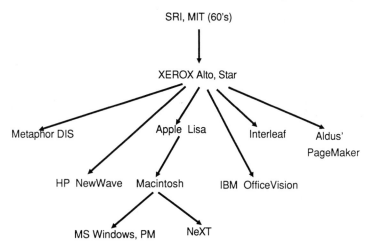

Figure 9.3 Evolution of object-oriented user interfaces.

of an application programming interface (API) to simplify the design and the development of user interfaces.

These object-oriented layers provide a hierarchy of predefined classes. These classes encapsulate the behavior of screen objects such as windows, menus, and icons. Each class definition handles events such as drawing screen elements or clicking and dragging the mouse. Methods attached to a class definition allow the application developer to:

a. specify which control options should be present, set, or reset

b. draw the screen objects

c. handle the events such as mouse click

d. and communicate with the GUI

Subclasses, within a hierarchy, inherit behavior and functionality from their superclasses. In addition, they can override, refine or extend both behavior and functionality.

2. *Presentation*. Direct manipulation of the computer is more intuitive than traditional command-based interfaces. Users perform their day-to-day work on the computer by simply selecting or moving the icons and objects on the screen.

3. *Integration*. Object-oriented concepts such as complex objects and object identity can be employed to enhance the capabilities of a user interface. Users develop complex applications by integrating information from a set of applications. An end-user can develop a document with information drawn from a set of applications such as database, spreadsheet, and word processor.

We covered graphical user interfaces by concentrating on popular Microsoft Windows and Macintosh Toolbox. The GUIs provide programming interfaces that allow users to create screen objects, draw screen objects, monitor mouse activations, and report screen events to the user. Most of GUIs use an object-oriented approach to deal with screen object manipulation. Communication, about the state of screen objects, is accomplished through messages to be sent between the application and the user-interface engine.

As demonstrated, Windows has some object-oriented features. In order to create screen objects such as windows, the application developer defines a class specifying the necessary properties. Instances of the window class can then be created. Several applications can share the same window definitions simultaneously. To communicate with instances of a window class, messages are sent and received by a special function called the *window function*. The window function handles all messages such as redrawing screens, displaying icons, or pop-up menus, and changing the contents of the client area.

The Macintosh Toolbox provides a collection of utilities to access and manipulate Macintosh's hardware and software resources. It provides a set of utilities to manipulate user-interface components such as windows, menu bar, and dialog boxes.

Just like Microsoft Windows, the Macintosh Toolbox has object-oriented features. For example, the application developer defines a new type of window by defining a template for a new class of windows. Messages are sent between Toolbox and the application to change the behavior of screen objects such as windows and cursors. For each class of windows defined by the system or the user, there exists a function called the *window definition function*. When a window needs to be drawn or resized, a message is sent to the *window definition function* to perform the appropriate action.

Object orientation also comes to the rescue of the software engineer, by lightening the burden of user-interface development. Development environments such as MacApp and Actor provide libraries composed of object hierarchies. Each class within the hierarchy defines the attributes necessary for its objects in addition to inheriting features from its superclasses. Each object within the hierarchy communicates with other objects in the system through transmission of messages. The user-interface designer can further extend the class hierarchy by adding their own screen object designs. These new screen objects can inherit properties from existing classes. In addition, they can refine old properties or define new properties as needed.

MacApp is an object-oriented layer on top of Macintosh Toolbox. MacApp is a library providing a large collection of classes defined using Object Pascal and MPW Assembly Language. This large collection of classes provides services for creating windows, handling File I/O, handling icons and cursors, and control components such as button, dials, and scroll bars.

If you program directly in the Toolbox you will need a large body of code just to manipulate user-interface objects. But MacApp provides prebuilt class definitions that simplify creation and manipulation of user interfaces for Macintosh. Some of the operations automatically handled by these predefined classes are:

- Managing windows, menus, and mouse
- Handling Errors
- Editing text within windows
- Filing documents

Besides managing screen objects, event handling for each class definition is a major feature of MacApp. MacApp also provides powerful debugging tools such as: the Inspector window, the Interactive Debugger, and the Debug Menu.

Actor is an object-oriented environment tailored for designing MS Windows applications (Whitewater Group, 1987). The major components of the Actor environment are the Actor language, its development environment, and the class hierarchy.

The Actor, just like Smalltalk, is a novel object-oriented language. The language supports abstract data typing, data hiding, single inheritance, and polymorphism (overriding of methods within the hierarchy). The language comes with a predefined hierarchy of classes. Everything in Actor is an object: numbers, windows, and even a class. Just like instances of a class, a class object has instance variables and methods.

In addition to the language, Actor comes with a powerful development environment consisting of: the Inspector, the Browser, and the Debugger.

Actor also provides an extensive library of class definitions. Some of the functions supported with this library include: easy manipulation of MS Windows, set and collection objects, File I/O, parsing, and string handling.

The NeXT user-interface development environment demonstrated how direct manipulation can come to the rescue of programmers and application developers. The tools presented in the NeXT environment clearly show the future of user-interface design. Tools such as the NeXT *Interface Builder* will soon be incorporated in other platforms.

NextStep is the most impressive piece of technology offered with the NeXT computer. NextStep permits the developer to design the user interface directly on the screen. The NeXT user interface draws heavily on direct manipulation and modern graphic user interfaces. The developer simply selects the menu, control, and screen objects from a palette, then moves the controls to the desired location; and, can resize the controls to the desired dimension.

In Chapter 8, we presented object-oriented user-interface environments and tools available to the end-user such as HP NewWave and Metaphor DIS. Both of these environments permit the end-user to directly manipulate objects that are familiar to them. Also, the NewWave Object Management Facility allows creation and manipulation of objects composed of a variety of user-defined types, including text, graphics and images. In addition, Metaphor DIS allows the end-user to graphically construct applications by connecting predefined components. This puts broad flexibility and power in the hands of the end-user.

HP's NewWave comes with a set of utilities including the NewWave Office. NewWave allows end-users to create compound documents composed of text, graphics, images, and voice. NewWave applies the desktop metaphor and object orientation throughout its environment.

Metaphor Data Interpretation System (DIS) provides an office manager or corporate executive a computing environment tailored to their needs. It enables them to manipulate data and even develop applications without the help of their MIS department.

The DIS provides an end-user environment with emphasis on the desktop metaphor paradigm. The end-user simply sees the entire tools collection as a set of icons. By manipulating these icons and a set of graphically oriented tools, the end-user can develop applications for their own needs.

Graphical user interfaces will play a dominant role in the industry. Direct manipulation of objects will be widespread and will make computers accessible to a broader audience. In the future, direct manipulation will allow developers to design user interfaces by selecting and resizing screen objects directly on the screen. Tools such as NextStep will be commonly used to develop sophisticated user interfaces. Also, the end-user will be able to build an application graphically by connecting preconstructed parameterized components.

■ 9.7 OBJECT ORIENTATION IN THE 1990s

The preceding sections summarized the object-oriented concepts, languages, databases, and user interfaces. In this final section, we summarize the object orientation directions of user interfaces, databases, and programming languages.

As far as user interfaces, object orientation will manifest itself in:

1. *Graphical UI operating system environments.* As discussed in Chapter 8, the graphical user interfaces of operating systems such as the Windows environment of DOS, the Macintosh Toolbox, NextStep of Next, and so on, exhibit the Object/Message "point and click" object-oriented paradigm. The user's interaction is with objects (windows, menus, dialogs) and each object responds to a number of commands. The trend of object-oriented graphical interfaces is permeating almost all platforms and areas of computation.

2. *Visual programming.* Visual programming is replacing mundane and repetitious character/procedure-based programming habits. Visual programming techniques to create or browse class hierarchies, to construct flow of control, and even to query persistent databases are providing much friendlier programming environments. The benefits are increased productivity of programmers and increased maintainability of complex code bases.

3. *Hypermedia documents*. The trend in the 90s is toward *sharing*: sharing between products, sharing across different platforms, and sharing between different users. One requirement for sharing is the ability to *navigate* or link from one product/object node to another. Another is to allow the construction of "heterogeneous" object spaces, where different sub-objects are obtained from different sources. To achieve these goals in an environment that manipulates multimedia (text, graphics, voice) objects, *hypermedia* systems are controlling the construction and maintenance of hypermedia links across different objects.

The object-oriented features of user interfaces will support the capabilities of underlying object-oriented languages and databases.

In databases, besides some novel object-oriented database products, relational database management systems are *starting to incorporate* object orientation features. Many companies involved in the development of relational systems are incorporating object orientation features in their products.

When discussing databases however, we should look at the broader perspective and remember that the future of databases is, in fact, with *intelligent databases* (Parsaye et al., 1989). Intelligent databases will tightly integrate artificial intelligence, information retrieval, object-oriented and multimedia technologies, with traditional databases. Therefore the *extension* of databases with additional capabilities is not limited to object orientation. Support of inferencing (artificial intelligence), full-text retrieval (information retrieval) and multimedia data types (voice, text, graphics) are equally important. Yet, the high-level hypermedia user interfaces and high-level tools of intelligent databases will all manifest object-oriented capabilities.

Most software development will be affected by object orientation one way or another. This will take the form of:

1. *Object-oriented design methodologies*. These methodologies encourage the developer to design and implement more modularized and extensible code bases *independent of the underlying language*.
2. *Object-oriented languages*. To facilitate the application of object-oriented design methodologies, developers are using object-oriented languages. The most popular languages will continue to be C++ and Ada.
3. *Object-oriented environments*. Similar to the Smalltalk environment, integrated graphical programming environments have been developed for other programming languages, including C++, Objective C, and Actor. These environments integrate object-oriented user-interface capabilities in the development effort.

The 1990s will be the decade of the proliferation of object-oriented languages and technologies.

■ 9.8 OTHER REFERENCES

This book covered object-oriented concepts, languages, databases, and user interfaces. Along with this book, there are other materials that should prove useful to our readers. This section enlists some of these references.

For object-oriented concepts:

Object-Oriented Computing Volume I and II (1987) by G. Peterson. Washington, DC: IEEE Press.

Object-Oriented Concepts, Databases, and Applications (1989) by W. Kim and F. H. Lochovsky. New York: ACM Press.

Object-Oriented Concurrent Programming (1987) by A. Yonezawa and M. Tokoro. Cambridge, MA: The MIT Press.

Research Directions in Object-Oriented Programming (1987) by B. Shriver and P. Wegner (eds.). Cambridge, MA: The MIT Press.

For object-oriented directions:

Object-Oriented Systems: The Commercial Benefits (1989) by J. Jeffcoate et al. Ovum Report. London: Dudley Ltd.

Release 1.0 (September 1989) by E. Dyson.

For object-oriented design:

Object-Oriented Analysis (1990) by P. Coad and E. Yourdon. Englewood Cliffs, NJ: Prentice-Hall.

Object-Oriented Systems Analysis (1990) by S. Shlaer and S. Mellor. Englewood Cliffs, NJ: Prentice-Hall.

For object-oriented languages:

Object-Oriented Programming Design with Examples in C++ (1990) by M. Mulen. Reading, MA: Addison-Wesley.

Object-Oriented Programming—An Evolutionary Approach (1987) by B. Cox. Reading, MA; Addison-Wesley.

Object-Oriented Software Construction (1988) by B. Meyer. Englewood Cliffs, NJ: Prentice-Hall.

For Ada:

Ada Language and Methodology (1987) by D.A. Watt et al. Englewood Cliffs, NJ: Prentice-Hall.

Software Engineering with Ada (1986) by G. Booch. Menlo Park, CA: Benjamin/Cummings.

For C++:

The C++ Programming Language (1986) by B. Stroustrup. Reading, MA: Addison-Wesley.

The Complete C++ Primer (1990) by K. Weiskamp and B. Flamig. San Diego: Academic Press.

C++ Primer (1989) by S. B. Lippman. Reading, MA: Addison-Wesley.

For Smalltalk:

Smalltalk-80: The Language and Its Implementation (1983) by A. Goldberg and D. Robson. Reading, MA: Addison-Wesley

For object-oriented databases:

Intelligent Databases (1989) K. Parsaye et al. New York: John Wiley & Sons.

Principles of Databases and Knowledge-Base Systems (1988) by J. D. Ullman. Rockville, MD: Computer Science Press.

Readings in Object-Oriented Database Systems (1990) by S. B. Zdonik and D. Maier (eds.). San Mateo, CA: Morgan Kaufmann Publishers.

Relational Databases and Knowledge Bases (1989) G. Gardarin and P. Valduriez. Reading, MA: Addison Wesley.

For object-oriented user interfaces:

Designing the User Interface (1987) by B. Schneiderman. Reading, MA: Addison Wesley.

Programming the User Interface (1989) by J. R. Brown and S. Cunningham. New York: John Wiley & Sons.

Object-Oriented Programming for the Macintosh (1986) by K. J. Schmucker. Hasbrouck Heights, NJ: Hayden Book Co.

Visual Information Systems (1988) by R. H. Veith. Boston: G. K. Hall & Co.

Visual Programming (1988) by N. C. Shu. New York: Van Nostrand Reinhold Co.

Other references include the OOPSLA proceedings from the ACM, the *Journal of Object-Oriented Programming*, and the *C++ Report*.

REFERENCES

Abiteboul, S., and Bidoit, N. (1984) An algebra for non-normalized relations. *ACM International Symposium on PODS*, March.

Abiteboul, S.; Grumbach, S.; Voisard, A.; and Walter, S. (1990) An extensible rule-based language with complex objects and data-functions. *Proceedings of 2nd International Workshop on Database Programming Languages,* R. Hall, R. Morrison, and D. Stemples (eds.). San Mateo, CA: Morgan Kaufmann Publishers.

Abiteboul, S., and Hull, R. (1984) IFO: A formal semantic database model. *Proceedings of the ACM SIGACT-SIGMOD Symposium on Principles of Database Systems.*

Abrial, J. R. (1974) Data semantics. In *Data Base Management*, J. W. Klimbie and K. L. Koffeman (eds.). New York: North-Holland Publishing Co.

Agha, G., and Hewitt, C. (1987) Concurrent programming using actors. In A. Yonezawa and M. Tokoro (eds.). *Object-Oriented Concurrent Programming.* Cambridge, MA: The MIT Press.

Ait-Kaci, H., and Nasr, R. (1986) Logic and inheritance. *ACM Symposium on Principles of Programming Languages*, January.

Albano, A.; Cardelli, L.; and Orsini, R. (1985) Galileo: A strongly-typed interactive conceptual language. *ACM Transactions on Database Systems, 10*(2), (June).

American National Standards Institute-MIL-STD-1815A-1983 (1983) *The Ada Reference Manual.* Summit, NJ: Silicon Press.

American National Standards Institute (1966) *American National Standard FORTRAN* (ANSX 3.9-1966), New York.

Anderson, L; Echland, E.; and Maier, D. (1986) Proteus; objectifying the DBMS user interface. *Proceedings of 1986 International Workshop on Object-Oriented Database Systems.* K. Dittrich and U. Dayal. IEEE Computer Society.

Andrews, T., and Harris, C. (1987) Combining language and database advances in an object-oriented environment. *Proceedings of OOPSLA-87.*

411

Apple Computer (1988) *The MacApp Interim Manual.* Apple Computer Inc., Cupertino, CA.

Apple Computer (1987) *MPW Pascal Reference Manual.* Apple Computer Inc., Cupertino, CA.

Apple Computer (1985–87) Inside Macintosh: volumes 1–5. Reading, MA: Addison-Wesley.

Astrahan, M. M., et al. (1976) System R: A relational approach to data management. *ACM Transactions on Database Systems, 1*(2), 97–137.

AT&T (1986) *The UNIX System User's Manual.* Englewood Cliffs, NJ: Prentice-Hall.

Atkinson, M. P.; Bailey, P. J.; Cockshott, W. P.; Chisholm, K. J.; and Morrison, R. (1983) An approach to persistent programming. *Computer Journal, 26,* (November).

Atkinson, M.; Buneman, P.; and Morrison, R. (eds.) (1985) *Persistence and Data Types* Papers from the Appin Workshop, University of Glasgow.

Backus, J. (1978) The history of FORTRAN I, II and III. *ACM Sigplan Notices, 13*(8), (August), 165–180.

Baker, H. G. (1978) List processing in real time on a serial computer. *Communications of the ACM, 21*(4), (April).

Ballard, S. and Shirron, S. (1983) The design and implementation of VAX/Smalltalk-80. In *Smalltalk-80: Bits of History, Word of Advice,* G. Krasner (ed.). Reading, MA: Addison-Wesley.

Bancilhon, F., et al. (1988) The design and implementation of O_2, an object-oriented database system. *Advances in Object-Oriented Database Systems.* Proc. Second Int. Workshop on Object-Oriented Database Syst., K. Dittrich (ed.). Bad Munster, FRG, Sept. 88.

Bancilhon, F., et al. (1983) VERSO: A relational back end data base machine. *Proceedings of 2nd International Workshop on Database Machines.*

Bancilhon, F.; Briggs, T.; Khoshafian, S.; and Valduriez, P. (1987) FAD—a simple and powerful database language. *Proceedings of VLDB 1987.*

Bancilhon, F. and Khoshafian, S. (1989) A calculus for complex objects. *Journal of Computer and System Sciences, 38*(2), 326–340.

Bancilhon, F., and Khoshafian, S. (1986) A calculus for complex objects. *ACM International Symposium on PODS*, March.

Banerjee, J., et al. (1987) Data model issues for object-oriented applications. *ACM Transactions on Office Information Systems, 5*(1).

Barnes, J. G. P. (1980) An overview of Ada. *Software Practice and Experience, 10,* 851–887.

Barth, P. S. (1986) An object-oriented approach to graphical interfaces. *ACM Transactions on Graphics, 5*(2), April, 142–172.

Beech, D. (1988) A foundation for evolution from relational to object databases. *Advances in Database Technology—EDBT 1988,* J. W. Schmidt, S. Ceri, and M. Missikiff (eds.). In *Lecture Notes in Computer Science,* Springer-Verlag.

Bergman, N. J. (1989) First look at CommonView. *Dr. Dobb's Journal,* October 1989, 74–80.

Bernstein, P. A., and Goodman, N. (1980) Timestamp-based algorithms for concurrency control in distributed database systems. *Proceedings of VLDB 1987.*

Black, A.; Hutchinson, N.; Jul, E.; Levy, H.; and Carter, L. (1987) Distribution and abstract types in emerald. *IEEE Transactions on Software Engineering, 13*(1), 65–76.

Bobrow, D. G., et al. (1988) *Common LISP Object System Specification.* X3J13 Document 88-002R, (June).

Bobrow, D. G. et al. (1986) CommonLoops merging LISP and object-oriented programming. *Proceedings of OOPSLA-86*.

Booch, G. (1987) *Software Components with Ada*. Menlo Park, CA: Benjamin/Cummings Series.

Booch, G. (1986) Object-oriented development. *IEEE Transactions on Software Engineering*, Feb. 1986.

Booch, G. (1986) *Software Engineering with Ada*. (Second Edition) Menlo Park, CA: Benjamin/Cummings Publishing Co.

Borning, A., and O'Shea, T. (1987) DeltaTalk: An empirically and aesthetically motivated simplification of the Smalltalk-80 language, ECOOP '87, Paris, France (June).

Brachman, R. J. (1985) I lied about the trees—or, defaults and definitions in knowledge representation. *AI Magazine 6*(3), 80–93.

Brown, J. R., and Cunningham, S. (1989) *Programming the User Interface. Principles and Examples*. New York: John Wiley & Sons, Inc.

Burstall, R. M., and Goguen, J. A. (1977) Putting theories together to make specifications. *Proceedings of ICJAI-77*.

Buzzard, G. D., and Mudge, T. N. (1985) Object-based computing and the Ada programming language. *Computer*, (March) 1985.

Cardelli, L. (1987) *Building User Interfaces by Direct Manipulation*. Digital Equipment Corporation, Systems Research Center, Palo Alto, CA, (October).

Cardelli L. (1984*a*) *Amber*. AT&T Bell Labs Technical Memorandum 11271-840924-10TM.

Cardelli, L. (1984*b*) A semantics of multiple inheritance. K. Gills, D. B. McQueen, and G. Plotkin (eds.). In *Lecture Notes in Computer Science* (173), New York: Springer-Verlag.

Cardelli, L., and Wegner, P. (1985) On understanding types, data abstraction, and polymorphism. *Computing Surveys, 17*(4).

Cardenas, A. F. (1979) *Data Base Management Systems*. Boston: Allyn and Bacon.

Carey, M.; DeWitt, D.; and Vanderberg, S. (1988) A data model and query language for EXODUS. *Proc. of 1988 SIGMOD Conference*. Chicago, IL.

Carey, M. J., et al. (1990) The EXODUS DBMS project: An overview. In *Readings in Object-Oriented Databases*, S. T. Zdonik and D. Maier (eds.). San Mateo, CA: Morgan Kaufmann Publishers, Inc.

Caudill, P. J., and Wirfs-Brock, A. (1986) A third generation Smalltalk-80 implementation. *Proceedings of OOPSLA-86*, Portland, Oregon.

Cerri, S., and Pelagatti, G. (1984) *Distributed Databases: Principles and Systems*. New York: McGraw-Hill.

Chamberlin, D. D.; Astrahan, M. M.; et al. (1976) SEQUEL 2: A unified approach to data definition, manipulation, and control. *IBM Journal of Research and Development, 20,* 560–575.

Chang, C. L., and Walker, A. (1986) PROSQL: A prolog programming interface with SQL/DS. *Proc. First. International Workshop on Expert Data Systems*. L. Kerschberg (ed.). Menlo Park, CA: Benjamin/Cummings Inc.

Chen, P. P. (1976) The entity-relationship model—toward a unified view of data. *ACM Transactions on Database Systems, 1*(1).

Clifford, J., and Warren, D. S. (1983) Formal semantics for time in databases. *ACM Transactions on Database Systems, 8*(2).

Coad, P., and Yourdon, E. (1990) *Object-Oriented Analysis*. Englewood Cliffs, NJ: Prentice-Hall.

Cobb, A., and Weiner J. (1989) Examining NewWave, Hewlett-Packard's graphical object-oriented environment. *Microsoft Systems Journal*, (November), 1–18.

Codd, E. F. (1985) Is your DBMS really relational? *Computer World*, October 14, 1985.

Codd, E. F. (1979) Extending the database relational model to capture more meaning. *ACM Transactions on Database Systems, 4*, 397–434.

Codd, E. F. (1970) A relational model for large shared data banks. *Communications of the ACM, 13*, 377–387.

Cointe, P. (1987) Metaclasses are first class: the ObjVLisp model. *Proceedings of OOPSLA-87* (December).

Collard, P. (1989) Object-oriented programming techniques with Ada: An example. *ACM Ada LETTERS*, (6), September/October 1989, 119–126.

Collins, G. E. (1960) A method for overlapping and erasure of lists. *Communications of the ACM, 21*(4), (December).

Copeland, G. P. (1980) What if mass storage were free? *Proceedings of the Fifth Workshop on Computer Architecture for Non-Numeric Processing,* Pacific Grove, California.

Copeland, G. P., and Khoshafian, S. (1987) Identity and versions for complex objects. *Proceedings of Persistent Object Systems: Their Design, Implementation, and Use*. Research Report No. 44. University of St. Andrews, Scotland.

Copeland, G. P., and Khoshafian, S. (1985) A decomposition storage model. *Proc. ACM/SIGMOD International Conference on the Management of Data*.

Copeland, G. P., and Maier, D. (1984) Making Smalltalk a database system. *Proceedings of the SIGMOD Conference,* ACM, Boston.

Conklin, J. (1987) Hypertext: A survey and introduction. *IEEE Computer, 20*(9), 17–41.

Cox, B. (1986) *Object-Oriented Programming: An Evolutionary Approach*. Reading, MA: Addison-Wesley.

Cox, B. (1984) Message/object programming: An evolutionary change in programming technology. *IEEE Software*, January 1984, 50–61.

Cox, B., and Hunt, B. (1986) Objects, icons, and software ICs. *BYTE*, (August).

Cuadra, J. (1987) *Directory of Online Databases, Vol. 8.* New York: Cuadra/Elsevier.

Dahl, O-J., and Nygaard, K. (1966) Simula—an ALGOL-based simulation language. *Communications of the ACM, 9*, 671–678.

Dahl, O-J.; Myhrhaug, B.; and Nygaard, K. (1970) *The Simula 67 Common Base Language*. Publication S22, Norwegian Computing Centre, Oslo.

Date, C. J. (1987) *A Guide to SQL Standards*. Reading, MA: Addison-Wesley.

Date, C. J. (1986) *An Introduction to Database Systems*. Reading, MA: Addison-Wesley.

Dayal, U.; Goodman, N.; and Katz, R. (1982) An extended relational algebra with control over duplicate elimination. *Proceedings of PODS, 1982*.

Deppsich, U.; Paul, H-B.; and Schek, H-J. (1986) A storage system for complex object. *Proceedings of 1986 International Workshop on Object-Oriented Database Systems*, Pacific Grove, California, September, 1986.

Deutsch, L. P., and Bobrow, D. G. (1976) An efficient incremental automatic garbage collector. *Communications of the ACM, 19*(9), (September).

Deux, O., et al. (1990) The story of O₂ *IEEE Transactions on Knowledge and Data Engineering*. 2(1), March 1990.

Dewhurst, S. C., and Stark, K. T. (1989) *Programming in C++*. Englewood Cliffs, NJ: Prentice-Hall.

Dewitt, D., and Gerber, R. (1985) Multiprocessor Hash-Based Join Algorithms. *Proceedings of VLDB*.

Dittrich, K. R. (1986) Object-oriented database systems: The notion and the issues. *Proceedings of the International Workshop on Object-Oriented Database Systems*, Pacific Grove, California, September, 1986.

Dittrich, K., and Dayal, U. (eds.) (1986) *Proceedings of 1986 International Workshop on Object-Oriented Database Systems*. Pacific Grove, CA, IEEE Computer Society Press.

Dion, J. (1980) The cambridge file server. *Operating Systems Review,* ACM SIGOPS, 14(4), (October).

Dyson E. (1989) *Release 1.0:* Special issue on object-oriented databases. September 1989.

Ehrig, H.; Kreowski, H.; and Padawiz, P. (1978) Stepwise specification and implementation of abstract data types. *Proceedings of the 5th ICALP*.

Eswaran, K. P.; Gray, J. N.; Lorie, R. A.; and Traiger, I. L. (1976) The notions of consistency and predicate locks in a database system. *Communications of the ACM, 19,* 624–633.

Fagin, R. (1980) Horn clauses as relational dependencies. *Proceedings of the ACM Conference on Foundations of Computer Science,* Los Angeles, April.

Fishman, D., et al. (1989) *Overview of the Iris DBMS*. Hewlett-Packard Technical report HPL-SAL-89-15.

Fishman, D., et al. (1987) Iris: An object oriented database management system, *ACM Transactions on Database Systems, 5*(1).

Gardarin, G., and Valduriez, P. (1989) *Relational Databases and Knowledge Bases*. Reading, MA: Addison-Wesley Publishing Company.

Goguen, J. A.; Thatcher, J. W.; Wegner, E. G.; and Wright, J. B. (1975) Abstract data types as initial algebras and correctness of data representation. *Proceedings of the Conference on Computer Graphics, Pattern Recognition and Data Structures*.

Goldberg, A. (ed.) (1988) *A History of Personal Workstations*. New York: ACM Press.

Goldberg, A. and Robson, D. (1983) *Smalltalk-80: The Language and its Implementation*. Reading, MA: Addison-Wesley.

Goldstein, I. P., and Bobrow, D. G. (1984) A layered approach to software design. In D. Barstow, H. Shrobe, and E. Sandewall (eds.). *Interactive Programming Environments*. New York: McGraw-Hill, pp. 387–413.

Goodman, D. (1987) *The Complete HyperCard Handbook*. New York: Bantam Books.

Gray, J. (1978) Notes on database operating systems. *IBM research report RJ2188,* IBM Research Center, San Jose, CA.

Güting, R. H. (1988) Geo-Relational Algebra: A Model and Query Language for Geometric Database Systems. Springer Verlag 303, *Extending Database Technology,* 1988, Venice.

Guttag, J. (1977) Abstract data types and the development of data structures. *Communications of the ACM, 20.*

Halasz, F. (1988) Reflections on NoteCards: Seven issues for the next generation of hypermedia systems. *Communications of the ACM,* July, 1988.

Hall, P. A. V.; Owlett, J.; and Todd, S. J. P. (1976) Relations and entities. *Modeling In Data Base Management Systems,* G. M. Nijssen (ed.). New York: North-Holland Publishing Co.

Hammer, M., and McLeod, D. (1981) Database description with SDM: a semantic database model. *ACM Trans. Database Syst. 6*(3).

Harper, R.; MacQueen, D.; and Milner, R. (1986) *Standard ML.* ECS-LFCS-86-2, Department of Computer Science, University of Edinburgh.

Hayes, F., and Baran, N. (1989) A guide to GUI. *BYTE,* (July), 250–257.

Hayes-Roth, F.; Waterman, D. A.; and Lenat, D. B. (1983) *Building Expert Systems.* Reading, MA: Addison-Wesley.

Herot, C. F. (1980) Spatial management of data. *ACM Transactions on Database Systems, 5,* 493–514.

Hewitt, C. (1977) Viewing control structures as patterns of passing messages. *Artificial Intelligence, 8*(3).

Hewitt, C.; Bishop, P.; and Steiger, R. (1973) A universal, modular actor formalism for artificial intelligence. *Proceedings of IJCAI,* August.

Hewlett-Packard (1988) *HP NewWave Environment General Information Manual,* Cupertino, CA.

Howe, G. R., and Lindsay, J. (1981) A generalized iterative record linkage. *Computer System For Use In Medical Follow-up Studies,* Computers and Biomedical Research, Vol. 14.

Hull, R., and King R. (1987) Semantic database modeling: Survey, application, and research issues. *ACM Computing Surveys, 19*(3).

Hull, R., and Yap, C. K. (1984) The format model: A theory of database organization. *Journal of the ACM, 31*(3), (July).

International Business Machines (1988*a*) *Systems Application Architecture: An Overview.* IBM Doc Number GC26-4341-3.

International Business Machines (1988*b*) *Systems Application Architecture: Common User Access Advanced Interface Design.* IBM Doc Number 0328-300-R00-1089.

Jacobs, B. E. (1982) On database logic. *Journal of the ACM, 29*(2), (April).

Jaeschke, G., and Schek, H. (1982) Remarks on the algebra of non-first normal form relations. *Proceedings of the ACM International Symposium on PODS,* Los Angeles, 124–138.

Jagannathan, D.; Guck, R. L.; Fritchman, B. L.; Thompson, J. P.; and Tolbert, D. M. (1988) SIM: A database system based on the semantic data model. *Proceedings of ACM SIGMOD 1988.*

Jeffcoate, J.; Hales, K.; and Downes, V. (1989) *Object-Oriented Systems: The Commercial Benefits.* Ovum Report. London: Dudley Ltd.

Johnson, J.; Roberts, T.; Verplank, W.; Smith, D. C.; Irby, C. H.; Beard, M.; and Mackey, K. (1989) The Xerox Star: A retrospective. *IEEE Computer,* (September), 11–26.

Kaehler, T., and Krasner, G. (1983) LOOM—large object-oriented memory for Smalltalk-80 systems. *Smalltalk-80: Bits Of History, Words Of Advice,* G. Krasner (ed.). Reading, MA: Addison-Wesley.

Katz, R. H. (1987) *Information Management for Engineering Design.* Berlin: Springer-Verlag.

Katz, R. H., and Lehman, T. J. (1984) Database support for versions and alternatives of large design files. *IEEE Transactions on Software Engineering, SE-10,* No. 2.

Kernighan, B. W., and Ritchie, D. M. (1988) *The C Programming Language.* Englewood Cliffs, NJ: Prentice-Hall.

Kerschberg, L., and Pacheco, J. E. S. (1976) A functional data base model. *Tech. Rep.*, Pontificia Univ. Catolica do Rio de Janeiro, Rio de Janeiro, Brazil.

Ketabchi, M. A. (1985) *On the Management of Computer Aided Design Databases.* PhD Dissertation, University of Minnesota.

Khoshafian, S. (1990) Intelligent SQL. Submitted to X3/SPARC/DBSSG OODB Task Group Workshop, Atlantic City, N.J. (May).

Khoshafian, S. (1989) A persistent complex object database language. *Data and Knowledge Engineering, 3* (1988/89).

Khoshafian, S., and Briggs, T. (1988) Schema Design and Mapping Strategies for Persistent Object Models. *Information and Software Technology,* December.

Khoshafian, S., and Copeland, G. (1986) Object Identity. *Proceedings of OOPSLA-86,* Portland, Oregon.

Khoshafian, S., and Frank, D. (1988) Implementation techniques for object oriented databases. *Proceedings of the Second International Workshop on Object-Oriented Database Systems,* Germany, September.

Khoshafian, S.; Franklin, M. J.; and Carey, M. J. (1990*a*) Storage management for persistent complex objects. *Information Systems, 15*(3).

Khoshafian, S.; Franklin, M. J.; and Carey, M. J. (1988*b*) Storage management for persistent complex objects, *MCC Tech Report* ACA-ST-118-88, (April).

Khoshafian, S.; Parsaye, K.; and Wong, H. (1990*b*) Intelligent database engines. *Database Programming and Design* (July).

Khoshafian, S., and Valduriez, P. (1987*a*) Persistence, sharing, and object orientation: A database perspective. *Proceedings of the Workshop on Database Programming Languages,* Roscoff, France, 1987.

Khoshafian, S., and Valduriez, P. (1987*b*) Parallel execution strategies for declustered databases. *Proceedings of IWDM '87.*

Khoshafian, S.; Valduriez, P.; and Copeland, G. (1988) Parallel processing for complex objects. *Proceedings of the Fourth International Conference on Data Engineering,* February, 1988.

Kim, W., et al. (1987) Composite object support in an object-oriented database system. *Proceedings of OOPSLA-87.*

Kim, W.; Garza, J. F.; Ballou, N.; and Woelk, D. (1990) Architecture of the ORION next-generation database system. *IEEE Transactions on Knowledge and Data Engineering, 2*(1), March 1990.

Kim, W., and Lochovsky, F. H. (eds.) (1989) *Object-Oriented Concepts, Databases, and Applications.* New York: ACM Press.

King, R., and McLeod, D. (1985) Semantic database models. In S. B. Yao (ed.). *Database Design.* New York: Springer-Verlag.

King, R., and McLeod, D. (1984) A unified model and methodology for conceptual database design. In M. L. Brodie, J. Mylopoulos, and J. W. Schmidt (eds.). *On Conceptual Modeling: Perspectives from Artificial Intelligence, Databases, and Programming Language.* New York: Springer-Verlag.

Kitsuregawa, M.: Tanaka, H.; and Moto-oka, T. (1983) Application of hash to a database machine and its architecture. *New Generation Computing, 1*(1).

Klausner, A., and Goodman, N. (1985) Multi-relations—semantics and languages. *Proceedings of VLDB 1985.*

Knor, E. (1990) Software's next wave: Putting the user first. *PC World,* January, 134–143.

Knuth, D. (1973) *The Art of Computer Programming, Volume I.* Reading MA: Addison-Wesley.

Korth, H. F.; Kim, W.; and Bancilhon, F. (1990) On long-duration CAD transactions. In *Readings in Object-Oriented Databases,* S. T. Zdonik and D. Maier (eds.). San Mateo, CA: Morgan Kaufmann Publishers, Inc.

Kowalski, R. (1979) *Logic for Problem Solving.* New York: North-Holland.

Krasner G. E., and Pope S. T. (1988) A cookbook for using the model-view-controller user interface paradigm in Smalltalk-80. *Journal of Object Oriented Programming,* (August/September), 26–49.

Kulkarni, K. G., and Atkinson, M. P. (1986) EFDM: Extended functional data model. *The Computer Journal, 29*(1).

Kung, H. T., and Robinson, J. (1981) On optimistic methods for concurrency control. *ACM TODS, 6*(2) (June).

Kuper, G. M., and Vardi, M. Y. (1985) On the expressive power of the logic data model. *Proceedings of the ACM SIGMOD,* 180–187, Austin, TX.

Kuper, G. M., and Vardi, M. Y. (1984) A new approach to database logic. *Proceedings of the ACM International Symposium on PODS,* Waterloo, Canada, 1984.

Lambert, S., and Ropiequet, S. (1986) *CD ROM: The New Papyrus.* Redmond, WA: Microsoft Press.

Larson, J. (1986) A visual approach to browsing in a database environment. *IEEE Computer,* (June), 1986.

Leach, P. J.; Stumpf, B. L.; Hamilton, J. A.; and Levine, P. H. (1982) UIDS as internal names in a distributed file system. *Proceedings of the First Symposium On Principles Of Distributed Computing,* Ottawa, Canada.

Lecluse, C., and Richard, P. (1989) The O$_2$ database programming language, *Proceedings of VLDB 1989.*

Lecluse, C.; Richard, P.; and Velez, F. (1988) O$_2$, an object-oriented data model. *Proceedings of ACM SIGMOD,* Chicago, IL.

Ledbetter, L., and Cox, B. (1985) Software-IC's, *BYTE,* (June) 1985.

Lee, E. S., and McGregor, J. N. (1985) Minimizing menu search time in menu retrieval systems. *Human Factors, 27,* 157–162.

Lieberman, H. (1986) Using prototypical objects to implement shared behavior in object-oriented systems. *Proceedings of OOPSLA-86,* Portland, Oregon.

Lieberman, H. (1981) *A Preview of Act 1.* MIT AI Lab Memo No. 625.

Lieberman, H., and Hewitt, C. (1983) A real-time garbage collector based on the lifetimes of objects. *Communications of the ACM, 26*(6).

Lippman, S. B. (1989) *C++ Primer.* Reading, MA: Addison-Wesley.

Liskov, B., and Guttag, J. (1986) *Abstraction and Specification in Program Development.* Cambridge, MA: The MIT Press.

Liskov., B.; Snyder, A.; Atkinson, R.; and Schaffert, C. (1977). Abstraction Mechanisms in CLU. *Communications of the ACM, 20*(8).

Liskov, B. H., and Zilles, S. M. (1975) Specification techniques for data abstractions. *IEEE Transactions on Software Engineering, SE-1.*

Maier, D. (1983) *The Theory of Relational Databases.* Rockville, MA: Computer Science Press.

Maier, D., and Stein, J. C. (1990) Development and implementation of an object-oriented DBMS. *Readings in Object-Oriented Database Systems,* S. Zdonik and D. Maier (eds.). San Mateo, CA: Morgan Kaufmann Publishers.

Maier, D., and Stein, J. (1986) Indexing in an object-oriented DMBS. *Proceedings of 1986 International Workshop on Object-Oriented Database Systems*, Pacific Grove, California, 1986.

Maier, D.; Stein, J.; Ottis, A.; and Purdy, A. (1986) Development of an object-oriented DBMS. *Proceedings of OOPSLA-86,* Portland, Oregon.

Manola, F., and Dayal, U. (1986) PDM: An object-oriented data model. *Proceedings of 1986 International Workshop on Object-Oriented Database Systems*, Pacific Grove, California.

McCarthy, J. (1960) Recursive functions of symbolic expressions and their computation by machine, I. *Communications of the ACM, 3.*

McCarthy, J., et al. (1965) *LISP 1.5 Programmer's Manual.* Cambridge, MA: The MIT Press.

Metaphor Computer Systems (1988) *Workstation Tools.* Mountain View, CA.

Meyer, B. (1988) *Object-Oriented Software Construction.* Englewood Cliffs, NJ: Prentice-Hall.

Meyrowitz, N. (1986) Intermedia: The architecture and construction of an object-oriented hypertext/hypermedia system and applications framework. *Proceedings of OOPSLA '86,* Portland, Oregon.

Minoura, T., and Parsaye, K. (1984) Version based concurrency control of a database system. *Proceedings of the 1984 ACM/IEEE Conference on Data Engineering*, Los Angeles.

Minsky, M. (1975) A framework for representing knowledge. In P. H. Winston (ed.). *The Psychology of Computer Vision.* New York: McGraw-Hill.

Minsky, M. (ed.) (1968) *Semantic Information Processing.* Cambridge, MA: The MIT Press.

Moon, D.A. (1986) Object-oriented programming with flavors. *Proceedings of OOPSLA-86,* Portland, Oregon.

Moss, E. (1981) *Nested Transactions: An Approach to Reliable Distributed Computing.* PhD dissertation, MIT, Cambridge, MA.

Moss, E., and Wolf, A. (1988) *Toward Principles of Inheritance and Subtyping in Programming Languages.* COINS Technical Report 88-95, University of Massachusetts.

Mullen, M. (1989) *Object-Oriented Program Design with Examples in C++.* Reading, MA: Addison-Wesley.

Mylopoulos, J.; Bernstein, P. A.; and Wong, H. K. T. (1980) A language facility for designing database-intensive applications. *ACM Transactions on Database Systems, 5(2).*

Mylopoulos, J. and Wong, H. K. T. (1980) Some features of the taxis data model. *Proceedings of the 6th VLDB Conference.*

Naur, P. (ed.) (1960) Report on the algorithmic language ALGOL 60. *Communications of the ACM,* (May).

O'Brien, P. (1985) *Trellis Object-Oriented Environment Language Tutorial.* DEC Eastern Research Lab Report, DEC-TR-373, (November).

Ontologic (1989) *Client Library Reference,* Ontologic, Inc., Billerica, MA.

Ontologic (1988) *Vbase, Integrated Object Database Manual,* Ontologic, Inc., Billerica, MA.

Ozsoyoglu, M. Z. and Ozsoyoglu, G. (1983) An extension of relational algebra for summary tables. *Proceedings of the 2nd International Conference on Statistical Database Management*, Los Angeles, 202–211.

Papadimitriou, C. H. (1979) The serializability of concurrent database updates. *Journal of the ACM, 26*, 631–653.

Parnas, D. L. (1972) On the criteria to be used in decomposing systems into modules. *Communications of the ACM, 12* (December).

Parsaye, K. (1982) *Higher Order Abstract Data Types.* PhD Dissertation, Department of Computer Science, University of California at Los Angeles, Report No. CSD-820112.

Parsaye, K., and Chignell, M. (1988) *Expert Systems for Experts.* New York: Wiley & Sons, Inc.

Parsaye, K.; Chignell M.; Khoshafian, S.; and Wong H. (1989) *Intelligent Databases.* New York: Wiley & Sons, Inc.

Perry T. S., and Voelcker J. (1989) Of mice and menus: Designing the user-friendly interface. *IEEE Spectrum*, (September), 46–51.

Pertzold, C. (1988) *Programming Windows.* Redmon, WA: Microsoft Press.

Peterson, G. (1987) *Object-Oriented Computing* Volume I and II. Washington, DC: IEEE Society Press.

Pfaff, G. E. (ed.) (1985) *User Interface Management Systems.* New York: Springer-Verlag.

Pooley, R. J. (1989) *An Introduction to Programming in SIMULA.* Blackwell Scientific Publications.

Popek, P., et al. (1981) LOCUS: A network transparent, high reliability distributed system. *Proceedings of the Eighth Symposium On Operating Systems Principles,* December.

Quillian, M. R. (1968) Semantic memory. In M. Minsky (ed.). *Semantic Information Processing.* Cambridge, MA: The MIT Press, 227–270.

Randell, B., and Russell, L. (1964) *ALGOL 60 Implementation*, New York: Academic Press.

Rentsch, T. (1982) Object-oriented programming. *SIGPLAN Notices*, (September).

Richardson, J. E.; Carey, M. J.; and Schuh, D. T. (1989) *The Design of the E Programming Language.* Computer Sciences Tech. Report #824, University of Wisconsin, Madison.

Risch, T.; Reboh, R.; Hart, P.; and Duda, R. A. (1988) Functional approach to integrating database and expert systems. *Communications of the ACM, 31*, 1424–1437.

Ritchie, D. M.; Johnson, D. M.; Lesk, M. E.; and Kernighan, B. W. (1978) *The C Programming Language.* Bell System Technical Journal, AT&T, (August), 179–219.

Roussopoulos, N; Faloutsos, C.; and Sellis, T. (1988) An efficient pictorial database system for PSQL. *IEEE Transactions on Software Engineering, SE-14(5)* (May).

Roth, M.; Korth, H.; and Siberschatz, A. (1984) *Theory of Non-First-Normal-Form Relational Databases.* TR-84-36, Department of Computer Science, University of Texas at Austin.

Salton, G., and McGill, M. J. (1983) *An Introduction to Modern Information Retrieval.* New York: McGraw-Hill.

Saltzer, J. H. (1978) Naming and binding of objects. In Goos and Harman (eds.). *Lecture Notes in Computer Science.* Berlin: Springer-Verlag.

Schaffert, C.; Cooper, T.; Bullis, B.; Kilian, M.; and Wilpolt, C. (1986) An introduction to Trellis/Owl. *OOPSLA-86 Proceedings,* 9–16.

Schek, H. J., and Scholl, M. H. (1986) The relational model with relational valued attributes. *Information Systems, 11*(2).

Schmucker, K. J. (1986) *Object-Oriented Programming for the Macintosh*, Hasbrouck Heights, NJ: Hayden Book Co.

Schneiderman, B. (1987) *Designing the User Interface*. Reading, MA: Addison-Wesley.

Schriver, B., and Wegner, P. (eds.) (1987) *Research Directions in Object-Oriented Programming*. Cambridge, MA: The MIT Press.

Selinger, P. G.; Astrahan, M. M.; Chamberlin, D. D.; Lorie, R. A.; and Price, T. G. (1979) Access path selection in relational database management system. *Proc. ACM/SIGMOD*, June.

Servio Logic (1989) *Programming in OPAL*. Servio Logic Development Corporation. Beaverton, Oregon.

Servio Logic (1987) *OPAL Programming Environment manual*. Servio Logic Development Corporation. Beaverton, Oregon.

Seidewitz, E. (1987) Object-oriented programming in Smalltalk and Ada. *Proceedings of 1987 OOPSLA*, October 1987.

Seymour, J. (1989*a*) The GUI, an interface you won't outgrow. *PC Magazine*, (September), 97–109.

Seymour, J. (1989*b*) GUIs for DOS and OS/2. *PC Magazine*, (September), 111–131.

Shibayama, E., and Yonezawa, A. (1987) Distributed computing in ABCL/1. In A. Yonezawa and M. Tokora (eds.). *Object-Oriented Concurrent Programming*. Cambridge, MA: The MIT Press.

Shipman, J. (1981) The functional data model and the data language DAPLEX. *ACM Transactions on Database Systems, 6*(1).

Shlaer, S., and Mellor, S. (1990) *Object-Oriented Systems Analysis*. Englewood Cliffs, NJ: Prentice-Hall.

Shriver, B., and Wegner, P. (1987) *Research Directions in Object-Oriented Programming*, Cambridge, MA: The MIT Press.

Shu, N. C. (1988) *Visual Programming*. New York: Van Nostrand Reinhold Company.

Smith, J. M. and Smith, D. C. P. (1977) Database abstractions: Aggregations and generalizations. *ACM Transactions on Database Systems, 2*(2), 105–133.

Smith, K. E., and Zdonik, S. B. (1987) Intermedia: A case study of the differences between relational and object-oriented database systems. *Proceedings of OOPSLA '87*, Orlando, Florida.

Snyder, A. (1986*a*) Encapsulation and inheritance in object-oriented programming languages. *Proceedings of OOPSLA '86*, Portland, Oregon.

Snyder, A. (1986*b*) CommonObjects: An overview. *ACM SIGPLAN Notices 21*(10), 19–28.

Snyder, A. (1985) *Object-Oriented Programming for CommonLisp*. Hewlett-Packard Technical Report ATC-85-1.

Stadish, T. A. (1980) *Data Structure Techniques*. Reading, MA: Addison-Wesley.

Stamos, J. W. (1982) A large object-oriented virtual memory: Grouping strategies, measurements, and performance. Xerox Technical Report, SCG-82-2, Xerox, Palo Alto Research Center.

Stefik, M., and Bobrow, D. G. (1986) Object-oriented programming: Themes and variations. *AI Magazine, 6*(4).

Stein, L. A. (1987) Delegation is inheritance. *Proceedings of OOPSLA-87*.

Stein, L. A.; Lieberman, H.; and Ungar, D. (1989) A shared view of sharing: The treaty of Orlando. In *Object-Oriented Concepts, Databases, and Applications*. W. Kim and F.H. Lochovsky (eds.). New York: ACM Press.

Stemple, D.; Sheard, T.; and Bunker, R. (1990) Abstract data types in databases: Specification, manipulation, and access. *Readings in Object-Oriented Databases*, S. T. Zdonik and D. Maier (eds.). San Mateo, CA: Morgan Kaufmann Publishers, Inc.

Stonebraker, M. (1986) Triggers and inference in database systems. In M. L. Brodie and J. Mylopoulos (eds.). *On Knowledge Base Management Systems*. New York: Springer-Verlag.

Stonebraker, M., and Rowe, L.A. (1986) The design of POSTGRES. *Proceedings of SIGMOD-86*.

Stonebraker, M.; Rowe, L.; and Hiohama, M. (1990) The implementation of POSTGRES. *IEEE Transactions on Knowledge and Data Engineering, 2*(1), March 1990.

Stonebraker, M.; Wong, E.; Kreps, P.; and Held, G. (1976) The design and implementation of INGRES. *ACM Transactions on Database Systems, 1,* 189–222.

Stroustrup, B. (1989) *C++ Reference Manual*. AT&T Bell Laboratories, Murray Hill, NJ.

Stroustrup, B. (1986) *The C++ Programming Language*. Reading, MA: Addison-Wesley.

Symbolics, Inc. (1988) *Statice*. Cambridge, MA.

Tanaka, M., and Ichikawa, T. (1988) A visual user interface for map information retrieval based on semantic significance. *IEEE Transactions on Software Engineering, SE-14,* 666–671.

Tanenbaum, A. S. (1976) A tutorial on ALGOL 68. *Computing Surveys 8*(2), (June).

Thomas, S. (1982) *A Non-First-Normal-Form Relational Database Model*. PhD Dissertation, Vanderbilt University.

Trimble, J., and Chappell, D. (1989) *A Visual Introduction to SQL*. New York: John Wiley & Sons.

Tsur, S., and Zaniolo, C. (1986) LDL: A logic based data language. *Proceedings of VLDB '86*.

Ullman, J. D. (1988) *Principles of Database and Knowledge-Base Systems*. Rockville, MA: Computer Science Press.

Ullman, J. D. (1987) Database theory—past and future. *Proceedings of 6th PODS*, San Diego.

Ullman, J. (1980) *Principles of Relational Database Systems*. New York: Computer Science Press.

Ungar, D. M. (1987) *The Design and Evaluation of High Performance Smalltalk Systems*. Cambridge, MA: The MIT Press.

Ungar, D. M., and Patterson, D. A. (1983) Berkeley Smalltalk: Who knows where the time goes? In *Smalltalk-80: Bits of History, Word of Advice*. G. Krasner (ed.). Reading, MA: Addison-Wesley.

UNISYS (1987) *A Series InfoExec Semantic Information Manager*. Technical Overview and Functional Overview Manuals, UNISYS corporation.

Valduriez, P. (1987) Join indices. *ACM Transactions on Database Systems, 12*(2).

Valduriez, P.; Khoshafian, S.; and Copeland, G. (1986) Implementation techniques of complex objects. *Proceedings of VLDB*, Kyoto, Japan.

Veith, R. H. (1988) *Visual Information Systems: The Power of Graphics And Video*. Boston, MA: G. K. Hall & Co.

Warren, D. H. D. (1977) Implementing Prolog: Compiling predicate logic programs. *AI Report*. Edinburgh University, Edinburgh.

Watt, D. A.; Wichmann, B. A.; and Findlay, W. (1987) *Ada Language and Methodology*. Englewood Cliffs, NJ: Prentice-Hall International.

Webster, B. F. (1989) *The NeXT Book*. Reading, MA: Addison-Wesley.

Wegner, P. (1987) Dimensions of object-oriented language design. *Proceedings of OOPSLA-87*, Orlando.

Weiskamp, K., and Flamig, B. (1990) *The Complete C++ Primer* San Diego: Academic Press.

White, G. M. (1983) The desktop metaphor. *Byte*, (December).

Whitewater Group (1989*a*) *Actor Language Manual*. The Whitewater Group, Inc., Evanston, IL.

Whitewater Group (1989*b*) *Whitewater Resource Toolkit for Windows*. The Whitewater Group, Inc., Evanston, IL.

Wiederhold, G. (1983) *Database Design*. New York: McGraw-Hill.

Wiener, K. A., and Pinson, L. J. (1989) A practical example of multiple inheritance in C++. *ACM SIGPLAN Notices, 14*(9) September 1989.

Wilson, P. R. (1988) Opportunistic garbage collection. *SIGPLAN Notices, 23*(12), (December).

Wirth, N. (1971) The programming language Pascal. *Acta Informatica 1*, Vol.1 (May).

Wong, H. T. (1983) *Design and Verification of Information Systems*. PhD Thesis, University of Toronto.

Wrigley, E. A. (ed.) (1973) *Identifying People in the Past*. London: Edward Arnold.

Wulf, W. A.; London, R. L.; and Shaw, M. (1976) An introduction to the construction and verification of alphard programs, *IEEE Transactions on Software Engineering, SE-2*.

Yokote, Y., and Tokoro, M. (1987) Concurrent Programming in ConcurrentSmalltalk. In A. Yonezawa and M. Tokoro (eds.). *Object-Oriented Concurrent Programming*. Cambridge, MA: The MIT Press.

Yonezawa, A., et al. (1987) Modeling and programming in an object-oriented concurrent language ABCL/1. In A. Yonezawa and M. Tokoro (eds.). *Object-Oriented Concurrent Programming*. Cambridge, MA: The MIT Press.

Young, R. L. (1987) An object-oriented framework for interactive data graphics. *OOPSLA '87 Proceedings*, 78–90.

Zaniolo, C. (1985) The representation and deductive retrieval of complex objects. *Proceedings of VLDB '85*.

Zaniolo, C. (1983) The database language GEM. *Proceedings of the ACM SIGMOD Conference*, San Jose.

Zdonik, S. (1984) Object management system concepts. *Proceedings of the Conference on Office Information Systems, ACM/SIGOA*, Toronto, Canada.

Zdonik, S., and Maier, D. (eds.) (1990) *Readings in Object-Oriented Database Systems*. San Mateo, CA: Morgan Kaufmann Publishers.

Zdonik, S., and Wegner, P. (1986) Language and Methodology for Object-Oriented Database Environments. *Proceedings of the Nineteenth Annual Hawaii International Conference on System Sciences*.

Zloof, M. M. (1977) Query-by-example: A data base language. *IBM Systems Journal, 16*, 324–343.

Zloof, M. M. (1975) *Query-by-Example: Operations on the Transitive Closure*. IBM RC 5526. Yorktown Heights, New York.

Zortech (1989) *C++ Compiler Reference*. Zortech Inc., Arlington, MA.

INDEX

■ ABOUT THE AUTHORS

Dr. Setrag Khoshafian is the architect and manager of the intelligent database engine project at the Walnut Creek Advanced Development Center of Ashton-Tate. He is the principal designer of Intelligent SQL. Dr. Khoshafian has made significant contributions in the areas of object-oriented and intelligent database technologies. He was a designer and architect of one of the earliest object-oriented database language implementations, FAD. He is a co-author of *Intelligent Databases*, also by Wiley publications. He received his BS and MS degrees in Mathematics from the American University of Beirut. He received his MS and PhD in Computer Science from the University of Wisconsin, Madison. His current research interests span object-oriented systems, intelligent database engines, intelligent user interfaces, and visual programming.

Razmik Abnous is a senior software designer and a project leader at Ashton-Tate Corporation. He received his BS and MEng degrees in Applied Mathematics and Computer Science from the University of Louisville in Kentucky. Also, he teaches object orientation at the University of California, Berkeley extension. Prior to Ashton-Tate, he was a principal software engineer in the Artificial Intelligence Technology Group of Digital Equipment Corporation. In the past several years, he has been a designer of database systems applying object orientation, inferencing, and the client/server model. His current research interests are in object orientation, intelligent databases, client/server databases, and user interfaces.